W9-DIJ-879

ALL THE RAGE

ALL THE RAGE

STORIES FROM THE FRONTLINE OF BEAUTY:
A HISTORY OF PAIN, PLEASURE, AND POWER
1860–1960

VIRGINIA NICHOLSON

PEGASUS BOOKS
NEW YORK LONDON

ALL THE RAGE

Pegasus Books, Ltd.
148 West 37th Street, 13th Floor
New York, NY 10018

First Pegasus Books cloth edition August 2024

ISBN: 978-1-63936-706-1

10 9 8 7 6 5 4 3 2 1

Printed in the United States of America
Distributed by Simon & Schuster
www.pegasusbooks.com

Contents

3. New Century

4. Jazz Age

5. Modern Girls

6. Beauty is a Duty

The author aged four, dressed up as a princess,
in the garden at Charleston, 1959

Prologue

Until I was twelve, my family spent every summer holiday at a pretty farmhouse under the South Downs, called Charleston. It was here that my grandmother, the artist Vanessa Bell, lived, loved and painted until her death in 1961. Today, Charleston is a museum – 'the Sussex home of the Bloomsbury Group' – where thousands of visitors come to admire the miscellany of paintings, textiles, ceramics and furniture that she accumulated in this rural retreat, with its simple rooms transfigured by glowing pattern, ample goddesses and Matisse-style goldfish. This was 'Nessa's' house: a place of colourful creativity, smelling of turpentine, lavender and old books. A place of freedom to dream, and limitless horizons.

As children we slept in the roomy attic. Its corner was curtained off, and if you pulled the drape aside it revealed a forgotten jumble of fantastical, musty dressing-up things: medieval-style gowns with jagged sleeves, velvet cloaks with sequinned collars, brocaded skirts, kimonos, cummerbunds and caftans, all of them promising fantasy-fulfilment and fairy-tale adventure. I don't know who these gaudy garments had been created for. The visitors to Charleston – writers, intellectuals, artists and performers – loved theatricals, so maybe my great-aunt Virginia Woolf, Vanessa's younger sister, dressed up in them. The economist John Maynard Keynes was a regular guest, with his flamboyant Russian ballerina wife, Lydia Lopokova, so it's possible that she danced in them. In the photograph my mother took of me in 1959, I'm decked out as a rather stagy princess. At other times I might have been Maid Marian, a mermaid, a ghost or the goddess Athene.

The world I grew up in was one in which art and make-believe were nourished, where everyday objects were decorated. I think I was born with a consuming interest both in what we wear and in how we look. Or perhaps the seeds of that fascination were planted sixty-odd years ago as I pulled a motley, moth-eaten gown off its hanger and struggled to find the sleeves, or when my older cousin gave me the tempting gift of a box of Leichner greasepaints. Either way, clothes, hairstyles and make-up have always had, for me, the character of an adventure.

My father, Quentin Bell, was an intellectually voracious man: an art historian, a painter and sculptor, a biographer and a teacher – and as I grew up I began to learn from him about one of his special subjects, the history and iconography of female finery. My mother, Anne Olivier Bell, whose reputation as an editor and scholar rests on her ground-breaking work editing Virginia Woolf's diaries, was equally formative; she taught me to sew, and steered my taste in clothes. Thanks to them, it's second nature for me to notice people's choice of dress, and to speculate about how they choose to present themselves and their bodies to the world.

This book has grown out of that fixation. And – focussing specifically on women's relationship with their appearance – it has become a quest to discover what their daily choices declare. More precisely, it also asks, is our style our own, or has it been historically determined by external, often political forces? Who decides on the kind of face we show to the world, and whose approval are we seeking when we get ready to confront it each day? What are the roles played by custom, colour and class?

Since the mid-nineteenth century the mutations of the ideal woman's body shape have perhaps been more extreme than at any period of history. The female silhouette has expanded and contracted, metamorphosing from the outline of a lampshade to that of an hourglass, from a cone to a column. Women's busts were lowered and raised, inflated and flattened. Until the turn of the twentieth century legs and feet were suppressed, after which – with several interruptions – they became increasingly visible. My research has taken me on a joyful and multi-storeyed quest in search of the tea gown, 'enamelling', bust developers, 'rational' dress, the Marcel wave, the waspie, beauty contests, Gibson girls, the bob, the banana skirt, knickers, suntans, radioactive corsets and 'Flatterettes'.

This is not an academic treatise, more a voyage of exploration, as en route I discovered that the African American entertainer Aida Overton Walker danced the cakewalk in front of the king at Buckingham Palace in 1903, and was rewarded with a diamond brooch; that the first female plastic surgeon in the world was a French feminist who wore a lapel button reading *'Je veux voter'*; and that the queen of cosmetics Elizabeth Arden supplied lipsticks to suffragettes as a sign of solidarity. I was also shocked to find out that in 1913 one Mrs Lanning of Atlantic City was attacked and beaten unconscious by a mob who disapproved of her too-revealing beachwear. Then there was the memoir written by a lady's maid in the 1920s, describing how she not only had to memorise her mistress's hairpins but also had to help in administering her enemas. More comical was the story of how the artist Kathleen Hale furtively disposed of her uncomfortable corset by shoving it into a prickly hedge, as was the discovery of the 'Turkobath', a plastic cape that clipped onto the sides of the bathtub and supposedly melted the fat off you by creating a steam bath effect. For me, such delectable trivia has always been at the very heart of history – telling us what it was like to live in past times.

But as I explored, I found there was a more complex story to tell – because dress, beauty and self-adornment have always reflected social change. Virginia Woolf's aphorism seems to me eternally relevant: 'Vain trifles as they seem, clothes have, they say, more important offices than to merely keep us warm. They change our view of the world, and the world's view of us.'

It's almost a century since Woolf wrote those words (in *Orlando* [1928]), and her insight on clothes applies equally to the inessentials with which we adorn our bodies, such as hairstyles, make-up and ornaments. Disguises or uniforms, badges of allegiance or declarations of non-conformity, mating plumage or workwear, rich or poor: though there are innumerable variables, they are not 'vain trifles'. Factors bigger than ourselves – like fashion, sex, gender and class status – have bearings on how we look. Thus our outward appearance is a label we attach to ourselves each day, telling the world who we truly are.

———

At the centre of this story is the female body, in all its diversity, fat, thin, short, tall, brown, white, black, pink, smooth, hairy, wrinkly, youthful, crooked or symmetrical; and – relevant as ever in this context – the vexed issues of body image and bodily autonomy. We may even find ourselves wondering, whose body is it? Are our legs really our own, to conceal or display as we please? In the hundred years from 1860 to 1960, textile industrialisation changed the game for fashion, and saw it move into the fast lane. That happened concurrent with a social revolution, which saw unprecedented progress in female emancipation. One after another, the fences that kept women out were starting to fall, allowing them to break through into the economic, educational, sexual and political strongholds previously reserved for men. At the same time feminist movements were defying the 'morality police' of their day. This same hundred years saw the rapid introduction of new technologies like photography, film and, eventually, TV, which (for better and worse) thrust women – and female imagery – out of the private and into the public gaze.

From the mid-nineteenth century, for the best part of fifty years, women's anatomical realities were refashioned from the exterior, via sharp steel and galling whalebone. By the 1920s the creation of an attractive image could no longer be achieved by webbing, boning and a rearrangement of petticoats. Our newly enfranchised great-grandmothers had thrown off their corsets and might be seen in swimsuits gaily leaping off diving boards or shaking their released legs in time to a jazz band. The Second World War then offered them access to a 'man's world' which seemed to point in the direction of even greater freedom, and by 1960 real equality appeared to be on the horizon. My chosen hundred-year timeframe presents a panorama in which the female body was revealed, going from almost complete cover-up to a point – around 1960 – where women were able to appear in public places wearing a bare minimum of clothing: a convincing transformation from captivity to liberation – or was it? Things weren't so simple, especially since that same period was also one of huge technological advance. Under the spotlight of electricity, photography and film, women's bodies were illuminated more brightly (and also more unflatteringly) than at any other time in human history. By 1960, imagery of the 'ideal' – but unattainable – female body was omnipresent.

———

Ironically, as women's limbs and flesh emerged from the darkness, new, more punitive controls were imposed on their bodies.

Fashions that exposed one's legs and arms demanded that those legs and arms be presentable. Freedom from petticoats came with a price tag, just as gaining political rights and joining the workplace had implications – not always positive ones – for the way women dressed and groomed themselves. The transition from the privacy of home to the exposure of the wider world laid a woman's appearance open to public scrutiny, and often hostility. In the pages that follow we will track the historical 'undressing' of women, as the anxiety surrounding the fashioning of beauty shifts from their outer garments to the human body itself.

For how is it, in an age of unisex and Lycra, that even brave, creative women can often feel condemned and tyrannised? For as long as popular belief subscribes to a particular, limited ideal of beauty, we are liable to feel a nagging discontent with how we look. Some women opt out of the pressures that modern beauty imposes, like twenty-five-year-old Asha Hussein, who in 2021 told *Glamour* magazine why she chose to wear the hijab. 'I am not my hair. I am not my beauty, I am not my body. I am me,' she explained. She might argue that under the patriarchy the wearing of a hijab – or a veil, or a crinoline – is one way to find freedom.

It seems to me that, as women, a high proportion of us have never been comfortable with our bodies – which is hardly surprising when we reflect that for years they have been a battleground for commercial interests, as well as a site for guilt, anger and harm. Today's beauty-seekers have high-tech options. We may decide to have the body we were born with straightened, corrected, lifted or realigned. We may submit to needles and scalpels, and do it willingly, because we believe it improves our appearance. But isn't this just a variant on how previous generations chastised their bodies and mortified their flesh? Nineteenth-century women squeezed their figures into hourglass-shaped corsets; their twentieth-century descendants had their faces injected with paraffin wax, lived off black coffee and lettuce, and paid surgeons to excise their wrinkles. How many of us, I wonder, would turn the clock back to that bygone age of the total cover-up, when women's frocks were fashioned by crinolines and their waistlines by tight-lacing?

All the Rage aims in part to disentangle some of these inconsistencies; it is also an attempt to understand and to reconcile the history of the liberation of the female body in light of an incongruity: that, at the very time that women's economic, educational, sexual and political chains were being unlocked, the shackles of perceived 'femininity' were tightening their grip.

———

This story is told chronologically, and to open each chapter I've selected the full-length image of a clothed woman who I believe – subjectively – to encapsulate the aesthetic and the zeitgeist of her era. Alexandra, Lillie, Diana, Freda, Prunella, Betty and Brigitte: each one stands (or reclines) as a representative of a moment in women's history. These are the white, Western celebrity influencers, movie stars, icons – the so-called 'Professional Beauties' of their day. In the period I'm addressing, beauty, privilege and whiteness all – largely – belonged together. But obviously that is not a denial of the fact that women of colour both influenced, and were influenced by, trends in beauty and fashion.

Many 'ordinary' women looked at such icons of loveliness with a mixture of envy and despair. This century-long progression of photographs demonstrates other facets of the revolution in progress. The beauty and advertising industries were expanding in tandem with fluctuations of fashion: it was in their interests to play on women's bodily insecurities. Not all of our grandmothers and great-grandmothers submitted without a fight, and the 'beauty' battles fought by feminists have often been bloody. A hundred or more years ago, cutting your hair short was regarded almost as an act of aggression, while the wearing of trousers, if not ridiculed, was a trigger for verbal abuse and derision. Nonetheless, it was simply a matter of time before both cropped hair and jeans went mainstream. Today, the Real Beauty Campaign, the 'body positivity' movement, and 'fat pride' co-exist with body dysmorphia, voyeurism and extreme misogyny. Indisputably, we still have a long way to go.

This is also a personal book for me. Instinctively, all my sympathies are aroused by the human impulse towards self-adornment – the pursuit of loveliness. I love putting on make-up, choosing jewellery and shopping. I rejoice at pink hair and blue lipstick, even if I don't wear them myself. But in my sixties I'm as anxious about how I look as many women I know. I spend money on face cream, I read beauty columns and I often wish my legs were lovelier. My own doubts and insecurities about my body – about how I dress it and groom it – surface in the narrative that follows.

My 'imperfections' may not keep me awake at night, yet I often puzzle about why I care. There's no easy answer. I'm not seeking a husband. I don't have a public role. Is it because I want to be admired by other women? Is it because I too have bought into the myths about youth and beauty? What I suspect is that many of us, when we choose our clothes and 'do' our faces, are confronted with an inescapable and deep-rooted inheritance: a status quo whereby we are judged on our looks, and that judgement is delivered by men. These factors have bedevilled our relationship with our appearance.

And yet I know I am not alone in feeling that troubling to look nice, and dressing in clothes that I love, sends a powerful message about who I am. I also strongly believe that self-adornment is one of the fun sides of being a woman – in fact, of being a human being!

————

When I was young, I had a friend whose remedy for *everything* bad – heartbreak, overdrafts, pests and plagues – was 'have a bath and put on make-up', and it's proved good advice. Doing your hair, putting on your war paint, a brightly coloured dress, choosing the right scarf, necklace and earrings is pure fun – party time! And playing at being Cinderella at the ball, just to feel good about yourself, can also send out an explicit message of courage, confidence, joy and renewal to others. Frocks and furbelows may be 'vain trifles', but I don't accept that playing dress-up makes me irredeemably frivolous. Though I often sigh at my reflection in the mirror as I grow older, somewhere inside me there is still the little girl trying on my mother's high-heeled shoes and discovering the neglected treasures in the recesses of the Charleston attic.

The photograph of Princess Alexandra of Denmark, taken in 1860,
that secured her engagement to Albert Edward, the Prince of Wales

1

Victoriana

Alexandra

This is Alexandra: the chaste young princess who will be chosen to be Queen of the United Kingdom and the British Dominions. It is one of the earliest official photographs of a woman who was to become an icon of her age, a beauty to whom countless other women aspired.

It's 1860, nearly the mid-point of the Victorian era. Photography, cumbersome, expensive and slow, has not yet become a mass medium, but it's beginning to change how people see themselves. With the ability to reproduce and distribute pictures that seemed like magic mirrors, imagery was transformed. At this time a photographic portrait session was a luxury, requiring a professional operator to handle the toxic chemicals involved, and the exposure time of twenty seconds or more meant that the model needed to remain motionless, and not smile. Alexandra's static, solemn pose, with its fanciful reflection device, may have been in a studio, or it may have been staged in the Yellow Palace in Copenhagen where the sixteen-year-old then lived. The princess has a resigned, almost apprehensive air. She must know that the carefully presented result will be despatched to the nineteen-year-old

Prince of Wales, heir to Victoria's throne, who is being prepared by his zealous parents for marriage – and who knows how he will react when he sees it? Though Alexandra's father was next in line to the throne of Denmark, he was not rich. The princess had been brought up in a grace-and-favour dwelling, but played her part in the household's economies by dressmaking and helping in the home. Her family did not participate in court life, and Alexandra would have been aware that she needed to make a good match. The photograph is a bid for her future.

With this in mind her image has been constructed with the utmost care; her dynastically ambitious mother, Princess Louise of Hesse-Kassel, would certainly have had a hand in advising her daughter. Nothing has been left to chance. She has had her hair done in two symmetrical pendant ringlets (a style known as a *repentir*), put on her best hat and chosen her most fashionable outfit: modestly high-necked, of a bold checked design ornamented with fancy braid, with bell sleeves and under-sleeves.* Their cut, low-set on the shoulder, looks as if it would constrict arm movement. One can only guess what colour the dress was. The first synthetic aniline dyes had recently come into production, so perhaps a fashion-conscious sixteen-year-old might have chosen a fabric checked in vibrant mauve or magenta.

Unquestionably, the skirt's beehive form is supported by the metal-hooped framework known as a crinoline: in 1860, they were the height of fashion. Alexandra's slender figure, emphasised by the longitudinal fabric design, is also strained in at the waist by an infrastructure of corsetry, which makes her bust a solid, indivisible form. Her overall shape is that of a bell: arms and trunk subsumed into a gently curvaceous pyramidical form

---

* They were probably of a type known as *engageantes*, lightweight detachable sleeves worn under the wide-open bell sleeves of the main dress.

which takes little account of human anatomy. Her feet are invisible; she appears to hover half an inch above the floor, not walking, but gliding – demonstrating the magic of what one might describe as the 'no-legs' woman. Her hands are little, white and show no sign of manual labour. Her facial features appear to be as nature created them, though the photographer's assistant has most likely touched them up with a fine paintbrush. She stares at the camera, stretches out her pale hand to rest on the architectural studio prop to her right and appeals to the young prince to admire her.

And Prince Edward and his parents *did* admire the look of this carefully packaged Danish princess. Already, they knew that Alexandra was well-born, devout and unaffected. But apart from that – as with so many women – her clothes and appearance had to bear the burden of the narrative. Regarding her actual physical qualities, the royal family had little to go on, because not only is she covered from head to foot, she is also shaped and sculpted: customised by the forces of society and fashion to conform to a mid-nineteenth-century ideal of womanhood.

On 10 March 1863 Prince Edward ('Bertie') and Princess Alexandra were married at Windsor. Status, wealth and security were now hers; she was just eighteen. Press and public gave their new princess the kind of ecstatic reception that was given to the young Diana Spencer over a century later.* The similarity continues. As Princess of Wales, Alexandra would become an admired and imitated icon for fashion-conscious women. The newspapers reported that she was 'an acknowledged Queen of beauty', with 'fine full eyes' and a 'fine full forehead'; 'the most charming of brides'.

---

* When Diana became Princess of Wales on her wedding day in 1981, some of her friends – apparently – made her the gift of Georgina Battiscombe's biography of Alexandra, in the hope she would benefit from the example of her husband's great-great-grandmother.

> She glittered like the morning star, full of life, and splendour, and
> joy, a bright vision that will long be imprinted on the memory of
> those who are fortunate enough to catch a glimpse of the Princess
> Alexandra.

The hyperbole is familiar. It speaks of a nation eager to clasp
a blameless, impeccable virgin to its collective bosom. But history and fashion play tricks with our perceptions: physically,
Alexandra seems to have little or nothing in common with
today's icons. Nevertheless – beneath the billowing yards of
fabric, the bolster bust and the immaculately twirled locks –
there was a body. In imagination, the supporting infrastructure
can be dismantled.

———

It is the job of a lady's maid to assist Princess Alexandra of
Schleswig-Holstein-Sonderburg-Glücksburg in her chamber,
and it's a lengthy and elaborate procedure. First of all her
dress must be unbuttoned. The checked confection is rever-
ently removed. Beneath, as when one unmoulds a pudding
from its basin, the form is retained. She has on a voluminous
petticoat: it covers the framework of her crinoline, and its
job is to soften the structural ridges that would otherwise be
visible through the dress fabric. Above, made to match, she
wears a well-fitting petticoat bodice which protects her dress
from her corset.

Next, the maid helps Alexandra to remove the bodice and
petticoat, and the crinoline itself is revealed. Surprisingly flexible, it's a hooped cage of tempered steel linked by tapes and
secured at the waist. And it's light, weighing less than a pound.
This is followed by the corset, made from starched buckram or

heavy linen with whalebone inserts. Imposing its rigid form on the flesh beneath, it is like the shell of a crustacean, encasing a soft, edible delicacy. It is hooked at the front and tight-laced at the back.

Through the bars of the crinoline cage a further garment is visible. It resembles a pair of long, wide-legged trousers. Older women – from the generation born in the eighteenth century – did not differentiate their legs, not even invisibly, under their skirts, unless they wanted to be thought depraved. Underpants – 'pantalettes' – for women were introduced in the early decades of the nineteenth century. Assuming she wore them, Alexandra would have been in the vanguard of pants-wearers: a pair of ample tucked and lace-trimmed drawers, reaching to mid-calf. The legs don't join at the crotch: instead, this seam was left open – far more convenient when using the lavatory. Below, there's a pair of ankles clad in white stockings, held up by ribboned garters. The feet, previously invisible, are shod in elegant kitten-heeled button-up ankle boots.

It takes skilled hands to help unpin her hat, to extricate the fancy tortoiseshell combs which keep her coiffure in place, and to allow her long, light brown tresses to unravel and float free. Her fingernails are clean and buffed.

Alexandra's maid is familiar with which ribbons to untie and which buttons to undo, in order to remove, first, the crinoline and then – accompanied by an audible exhalation of relief – the corset, revealing one further layer below, next to the skin, the chemise: a fragile and flimsy piece of underwear made from prettily embroidered white cotton. With tact and intimacy, the young woman next helps her mistress to take off her boots, her stockings, her garters, drawers and chemise. The 1860s woman is undressed.

Is this beautiful princess different from her twenty-first-century descendant? Mostly, no. Her fingers and toes are unadorned. Her figure, no longer distorted by undergarments, has the generous elasticity and bounce of a very young woman; nevertheless, without the cantilevered support of her corset, her stomach and breasts – now identifiable one from the other – settle naturally. It is hard to tell whether those central sections of her body are small, medium or large. Sixteen-year-old Alexandra might have been covered in puppy fat, for the corset was not intended to make a woman thinner; instead it redistributed her fatness, pushing it around into whatever position happened to suit the fashion of the day. But this is not something she needs to think about, as few will ever see her tummy, or her breasts. It's also impossible to know whether she has gone to the trouble of shaving or otherwise removing any growth of hair from armpits, legs or groin. As these are certainly areas which will remain hidden, and since it was not yet common practice to attempt depilation on areas of the body other than the face, it is highly probable that she has not. The transparent pallor of her Nordic skin shows that it has rarely been exposed to sunshine.

Thinking about the complex infrastructure that has squashed and imprisoned Alexandra's tender body, it is hard not to feel a sense of release; to want to cry good riddance to all those hooks, buttons and fancy accessories. They seem horrifying. Nineteenth-century women were restricted in what they could do, where they could go. Nevertheless, Victorian women retained a kind of ownership of their bodies – giving them a measure of wholeness and even integrity – that many women today may feel they no longer have.

Covering, corseting and confining was inconvenient, laborious, time-consuming and often very uncomfortable. It was also conformist, discriminatory and perpetuated the myth of the

subservient, decorative, powerless woman. And yet – the body
beneath had honesty. It might be fat and it might be thin. In
1860, there was talk of dieting, but it was far from mainstream.
Self-starvation was rare, and had no medical name. Body hair
was left in situ; pedicures were irrelevant, and respectable women
didn't use make-up. It was impossible to make unfavourable
bodily comparisons on the beach, when your swimwear – including black stockings – hid everything from sight.

Alexandra was regarded as a beauty. To modern eyes, however,
her features may seem more handsome than attractive; her jawline looks rather heavy. But her complexion is smooth, flawless
and completely free from make-up.

She was an active young woman, a lover of riding, swimming
and skating. So her undressed limbs are likely to show more
muscularity than is usual for a woman of her class; her bottom
may be hefty, and she may have cellulite on her thighs. We'll
never know, because the nineteenth century fostered a culture
of bodily privacy. Even her husband was unlikely to see her with
nothing on; wives were often advised to remain clothed in the
marital bed.

But Alexandra is in every respect as much a flesh-and-blood
human being as you or me. Her skin may erupt with blemishes,
she may give off odours, sweat or tremble with cold; childbirth
and hormones will wreak changes to her skin and muscles.
She may grow fat, her hair may turn white, she may wrinkle,
shrivel and become spotted with the stains of old age. Calluses
and pigmentation will appear. But – with corsetry, floor-length
dresses, ample sleeves and cover-up necklines – she can mitigate
the signs of advancing years. True, she may subtly tint her hair,

or seek to smooth out facial wrinkles with balsams and lotions made from strawberry leaves, or use tincture of benzoin to impart a rosy hue to the skin. But so long as she could lace in her waist, cloak her arms and sheathe her legs under long skirts, she retained some control over how the world saw her.

Alexandra will do everything in her power to keep her beauty. As she matures, the queen will become hugely admired for her statuesque elegance, famed for a wasp waist and a majestic bejewelled bust, cinched in and held aloft by gravity-defying corsetry. There was a small scar on her neck, left over from a childhood operation; it was for this reason that she always preferred to wear high-necked dresses or, failing that, a pearl choker; thus influencing the look of a generation of society ladies.

As Princess of Wales and later as Queen Consort, Alexandra lived up to the British people's hopes. She became a fashion leader, a favourite and a model of virtue, wifehood and motherhood. She bore her husband six children, remained steadfastly faithful to him while enduring his serial infidelities and, when not enclosed within the domestic sphere or suffering from a series of unlucky ailments, devoted herself to church and charity. But above all, like so many women, she did what was expected of her, and kept up appearances.

Vanity Fair

It's 1858. Queen Victoria's reign is at its zenith. On a late-autumn afternoon, the London light is dimming and a youngish, stocky, pasty-faced man-about-town with a copious moustache is leaning against the wooden rails that surround Hyde Park. Fallen leaves lie in the path of a colourful parade of fashionably dressed equestrians, prancing on their mounts down the tree-lined alley of Rotten Row. The parallel walkways that flank the Row are thick with the cream of London society, taking the air. The rakish male onlooker is entranced:

> Ladies ... real ladies – promenade in an amplitude of crinoline difficult to imagine and impossible to describe; some of them with stalwart footmen following them, whose looks beam forth with conscious pride at the superlative toilettes of their distinguished proprietresses; some escorted by their bedizened beaux.

The journalist George Augustus Sala, who often signed off as G.A.S., prided himself on his flamboyant literary style. But there is a touch of lip-smacking prurience in the description of the 'real ladies' on display that afternoon. Above all, it is the 'beautiful women on horseback' who whet his appetite, decked out in their 'ravishing riding-habits' and a kaleidoscopic array of hats –

> And as the joyous cavalcade streams past ... from time to time the naughty wind will flutter the skirt of a habit, and display a tiny, coquettish, brilliant little boot, with a military heel, and tightly strapped over it the Amazonian riding-trouser.*

Sala's peephole onto the pageant of mid-nineteenth-century society reveals a parade of women seen through men's eyes. And, knowing that they were the spectacle, each of them – whether strolling or on horseback – would have put her best boot forward.

---

* The 'riding-trouser' was an innovation; a modesty guard worn under the skirt. For respectable women, actual trousers were unthinkable. In 1851 the American reformer Amelia Bloomer gave her name to 'bloomers' – or bifurcated garments – which she promoted as liberatingly practical. But her campaign quickly unravelled under sustained derision and harassment.

Just two years earlier, cage crinolines had been introduced. They were perhaps the most unwieldy garments ever invented. They swept things off tables, broke them, impeded movement through doors and up stairs, and presented serious challenges in mounting and alighting from carriages or omnibuses. But their popularity was all-embracing. 'Your lady's maid must now have her crinoline and it has even become essential to factory girls,' sniffed one snobbish journalist. More to the point, the crinoline put working women at risk. Their width and their design – which created an upward draught as with a chimney – made them deadly fire hazards for the servant class, whose work involved lighting fires and cooking stoves. Although there are no exact statistics,* many hundreds of deaths by fire in the 1860s can probably be blamed on crinolines. Mistresses were also sometimes set alight. When the society hostess Lady Dorothy Nevill's voluminous skirt caught fire, she narrowly avoided being burnt to death by rolling on the hearthrug.

Nonetheless these metal-hooped frameworks (which had stimulated the Sheffield steel industry) came – for many women – as a deliverance from the horrible weight of countless petticoats. The legs now existed in a spacious vacuum. 'Oh, [they were] delightful,' recalled Henrietta Litchfield, daughter of Charles Darwin. 'I've never been so comfortable since they went out. [They] made walking so light and easy.' A crinoline also swung seductively from side to side, revealing occasional tantalising glimpses of ankle and calf. There were other advantages. In a society which regarded women as weak and inferior, the crinoline made them conspicuous while also enforcing a

---

*   An author writing in the *Lancet* in October 1860 noted that the registrar general had recorded in excess of three thousand deaths annually by fire, many of which were attributable to clothes catching alight. See Alison Matthews David, *Fashion Victims – The Danger of Dress Past and Present* (2015).

distance between the wearer and potential molesters. They could also be artfully arranged to conceal pregnancy.

Crinolines aside, looking like a 'real lady' took effort. The 'superlative toilette' noted by G.A.S. will have been the result of much time and expenditure. Soap, perfume, pomatums, creams and essences, polishes and emulsions gave every beauty her bloom. But the blessed sight of the lady on parade concealed a hidden army of low-paid female labour. The elegant figures of those horsewomen on Rotten Row were boosted by women workers in the staymaking industry, who painstakingly stitched together the layers of heavy-duty linen around the inserts of whalebone which formed their complex and constricting under-garments – while those same corsets often owed their flattering shape to the exertions of a lady's maid, tugging on the unfor-giving laces to bring about the desired curves.

Meanwhile, fluttering skirts, embroidered pelisses and fancy millinery represented hours of work by innumerable needlewomen satisfying an insatiable appetite for finery. By the late 1850s nearly three hundred thousand British women were employed in dressmaking and millinery alone, with rising one million overall working in the clothing trades. In 1863 an outcry erupted over the case of Mary Ann Walkley, aged twenty, who was one of fifty seam-stresses employed in the Regent Street workshop of the court dressmaker Madame Elise. Mary Ann and the others had been stitching ballgowns for a very special occasion: a celebration for Princess Alexandra of Denmark, who had recently become Princess of Wales following her mar-riage to Prince Edward. The pressure was on, and for over twenty-six hours Mary Ann didn't get a break. Over the night of Friday 19 June she became ill. By Sunday she was worse, and on Monday morning her roommate found her dead in the bed beside her.

A post-mortem determined that Mary Ann Walkley had died of apoplexy – a stroke – and the surgeon stated that 'long hours of work in a crowded apartment, and sleeping in a close, badly ventilated room, would have a great tendency to produce the symptoms'. Questions were asked in Parliament, the women's conditions were compared to slavery, and press commentary agreed that Mary Ann had been worked to death.* Was the beautiful princess aware that a woman just a couple of years older than her had died, getting those magnificent ballgowns ready to greet her?

————

The Victorians were fascinated by finery, by its extravagance and its voluptuousness. Sala resorts to his classical dictionary to describe the overwhelming effect of the fashion parade: 'The Danaës! The Amazons! The lady cavaliers! The horsewomen! Can any scene in the world equal Rotten Row at four in the afternoon, and in the full tide of the season?' A marketplace of gloriously apparelled lovelies, tripping by smelling of roses and flaunting their sexy footwear. Make no mistake, this was a shop window, with young women for sale to potential husbands. And – like the Danish princess – each one of them knew that her face was her fortune.

This is Vanity Fair. But it is more than that – it's a morality play. For Sala's titillating afternoon stroll comes with a warning. 'All is not gold that glitters, my son,' he reminds his reader. 'Those are not all countesses' or earls' daughters.' Beware. Women in the street had other connotations. And

---

* No laws were ever enacted to improve working conditions for seamstresses. More than a century and a half later, pay and conditions for many workers (mostly women) in the garment trade remain inhumane and unacceptable.

Sala identifies three such women of easy virtue, two of them on horseback, and the third visible through the windows of a brougham: 'Some of those dashing delightful creatures have covered themselves with shame, and their mothers with grief, and have brought their fathers' gray hair with sorrow to the grave.'

Sala's comments go to the heart of what was seen as the natural order of things in the Victorian era. Sexual respectability meant dialling down showy accessories, and not strutting around like a street-walker. It meant covering up or only venturing out with a male protector. Where restrictions on women are concerned, Victorian England has many echoes in political regimes where virtue and fashionable elegance are seen as incompatible. Basically, it meant being regulated and restricted, whether indoors or out.

On 7 January 1862 a father describing himself as 'Paterfamilias from the Provinces', who had recently moved his family to London and whose two young daughters were not long out of the schoolroom, wrote an angry letter to *The Times* to complain that his girls had been subjected to lascivious comments by a group of deplorable scoundrels while out walking. 'London [is] infested by a number of ill-conditioned blackguards who [make] it a business to insult and terrify young ladies by following them and even being daring enough at times to attempt to speak to them.' This was a disgrace and he intended to beat the villains' brains out. The follow-up correspondence has a familiar ring. Were the girls asking for it, by dressing provocatively, a female correspondent retorted unsympathetically. She claimed she had never had any trouble herself, because she dressed modestly:

If young ladies from the country ... will walk down Oxford Street dressed in red cloaks and pork-pie hats with white feathers ...

they cannot expect to escape the notice of those few despicable idlers, unworthy the name of men, who take advantage of the weakness of women.

To which 'A London Man' responded, saying that some young ladies he knew had endured a similar experience, and lamenting, 'No good-looking girl or woman is safe from this sort of molestation unless she be under male protection.' Mr 'Common Sense', however, countered with his view that the young ladies had brought it on themselves by their attention-seeking dress and behaviour:

> It never occurs to [their fathers] that bonnets of the 'kiss me quick' build, loud stockings, exaggerated *tournures*,* capes, and crinolines; vagrant ringlets straying over the shoulder, better known by the name of 'follow me, lads', and such like decoys, are all unmistakably intended to attract the notice and attentions of the male sex.

Paterfamilias, he said, would do better if he sent his girls out properly protected, or protected them himself. Another female correspondent suggested helpfully that women on their own were always safe until about half past ten in the morning – but probably not after that.

How easy it is to imagine a pair of carefree young women in pork-pie hats with untidy ringlets laughing and tripping along Oxford Street – it could be today. The smothering, obnoxious male stags sniffing and baying around them may also be familiar. But the underlying narrative has an alien ring, with the women seen, above all, as powerless.

In the 1860s the bargain was status and security in return

---

* A bustle, or similar padded undergarment used to add fullness to the costume and enhance a woman's figure.

for captivity – a pact not agreed but imposed. Any woman who defaulted tainted her honour and reputation, and that of her family.

––––––––

The class of women who took this step are little heard. But in 1858 two 'unfortunates' who wrote letters to *The Times* were given space by the editor to tell their side of the story. Their voices testify to a social climate of oppression, hypocrisy, injustice, inequality and stigma linked to their appearance. On 4 February a letter was printed from 'One More Unfortunate' – who, having disgraced herself, did not feel able to give her name or go into detail about how she came to be making a living as a prostitute. She acknowledges, however, that she and her kind have lost all claim to social acceptance – 'We are cut off from the moral, social and religious worlds ... People shrink from us as they would from loathsome things.' But she is incensed: the fault lies with society. Her purpose is to remind the male reader of his complicity: 'Recollect it was man who made us what we are. It is man who pays for the finery, the rouge, and the gin ... Say, then, is it for man to persecute even the most profligate among us?'

The conversation was promptly joined by 'Another Unfortunate'. An uneducated woman, but pretty, cunning and streetwise from an early age, the height of her ambition was to be like the girls who had fled her deprived provincial neighbourhood and returned decked out in dazzling 'ribands and fine clothes'. At the age of fifteen she joined their ranks – 'and thus commenced my career as what you better classes call a prostitute'. And she vents indignation as she continues to highlight society's worst fear – that nobody would be able to tell the good woman apart from the bad woman:

I behave myself with as much propriety as society can exact.
I pay business visits to my tradespeople, the most fashionable
of the West-end. My milliners, my silk-mercers, my bootmak-
ers, know, all of them, who I am and how I live, and they
solicit my patronage as earnestly and cringingly as if I were
Madam, my Lady.

At what level did the good woman become bad? It took skill
to decipher the nuances of appearance. A blush, a flounce, a
ringlet or an inch of hemline could spell the difference between
vice and virtue, between a gentlewoman and a sex worker.
And those pretty young ladies in Oxford Street – were they out
shopping, or being bought?

Lady-like

Society was a marketplace. The merchandise was women. The
currency was dress, and beauty.

But there were voices who challenged this view of the world.
In the late eighteenth century Mary Wollstonecraft had looked
around her and saw that women were condemned to lead fatu-
ous lives. They were weak, frivolous and concerned only with
fripperies and dress. 'Confined … in cages, like the feathered
race, they have nothing to do but to plume themselves, and
stalk with mock-majesty from perch to perch': 'Taught from
their infancy, that beauty is woman's sceptre, the mind shapes
itself to the body, and, roaming round its gilt cage, only seeks
to adorn its prison.'

The dress reform movement, spearheaded by Florence
Harberton, would gather pace as the century progressed

(there will be more on this in Chapter 2). But behind it was the belief that liberty of movement complemented and aided women's political and social liberty. In the United States in the mid-nineteenth century, advanced thinking on clothes tended towards a theory of male conspiracy: that men were hampering women's progress towards equality and ensuring they would never be able to operate in the workplace by purposefully putting them into cumbersome and complicated garments.

'I can see no business avocation, in which woman in her present dress can possibly earn equal wages with man,' wrote the Massachusetts-born social reformer Susan B. Anthony, while her close colleague and contemporary in the American women's movement, Elizabeth Cady Stanton, argued that women could only be freed from their economic dependency on men when they were no longer forced to charm and beguile them with pretty frocks. Mrs Stanton, herself short and plump of stature, was an early adopter of bloomers; she both wore them and took every opportunity to promote them in print. Unfortunately the bloomer campaign never took off: the pair and their followers incurred ridicule and taunts, and by 1860 bloomers were effectively dead, on both sides of the Atlantic. But though long skirts and petticoats seemed – temporarily – to have won, and though the word 'feminism' would not appear in Britain until late in the nineteenth century, the women's movement was still simmering on the back burner. Harriet Taylor Mill, writing under the name of her husband, John Stuart Mill, argued in favour of the enfranchisement of women. The mid-nineteenth century also saw the emergence of the first 'feminist' forum, based in Langham Place in London – the eventual cradle of the suffrage movement.

There was much to fight for. For the greater part of Victoria's reign women – even princesses – were regarded as commodities, lacking rights, agency and autonomy; they were, effectively, chattels. Until 1882 a married woman was regarded in law as having no separate existence from that of her husband; she became his property, and anything she earned, owned or inherited became his. But not being a wife was even worse. The spinster – a Dickensian caricature – may have been permitted to own property, but she was treated with contempt. The competition for husbands was fierce. The 1861 census recorded a gender imbalance of only 879 men for every 1,000 women. Getting a man meant the difference between success and failure, security and destitution. 'Reader, I married him,' concludes the eponymous heroine of Charlotte Brontë's *Jane Eyre* (1847). After terrible trials, she has made a match in which both partners are worthy of each other. It is the biggest sigh of relief in English literature.

These factors, along with the divorce laws, made it prohibitive for any woman to escape from an unhappy marriage. A spinster might be regarded as unlucky, but a divorcée was unacceptable. Few with children would risk it, as they were also legally her husband's property.

There was huge demand for female labour, but – as mentioned earlier – it tended to be menial and low-paid, with the largest number of women employed as domestic servants, followed a close second by those working in the textile and clothing trades. Here too, a woman's personal attractions were marketable (as they still are). Better-looking women got better jobs; a pretty young woman was more likely to find employment as a parlourmaid, creating a good impression by opening the front door to her employer's visitors. Shops liked bright, bonny girls with good figures to work in their showrooms. These were also situations in which a working woman – if she was attractive and had domestic skills – might meet her future husband: the man who would rescue her from hard labour and penury.

There was no method of controlling women's reproduction. Why would there be, when a woman's prime purpose was to bear children? Giving birth to and bringing up the human race was seen as a 'sweet vocation'. But it was also a terrifying responsibility: 'Narrow indeed is the path in which a mother must walk,' wrote Eliza Warren, the author of an 1865 manual on childcare, 'knowing that she holds in her hand and cherishes at her breast an immortal spirit. Through her the germ of future happiness or misery has budded: through her a blessing or a curse has been cast upon the world: on earth she has created either a follower of Christ or a companion of fiends.'

What destiny could possibly be of greater consequence than this?

It was also generally believed that women's minds – having little capacity for topics beyond the all-consuming ones of babies, bonnets, romance and trinkets – were unable to cope with politics or national affairs. Thus women could not vote. At just over 50 per cent (in 1851), women's literacy was lower than that of men; even among more privileged women, their education fitted them only for the society circuit. Recalling her youth in the 1840s, Lady Dorothy Nevill outlined her own schoolroom years:

> ... a little French – some knowledge of piano playing, singing and painting in water colours, was considered a sufficient equipment. As for occupations and amusements, crochet and worsted work, together with archery and croquet, were the main relaxations of well-to-do girls.

> The true empire of woman in old days was declared to be one
> of softness, dignity and compliance – her commands were caresses
> and her menaces tears.

In other words, the sole areas where a female might claim superiority were her virtue, her vulnerability, her delicacy and her
beauty. Her capital was her femininity; and her elaborate, lacy
clothes accentuated this in every respect. The box that imprisoned this porcelain goddess was marked 'Fragile'; and everyone
knew the shop rules: 'All breakages must be paid for.'

––––––––

Morality had to be carefully codified. In *How to Behave – A
Pocket Manual of Etiquette* (1865), 'Mrs Manners' advised
her readers that a person's moral standing could be gauged by
their decorum in dress: 'Dress has its language, which is, or
may be, read and understood by all ... The choice we make
indicates our prominent traits of character.' Therefore a lady
who wished to be considered proper had to understand the
rules of taste:

> Highly ornamented clothes worn to church, or to shop in, are in
> bad taste ...
>   Deep and bright-coloured gloves are always in bad taste ...
> White stockings and dark dresses ... are not indicative of good
> taste. A girl with neatly and properly dressed feet, with neat, well-
> fitting gloves, smoothly arranged hair, and a clean, well-made
> dress, who walks well, and speaks well, and, above all, acts politely
> and kindly, *is a lady*.

Mourning dress had a complex geology of its own, strati-
fied into levels from inky jet and black bombazine to shadowy

grey. A widow must mourn for two years – but if it was only your aunt who had died, you might get away with just a couple of months.

A lady's coiffure – or lack of – had its own semantics. Loose hair denoted loose morals. Pinned, combed, brushed and tamed, styled hair was obedient hair, the hallmark of the disciplined and respectable lady. Remember the petrifying episode in *Jane Eyre* when the school inspector Mr Brocklehurst insists to the teacher that a pupil's hair must be shorn:

> 'Red hair, ma'am, curled – curled all over?' And extending his cane he pointed to the awful object, his hand shaking as he did so ...
>
> 'Miss Temple, that girl's hair must be cut off entirely; I will send a barber to-morrow.'

This is an extreme case, but it serves to illustrate the anger which supposedly 'uncontrolled' hair could provoke.* Normally, an innocent Victorian Alice in Wonderland might wear her hair loose without fear of reproach, just as she would wear shorter skirts than her mother. But as soon as she reached the danger zone of puberty, up went her hair and down went her skirts.

———

It's the summer of 1873. River steamers carry passengers down the loops of the Seine from inland Rouen to Honfleur on the

---

* It still can. In 2016 Pretoria Girls' High School in South Africa told their pupils that Afro hair was 'messy' and 'exotic', and must be tamed. Thirteen-year-old Zulaikha Patel was threatened with arrest for leading a protest against the hair policy. The school backed down. Emma Dabiri, in *Don't Touch My Hair* (2019) writes, 'The only way Afro hair can seemingly fulfil the criteria for beauty is if we make it look like European hair – if we make ourselves look like something we are not.'

coast. On board one of these, a middle-aged lady wearing a modest grey dress softly frilled at the neck, and a blue jacket, is seated with her husband. She's tall and shapely, with a strong build, blue eyes and a reddish complexion; in her kid-gloved hand she carries a striped parasol to guard against the sun, and her soft brown hair is swept underneath a polite hat trimmed with a plume of cock's feathers. The gentleman is a little older than she is, in his mid-forties, with a luxuriant pepper-and-salt beard and moustache, noticeably shiny boots, a mild demeanour and the easy, entitled manner of a man who knows that, however frumpy and nondescript his suit and hat may be, he belongs to the upper class of the top nation in the world. If you have been to Trinity College, Cambridge, nothing can take that away from you. On the lady's finger there's a gold band; they are recently married. This is their honeymoon voyage, and it is the first time the lady has been abroad.

But the happy English couple were not all they appeared to be. Arthur Joseph Munby and Hannah Cullwick had first met nineteen years earlier; at that time Munby was a working barrister, and Hannah, born in Shropshire to a saddler and a servant, was a lowly servant in the household of Lady Louisa Cotes, who had been a bridesmaid to Queen Victoria. Hannah was at the bottom of the social pile. Regardless of the plumed hat and kid gloves, she was not, and never would be, a lady.

The facts of this unconventional relationship came to light after both their deaths, when their papers were made public. Again and again Munby's writings return to his fascination with the lower castes of Victorian women. His first meeting with Hannah had set him on the road to a lifelong love affair with her steely physique and statuesque strength. Years later he described that encounter:

A country girl, she was, a scullion at the Squire's ...

A robust hardworking peasant lass, with the marks of labour and servitude upon her everywhere: yet endowed with a grace and beauty, an obvious intelligence, that would have become a lady of the highest.

Their love endured: a clandestine, fetishistic playing-out of roles, in which Hannah willingly acted the submissive. She loved to be the drudge: to clean his boots, wash his feet and be with him 'in her dirt' – as she described the mess she was in after a long day sweeping chimneys, cleaning knives, emptying slops and gutting fowl.

Hannah Cullwick, dressed as a servant

But if the two of them were ever to go out together, Hannah had to maintain the pretence that she was a lady – for example, it was essential for her to conceal her rough, reddened and callused hands by wearing gloves. But Hannah never felt comfortable in this guise. She may have been an under-servant, but she was also a super-competent and independent woman who despised the fussy gentility and uncomfortable clothes that went with being ladylike. As she saw it, not appearing genteel had all the advantages:

> I wound my way through the crowd o' passing folk in Fleet Street & the Strand but they only star'd & pass'd on ... That's the best o' being drest rough, & looking 'nobody' – you can go anywhere & not be wonder'd at.

For Hannah, this was about personal liberty – and she could see for herself that 'born-and-bred' ladies had precious little of that. She didn't own a mirror. As far as she could, she wore the clothes she chose to wear, and those clothes were *not* veils, gloves and fancy millinery. Munby sadly recognised Hannah's reluctance to submit to ladylike ways:

> 'I say, Massa,' she exclaimed, '*what* a good job I aren'a a lady! One thing, I should hate to be stuck up, an' dress fine, an' keep that nesh* an' prim, an' talk affected, like ladies do by what I've heerd, an' sit on sofas, an' have soft hands, an' have company, an' all such as that.

Hannah Cullwick took pride in being muscular, unkempt, plain-speaking and dirty; a pride which runs counter to

---

* A dialect word meaning a) 'unable to endure fatigue or exposure; susceptible to cold; delicate, weak. b) Dainty, fastidious, squeamish' (*OED*).

everything Victorian womanhood was taught to aspire to. Her defiant, uninhibited behaviour, and the latitude of her love life, come from a different world than that of the frilly feminine ladies whose disguise she was forced to adopt in public. A hundred years later, and Hannah might have been a hippie, a feminist rebel, a dropout. But articulate though she was, her circumstances left her, in the 1870s, with few options. Her extraordinary story – in which a working woman could only find real freedom through soiling and defacing her appearance – is a measure of just how imprisoned Victorian women were. And in all her soot and squalor, Hannah didn't envy them – 'Eh, I wouldna be a lady, not for a thousand pound!'

Victorian England harboured a multitude of shocking and compromising secrets. Behind closed doors, scores of pornographic publications catered for every caprice of the male imagination, from slave porn to paedophile porn, actress porn to flagellation. Undercover appetites for female flesh didn't have to look far to be aroused and satisfied.

But town halls, law courts, art galleries, city squares and stately homes were also public exhibition spaces for the unclothed female: on walls, pediments and in courtyards, her divine bosom and silky thighs reposed in bronze and marble splendour.

It is hard to imagine, now, the visual impact of a naked woman set against the squadrons of veiled and secluded Vestal Virgins, wives and mothers of Victorian England. And yet the contradiction was everywhere: for naked female imagery had rarely been more triumphant than in England in the late nineteenth and early twentieth centuries.*

Allowances could be made for the Old Masters. Greek marble, and the Aphrodites of Michelangelo, Titian, Canova and Rubens, had long earned the artistic stamp of approval. The nineteenth century would introduce a new beauty parade. At Osborne House, her country home on the Isle of Wight, Queen Victoria furnished the royal apartments with artworks of sensuous nudes. It appears that she and Albert rejoiced in sexy, scantily draped nymphettes.

But lest the queen be open to accusations of indecency the subjects – without exception – derive from history, mythology and romance. Fiction and fable blurred their impact and kept their erotic charge at a distance – but set the bar high in terms of feminine, fairy-tale perfection.

The artists were all male. From Rossetti's suffocatingly languorous goddesses to Etty's fleshy nudes, Leighton's saccharine mythological pin-ups to Alma-Tadema's titillatingly voyeuristic portrayals of ancient Rome, a wealth of artwork gave visibility to the disrobed curves of innumerable artists' models. No 'lady' would have stripped naked to pose for an artist, not even a Royal Academician. But their 'classical' subject matter conferred respectability on a heavenly host of women who – as studio models – had sacrificed that

---

* An extreme example of this has a personal resonance for me. The 1950s and early 60s were also an era of prudery, and at this time authorities in Leeds ordered the removal of one of the city's most distinctive public sculptural features – a ring of eight bare-breasted nymphs holding lamps. My father Quentin Bell, at that time Professor of Fine Art at the University of Leeds, and an authority on Victorian art, headed a campaign to reinstate the nymphs where they had stood in City Square. Alfred Drury's bronze nudes are now one of the city's iconic landmarks. However, some complaints have been received that they objectify women, and following the protests and toppling of statues associated with colonialism and slavery, Leeds City Council has commissioned a Statues Review Report to recommend on the fate of the city's public art. There is no guarantee that the nymphs will not be removed again.

attribute in their own lives. Through art, nudity was made palatable to the public of both sexes, with Aphrodites and Ariadnes depicted as white, perky-breasted, irreproachably hairless nymphs, often teasingly veiled with gossamer wisps of drapery.

Perceptions of a woman's body were mediated – and commodified – through high culture, and inevitably the goddesses' flawlessness made some women feel that their own bodies were suboptimal. The fear of standing revealed could be crippling. In her autobiography, the artist Kathleen Hale tells how her mother, as the date of her wedding approached (in 1891), was consumed with dread at the thought of the inevitable discovery of her pubic hair, which she imagined to be 'a monstrous disfigurement, peculiar to herself alone'. And she must surely have been one of many – as is also illustrated by the sad story of the art and social critic John Ruskin and his bride Euphemia ('Effie') Gray. In 1848 nineteen-year-old Effie married Ruskin, who was eleven years her senior. A legend, perhaps apocryphal, endures, that Ruskin refused to consummate the marriage because he was so horrified to discover that the intimate parts of her body did not correspond to the smooth hairlessness with which he was familiar from classical nudes. Effie later gave an account of the motives to which Ruskin attributed his abstinence from a sexual relationship within their marriage:

> He alleged various reasons, hatred to children, religious motives, a desire to preserve my beauty, and finally this last year told me his true reason (and this to me is as villainous as all the rest) that he had imagined women were quite different to what he saw I was, and that the reason he did not make me his Wife was that he was disgusted with my person the first evening 10th April.

There are many possible interpretations, and the pubic hair theory is just a theory. But the legend's very existence, in fact its essential component – that Effie felt she had disappointed her husband, and that for whatever reason he would not have sex with her – points to the Victorian lady's predicament. Covered up, gift-wrapped, she promises every divine satisfaction to the prospective purchaser. Uncovered, he wants his money back.

In 1854, after six years of phantom marriage, a huge scandal erupted when Effie – still a virgin – filed for an annulment, and soon after married Ruskin's close friend and disciple John Everett Millais (by whom she would proceed to bear eight children). Millais was one of the nineteenth century's most admired artists. And in 1870 his spectacular canvas *The Knight Errant* topped the bill at the Royal Academy's annual exhibition.

This striking erotic fantasy is set safely in the bygone days of chivalry and courtly love. It depicts a handsome knight taking up his mighty sword to slash the bonds strapping a naked woman to a tree; both are life-size. The hero has slain the maiden's attacker, who lies dead in the background. Her breasts and thighs shimmer with reflections from his glittering armour, in which he is fortified from head to toe.

The Knight Errant by Sir John Everett Millais, 1870

Millais's Arthurian tableau offers up some revealing readings from the Victorian beauty barometer. His conceit speaks eloquently of defencelessness, vulnerability, capture, control and rescue. To ensure her survival, the Victorian woman needed to arouse protective instincts in the Victorian man. A woman with a strong physique had less chance of finding someone to look after her, because she appeared able to look after herself. Millais's rather strapping damsel in distress could probably have seen off her assailants with a sharp kick, put her clothes back on and run away. But that didn't get anyone a knight in armour. As for the look in his eye; that's also unambiguous. Millais seems to be telling a story of manly honour. But is that believable, in the circumstances? The perfect hairlessness of the maiden's creamy-white body, clothed only in a cascade of undisciplined golden tresses which descend like a torrent, caressing her pelvis, seems to emphasise her vulnerability. Though Millais, unlike his mentor, seems not to have been disgusted by Effie's 'person', it appears that the existence of pubic hair ran counter to the prevailing aesthetic – just as it does today.

Binaries and Boundaries

What was that prevailing aesthetic?

The nineteenth century set great store by telling the sexes apart. It's a point that may seem obvious, but the fear that women might be masquerading as men, behaving in a masculine way and seizing power by stealth, was a real one. Over the century and a half that has passed since then, the sexes' distinctiveness has become massively blurred. But back then you *had* to be able to differentiate women, sartorially, from men.

Mid-Victorian England was so consumed with the imperative for women to look like women that when they didn't there

was uproar. In 1868 a row broke out in the morning papers
about the 'pit-brow lassies' or 'broo-wenches' employed by
the Wigan coalmines, because they wore trousers to protect
themselves.

> They generally wear a peculiar description of attire, consisting
> of coarse trousers, *resembling those worn by men* [my ital-
> ics], fastened by a belt round the waist, a soft bonnet, and a
> shawl. The petticoats are generally tucked into the trousers.
> Sometimes they may be seen wearing jackets *like the men*
> [my italics], smoking, drinking, and behaving as if completely
> unsexed.

What's striking is the narrative of male ownership. Even the
miners' union reported that it was

> a most sickening sight to see girls and women who had been cre-
> ated for a much nobler sphere of action, clad *in men's attire* [my
> italics] on the pit banks, but it is a much sadder sight to see them,
> day by day losing everything modest and womanly.

There were only five hundred broo-wenches, but their defem-
inisation made them famous, particularly after the 'social
explorer' Arthur Joseph Munby* visited Wigan and persuaded
a number of the lasses to have their photographs taken. The
pictures quickly became collectibles, while the women themselves, in their 'unmentionable nether garments', became a local
tourist attraction.

---

*   As we have seen, Arthur Joseph Munby, though of the 'gentleman' class,
nurtured a fascination with the lives of the working classes, particularly servants and 'unbecoming women'.

Female colliery workers in Wigan, c. 1870s

Thus Victorian Britain was strikingly gendered. Unless they landed in Wigan, the visitor from Mars would have no difficulty telling which Earth-dweller was male and which female. Seen from a distance, a clothed Victorian man resembled a lamp post: straight up and down, topped with a shiny cylindrical structure. His opposite number was all curves, billows and undulations. While he appeared black, unembellished and vertical, she was all colourful swags and sweeps, sinuous and S-shaped. Above all, like Princess Alexandra, she was the possessor of an 'hourglass' figure. Attention was focussed on her tiny waist.

In the 1860s, as men's clothing became increasingly neutral and easy to wear, the packaging surrounding the average woman was growing ever more complicated, protective and unassailable. The crinoline, which – for all its drawbacks – had briefly permitted such delightful ease of walking, was on the wane. Petticoats were piling back on.

As the century progresses the Victorian woman is putty, her contour swelling or contracting according to the whim of the decade: in, out; curved, flat; circular or asymmetrical; bottom or bosom. From 1870, fashion had abandoned the crinoline, and decreed a new emphasis on a lady's rump and hips, just as it does today. But while twenty-first-century women who want to look like Kim Kardashian may choose to have their behinds re-sculpted under anaesthetic, the nineteenth-century lady attached a bustle, or tournure, to her rear. This took up the slack, scooping up yards and yards of excess drapery to create a waterfall effect, cascading down into a foaming train of ruffles and flounces.

Appearing billowy and curvy required complex infrastructure. A cantilevered panier of steel, whalebone bands, or a horsehair and buckram 'dress improver', projecting up to two feet, then buckled or buttoned around the waist, was needed to support the bustle. And a standard trousseau consisted of sixty-five items of assorted underwear, including chemises, drawers, multitudinous petticoats, camisoles, vests and hose.

————

And corsets.

In the early 1860s British women bought twelve million of them. 'No discussion of the feminine body in the Western world can make much sense without getting a grip on the corset,' wrote the American feminist commentator Susan Brownmiller in the 1980s.

From corset design to decoration, from debates about damage to health to discussions about their alleged benefits, from dress reform to the dilemmas of marriageability, the discourse around corsets illuminates a subject packed with contradictions and controversy. The Australian academic Leigh Summers debunks the idea that tight-laced corsets were worn only by the privileged classes, and argues that the resulting debility was seen as desirable by a society that prized female fragility. Here, the corset can also be understood as a device – in a sense, a straitjacket – used by men to contain and suppress female flesh, with all its connotations of sexuality and the corporeal. Later, Dr Summers explores the entrenched myth, which would prevail for at least another hundred years, that the female body was inherently weak and in need of support and stabilisation. Pressing in on the flesh, torturing the skeleton, these rigid body-scaffolds defied any part of the anatomy to wobble or collapse. Perceived defects were smoothed out. Fat was squashed. It is hard at this distance in time to assess the impact of corsets on health. It is likely that, tight-laced, they caused – at the very least – fainting, respiratory and digestive problems. And despite its evidently injurious effects, there was no consensus either among the public or the medical profession about the evils of the corset. We may think of it as a cruel tyrant. At this time the body was made malleable by disciplining it from the outside. Later, that malleability would involve scalpels and sutures.

Typically, it would seem that the corset-wearing damsel was liable to be swooning or incapacitated. The whalebone armature served as a chastity belt while also stimulating panting, the heaving of breasts, flushing or pallor – an outlet, perhaps, for suppressed female desires? To this day, tight-laced corsets are associated with the *femme fatale*: submissive, but excitingly erotic; impregnable but also pregnable. The American fashion historian Valerie Steele has a cautious take on tight-lacing. She believes that it was rarely carried to the extremes that are sometimes supposed. In *Fashion and Eroticism* (1985), however, she explores the complex relationship between tiny waists and fetishism, and shows how corsetry could enhance sexual pleasure for both men and women.

In the context of Victorian society – whether in the ballroom or on the street – the unyielding, uncomfortable corset was non-negotiable. Above all, corsetry contained and mastered the wilful body. To put it simply, if you were tight, you were not loose.

Many authors have commented on the corset's important role in incapacitating the wearer for manual labour. 'No young lady could go into good society with a coarse clumsy waist *like a rustic*' (my italics). That included getting themselves dressed in the morning. Society was full of privileged ladies who needed a lady's maid to help tighten their stays before they could be deemed presentable. Once strapped in and swathed in flounces, a woman's ability to perform useful tasks was substantially reduced. This made her husband feel all the more alpha and able to congratulate himself on his dauntless prowess in providing for the decorous dead weight – the beautiful *thing* – who adorned his drawing room, embroidered his firescreens and fed his canary. Female beauty, class and male economic status were co-dependent.

So the man's approval of a woman's self-presentation was all-important. If straight up-and-down gentlemen liked curvy in-and-out ladies, that is what they must have. 'As a gentleman I admire exceedingly, not only a small, but a well-laced-in waist in a lady ... and I believe nine out of ten of us do the same,' explained one. In 1868 a woman wrote about her marriage, and her corset, to the *Englishwoman's Domestic Magazine*. The correspondence to this publication has long interested historians of the corset, and it has proved controversial. For convenience I'll call the woman Matilda. Her husband, she explained, was one of those who was 'particularly fond of a small waist'. Matilda recounts how she bought some new stays, made to measure for a *fourteen-inch* waist, and enlisted the help of her maid. Gradually, over weeks, the maid helped to reduce her mistress's waist measurement, inch by inch. 'For the first few days, the pain was very great,' but Matilda was determined. So they proceeded –

> [And] as soon as the stays were laced to close, and I had worn them so for a few days, I began to care nothing about [the pain], and in a month or so I would not have taken them off on any account. For I quite enjoyed the sensation, and when I let my husband see me in a dress to fit I was amply repaid for my trouble.

However, as Valerie Steele points out, accounts of this kind were unreliable and atypical. Her careful research shows that while the majority of women across the social spectrum wore corsets, most of their waistlines were around twenty-one or twenty-two inches. Strikingly small, yes. Dangerously distorted, no.

———

The gendering of Victorian society was accomplished through bustles, petticoats and corsetry. But it was also accomplished through hair. Think of the Victorian man. He is bushy. Unruly facial foliage sprouts in all directions around his chin and chops, and from beneath his top hat; his jawline is furnished with out-of-control 'dundrearies'. The sight of the fashionable men in Hyde Park with their 'Brobdingnagian moustaches and whiskers!'* left George Augustus Sala astounded. Like Samson, a man's hair was the expression of his virility. His female counterpart also boasted

---

*   Brobdingnagian: an elaborate adjective denoting exaggerated size, a reference to the race of giants living in the land of Brobdingnag described in Jonathan Swift's satirical novel *Gulliver's Travels* (1726).

large quantities of hair – mothers often prided themselves on having daughters whose hair reached beyond their waist. But that 'crowning glory' had to be tamed and controlled, and it was a formidable task. Ringlets and fringes (or 'fronts') made complex demands on the fashionable lady, and on her maid, for hair salons were mostly unknown in the nineteenth century; the fashion-conscious courtesan Lola Montez was adamant that a woman's hair should be brushed for at least ten minutes, *four* times a day.

As for hair in the wrong place, hairy women – like the bearded ladies gawped at and abused in circus sideshows – were seen as an offence against nature. God did not intend women to resemble men.

Science endorsed this perception. Charles Darwin (who himself boasted a notably hirsute chin) regarded prehistoric human beings as being hairy by default. He saw females, however, as having evolved to attract men by losing their mammalian fur – as if lack of some essential human factor was what made a female feminine. Natural selection? The idea that women must work on their appearance and distort its nature to please men, while men do the selecting, goes deep.*

In recognition that superfluous hair, particularly on the face, was 'a source of extreme annoyance and mortification', the beauty manuals had words of advice. Tweezers and razor were at the ready. Pitch-plaster – which worked like a waxed strip – painfully ripped unwanted hair out by the roots. A leather pad made sticky with gum or resin could serve the same purpose. Recipes for depilatories abounded. Mix together quicklime, lye and arsenic ... Or, if that felt too violent, try 'singeing with glowing nut-shells'.

---

* This idea is more rigorously explored in Karin Lesnik-Oberstein (ed.), *The Last Taboo: Women and Body Hair* (2006).

Ideas of femininity carried over into the areas of comportment and poise. Vigorous activity was not thought feminine. For example, Queen Victoria disapproved of her new daughter-in-law's love of energetic activities. This view was rooted in the commonly held belief that a woman's physiology was uniquely unstable. In the first half of the nineteenth century the feverish symptoms of tuberculosis – pallor, glittering eyes and heightened colour in the lips – were positively sought after; La Traviata caught the moment, at a time when the disease was ravaging Europe and the woman of fashion wanted to look as if she was wasting away.* 'Consumption is ... a flattering malady,' wrote Charlotte Brontë of her dying sister Anne.†Though health is a priority for beauty writers of the later Victorian era, physicians continued to see female debility as inevitable. Some doctors believed that gynaecological diseases were brought on not just by corseting too tightly, but also by studying, and neglect of the home. William Goodell, author of *Lessons in Gynaecology* (1880), believed that 'too much brain work and too little housework' were responsible for diseases of the uterus – a convergence of fears around women's invasion of the male, and neglect of the female realms. The view that 'fatiguing activities' might endanger those all-important reproductive organs caused true ladies to avoid exercise. Think back to Fanny Price in Jane Austen's *Mansfield Park* (1814), forever suffering from headaches, or 'knocked up' from dancing

---

* See Carolyn A. Day, *Consumptive Chic: A History of Beauty, Fashion and Disease* (2017).
† Echoed in the 1990s by so-called 'heroin chic' epitomised by model Kate Moss. More recently iconic beauties have been fuller in figure, but the signs of a return to skinny are ominous. In December 2022 the *New York Post* ran an article entitled 'Bye-bye booty: Heroin chic is back'.

too vigorously at a ball. Moderate exercise was acceptable and had its advocates – like the writer Matilda Pullan, who thought there was 'no better exercise in the world than rubbing a table or sideboard, or sweeping a room'. A lady, well covered up, might enjoy exercise on foot or on horseback (side-saddle of course – a woman who rode astride was courting disaster, and might suffer prolapse). Fanny Price took the air on a good-tempered mare. But energetic mid-Victorian sportswomen were few and far between.

'Ladies do not work, and therefore cannot play,' wrote the philosopher and social reformer Frances Power Cobbe in 1870. Cobbe would become a leading voice in the early years of women's suffrage and, like more modern feminists, she believed that women who were in control of their bodies were also in control of their destinies. She advised them to take up swimming, archery and croquet. However, her advice went largely unheeded by the majority. Most ladies made do with strolling elegantly in the park under the shade of their parasols. Inactivity, uselessness and infantilism were essential ingredients in the middle- and upper-class femininity mix.

Femininity. Wordsworth's lines from 'She Was a Phantom of Delight', written in 1804, had entered the national psyche:

> I saw her, upon nearer view,
> A Spirit, yet a Woman too!

Victorians drank in this mystical ideal with their mother's milk. *The Angel in the House*, a hugely popular narrative poem by star poet Coventry Patmore, expanded the idea of the 'spirit' woman to include the woman as 'helpmeet':

> Man must be pleased; but him to please
> Is woman's pleasure ...

Womankind was otherworldly, but she was also domestic, docile, passive. These ideals were absorbed through poetry, but also through advertisements, magazines, art, fashion and fiction. The illusion had to be maintained. Dora Spenlow, Dickens's heroine in *David Copperfield*, famously exemplifies the female's enchanting delicacy, alongside the fatuity of her existence. Copperfield's child bride is 'Little Blossom', tiny of stature: a frivolous, elflike baby who bursts into tears over trifles, counts on her fingers, and in due course expires, innocent, incompetent, capricious and curly-haired to the last.

Dora was just one of Dickens's mid-century feminine archetypes: fragile and dependent in her frilly, uncomfortable clothes and elaborate hairstyles. Meanwhile, men's wear, dark, practical and uniform, was moving in the opposite direction. These were the expressions of power, and of freedom.

Maintaining the distinction between man and woman was not just about fulfilling one's domestic destiny with an adorable child bride; it was about power, fear and control. And it gives context to the later shock waves caused by women wearing trousers, cutting their hair short, behaving 'mannishly', or in other ways advancing into male territory, as they began to step out of the home and into the wide world.

English Rose

White femininity had another card to play. For while an Englishman's prowess might be demonstrated by his swarthy or florid skin – an indicator of health and miscellaneous outdoorsy feats of energetic machismo – his wife's quality was judged by the pinkness and alabaster whiteness of hers. 'Englishwomen are famed for their dazzlingly fair complexions,' declared a beauty advice manual from the

1880s. The author of *The Toilet* (1897) took it arrogantly further: Englishwomen were the 'favourites of nature'. Their 'matchless purity and freshness of complexion' was held up in comparison to that of Mediterranean women who, it was believed, had ruined their delicate cheeks by eating highly seasoned food and drinking too much coffee.*

When the Royal Academician William Edward Frost represented the mythological subject of the disarming of Cupid, the bewitching goddess stealing his quiver-full of arrows while he sleeps appears to have lived all her life under a stone; and so do her lovely companions. *The Toilet* again: 'Naturally, all women are anxious to possess a white, fine skin ... We, in England, are justly proud of the delicate pink-and-white and rose-leaf complexions of our "rosebud garden of girls".'

The Disarming of Cupid by William Edward Frost, 1850

---

* Does this explain the puritanical, dispiriting blandness of English food in the days before we woke up to garlic and espressos?

The floral metaphor was a common one. Whiteness had long been an indicator of purity and virginity, while the roseate bloom on a young woman's cheek could be understood as a sign that she was 'ripe' and ready. Other visible parts of the body were expected to be equally pearly and perfect. 'Round, white, and smooth shoulders, with suggestions of dimples above the arm, form the ideal beauty of this part of a woman's frame,' urged *The Toilet*. Certain subtle paint-on colourings could be used to enhance the appearance of aristocratic-looking blue veins across a fine lady's décolletage or around her temples.

To stay pink-and-white, a lady's skin needed to remain under cover, clothed from neck to toe, shielded from the sun's rays behind walls, doors and curtains, or visible only after the sun has set, and its owner was regarded as safe from vulgar, covetous eyes. Sunshine and outdoor work printed indelible messages on the hands, telling the world that you were plebeian, and not of the drawing-room breed. Beauty and class were synonymous. 'The most beautiful hands are those that do little work,' claimed the author of *How to be Pretty Though Plain*, while *The Lady's Guide to Perfect Gentility* (1856) stated that 'Gentlemen make the hand a test of beauty calling a lady pretty if she can display a beautiful hand.'

The great outdoors was even more damaging to the face. 'Freckles are the enemy ... they are ugly and most difficult to get rid of.' Being lovely was a dependent state, involving gloves, idleness and, above all, staying indoors. If that didn't work, try emulsion of cucumbers. As for the unlucky possessor of pimples – often thought to be caused by 'impure blood', or, worse, by 'lascivious thoughts' – the Victorian lady had many products she could turn to: Alex Ross's Vegetable Skin Pill, Cuticura soap, Vinolia soap, Sulpholine lotion, Sarsaparilla, Cullwick's Skin Ointment or Dr Mackenzie's Arsenical Soap ('perfectly harmless'). 'You can't blame men for not being attracted to women whose faces are disfigured with pimples, blotches, blackheads and other unnecessary blemishes,' declared the American 'beauty doctor' Mrs Cervais Graham, speaking out on behalf of Kosmeo Cream. 'When a man marries, nine times out of ten he chooses a girl with a pretty complexion.'

In the mid-nineteenth century the British cosmetics industry was in its infancy; it would soon be galloping. Chemists and manufacturers were springing into action to supply a growing demand for toiletries. At the Great Exhibition, the world's first industrial and cultural fair held in London in 1851, British manufacturers of these items were prominent. Hair products, anti-freckle cream and pimple removers had dedicated stands and won prizes. By the 1890s such products were keeping a sizeable sector of the economy afloat.

Grandmother's hints were still preserved in many a household. Combine honey, rose water and Florentine iris powder, daub the mixture thickly inside a pair of chamois leather gloves and wear the gloves to bed: 'on taking them off the hands will feel like velvet to the touch and be of a most exquisite whiteness'. Rub the skin with attar of roses, spirits of wine and hazeline. Always wear a gauze veil and carry a parasol. Eat white meat. Drink milk. Drink vinegar. Do whatever it takes – including applying lethal arsenic lotions – to promote that coveted ethereal translucency. And the beauty writers were all in agreement: 'It is impossible to have a fine complexion if care is not taken to diet oneself properly, and to avoid anything that is harmful, such as salt meat or fish, curries and all highly spiced dishes.'

———

Keep off the curry! – an injunction that generations of colonial wives often failed to note and observe. In the age of the British

Empire, where the rulers had paler skin than the ruled, whiteness was the conspicuous marker of imperialism.

Racism ran deep. Pears showed how dramatically its soap could 'improve the complexion' with an illustration of a Black child in the bathtub, shockingly having his or her 'dirt' washed off, and transformed into a white child. This was an historical moment when white people gladly shouldered their burden of bringing religion and civilisation to the non-Christian regions of the world. Light skin – to them – demonstrated moral worth, class and virtue.

Few were unaffected by the collision of cultures, and colours, in the age of Empire. The impact colonialism had on the subjected populations was complex and insidious; in time, it would build a huge market for products such as Fair and Lovely skin-lightening cream.

———

In 1857 a little girl aged seven was being made ready for her wedding – her *gauridaan*, the Hindi term for a marriage in which the bride was a child. She most likely wore an ornately embroidered red saree for luck, and would have been draped from head to foot in heavy jewellery. Born in 1850, Jnanadanandini Devi grew up in a village in Bengal. The prestigious match would see her settled, for Jnanadanandini's bridegroom Satyendranath – eight years her senior – had been born into the esteemed and influential Tagore family of Kolkata (known at the time as Calcutta);* he was a sensitive, artistic young man who would become the first Indian to be

---

* The most internationally famous and forward-looking member of this important family was Satyendranath's younger brother, the poet, writer, dramatist, moderniser and thinker Rabindranath Tagore, who would become the first Asian to win the Nobel Prize for Literature.

appointed to the Imperial Civil Service. But – starting with their clothes – Jnanadanandini too could claim to be a pioneer, as one of the earliest Indian women to blaze a progressive trail through centuries of hidebound sumptuary codes.

After the wedding the new bride joined the female household of the Tagore mansion. Custom decreed that she must now stay within the walls of the *zenana* (more often known as *purdah*), the section of the house where the women lived, strictly separated from the men and attended by female servants and eunuchs. In these all-female rooms and courtyards, women wandered barefoot, dressed – as tradition required – in fine transparent sarees worn without undergarments. On the rare occasions when they left the zenana, women were transported in palanquins, veiled and invisible. Their dress effectively barred them from all contact with outside society, whether Indian or European: 'We are trapped like birds in a cage,' recalled one woman. But Jnanadanandini's new husband had startlingly liberal views about the role of women in Bengali society. He engaged tutors to teach Jnanadanandini to read and write. He also believed – contrary to custom – that a wife should accompany her husband when he travelled for work. And perhaps it was while she was still in Kolkata that Jnanadanandini Tagore started, under the influence of her husband and her newfound education, to nurture a dream of bettering her sex. It seems that buried beneath the shy exterior, an independent spirit was awaiting release.

In 1864, Satyendranath decided that Jnanadanandini should accompany him to his posting in Gujarat, on the other side of India. In Mumbai, she was thrown into the midst of a very different society. Most significantly, she observed that the Parsi sect of women wore their sarees in a style which allowed them to go out in public places; unlike the gossamer-thin sarees worn in the Bengali *zenana*, these sarees were respectable, and could be worn with a jacket, over a European-style blouse and petticoat. Copying them, Jnanadanandini could socialise with the Englishwomen and Europeans who lived in the city. Two years later Jnanadanandini returned to Kolkata, wearing her new-look, easy-to-wear Mumbai-style saree, with its pallu or loose end pinned over the left shoulder, leaving the right hand free. As her husband's sister, Swarnakumari Devi, remembered, 'this attire [was] an integral combination of indigenousness, decorum and modesty ...' And soon, all the Tagore women wanted one too.

Jnanadanandini Tagore, aged around sixteen,
wearing the Brahmika saree and a Western-style
blouse with cuffs, about 1866

This fashion – so liberating and sophisticated – swept through Kolkata's upper classes, and with new-found confidence Jnanadanandini publicised her discovery, teaching the women of her caste to dress in a more Western way, with lacy blouses, jackets, hats and shoes. It was, of course, controversial. The tradition among Hindus was that no sacred rites could be attended by worshippers wearing clothes that had been stitched. Many Bengali women struggled with putting fashion above their beliefs.

It is ironic that, at a time when British and American women were hampered and held captive by their clothes, Jnanadanandini Tagore was adding several ladylike and modesty-protecting layers to Bengali woman's dress. The 'Western' style denoted decency and progress, and freed the conquered race to frequent the 'polite' society of their conquerors. But that is not how it felt for the women finally released from the imprisonment of the zenana. For this, and for her passionate advocacy of women's education, Jnanadanandini is now remembered as one of the early liberators of Indian women.

In 1877, when Jnanadanandini was twenty-seven years old, she undertook the long sea journey to England, accompanied only by her three small children. It was typically brave of her. But although we know that she wanted to visit England to pursue her interest in the advancement of women, we don't have her own account of how an Indian woman of high caste reacted to the culture of this wet, grey island nation – the 'motherland' and the nucleus of Empire.

———

For an Indian woman's insights into high-Victorian society, turn instead to *Englande Bangamahila* (1885), or 'A Bengali Lady in England', by Krishnabhabini Das.

Like Jnanadanandini Tagore, Krishnabhabini had grown up in a small Bengali village; by the age of nine she too was married, and was fortunate in her husband, Devendranath Das, who was progressive and encouraged his child bride to read and write. In 1882, Das decided to pursue a career in England; thus, when Krishnabhabini was just eighteen, the couple made the journey, and settled in London for the next seven years. The book she wrote about her experiences was directed at a Bengali readership. Fiery and fervent in her views, Krishnabhabini offers up a consciousness-raising commentary not only on her colonial masters and mistresses, but also on her own country, which she saw as backward and stagnant.

The public life of Englishwomen astounded her. Her description echoes that of George Augustus Sala a couple of decades earlier. Spend some time around Hyde Park, she suggested, and observe the display of wealthy women in their excessive finery. This outdoor procession of ladies spared no expense on hats, gowns and jewellery:

> On coming to England, one is quite amazed on seeing the apparel of women. English ladies are very fond of showy clothes. Both the rich and poor are obsessed by clothes and appearances ... These are quite fancy and gorgeous, and when going out, they always wear good and expensive clothes ... But I cannot praise the taste of English ladies. Very few ladies dress elegantly, as the ordinary English women have no idea what will look good on them.

Krishnabhabini was shocked by the lengths that Englishwomen went to, to 'improve' their appearance:

> Corsets, crinolines and such products can make such changes to the structure and dimension of the body that it becomes impossible to discern who is a real beauty and who an artificial one. To present themselves as attractive, they even tolerate pain that distorts their natural physique.

And she proceeded to explain that, while in India bangles and jewelled ornaments signified high caste, in England sumptuous dress was the code by which a woman's wealth and status were judged. In Krishnabhabini's view, this obsession with fashion was reaching dangerous levels: 'I believe the lure of clothes is an enemy lurking in the minds of English women. They are just not able to get rid of this temptation.'

And yet, for a young Englishwoman seeking to secure a husband, looking her best was a necessity. English women seeking husbands had to fend for themselves in the scramble and rivalry of the marriage marketplace. To Krishnabhabini this felt exhausting, and smacked of desperation. Young Englishwomen were brazen. They stepped out in their glad rags, entirely lacking in coyness or suitable feminine modesty. Where was their humility? What had become of their veils, their chaperones? 'They frequent roads, gardens, theatres, venues visited by gatherings of men, and try to show off their beauty and their talents ... The ugly have a serious problem.'

And yet – for Krishnabhabini – the glory of England was the possibility for its womenfolk to mix equally with men, to build relationships with their fathers and brothers, to learn and to grow, mentally and morally. Above all, they were educated. Krishnabhabini Das saw the seat of empire as a beacon of freedom and tolerance. In the 1880s she was waving the flag of feminism, hoping that her words would be heeded by those in power, who could help guide Indian women on the path to freedom and uplift.

The freedoms she dreamt of would be slow to emerge. Still today more than half of brides in West Bengal are aged under twenty-one. And even in sophisticated metropolitan areas, it remains, controversially, a necessity for Indian women to be offered modern-day *zenanas* – safe spaces – where they can travel, work, exercise and socialise without risk of male moles-tation or intrusive comments.

Officials of the Raj banned *Englande Bangamahila*. Das's book was deemed too critical of India's colonial rulers to remain available to the subjugated race. But the foundations of what might one day become a more liberal India had been laid.

Secrets and Lies

Interested and inquisitive, Krishnabhabini Das takes us on her journey to England in the 1880s and we see it through her eyes. She is critical and admiring in equal measure: 'The ordinary Englishwoman is not ugly ... English ladies have beautiful, flawless, pinkish complexions, and usually it is this that makes several of them seem pretty.' But that pink flawlessness was often achieved through artifice.

The Victorian woman's relationship with cosmetics enters the territory of sexual morality, disguise, secrets and lies – and it is one of the foundation myths of the beauty story. Here, it helps to distinguish between potions and lotions that preserved a lady's natural charms, and those that used artifice to camou-flage or conceal. While a woman wasn't condemned for using a preventive – a veil, a parasol or glycerine creams to retain her alabaster skin and youthful radiance – judgement was harsh on anyone who 'painted' or dyed. To seek to embellish nature – to improve on what God had given you – was heresy. Rouge was the badge of the harlot or the actress: a woman who pretended to be what she was not, a Jezebel, a liar, who faked the 'innocent', 'blameless' blush of the modest virgin. Beauty writers urged restraint: 'Do not begin to paint the face: it never looks pretty, and always gives a hard, unnatural expression.'

'A violently rouged woman is a disgusting sight ... Excessive use of powder is also a vulgar trick.' And even Lola Montez was unequivocally damning: 'If Satan has ever had any direct agency in inducing woman to spoil or deform her own beauty, it must have been in tempting her to use *paints*.'

They may have been justified: cosmetics frequently contained damaging chemicals. Face powder might be adulterated with poisonous carbonate of lead or subchloride of bismuth – and the skin of women who used bismuth preparations sometimes turned ghostly grey when exposed to certain gases, for example from a coal fire. Ceruse was often added to skin-brighteners; it was a pigment derived from white lead, and dangerously toxic.

In America a notorious case of poisoning was reported, in which three young women needed treatment for 'lead palsy' after using a cosmetic brand named Laird's Bloom of Youth. After applying it lavishly, their arms and hands became contorted and paralysed.

But looking like a rosebud remained high on white women's wish lists, and Lola Montez considered that 'a little vegetable *rouge* tinging the cheek of a beautiful woman, who, from ill health or an anxious mind, loses her roses, may be excusable'. Unfortunately, liquid rouge, or 'bloom', usually contained ammonia or potash – both corrosive unless used in controlled moderation. But if that was a deterrent, you could touch up the blush on your cheeks with a preparation of red sandalwood and pounded alum. Alternately, a piece of silk dyed crimson and dipped in wine was thought to work well – 'It defies detection.' For eyes, kohl was available. You could also make your own mascara or eyebrow pencil from lamp-black. For the next forty-odd years the spectacle of a fashionable woman required suspension of disbelief: in reality, the lady of leisure was a deception, a construct, a projection – moulded in whalebone, tinted, titivated, disguised and upholstered.

But who could blame the women who sought to give their looks an upgrade? Ordinary women craved this perfection. And in the mid-1860s, fearful of losing their looks, many of them who could afford it flocked (discreetly) to an address in London's Bond Street which promised to supply exactly that. Mrs Sarah Rachel Leverson had opened her salon in 1863 and advertised its wares under the fascia 'Beautiful for Ever' – a guarantee which might have roused suspicions. Beautiful for Ever's shop window was temptingly dressed with colourful bottles and little pots. Inside, 'Madame Rachel' had furnished her 'Temple of Renovation' with Eastern artefacts and embellishments reminiscent of the harem. Word soon spread. Customers were charged steeply for Arabian Face Cream, Honey of Mount Hymettus soap, Favourite of the Harem's Pearl White face powder and Magnetic Rock Dew Water for removing wrinkles. In reality, Rachel Leverson was a fraud and con artist. She had started out selling fried fish, and switched to bogus cosmetics on impulse. For a while she had a lucrative line in 'enamelling': a procedure often chosen by prominent society ladies who submitted to having their face, neck and décolleté 'whitewashed' with a dense paste of *blanc de perle* in order to appear perfect on special occasions. Once enamelled (as described by the German cosmetician Dr Edmund Saalfeld), 'laughing was strictly forbidden and speaking reduced to a minimum'.

In due course Leverson opened her Bond Street shop. She now discovered a rich market in blackmailing wealthy society ladies, who, in return for not having their expensive secret pampering and beauty sessions revealed to their husbands, handed over their jewellery. In 1868 Rachel was convicted of fraud and imprisoned for four years. By 1872 she was back in business, fleecing the gullible, needy women who came to her for Jordan water and Circassian shampoo; but in 1878 she was again successfully sued by a prominent fashionable lady who claimed to have paid £200 for a series of face washes which had brought her out in a disastrous rash. Madame Rachel died in Woking Prison in 1880.

Press reaction to Madame Rachel's misdeeds was predictable. The columnists indulged in an orgy of antisemitic and puritanical gloating at fashionable folly and the 'foul and filthy doings' of the 'Bond Street Jewess'. The English have always loved a spot of *schadenfreude* at the spectacle of a charlatan outsmarting vain rich women, and in turn paying the price. The case of Madame Rachel seemed a victimless crime, and gave full satisfaction.

In 1868, at the height of the scandal, a journalist named Eliza Lynn Linton created her own stir with a tirade, in the *Saturday Review*, against 'the Girl of the Period'. Mrs Linton's article is a censorious onslaught on frivolity, ostentation and the collapse of morals, coupled with a lament that things weren't what they used to be:

> We prided ourselves as a nation on our women. We thought we had the pick of creation in this fair young English girl of ours ... This was in the old time ... when English girls were content to be what God and nature had made them ...
>
> The Girl of the Period is a creature who dyes her hair and paints her face ... a creature whose sole idea of life is fun; whose sole aim is unbounded luxury.

These wayward girls appeared dead set on carrying every fashion to extremes. If bonnets were scaled down, the Girl of the Period went for miniature fascinators ('four straws and a rosebud'); if modish women decided to wear their hair curled, she adopts a preposterous frizz. In another of Eliza Linton's essays she denounces uppity, 'man-hating' women who tried to upend the God-ordained relationship of the sexes:

> Nature framed men for power and women for tenderness ... the natural division of things is protection on the one side and a reasonable measure of – we will not mince the word – obedience on the other.

———

Eliza Linton's journalism plays into the familiar fear that the lines were becoming blurred between good women and bad ('fast') women – or even prostitutes. But she also gave voice to another, specifically male, source of alarm, that uncontrolled women threaten societal order. These girls were evidence of a 'national madness' that jeopardised stability. And in the 1860s there were already signs that women were starting to rock the boat. In 1866 1,499 women signed the petition presented to Parliament calling for women's suffrage. Meanwhile, one of the petition organisers, Emily Davies, was campaigning for the admission of women to universities; she was also working towards the opening of Girton College, the first women's university college, in Cambridge in 1869. Mrs Linton's abuse of 'the shrieking sisterhood' would have been aimed at Davies and her feminist colleagues from the Langham Place group who were gradually raising awareness of the need to improve women's situation. And – also in 1869 – John Stuart Mill published a powerful advocacy of women's equality, *The Subjection of Women* (inspired by his late wife Harriet Taylor), in which he put forward the controversial view that one sex should not dominate the other. Women are as able as men, he claimed, but society drained them of their natural capacities. Domesticity and childcare absorbed hours of the day, while the time that remained was consumed with social life and 'the engrossing duty, which society imposes exclusively on women, of making themselves charming'. Think of all that wasted potential, given over to dressing, prettifying, embellishing, whitening, curling and tight-lacing – because male patronage demanded it, and because a woman was nothing without that patronage. And then think how that time might have been spent – 'towards achieving respectable results in art, or science, or literature'.

The feminist ideas of Mill and Taylor, of Davies, the Langham Place group and others fell on fertile ground. Women would, over time, become writers, scientists and artists, and achieve much else besides. But the desire – and the pressure – to be beautiful would remain as deep-rooted as ever.

Lillie Langtry in 1885, aged thirty-two, after her relationship with
the Prince of Wales had ended

2

Belle Epoque

Lillie

'Those were the days of the great beauties,' recalled Margot Asquith, looking back at her youth in the 1870s and 80s. In the late Victorian era society was in thrall to the so-called 'Professional Beauties': white women of surpassing loveliness whose images became currency, and whose faces were their passport to Mayfair's ballrooms. Artists competed to paint them, and to love them. In Hyde Park the public jostled to catch a glimpse of these spellbinders on horseback. Lady Randolph Churchill commented, 'No party was complete or successful without these ladies. People would receive invitations with "Do come; the P.B.s will be there." This meant the certain attendance of society.'

Of all the P.B.s who embellished society in those decades, the most famously dazzling was Lillie Langtry. Lillie's celebrity rested not only on her lustrous beauty, but also on her relationship with 'Bertie', the Prince of Wales, who, a dozen or more years into his marriage with Princess Alexandra, had earned the reputation of a libertine. But who was this beauty?

Lovely Lillie was born in 1853, and arrived in London from Jersey in 1877; she was the daughter of a clergyman and respectably married, but soon it was not only artists and social-ites who were buzzing around her like bees round a jampot; she was mobbed in the park and pursued in the street. Tall (five feet eight inches) and curvaceous, her features were described as Greek in their perfection. Lillie's celebrity was comparable to that of today's supermodels or screen stars.

> There's a lovely lady in a plain black gown
> She isn't very rich, but she's taken all the town
> London Society has gone quite silly
> Fallen at the feet of the Jersey Lillie

> There's the Langtry this and the Langtry that,
> The Langtry bonnet and the Langtry hat
> The Langtry slipper and the Langtry shoe
> Langtry purple and Langtry blue
> The Langtry carriage and the Langtry cot,
> And every woman's hair in the Langtry knot.

Later that same year Lillie met the Prince of Wales at a dinner party; their three-year liaison began shortly afterwards. They were seen on horseback in Rotten Row together. Meanwhile Princess Alexandra, who took her husband's infatuations in her stride, made no exception with this one. It would blow over, and it did.

The photograph invites the spectator into what purports to be Lillie's boudoir. By the time it was taken, her glory days as the prince's mistress were past; she was in her thirties. On the advice of her friend Oscar Wilde, she had reinvented herself as an actress, and in 1882 made a coast-to-coast tour of America.

But a stage career was still regarded as morally questionable: actresses and dancers were women who made up their faces and wore frothy skirts that displayed their legs, and worse. Here, the image is of a glamorous courtesan – what was often known as a *grande horizontale* – reclined on her day bed in semi-*déshabille*. The setting is luxurious, a little stifling, replete with fanciful furnishings, chintz and velvet. A branch of foliage hints at the hothouse, while in the foreground a leopard skin adds a touch of exciting barbarity. Lillie's pose exudes eroticism. A fronded feather fan droops languidly from her right hand and comes to rest between her thighs, while with her left she idly fingers the hair at the nape of her neck (her nails are visibly unadorned). Lillie has adopted the abandoned pose of a woman submitting to a man. Her creamy skin is free of jewellery, and her corsage free of the customary frills and froth. But she appears serene, dreamy almost; not a perfectly coiffed hair is out of place. If the pose is her own choice, perhaps there is something in her expression which sends the message, 'I know what I'm doing.'

Her corset, or bodice, defines the tightly controlled, wasp-waisted silhouette still idolised by Victorian men. A wisp of gauze caresses her décolleté, but if she possesses a cleavage, it's been artistically brushed out. From the ample hips upwards, all is tight and impenetrable. The casual 'Langtry knot' has been replaced with crisp waves, for this was a time of laborious hairdressing extravaganzas, boosted with complex 'postiches' – artificial pads, plaits and switches. Her tightly curled fringe may even have been fake. But navigating her corset and coiffure would have presented a challenge to any admirer. What with hooks, laces, combs and pins, the lover would have needed determination to penetrate a stockade of prickly obstacles.

The skirts tell a different story, with their sexy ruffles, exaggerated brocade fabric and general air of dishevelment – what the poet Robert Herrick described as 'tempestuous petticoats'.* But the sexuality of her clothes betrays a paradox. While upper-body sexual characteristics were on lavish display, yet inaccessible, anything below the waist that might approach the revelation of female genitals was smothered, suppressed and buried under mounds of suggestive frou-frou. Meanwhile, the peeping 'Langtry slipper' and saucy black hose give a tiny unmissable hint of what lies beneath.

––––––––

So what does lie beneath?

A woman like Lillie Langtry required as much scaffolding below the surface as her predecessor in the 1860s. At the time of her London society debut, Lillie liked to wear her simple black dresses *au naturel*, uncorseted. But she grew to love fashion. In the 1880s the up-to-date silhouette remained curvaceously voluptuous. With the exception of the waist, a beautiful woman was expected to be well padded with flesh – and here Lillie's corset presents us with a triumphantly vertiginous shelf, transitioning seamlessly to the marmoreal bust known to fashion historians as the 'monobosom'. In 1881 Lillie had given birth to an illegitimate daughter. Maybe her breasts had increased greatly in size, but the comparison with a slimmer, slighter Lillie, as depicted in Millais's 1878 portrait, makes one think she may have inserted padded 'bust improvers', made from horsehair, rubber, satin pads or chamois leather; the 'falsies' could be pushed into specially fashioned circular pockets inserted into the corset. (Another way

––––––––

* Robert Herrick (1591–1674). His poem 'Delight in Disorder' begins: 'A sweet disorder in the dress / Kindles in clothes a wantonness ...'

of dealing with an inadequate chest was the 'patent palpitator', made from inflatable rubber; but these had the drawback that they often burst.) Meanwhile, the unruly tangle of fabric that foams beneath is also characteristic of the decade. Around 1870 the crinoline was replaced by the crinolette, or the bustle, and a plethora of petticoats. These were designed to enhance fullness in the dress, where it was required – and here they would have been copiously gathered and frilled at the back, and scooped over the bustle to aggressively emphasise the bottom, with further petti-coats beneath. Her horizontal pose makes it hard to tell whether or not Lillie was wearing a bustle. A standard bustle would have made reclining uncomfortable to say the least, but the ingenious Lillie found a solution, giving her name to the Langtry bustle – a 'reticulated' bottom-enhancer, engineered so that when you sat down its grid of hinged bands concertina'ed in on themselves, to give freedom of movement. Then, when you stood up, they re-opened.

Her theatrical ventures, a betting habit and product endorse-ments helped support Lillie's love of finery. The clothing merchant Stapley & Smith of London Wall would have sold many Langtry bustles to would-be imitators of the Langtry phenomenon, just as Pears sold quantities of its soap on the back of Lillie's championship: 'I have found it matchless for the hands and the complexion. Since using Pears Soap I have discarded all others.'

Beneath the petticoats Lillie wears long knickers. By the mid-1880s, the opening at the crotch was closed. Instead, the garment buttoned discreetly at a side placket. The majority of bourgeois women chose to wear long white cotton drawers edged with broderie anglaise next to the skin; others chose red flannel or alpaca. Silk was regarded with disapproval as only worn by actresses – it may have been Lillie's choice.

The market for what we call lingerie* – flattering, filmy underwear – was inhibited by women's own inhibitions. The bourgeoisie took the view that only loose women wore pretty knickers. 'A virtuous woman has a repugnance to excessive luxury in her underclothing.' Mostly, undergarments were made of serviceable linen or calico, which after washing became as scratchy and hard as planks. The common view was that chemises, drawers and the like should be exclusively hand-sewn, and adorned only with hand embroidery or handmade lace: an expression of modesty and authenticity. This norm was amplified by the *Englishwoman's Domestic Magazine*: 'A young lady spent a month in hemstitching and embroidering a garment which it was scarcely possible that any other human being, except her laundress, would ever see.'

This would soon change, but for now anything machine-made, overly decorated or extravagant was considered borderline immoral, and even coloured corsets were 'fast'. The relative plainness and purity of a lady's underwear speaks volumes about Victorian priorities. These were indeed garments that were only visible to the laundress. They had no function in reeling in or retaining a husband, thus there was no requirement for them to be ostentatious.

The later Victorian era also saw the arrival of 'combinations'. As the name suggests, this was an all-in-one chemise and knickerbocker garment, usually worn under the corset, comparable to a jumpsuit and just as unsatisfactory when visiting the lavatory. For this purpose, access was gained by way of a series of small linen-covered buttons running along the inside leg. Sometimes one can only marvel at the inconveniences of a Victorian woman's life!

---

* For Victorians, the word was more all-encompassing than it is today, and included collars, cuffs, handkerchiefs, nightclothes and all other white linen a woman might possess, apart from outdoor clothing and dresses.

Periods come into this category, and deserve a short digression. Like underwear, they were off limits: another area of life conducted with the strictest privacy and secrecy. Though scientific literature of the time discusses menstruation, the topic is taboo elsewhere, and it would be safe to presume that many men either ignored or were innocent of their wives' and daughters' gynaecological functions. What evidence there is indicates that some women treated menstruation as an illness and went to bed for a couple of days, while others just bled into their clothes. But it appears that most battled on with improvised napkins. The spirit quails as one contemplates the many wads, rags and clouts deployed, put together from old tablecloths, either safety-pinned in place, or secured by ribbons or cords tied around the hips.

From 1880 disposable sanitary pads began to be manufactured, made from cotton shoddy, a waste material used for cleaning brass; a number of companies advertised these (very discreetly) in women's magazines – 'highly recommended by members of the medical profession for their cleanliness, comfort, and antiseptic properties'. But a shilling a dozen was a prohibitive price for any but the well-off.

To return to the marginally more visible: in the costume she is wearing here, Lillie's stockings may have been supported by garters – bands tied with ribbons, worn around the legs – though in the 1880s suspenders attached to a belt or to the lower edge of the corset were the new-fangled way to keep your hosiery up.

It's likely that Lillie was wearing make-up for the photograph; her theatrical career meant a familiarity with cosmetics, and though 'painting' was still regarded with horror by the old-fashioned, condemnation was no longer universal. 'I do not wish to speak against the use of rouge and pearl powder,' wrote the author of *Beauty and How to Keep It* (1889), who published under the prestige-seeking *nom de plume* 'A Professional Beauty'. '[Their use] seems to have become more fashionable now than it has been for many years.' A careful look reveals that Lillie may have used a dark pencil to elongate the corners of her grey eyes and emphasise her brows. A little eye make-up wouldn't have been unusual, and nor would a subtle patina of powder and rouge. Cleansed, unenhanced, she appears paler and less polished. The likelihood is that her carefully coiffed hair, once it is let loose, descends halfway down her back. (Lillie's hair was naturally tawny-gold, but she was experimental, to her cost: on one misguided occasion she had it dyed black, only for the unstable colour to wash out in streaks, giving her a zebra appearance.)

This woman, whose face and body entranced the Prince of Wales, was regarded by many as the perfect beauty. The spectacle of her features, her hair, hands, arms and upper bosom were becoming familiar to thousands. In respect of this, they have been boosted, tended and enhanced to the full extent then acceptable.

Unsurprisingly, when all her clothes and cosmetics are removed, it becomes clear that they were a façade – behind which lies a flesh-and-blood woman of thirty, whose milky-white body still has the remnants of a girlish bloom. Lillie is also now a mother, and her breasts, her stomach and her thighs may reveal the aftermath of her pregnancy. Any woman in her middle years who has had a baby knows that the elasticity of youth is starting to pass, beyond recall. And does she have cellulite? Moles? Does she suffer from varicosity or thread veins, so often an after-effect of pregnancy? Stretch marks? Ragged toenails? Fat?

It will take some informed guesswork to calculate what will be revealed when Lillie's corset is unlaced, and the petticoats removed from her lower half. Certainly, there is no trace of a freckle or a suntan. What about the conundrum of unwanted hair? The 'Professional Beauty' advised women to resort to tweezers if facial hair was a problem, and sympathised with women who suffered from growth on their necks and arms, 'so much so that they are unable to wear a low-necked dress'. This still being the 'no-legs' era, the author made no mention of unwanted hair on lower limbs or other parts of the body, since there could be no possibility of them being on view. She also urged her readers to avoid potentially dangerous depilatory lotions. So Lillie's legs are probably sprinkled with downy filaments and, tracing the thigh upwards, the intimate area around her groin still sprouts an abundant growth – as one French writer put it, 'delicately shaded, at the summit, by the secret fleece of Venus'. Her underarms may or may not be shaved. Victorian representations of women rigorously eliminated armpit hair, and this photograph is a heavily staged collectible image. But the truth might have been different. Fascinatingly, another French writer, Émile Zola, created Nana – a fictional Parisian courtesan and *femme fatale* loosely based on the *demi-mondaine* Comtesse Valtesse de La Bigne. And the first sight of his heroine is on the stage of the Théâtre des Variétés:

A ripple of excitement ran through the auditorium. Nana was naked: naked, but with a quiet, bold conviction in the supremacy of her own flesh. Draped only with a light veil, it was possible to discern her shapely shoulders, her swelling bosom whose pink tips rose up like the points of spears, her broad, rolling hips with their voluptuous movement, her buttery thighs. Through the foamy, floating white gauze her entire body was revealed to all. Here was Venus arising from the waves, veiled only in her tresses. And when

Nana raised her arms, in the dazzle of the footlights, one could catch a glimpse of the golden hairs in her armpits ...

'Good grief!' was all Fauchery could find to say to la Faloise.

This is the male gaze of the *belle époque*, unmediated. Here, Zola provides the body historian with a rare – if voyeuristic – glimpse of a woman's scintillatingly sexy body: plump, rounded and voluptuous, but also unshaven. 'The golden hair in her armpits,' so delicately observed catching the light, is a thrilling reminder that – at least in Paris – nineteenth-century courtesans didn't shave them. And it's a reasonable extrapolation that Lillie Langtry didn't either.

It's also reasonable to assume that her perfection is limited to what is visible, from the bosom upwards, with everything below that unknowable. And that unknowableness, for Lillie, is a form of respite, a let-out from the endless scrutiny. Skirt lengths would rise slowly but inexorably after the turn of the century. But until then 'no-legs' women would continue to have the luxury of disguise.

Lillie Langtry (like Nana) was not thought to be a talented actress. But her striking looks changed the way the public perceived beauty – propagated through a multitude of portraits by Millais, Whistler, Frank Miles, Watts, Burne-Jones and Poynter. The young art of photography and advances in photographic reproduction also propelled her to fame. If Princess Alexandra comes high up the list of 'wife symbols' of the Victorian age, one of its most potent *sex* symbols was surely Lillie Langtry:* 'Mess

---

* The erotic impact of her image is immortalised in The Who's 1971 hit 'Pictures of Lily'. The teenage boy in the song can't sleep at night until his father gives him his old pin-ups of Lillie Langtry – 'Pictures of Lily made my life so wonderful / Pictures of Lily helped me sleep at night.' But the boy's desire to meet her in real life is frustrated when his father tells him, 'She's been dead since 1929.'

up my hair! Explore my stockings! Rumple my petticoats!' The incapacitating character of her dress, the welcoming, front-facing tilt of her hips, and her undemanding passivity all send out a silent message of non-resistance, perfectly attuned to the patriarchal assumptions of the time.

For as Victoria's reign reached its closing decades the major-ity of women remained as objectified, as devoid of rights and as enclosed within four walls as they had been at its start. But beauty, and the scrutiny that comes with it, had gone public.

Working Girls

The messages about beauty and fashion communicated by innu-merable working-class Victorian women are largely silent. Their images are few and far between. And yet working women, poor women, were intimately connected with the business of being beautiful.

If we could undress *them*, what would we see? *Not* Lillie Langtries. Malnourished, undergrown bodies. Bent spines. Dirt. Hands coarsened from washing, callused from scrub-bing, roughened from needlework, and nails snagged. Knees rubbed from the labour of scrubbing floors. Skin blemished and prematurely aged by insufficient diet; marked and scarred by accidents; displaying the pallor and thinness of a tubercular ailment; distended from child-bearing; darkened by exposure to the sun. Infrequently washed hair. Faces once pretty, but with features strained, wrinkled and reddened. Terrible teeth. Deformities. Perhaps it was as well for them that few house-holds possessed mirrors until the end of the nineteenth century.

And if we could hear them, what would they tell us? Beauty was a hard taskmaster – and perhaps hardest of all for over a million women and girls employed as domestic servants: those who witnessed at close quarters the vanities of life from which they were excluded. A servant was always visibly distinct from her mistress, marked out by her white cap and plain clothes; any 'Abigail'* who tried to look like her betters was doomed to failure. The lady's maid in particular was intimately acquainted with her mistress's cosmetics, curl-papers, lace and linen – and yet an unbridgeable gulf divided them.

For many other working women the economic connection with those same gracious refinements was more removed, but equally inextricable. Factory or piece-workers might talk of their long sedentary hours making beautiful lace, plaiting straw into elaborate bonnets, fashioning artificial flowers from velvet and satin, stitching kid gloves, sewing on buttons of bone, or constructing corsetry in airless rooms. Did they too wear whalebone? Fashion historians disagree about whether corset-wearing permeated all strata of society, but the likelihood is that it did; there are accounts of low-paid seamstresses suffering from the effects of tight-lacing, and the aggrieved mistress is to be heard complaining at the uppity maidservant who prances around aping her betters in cheap corsetry.

Fashion's grip on the female was tenacious. Being well-dressed mattered; it gave joy and self-esteem. Fashion choices in the nineteenth century weren't made randomly, any more than they are now. Class, gentility, perceived sex appeal and what the American theorist Thorstein Veblen described as 'conspicuous consumption' all play their part in driving those choices. Writing at the end of the nineteenth century, Veblen looked around him at the overblown, constricting clothes worn by the ladies of his home state, Minnesota, and argued that, on the evidence, people would rather be uncomfortable and handicapped than appear badly dressed. 'The need of

---

* The name Abigail was in common use as a reference to a lady's maid; it derives from the Bible (II Samuel, 24–28), in which Abigail is David's handmaid.

dress is eminently a "higher" or spiritual need,' he wrote. Nineteenth-century women were performing a balancing act between what was acceptably attractive and unacceptably showy. A working woman retained her self-respect by dressing as stylishly as she could afford.

Veblen doesn't allude to the Black servants of his Minnesota ladies, but another writer who travelled in America in the nineteenth century, the German Francis Lieber, introduced an interesting observation into his letters home:

> I wish you could see some negro servants dressed in their best. They go in heavy silks, with fashionable hats, fine gloves, worked stockings, elegant parasols, lace veils ... The good wages they receive enable them to go exceedingly well-dressed.

Clara Collet, who documented the lives of working women in the late nineteenth century, conjured up a similarly colourful picture of the East End factory girl on her day off, arm in arm with her friends, parading up and down the Bow Road, shrieking with laughter:

> On those occasions she is adorned and decked out, not so much for conquest as for her own personal delight and pleasure, and for the admiration of her fellow women. She wears a gorgeous plush hat with as many large ostrich feathers to match as her funds will run to – bright ruby or scarlet preferred. Like all the working women in the East End, she wears good tidy boots on all occasions, perhaps with high heels.

Unfortunately, Victorian fashions were accidents waiting to happen. In 1864 twenty-eight-year-old factory worker Matilda Davis was killed when her crinoline became entangled in machinery. The price of finery could be ill-health – long days spent in unventilated workshops were the norm. Female shop assistants or showroom workers, many of whom were expected to pay for their own cheap black silk dresses, might describe the long days spent on their feet behind the hosiery counter.

Looking back wryly at her childhood in the 1890s, Lady Violet Hardy recalled:

> The poor were people who had to work, obviously, for our enjoyment. When they were very poor, they were visited with the remains of the rice pudding, and given knitted cross-over shawls and flannel petticoats.

Back in the smoky, damp city, a housewife trying to make ends meet might also tell of the cold and chilblains of winter when a flannel petticoat could have provided very welcome warmth. Mrs O in Lambeth did her shopping after dark because she had no shoes and was ashamed to be seen in her slippers; her neighbour was thirty-eight, 'but her face is that of a woman of fifty ... [she] is tall and would be good-looking if her figure were not much misshapen'. Mrs Smith would buy one new dress which she expected to last for years; the rest of her clothes came from jumble sales.

A twenty-year-old woman who told her story to the journalist and reformer Henry Mayhew described working in a shirt-making factory from the age of twelve; at seventeen, after five years of being beaten and half-starved by her father, she left home – 'I had nothing but what I stood upright in.' This young woman lived largely by prostitution, and was jailed for stealing two dresses from a linen draper's shop – but not being seen in her shabby attire was worth it: 'Yes, sir, I liked prison very well, because I had such bad clothes, and was glad to be out of the way.'

'Ladies', who led the way where fashion and beauty were concerned, were in the minority. To the majority, the nineteenth century was unforgiving. Poverty, vagrancy, disease and the workhouse were ever-present threats. Working-class women were exempt from the assumption that ladies were required to be ornamental and futile.

The realities for wage-earning women were grim: an unmarried milliner might be paid 9 shillings a week. From this she would have to find 3 shillings a week for her rent, and eat and buy clothing from the remainder. This didn't leave a lot for face powder and finery. And yet ... For without financial prospects, what was a girl to do? Princesses and paupers alike knew that their faces were their fortunes, and working-class women were just as eager as their social superiors to send out the sartorial signals which might attract a husband, along with the economic security he could provide. Yet in many cases their freedom to do so was desperately restricted. Take the case of a rebellious group of live-in seamstresses who were accepting love letters from 'gentlemen' and arranging rendezvous. Reluctantly, and despite the fact that they seemed pretty and polite, the superintendent expelled them: 'The fondness for dress and admiration in young girls in their class of life is a terrible temptation.'

For domestic servants,* the obstacles were even greater. 'Followers' (as admirers were disparagingly known) were sternly discouraged, and a maidservant had to grab snatches of time 'at the area steps' to see her boyfriend, if she had one. The sumptuary laws imposed on live-in servants have a boarding-school flavour to them. Employers required maids joining their households to arrive properly equipped, at their own expense.

---

* In 1881 almost *a third of all girls* aged between fifteen and twenty were in service. In 1891 female indoor residential servants accounted for 34 per cent of all employed women; and most of them were young. Their numbers peaked that year at 1,386,167, and would not fall below one million until the late 1930s.

Morning wear was a dress in cotton print; black was for after-noons, with a white cap and apron. On Sundays the maids were expected to wear bonnets, not hats, in church – because hats were for the gentry. The rules against jewellery and fine feathers were rooted in class distinction: a parlourmaid must never be mistaken for her mistress. Not surprisingly the domestics didn't always comply, and it only takes a glance at some of the jour-nals and magazines aimed at housemaids and mill-girls (*Girls' Own Paper, Woman's Weekly, Woman's World*) to discover that their readers were as preoccupied with being attractive as those in higher social strata. The magazines catered for them with features such as 'Frocks and gowns for the month' or dec-orous suggestions in the advice columns for dress trimmings and beauty treatments:

> To dye gloves tan-colour ... steep saffron in boiling water.

> You will hardly find a better lotion for those bothering blackheads [than] ... an ounce of eau de cologne and one grain of corrosive sublimate.

> It is evident that your hair needs still more washing.

Many of the working-class correspondents also wrote in for romantic advice. 'Abigail' was as much in the business of enchanting the opposite sex as any debutante.

Rational Dress

Step by tiny step, Parliament and the law were moving towards a recognition that women were people, not chattels. It took years of patient perseverance, collecting signatures, string-pulling and persuading on the part of campaigners like Barbara Bodichon and Ursula Bright to push changes past an unwilling, male-only Parliament. Bodichon, who presided over the Langham Place group, lobbied for married women to be permitted to earn money for themselves, and to own property. Her efforts were rewarded with the passing of the Married Women's Property Act, 1870. Ursula Bright also worked tirelessly for over ten years, and in 1882 the Act was extended to encompass all property a woman might own. Courts were now compelled to recognise married women as being separate entities from men. The campaign for women's suffrage was on a slow burn, and would encounter greater obstacles. In America, the Statue of Liberty – an icon of freedom dressed as a robed goddess bearing a torch – was dedicated in October 1886, and there was a moment of delirious optimism, until it was declared that no representatives of women's suffrage groups would be allowed to attend the ceremony.

At the same time, though the old pattern of femininity would die a slow lingering death (it may even be indestructible?), the spiritual/mystical/submissive woman so beloved of poets and painters was starting to become angry and mutinous. She sought personal fulfilment, wrote books, shared lodgings with friends, got educated, spoke on political platforms. She even had unorthodox sexual relationships. Her type had a name: the 'New Woman', and she became a byword in 1895 when the author Grant Allen published his controversial bestseller, *The Woman Who Did*. The novel's provocative title gives an indication of Allen's broadly feminist intentions. His heroine, Herminia Barton, is portrayed as a woman with agency. She has been to Girton, lives on a higher plane, and breaks the rules of the bourgeoisie by having sex with a man to whom she is not married. And in Chapter 1 it is her clothes that mark her out:

She wore a curious Oriental-looking navy-blue robe of some soft
woollen stuff, that fell in natural folds ... It was a sort of sleeveless
sack, embroidered in front with arabesques in gold thread ... The
whole costume ... was charming in its novelty, charming too in
the way it permitted the utmost liberty and variety of movement
to the lithe limbs of its wearer.

The bohemian mindset will always find ways to stake out
new territory and challenge the conventions, and 'protest' clothing has an honourable lineage. Herminia's sleeveless sack tells
the world, 'I am not the type of woman who succumbs to the
slavery of marriage.'

Every woman knows that the way she chooses to present
herself gives off carefully coded messages about her identity.
It may or may not be about man-bait; it varies with age and
status. In the nineteenth century the conventions of dress
exerted an exceptional stranglehold over women. But along
with social conventions the tight-laced grip of dress was starting to loosen, falling 'in natural folds ... [with] liberty and
variety of movement'. Over the coming century the sartorial
choices women would make defined a battleground: on the
attack, progress and emancipation; on the defence, patriarchal
power and control.

————

The halting march of women's rights runs parallel with organised attempts to introduce so-called 'rational dress'. Thirty
years earlier, Amelia Bloomer's attempts to get women into
trousers had foundered. Now, in protest at ever tighter corsets,
ever more copious petticoats, higher heels and more cumbersome, constricting skirts, a group came together in 1881 and
formed the Rational Dress Society.

Its principal founder, Florence Harberton, was determined to spread the gospel about comfortable, lightweight and healthy clothing for women. In the context of fashionable wasp waists and frilly bustles, Lady Harberton in a combative pose, dressed in knee-length knickerbockers, flat lace-ups and a fancy hat may not have been the best advertisement for her cause: she comes across as doughty.

Nevertheless, she persisted, and in 1884 published *Reasons for Reform in Dress*, in which she argued persuasively against skirts. They were heavy but lacked warmth; they were immodest, hard to clean and unhygienic, and (as we have seen) they were dangerous:

[The skirt] is the cause of endless accidents from the highest to the lowest – the recent sprain of the Queen's ankle, according to the newspapers, having been caused by her stepping on her dress; and as for accidents to women walking or trying to run, and getting in and out of trains and carriages, their name is legion . . .

In truth, the skirt of a dress may be taken as the extremest type of ugliness in clothes.

Stays, hats, shoes and mantles were also grist to Lady Harberton's polemic, and in 1893 she started the Short Skirt League, whose members pledged to wear skirts of a length five inches above the ground. But though she may have seemed a pioneer, Lady Harberton was in reality latching onto an existing undercurrent of dissent, just as Herminia Barton had done in her sleeveless navy-blue sack. For decades, prevailing fashion had been opposed by small minorities of women, unwilling to sprain their ankles because of their skirts; and unwilling to be seen as silly, frivolous and vain.

As so often, artists took the lead. The sculptor Mary Thornycroft, who undertook numerous commissions to carve busts of all Queen Victoria's children, was resolute: crinolines were not for her. They got in the way. She took a firm stand against them, and was to be seen hammering away in her studio swathed in voluminous folds of silk falling unsupported to the floor. Mid-century, an 'artistic' style of dress was embraced by the Pre-Raphaelites' models: suffused with a Utopian spirit, women like Jane Morris and Elizabeth Siddall braved disapproval by abandoning their corsets, letting their hair loose and creating their own medieval gowns from vegetable-dyed drapery, hand-embroidered with lilies and daffodils. This ethereally droopy look appealed to a new generation of advanced and bohemian women: women like Agatha Cox and her three sisters.

Growing up in Tonbridge, Kent, in the early 1880s, Agatha, Margaret, Hilda and Dora were the belles of the town. Their older brothers had immersed themselves in the literature of socialism, Darwin and John Stuart Mill. The Cox boys gave their sisters progressive reading lists, and they grew up versed in 'enlightened' ideas, which spilled over into their dress choices. Bustles were top of the banned list. However, the girls' rigour didn't always go down well with their mother, a gentle, ringletted Victorian matriarch, who craved admiration for her four daughters. As Agatha Cox's daughter later recalled, 'She would beg them to wear bustles – "*just* a little something, dear . . ." They sternly refused.'

The Cox sisters chose beauty over fashion. They shopped for their *prêt-à-porter* 'art fabric' smocks and Indian shawls at the new emporium which had opened in Regent Street in 1875, Liberty: the mecca for the aesthetic movement.

'Aesthetes' – like the Coxes – were intense romantics who celebrated beauty and theatricality. To play Lady Macbeth, the dressmaker Ada Nettleship created for Ellen Terry a gown ornamented with the wings of over a thousand iridescent green beetles, while the illustrator Kate Greenaway popularised a more pastoral version of aestheticism: smocked, prettified and whimsical.

Violet Manners, the Duchess of Rutland, another gifted artist who was at the centre of the upper-class cultural coterie known as the Souls, typified the aesthete:

> She had great beauty. She was tall and frail with a complexion as delicate as the palest anemone ... She was greenery-yallery ... Always a sprig of bay was pinned high up to her neck by a green enamel tortoise.

An intriguing evolution of the rational dress movement was the lovely caprice of fashion known as the tea gown (or 'teagie'), adopted by the aesthetes and their sympathisers. In the looser moral climate of the *fin-de-siècle*, relaxed, languorous clothing seemed desirable; and so this filmy, feminine, draped garment came into being – often in light, silky green velvet with violet sashes – to be worn in a lady's own drawing room or boudoir, without a corset. Teatime – or *cinq-à-sept* – was also a good time to receive your lover, and the easy-to-take-off tea gown facilitated languid early evening intimacies, before the formalities of dinner and dancing demanded ballgowns and stays.

Meanwhile, the opponents of clothing that squeezed and mangled – people like Ruskin, Oscar Wilde, Charlotte Stopes, George Bernard Shaw and G. F. Watts – were becoming more vocal. As the climate turned against mortification of the flesh, novelist Margaret Oliphant denounced the excesses of 'bondage' fashion: 'A lady in full dress can hardly walk, can with difficulty get up stairs, and cannot by any possibility sit down.'

Health journalist Ada Ballin, author of *The Science of Dress in Theory and Practice* (1885), joined the growing Babel, lamenting fashion's folly as a cause of suffering and ill health. Ballin was a moderate; she spoke out for the re-education of girls: 'We want reform, not revolution.' Most people didn't need corsets, though she had her limits: 'A stout girl without stays looks very much like a shapeless and quivering mass of fat, and is by no means a charming spectacle.' But for outer clothing, Mrs Ballin saw trousers as the way forward – provided they were disguised *under* skirts: '[They] may be made so artfully that an outsider would not know the difference between them and an ordinary dress.'

Today, the Victorian woman appears blatantly imprisoned by her clothes, which prioritise femininity at the expense of liberty. But persistent as it was, there was no consensus within the movement. Some saw the folly of fashion as the culprit. Others were more fixated on health and modesty. In the end, healthy, woolly, flat-footed and unflattering as they were, rational clothes were doomed – because they were neither sexy nor beautiful.

Improving on Nature

The clothing debate would be equalled by the beauty debate. Eugenics was a topic that would pervade intellectual discourse for the next fifty years and beyond. Though the underlying beliefs go back centuries, the movement's nineteenth-century progenitor is generally agreed to be Sir Francis Galton, an eccentric half-cousin to Sir Charles Darwin. Galton loved to measure and analyse, and he took beauty seriously. His motto was, 'Whenever you can, count.' We are witnessing the genesis of a preoccupation with beauty statistics: one which would come to dominate our perceptions of how women look. During the 1880s Galton embarked on an unusual project:

> I use a needle mounted as a pricker, wherewith to prick holes, unseen, in a piece of paper, torn rudely into a cross with a long leg. I use its upper end for 'good', the cross-arm for 'medium', the lower end for 'bad'. The prick-holes keep distinct, and are easily read off at leisure ... I used this plan for my beauty data, classifying the girls I passed in streets or elsewhere as attractive, indifferent, or repellent.

The image of this bald gentleman in his sixties scanning the pavements of our towns and cities, and stealthily taking observational notes on female pedestrians, is a deeply sinister one. Back home, he noted the time and place where his data had been collected, and over months was able to create a 'Beauty Map' of Great Britain. He found 'London to rank highest for beauty; Aberdeen lowest'.

Galton's beauty survey was primitive, subjective and offensive. But his results reflect some important factors that underlie how beauty was and is perceived.* The women strolling in Hyde Park or around Grosvenor Square might well have had the resources that allowed them to appear attractive; and probably their groomed presentation implied in many cases the existence of a well-heeled husband. It's unpalatable, but axiomatic, that people's good looks are often a by-product of their wealth, and that rich men – as well as rich women – are magnets for the opposite sex. Galton probably noticed that this could have been an instance of selective breeding – of a cascade effect,

---

* In 2008 Viren Swami, Professor of Social Psychology at Anglia Ruskin University, with his colleague Eliana Hernandez, revisited Galton's Beauty Map, using more scientific methods than 'prickers', across a number of London boroughs. Richer boroughs like Westminster and Kensington were rated most attractive; more deprived boroughs such as Newham and Haringey the least.

whereby privileged beauty generated and perpetuated yet more privileged beauty.

Turning to the 'ugly' women of Aberdeen – as a letter to the *Aberdeen Evening Express* pointed out, the beauty and well-being of the haves in that city depended on the misery of the have-nots. The city's female millworkers earned as little as five or six shillings a week: 'Their plenty involves the poverty of working women ... every idle lady necessitates a factory slave.' On these meagre wages, just staying alive took precedence over looking pretty.

For Francis Galton, however, the 'pricker' project fed into one of broader significance; his object was the improvement of humanity itself. The 'best stock' would be encouraged to marry young and bring up their children healthily, while those 'afflicted by lunacy, feeble-mindedness, habitual criminality and pauperism' would be prevented from propagating. By the turn of the century, Galton would be hailed as the hero of a popular eugenics movement, whose aim was to craft a better race, by getting superior people to breed more and inferior people to breed less. And among those elements that constituted superiority, white female beauty was regarded as the most desirable.

––––––––

For anyone seeking style advice, ask a Frenchwoman. In 1891 'la Baronne Staffe'* published *Le Cabinet de Toilette*, a 'how-to' guide to womanly loveliness which became an instant success. The following year it was published in America as *My Lady's Dressing Room*, 'adapted' and with an introduction by

---

* This was the pseudonym of Blanche Soyer, who published a number of bibles of decorum and taste. Her sophisticated Parisian tone made her an authority for the French bourgeoisie. *The Lady's Dressing-Room* was published in England in 1893, in a translation by another *grande dame* of middle-class manners and morals, Lady Colin Campbell.

Harriet Hubbard Ayer,* who took the opportunity to reinforce the vital importance of beauty:

> One of the triumphs of our sex is that by legitimate means we have learned to care for ourselves physically ... We have learned how not to grow old, and we have learned ... that we may preserve the beauty of youth, or a delightful resemblance to it, far past the terrible middle age which we formerly so dreaded.

Alarm bells ring – are we re-entering Madame Rachel's fraudulent Beautiful for Ever territory? Or prefiguring a wonder-ingredient, wrinkle-reducing, anti-ageing miracle? La Baronne Staffe, though she was not peddling fake cosmetics, was peddling a dream; her books – which became bestsellers on both sides of the Atlantic – insisted that *'plus la femme est femme, plus l'homme l'aime'*: 'the more womanly a woman is, the more men love her'.

La Baronne illustrated her argument with an example of timeless perfection. The Marchioness of Londonderry was 'an English beauty, [who] retains her youthful charms, which defy the ravages of time'. Her ladyship's patent method was to spend every tenth day in bed in a darkened room doing absolutely nothing. Occasionally her maid read aloud to her from 'a light, unexciting romance'. Lady Londonderry was then in her mid-thirties. Expectations were changing. The London hostess Lady St Helier looked back at her youth: twenty years earlier a woman over thirty would have been considered past her prime, while by forty-five she was heading into her dotage. At that age her own mother 'had begun to wear caps' (the sign

---

* Harriet Hubbard Ayer was born privileged and rich, and – though not a feminist – achieved fame as the first, uncrowned queen of the American cosmetics industry. Ayer introduced the American consumer to game-changing face creams, soaps and perfumes. She was a skilled self-advertiser who also authored articles about health, beauty and etiquette.

of an old lady) and disposed of her youthful wardrobe as it was no longer needed.

Some village women in southern Mediterranean countries are still to be seen today, seated on rickety chairs in the hot sun, crocheting place mats, dressed from head to toe in black. These are women whose children have grown, they are widowed, and though they may only be in their forties they look much older. Their rusty black garments tell the world that they are, sexually, neutral – as if, now that their childbearing years have passed, the lights have been switched off. The classicist Dame Mary Beard has pointed out that conventions like this have grown up in patriarchal societies, as a way of dealing with a threat: 'Throughout many periods of history in the West there has been a real worry about what you do with women who are past their childbearing years. As I can confirm, women with long grey hair can make people anxious.'* At the turn of the twentieth century Lady St Helier looked at the changing world around her and saw that emancipation was speaking to older women too. And they were no longer content, at forty-five, to sit crocheting and wearing black:

> Nowadays mothers and daughters dress almost alike; and what is more common than the sight of a young and still beautiful mother dancing all through an evening as merrily, and as much sought after, as her daughter?

But as many of us know, clawing back youth, and trying to stay young, is hard work (unless we can spend every tenth day

---

* Dame Mary was famously attacked by the critic A. A. Gill for not taking more trouble to appear attractive while presenting a programme about ancient Rome. In his own restaurant column Gill customarily referred to his girlfriend as 'The Blonde'.

in bed). Fortunately, Baronne Staffe had a host of more practical tips: what to do about unwanted hair (tweezers or, failing that, a wash of distilled celandine leaves); freckles (pulverised camphor dissolved in oil of turpentine); and wax melted with alum and nut oil as a recipe for hardening the fingernails.

However, *The Lady's Dressing-Room* was also censorious. Staffe described making up as a 'deplorable and disfiguring habit'; wrinkles she attributed to sitting up late at night reading over-exciting novels; and outdoor pleasures like lawn tennis were held responsible for brown leathery hands. Pink corsets were in poor taste. Flowers in the house caused headaches. Violent emotions were to be avoided. Housework was better than gymnastics for exercise. No woman should let her skin become blotchy or spotty, or slouch around her home in a slovenly or faded gown.

For la Baronne, the issue was very simple: a woman who neglected herself would be repulsive to her husband. A fat woman with thick ankles should not be surprised if he started ogling other, more slender women. So beware: 'Your own happiness and that of your family may depend upon it.' Her book was explicit that it was a woman's sacred mission to 'remain beautiful . . . to be the delight of the eye and the joy of him who is the support of her womanly weakness . . . and to remain on the pedestal upon which she has been placed by him'.

Baronne Staffe stressed how important it was to preserve the mystique of femininity (a theme that will recur). Wordsworth's 'spirit' woman was an ever-present, if illusory, ideal.

The husband should always find the wife fresh, beautiful, sweet as a flower; but he should believe her to be so adorned by Nature, like the lilies of the field . . . He should not suspect she possesses means of enhancing it . . . which he might think foolish or ridiculous.

A woman's fresh, sweet, mystical aura was part of the gender pact. This state of affairs is perfectly defined by 'A Society Lady' from Chicago, the anonymous author of *The Secret Revealed – How to Acquire Personal Beauty* (1889):

Men who see only the stern realities of life in business often seek relaxation in the society of women whose whole object seems to be charming. They avoid women too much like themselves; the cold, exact, judicial, intellectual women who could discuss international politics or the law of supply and demand with him. He wants the wrinkles caressed out of his brain by soft rosy fingertips, and to forget sordid cares in the smile of coral lips.

There isn't any use to try to deny all of this. It is so. God made it so.

———

The well-bred lady owed much of her beauty to hours spent in the dressing-room. This was where the magic happened. In other words, no husband should ever be permitted to cross its threshold while his wife was engaged in such unpoetical pursuits as attaching hair pads or stuffing her bosom with horsehair wadding.

And talking of shapely bosoms, there was a growing perception that their primary purpose – lactation – conflicted with the aesthetic ideal. Physicians noted how young women's breasts were firm and uplifted, compared to post-pregnancy, when 'their breasts enlarge and hang loosely from the thorax'. The Victorian ideal of motherhood and its associated functions was becoming hard to reconcile with the exalted imagery of plump, firm, rounded breasts – for caressing not for suckling. Inevitably, manufacturers of products like the rub-on tonic Mother's Friend got in on the act:

> Many women go childless because they fear the ordeal will destroy their figures ... It need not be ... In cases where the breasts have withered and lost their graceful roundness ... it simply proved that Mother's Friend had not been used.

And if that didn't work there was Bust Cream or Food, or the Princess Bust Developer, a terrifying object that looked as if it was designed for unblocking sinks:

> If nature has not favored you with that greatest charm, a symmetrically rounded bosom, full and perfect, send for the Princess Bust Developer and you will be surprised, delighted and happy over the result of one week's use.

Victorian men liked their women 'womanly' – and that meant bountiful (except for round the waist).

> A wonderful joy our eyes to bless,
> In her magnificent comeliness,
> Is an English girl of eleven stone two,
> And five foot ten in her dancing shoe!

W. S. Gilbert wrote this lyric (for *Utopia, Limited*) in 1893. Youthfulness was sought-after – but youthfulness didn't mean adolescence. 'Maturity was the keynote of feminine beauty ... [These ladies] were imposing Boadiceas, figureheads on the prow of some Norse ship,' wrote the photographer and arbiter of elegance Cecil Beaton half a century later (in *The Glass of Fashion* (1954)). More crudely, the American journalist Henry Collins Brown recalled, 'We liked our women with plenty of meat on them.' Scrawny girls were not to his taste. Born in 1862, Brown grew up admiring the magnificent New York matrons of the 1880s: lush, curvaceous and Renoiresque. That did not mean fat. In 1897 an American journalist writing in *Harper's Bazaar* denounced fatness as a 'deformity'. Fat women were all very well in 'that burning clime where women, like pigs, are valued at so much a pound', but they were unacceptable in polite society. Thinness was also disparaged. It looked tubercular, which might be glamorous, but was inevitably regarded as a 'misfortune'. Baronne Staffe recommended a regular routine, a diet of soup and tapioca, and a glass of claret at breakfast in order to become 'fair, rosy and well rounded'. Clinicians had already noted that some (particularly young) women carried thinness to extremes; refusal to eat resulting in emaciation and sometimes death. In 1873 Sir William Gull gave this malady its name: anorexia nervosa. But he and his contemporaries did not observe any link between starvation and a desire by the sufferers either to change their appearance, or to control their lives. That was yet to come.

A slender woman was a virtuous woman, and for now, Staffe's sternest words were reserved for those who let themselves become too fat:

> A woman who is too stout cannot take a step without blowing like a grampus, without perspiring in torrents; she is as clumsy as an elephant ... Her cheeks and her eyelids, overcharged with fat, make a repulsive mass of her face.

Awareness of weight-loss diets had increased in the 1860s when William Banting, the obese executive of a funeral direction company, wrote a best-selling booklet describing how he had lost forty-six pounds by giving up sugar, carbohydrates and dairy products.* His *Letter on Corpulence* (1863) has been in print ever since, and his name would become so synonymous with his methodology that for a century afterwards if a person declined pudding they were liable to be met with the question, 'Are you banting?'

Domestic bathroom scales were not yet available; anyone who wanted to check their weight would need to find a public penny-slot machine. These were as popular as fairground amusements, and were often installed on the platforms of train stations. But by the 1880s there were signs that the goalposts were shifting. For women aspiring to be beautiful, it was no longer enough to pop in a bust-improver, tuck in a pad of false hair, tighten your stays and dab on some discreet powder. Women were being urged to modify their bodies, to edit what nature had given them. The intrinsic character of a woman's body was beginning to seem questionable, indeterminate – and at the mercy of others.

Certain interventions were being introduced, with the potential to improve a lady's appearance dramatically. 'Those persons afflicted with large noses may be glad to learn of a method of reducing their proportions,' wrote Baronne Staffe. She did not elaborate, but may have been alluding to the advances in cosmetic rhinoplasty being pioneered in America

---

* William Banting was preceded, a hundred years earlier, by the Georgians' diet guru Dr George Cheyne, who weighed over twenty-eight stone and nearly died from 'vertiginous paroxysms'. Subsequently he experimented with a diet based solely on milk and vegetables, which was so successful that it made his fortune.

at that time by the otolaryngologist John Orlando Roe. Refinements in the art of anaesthesia were also opening the door to surgeons offering painless procedures to people with protruding ears, or wrinkles. And relief was in sight for the hairy. Dr George Henry Fox of New York had observed at first hand the misery that women could endure from unwanted hair. They had come to him in distress, after years spent fruitlessly trying to tweezer out thousands of excess hairs. In his short book on the subject, *The Use of Electricity in the Removal of Superfluous Hair* (1886), Dr Fox described the hopeless predicament of the hirsute woman:

> This abnormal growth of hair is not always a trifling matter ... It is very apt to affect her disposition, and to injure her prospects in life, especially if she be young and unmarried.

Fox gave instances of women driven insane by their hairiness, and argued that his remedy could be life-changing. Though his procedure – electrolysis – was expensive, laborious and painful, it produced impressive results. And it was permanent!

Electrolysis was also being heralded as a possible antidote to wrinkles. Meanwhile, Parisian coiffeurs were exploring other ways in which technology could improve on nature: in 1883 the salon Monnet et Compagnie patented para-phenylene diamine, a compound that combined with peroxide to produce a range of hair colours. And the coiffeur Marcel Grateau was experimenting with iron tongs that he heated over a gas burner and applied to straight hair; Grateau's method resulted in spectacular parallel undulations – and would soon make him a fortune under the name of the Marcel wave. Women whose hearts were set on improving their appearance were a lucrative market. Beauty was so merged with a woman's identity that anyone promising to make her dreams come true could also make a gigantic profit. More than a century ago, the foundations were being laid for a global industry based on female psychology – and female biology.

The signs were also there that beauty itself was no longer an inner state, but was relocating, or being superimposed. A woman's hair, her nose, the ageing process itself could be refashioned and made to conform – by diet, by surgery, by technology. And even as women moved falteringly in the direction of winning the battle for equality and controlling their own destinies, so the control that they had over their own bodies was starting to slip from their grasp.

Dollar Princesses

Destiny appeared to beckon for Louise Montague, a twenty-one-year-old starlet from New York City. 'I am confident that I shall be successful, and you can say so if you wish!' she bragged to a journalist. 'And don't forget to state that I am the best-dressed woman on the variety stage.'

In 1881 the young singer and performer, whose modest reputation was based on assorted burlesque roles, was selected from over three thousand women who mailed in their photographs to become the 'Ten Thousand Dollar Beauty'.

> Miss Montague's claim to beauty is that she is a demi-blonde with classic features, a charming blue eye and a beautiful light complexion. Of medium height, she possesses a full and symmetrical figure. Her weight is 147 pounds. A mass of wavy dark chestnut hair,

combed well down over the narrow Grecian forehead, gives her somewhat of a matronly air, though it adds ten-fold to her beauty.

Louise Montague, the 'Ten Thousand
Dollar Beauty', 1890

The journalist's report ends on an uncomfortable note, as if he is making an appraisal of a horse: 'One of the charms of her face is her magnificent teeth, which she shows to advantage when in conversation.'

Circus entrepreneur Adam Forepaugh's nationwide call-out may make the claim to be the first commercial beauty contest. After her win, Louise Montague was awarded the title 'Queen of Beauty' and joined Forepaugh's troupe. She was allocated a part playing an 'Oriental' princess, and paraded through the streets of Philadelphia surrounded by circus animals:

> Seated in state upon the back of an elephant, Miss Louise Montague, the ex-variety star, now known as the 'handsomest lady in the world', carried herself with commendable grace and dignity . . . Following the '$10,000' face came a herd of seventeen handsomely caparizoned elephants.

The media now saw a huge promotional opportunity, and in tandem with the growth in the sale of cosmetics and beauty parlour treatments, the professional beauty pageant started to emerge in the late nineteenth century. Where America led Britain followed. And soon after the start of the next century we too would have our own cattle markets.

The *fin-de-siècle* saw an increase in transatlantic traffic. Scores of wealthy 'dollar princesses' arrived on these shores, seeking to marry impecunious members of the nobility; between 1880 and 1914 the number of American peeresses rose from four to fifty. This was the age of Edith Wharton's 'buccaneers'. One of them was Jennie Jerome.

With her ripe bosomy bloom Jennie was regarded – as her mother had been before her – as *la belle Américaine*. She secured Lord Randolph Spencer-Churchill, the syphilitic third son of the seventh Duke of Marlborough – possibly not a good bargain – though Jennie's place in history was secured by becoming mother to Winston Churchill.

Years later, and onto the second of three marriages, she published a memoir, *The Reminiscences of Lady Randolph Churchill* (1908), in which she recalled her glory days as a society beauty:

> A curious phase had come over society. Publicity became the fashion ... the craze for exhibiting the photographs of 'Ladies of Quality,' as they would have been called in the eighteenth century, was a novelty which brought forth much comment.

But it wasn't just a phase. High society was opening up (the Prince of Wales, who loved rich people, had a more relaxed attitude than his mother). Though the way was still largely barred for people of colour, Jews, Americans, industrialists and their daughters now had an entrée. And the public wanted a piece. Photography had been the entitlement of princesses and courtesans, but by 1900 there were more than a thousand photographic studios across Britain. Portraiture was no longer the preserve of the privileged who could commission a likeness from a painter: the second half of the nineteenth century saw an explosion of human imagery, for the rich and the less rich.

The bourgeoisie could now distribute pictures of themselves via *cartes de visite*, in a way comparable to the profile images so carefully curated and posted on social media today. *Cartes de visite* were hugely popular, avidly collected and pasted into albums.

Meanwhile, elegant ladies besieged fashionable photographers' studios, dreaming up coquettish poses: on swings, lounging in hammocks, cuddling kittens, wrapped in furs under fake snowstorms, garlanded with artificial flowers. In the last decades of the nineteenth century the Professional Beauties could scarcely keep pace with the demand. A stream of their luscious, lacy likenesses issued forth via magazines, advertisements, postcards and reproductions of works of art.

In the late nineteenth century 'Professional Beauty' picture postcards became popular collectibles

In Burlington Arcade crowds collected in front of the shop windows, where the photographs were exhibited alongside those of actresses (Lillie Langtry's image, as we have seen, was cultivated and distributed with care). Such self-promotion was of doubtful respectability; but we love, it appears, to announce our existence to the world. The relationship between subject and photographer, and the question of 'photogenicity' would now become additions to a growing range of appearance anxieties. Then as now, fashion and beauty, visual technology and appearance-worry were in lockstep – though Lady Randolph pleaded ignorance: 'The first time mine found its way into a shop, I was severely censured by my friends, and told I ought to prosecute the photographer.'

For just pennies, anyone could buy a celebrity beauty picture postcard from a stationer's, a brisk trade which demonstrated the public appetite for mass-produced female icons (and bust up many an artist's business plan). And with demand came supply, from both sides of the Atlantic.

In 1887 the young New York artist Charles Dana Gibson was hired as an illustrator by *Life*, a magazine then aimed principally at male readers. And it was foremost for them that he created the glamorous, confident, well-bred, seductive and improbably voluptuous 'Gibson Girl'. Effectively, she was a pin-up: 'a girl so alluring that other young men would want to climb into the picture and sit beside her'.

But women loved this male-generated ideal too, and wanted to be her. 'Fifth Avenue,' wrote one New York commentator, 'is like a procession of Gibsons.' For two decades, until the First World War, the name Gibson was given to everything from hats to handkerchiefs. In 1903 Gibson signed a $100,000 deal with *Collier's* to draw double-page spreads for the weekly. His Girl represented a way of life which captured the age. Her breezy outdoorsiness, vitality and sex appeal were a nod to America's progressive, can-do love of freedom: was this the woman of the twentieth century? But in case that seemed too emancipated, her desirability, decorum and updo kept her firmly within the bounds of nineteenth-century virtue and good breeding. Her independence was skin deep, for she rarely studied, or worked. Despite (or because of?) her voluminous bottom, visible legs, and the trade in souvenirs, the Gibson Girl was a lady, and would certainly end up as the bride of a Gibson Gentleman. There were also real-life Gibson Girls. One was Camille Clifford, who won a $2,000 prize for the best looka-like in a magazine competition sponsored by Gibson himself. Following her win, Clifford's eighteen-inch waist and dazzling deportment swept her to London, where she mingled in society and happily married a minor aristocrat.

OF COURSE THERE ARE MERMAIDS.

Charles Dana Gibson: *Of Course there are Mermaids*, 1902 – the 'Gibson Girl' at her most radiantly sexy in a beach outfit

The English aristocracy seemed to have a soft spot for American beauty; though their own beauties offered fierce competition. In November 1897 a gossip columnist from the *Brooklyn Daily Eagle* speculated as to how many of the female

English cast of *In Town* (playing that week in Montauk on Long Island) would eventually make a match with a hereditary peer. *In Town*, the creation of producer and impresario George Edwardes, had had its first hugely successful run at London's Gaiety Theatre in 1892, and was followed by a string of similarly frothy musical comedies with lightweight plots, jokes, songs and stylish costumes. But Edwardes's winning formula was the living, breathing, gorgeous Gaiety Girls themselves. Dressed in the latest fashions, the cast members had genuine cachet, became house-hold names for their beauty and elegance, and soon acquired an impressive track record of marrying into the nobility. It helped that their legs could be seen.

Denise Orme landed first a lord and then a duke. Gertie Millar became the Countess of Dudley. Connie Gilchrist got the Earl of Orkney and Rosie Boote got the Marquess of Headfort. Meanwhile, George Edwardes got a fortune touring his brand in the United States and worldwide.

Between them, the Gaiety Girls and the Gibson Girls were dreams made flesh.

———

If you were white, that is.

In 1898 a beautiful young African American woman named Aida Overton joined Black Patti's Troubadours,* a renowned singing and dancing group whose repertoire included a blend of high and low culture: operatic excerpts alongside ragtime songs, acrobatics, vaudeville comedy and 'minstrelsy' – the clichéd, demeaning presentation of Black stereotypes, which were what their white audience expected. This was an era when

———

* The troupe was named for its founder, Matilda Sissieretta Joyner Jones, a soprano often known as the Black Patti after the world-famous opera singer Adelina Patti.

many white people saw Black women as sexually free and easy. They were objectified as oversexed Jezebels, or caricatured as beaming plantation 'mammies'.

By the time she was eighteen Aida's physical grace and velvety mezzo-soprano had secured her reputation, above all for her smash hit performance of the ditty 'Miss Hannah from Savannah', in which her look – pearls, parasol, feathers and pompadour coiffure – were unmistakably modelled on the Gibson Girl. The song was a quaint send-up of a social climber trying to kick the ladder out from underneath her. Aida's stage pose as the super-respectable Hannah – with her thrown-out bust, ramrod stance and dainty wrists – was pitch perfect, and audiences loved her.

But Aida was on a mission to prove that a preconceived notion of Black femininity could and should be re-thought. Writing in *Colored American Magazine* in 1905, she would plead the cause of the Black female actor, whose reputation was so tarnished by public exhibitionism: 'Many well-meaning people dislike stage life, especially our women. On this point I would say, a woman does not lose her dignity today – as used to be the case – when she enters upon Stage life.'

Aida admitted that there were many dazzled, stage-struck girls who brought discredit to the profession. But serious, professionally minded girls who took up acting were in short supply and much needed: 'I should say to [them], "Come, for we need so many earnest workers in this field; and by hard work, I am sure the future will repay you and all of us."'

'Good acting' was, she claimed, as widespread among 'men and women of color' as it was in other races, and they deserved respect. Aida's own portrayal of Miss Hannah replaced sexualisation, exhibitionism, swagger and shamelessness with modesty, mystery and dignity. Her Gibson Girl get-up tells us that she was categorically rejecting the Black parody, and staking a claim for equality.

In 1899 Aida married the performer George Walker, who worked as one side of a famous vaudeville duo with his friend Bert Williams; Aida joined their company and started contributing both as a choreographer and producer. Their shows featured the cakewalk, a prancing, high-stepping, comical dance which had originated in the days of slavery – probably as a subtle mockery of the 'superior' white owners. With her career now skyrocketing, Aida made the cakewalk her own. In time, her skills would be in demand to teach the dance to nouveau riche high society ('the swell four hundred'). Here was an early example of how, in the Gilded Age, the white cultural elite were starting to dip into Black 'exoticism'; later in the century this would explode into fully fledged 'negrophilia'. Aida's perceived glamour, respectability and authenticity enabled her to target the patronage of the white upper classes. 'The fact of the matter is this,' she wrote, 'we come in contact with more white people in a week than other professional colored people meet in a year and more than some meet in a whole decade.'

At the turn of the century standing – or dancing – on a theatrical stage was a fast track to fame and prominence, and a visible way to make a political statement.* *In Dahomey*, created by Williams and Walker, was the first Broadway musical created entirely by writers and performers of colour, including Aida Overton Walker. In 1903, the team took this hugely successful show on tour to Britain, where the critics singled out Aida's performance: 'a dusky, vivacious young person whose dancing was very captivating'. Four months later the show was still going

---

*   Designer and architect Veronica Jackson offers a perceptive and well-researched take on Overton Walker's contribution, in her thesis 'Restructuring Respectability, Gender, and Power: Aida Overton Walker Performs a Black Feminist Resistance' (2019).

strong. In June Aida was invited to perform the cakewalk, and 'Miss Hannah', in Buckingham Palace gardens for the ninth birthday of the king's grandson, Prince Edward – and Edward VII, that famous lover of women, presented Aida with a diamond brooch in recognition of her talent.

Aida Overton Walker and her husband George Walker dancing the cakewalk for a number from *In Dahomey*, played at the Shaftesbury Theatre, London in 1903

Back in New York in 1904 Aida continued her work as both choreographer and leading lady in a run of hit Broadway shows. She had become a household name, and used her position to express her belief that Black women who chose the stage as a career had a vital role to play in the struggle for racial equality:

> In this age we are all fighting the one problem – that is the color problem ... As individuals we must strive all we can to show that we are as capable as white people ... [But] I venture to think and dare to state that our profession does more toward the alleviation of color prejudice than any other profession among colored people.

Aida was at the zenith of her stardom. But in 1909 her husband became ill; he died two years later, at the age of thirty-eight. Being widowed didn't stop Aida for long. After George's death she continued performing, and – unheard of till then – took bookings to appear at white venues across New York. In other ways too, she was ahead of the game. Aida was now winning fans for her appearances impersonating men. To begin with, she had filled in for George when he was ill, imitating his comedic manner, kitted out in a suit, spats, a cane and straw hat. Now, she beckoned her audiences to enter a make-believe masculine world, where the Black crooner sang of his childhood, his homeland and his soul. Her male dandy act was greeted with delight – the permissive atmosphere of the footlights, as always, taking the edge off its violation of the rules of femininity.

In 1912, in one of her most famous roles, Aida played Salome, in a lavish production with a thirty-six-piece symphony orchestra. Yet again, her interpretation of Herod's desirable wife changed the narrative. Given her outspoken intention to deflect the popular, over-eroticised image of the 'immoral' Black woman, her version was deliberately classy, artistic and modest. It attracted sell-out audiences.

And then, suddenly, it was all over.

October 24th 1914
AIDA OVERTON WALKER PASSES AWAY
In obedience to the summons of death there passed from the
American stage the greatest actress of the colored race and
one of the best comediennes of the age.

It was headline news across America. Aida was just thirty-four
years old, and had continued performing until two months
before her death, reported as being from kidney failure. But, in
her short career, Aida Overton Walker changed how audiences
saw Black performers, demonstrating that beauty, style, grace,
talent and fame could all be effective agents in the fight for
social justice and rights, above all for women of colour.

––––––––

Gilded Age grandeur didn't get more grandiose than New York's
Waldorf Hotel, situated on the corner of Fifth Avenue and 33rd
Street.* On Christmas Day 1909 two middle-aged high society
ladies, one American, the other English, shared a table in the
Waldorf's Empire Room restaurant, with its frescoed ceiling,
satin hangings and gilt-ornamented pale green marble pillars.
Lustrous silver-plated dish covers glittered beneath dozens of
electric lights. These two ladies were old friends, and it was a
meeting of minds. Elsie de Wolfe was interior designer to the
wealthy of Manhattan. In London Lucy Duff Gordon – dubbed
'Lucile' – had become the queen of cutting-edge couture for a
generation of stylish women. Crowded with well-heeled revel-
lers dressed in their Christmas best, the Empire Room was the

––––––––

*   The German Renaissance-style hotel was pulled down in 1929 to provide
the site for the Empire State Building.

perfect place for two fashion-conscious women to survey – and find fault with – their fellow diners.

'Of course Elsie and I began to talk about clothes and pick out the dresses we liked the best,' Lucy later recalled. Most of the women were dashingly attractive, and their dresses were expensive. But something was wrong with them. Elsie agreed with her friend that American women lacked taste and know-how, but explained that it wasn't their fault:

> 'We pay far more for clothes here than in Europe, but we have no really good designers, and we have to buy models brought over from France.'
>
> 'Some of these women are extraordinarily attractive,' I said, 'but they don't know how to dress. I wish I could teach them.'
>
> 'Why don't you? I have a splendid idea. You must open a shop over here. American women will love your dresses, and they will think it absolutely the last word in chic to be dressed by an English society woman.'
>
> From that moment I was fired with enthusiasm.

Lucy Duff Gordon was born Lucy Sutherland in London in 1863; her family later moved to Jersey. Bold and tomboyish as a child, Lucy's feminine and creative side found expression through dressing her family of dolls. She learnt to sew, and lavished hours of love on their miniature wardrobes. And at the age of fifteen she had an epiphany.

Lillie Langtry was then at the height of her fame. That summer she returned home to Jersey. The stunner who had 'gone away to London to be a great lady' was a local celebrity, and on her occasional visits she was always welcomed ecstatically by the island's population, with flags put out to greet her.

Lucy and her younger sister Elinor* were among those gripped by the arrival of this glamorous icon. As Lucy recalled:

> We were both very curious about this lovely creature, stories of whose romantic career as a court beauty used to be circulated all over the island. We were always hearing of what she had worn at the opera, of how she had set a new fashion in hats, and of how often the Prince of Wales had danced with her at the Devonshire House ball.
>
> Elinor and I determined that come what might we would see the 'Jersey Lily' and find out whether she was as beautiful as we had been told.

Mrs Langtry had been invited to a soirée by the governor, whose daughter, Ada, was the Sutherland girls' closest friend; she agreed to collaborate. On the night of the party, the sisters waited till after dark, then quietly crept out of their beds, dressed, stole from the house and made their way the short distance to Government House. Ada was waiting for them and let them in. With her guidance the pair of conspirators reached their goal – the ladies' cloakroom. Both were small; once there they took up position, cramped but thoroughly concealed underneath the draping folds of a muslin cloth which covered the dressing table. They had just a tiny peephole to spy on the lady guests who arrived to powder and titivate. Lillie was the last to come. A trill of musical laughter announced her arrival – and then she was in the room:

---

* Elinor Sutherland would grow up to become the hugely commercial and scandalous novelist Elinor Glyn. The sisters shared a racy, unconventional streak, and Lucy's career was advanced by Elinor's love of high fashion and entrée into wealthy circles.

I never saw any woman more divinely lovely than she looked in her white dress, with a scarlet flower in her hair nestling against one ear. She came and sat down at the dressing table while she arranged her dress and pinned a beautiful diamond brooch on one shoulder. We were so close to her that we did not move one inch, for fear of touching her dress and giving away the secret of our presence, but even through the folds of the muslin curtain we could see her perfect beauty. There was an extraordinary radiance about Lillie Langtry that I have never seen in any other woman.

Beautiful women would underpin Lucy's business. In due course she married, had a child, divorced and married again, to one of her investors, Sir Cosmo Duff Gordon. From small beginnings the talented dressmaker built up a following of devotees who couldn't resist the sex appeal of her low-necked, coffee-coloured tea gowns with their slit skirts. She also gave the gowns soulful names: 'The Sighing Sound of Lips Unsatisfied', or 'A Frenzied Song of Amorous Things', for example. But in the 1890s you had to be brave to wear them – vice and virtue, as we have seen, rode side by side along Rotten Row, and woe betide any woman who stepped in her high heels across the fine line that divided *comme il faut* from risqué! 'Are you quite sure, dear Lady Duff Gordon, that it does not look too suggestive?'

Lucy was romantic, self-promoting, enterprising, and a risk-taker. When she started her business she encountered a wall of prejudice. For a woman of her rank, 'keeping a shop' was déclassée, and even after her marriage to Sir Cosmo she could not be presented at court. But Lucy stood her ground. When her alluring designs were launched their Grecian simplicity shocked. Even more transgressive was the underwear she pro-duced – 'I hated the thought of my creations being worn over the ugly nun's veiling or linen-cum-Swiss embroidery which was all that the really virtuous woman of those days permitted herself.' At Maison Lucile in Hanover Square society ladies came to wonder at – and, if they were daring enough, buy – her cobwebby, pastel-coloured chiffon knickers and slips that now fully justified the name of lingerie. Lucy made no excuse:

> I was so sorry for the poor husbands, who had to see their wives looking so unattractive at night after taking off the romantic dresses I had created.

Evening gowns by Lucile, modelled by
two of her 'goddesses'

She also changed the fashion world for ever by introducing exclusive, invitation-only mannequin parades. The static modelling of dresses pre-existed this innovation, and had been practised by fashion houses such as Doucet, Worth and Redfern, who all had an American clientele. But Lucy wanted to put the soul back into clothes shopping. She had a strong sense of occasion, and her shows were different: theatrical and grandiose. With difficulty, she recruited six 'goddesses' to whom she gave fairy-tale names: Gamela, Dolores, Corisande, and so on; they were 'working girls' who lacked experience of high society. And they were beautiful: 'sinuous, dreamy [and] velvet-eyed', as one of them described her companions. This was blonde ingénue Elsie Kings, who joined Lucile's stable of models in the late 1890s, and was taught to walk with a book on her head:

> I soon learned the angle at which my hands appeared whitest, long and slender; at what degree my head best displayed my slender neck. Over and over it was impressed upon me that I had the gift of beauty, and never, never, must I do anything but enhance it!

Once Lucile had coiffed, manicured and trained them to walk with her trademark 'wonderful swaying step', the goddesses were dressed in her bewitchingly lovely dresses, decked in jewels and paraded before a glittering audience of princesses and duchesses. The show was a triumph. 'Orders flowed in by the dozen ... I knew that from that moment my career as a dressmaker would be smiled upon by fortune.' Lucy had opened a genie's bottle, for no one before had dreamed of selling dresses by exhibiting beautiful women as living clothes hangers.

According to the novelist Marie Corelli, much of the audience at Lucile's shows was actually formed of lecherous male spectators. 'They were invited to stare and smile, and they did it. But there was something remarkably offensive in their way of doing it.' 'Romance came very often to our house,' commented Elsie Kings.

Over the next half-century, the fashion model would become one of the most aspirational careers for women, as well as a commercial necessity in the high fashion ecosystem. In the service of businesses and brands, faces and bodies would be groomed, plucked and powdered.

But one of the most telling details to emerge from Lucy's fashion show experiment was her footnote about the models themselves. In 1900 the average woman was just over five feet tall, and 123 pounds (8 stone 11 lb). Thus the 'goddesses' were no more typical of their audience than today's models are of theirs, the difference being that while the lissom gazelles on the Paris or Milan runways present us with an ideal of ema-ciation, Lucile's mannequins expressed an ideal of matronly amplitude:

> The slimming craze had not been brought in at that time, and it amuses me to think of how different the figures of my goddesses were from the accepted standard of beauty today. Not one of them weighed much under eleven stone,* and several of them were considerably more. They were 'big girls' with 'fine figures' ... A woman was admired for looking like a woman, a thing with gen-erous curves and a full bust.

Lucile was reminiscing about her 'goddesses' in 1932, thirty years after the event – by which time show mannequins in clingy backless gowns and plunging necklines were super-slender and svelte. She had had a long and starry career; Paris, New York and Chicago had opened their doors to her, and she had dressed many of the most celebrated belles on both sides of the Atlantic. Yet still, for her, the tangibly lovely and curva-ceous Mrs Langtry remained in a class of her own. 'We have

---

* 154 pounds, or 70 kg.

no successor,' she wrote, adding, 'but then Lillie Langtry was a legend, she stood for romance.'

Freewheeling to Freedom

Little by little over the 1860s and 70s, equality movements had been gaining momentum. Local suffrage associations and groups like the Primrose League and the Women's Liberal Associations had lobbied for constitutional reform, but remained splintered until the formation of the National Society for Women's Suffrage in 1867. This laid the foundations for the centralised campaign which would burst into life under the leadership of Emmeline Pankhurst and her daughters Christabel, Sylvia and Adela, in the years before the First World War. And despite their cumbersome garments, women were starting to migrate beyond their parlours into the public world – and male terrain – of meadows, mountaintops and mixed bathing.

What sports and exercise *were* acceptable for the Victorian lady? Riding side-saddle had always been regarded as unimpeachable: everybody agreed that, provided the ankles were covered, every lady looked her best on horseback in an elegantly cut habit. Society was also unanimous that the tennis court offered a wonderful shop window for a marriageable young lady to show her wares, so long as she was protected from the sun. Lady Colin Campbell suggested female tennis players guard against chills by wearing a light cashmere or flannel dress, nicely embellished with ribbons and colourful trimmings, plus their choice of fashionable hat. She also advised on how to look chic while yachting or on the archery range: yet more niche shopping opportunities for the aspiring bride.

Mixed golf clubs offered matrimonial possibilities, but also brought in a sector of talented players, like Mabel Stringer, who were only hampered in their ambitions by the clothes:

> How on earth anyone of us ever managed to hit a ball, or get along at all in the outrageous garments with which fashion decreed we were to cover ourselves, is one of the great unsolved mysteries of that or any age.

Stringer, who would become a champion golfer, recalled stomping across the links wearing hats with veils, stiff collars that left sores on her neck, multitudinous petticoats, trailing skirts with leather-bound edges which collected the mud, tight belts and leg-o'-mutton sleeves so voluminous that they impeded visibility and had to be tethered down. One of her fellow golfers arrived to play a round or two wearing a skirt with a train and a hat trimmed with ostrich plumes. Despite this, male golfers met strong opposition among the female players. One of Mabel's male adversaries thought he was on safe ground when he challenged her, 'If you beat me, I shall have to support Women's Suffrage.' She did, and he kept his word.

But playing a round of golf was a breeze compared to going for a swim; preserving modesty in the water quite simply tied the body in knots. A woman hoping for a refreshing dip had first to retreat to a poky hut on wheels known as a bathing machine to unbutton all her petticoats et cetera, before re-buttoning herself into a knee-length, braid-trimmed tunic in serge or sateen with a frill at the neck and a sash around the waist, over pantalettes, black stockings and black India rubber bathing shoes. The ladies' page of the *Illustrated London News* recommended wearing a '*très chic*' straw bonnet tied under the chin with a large bow, on top of all this. Thus attired, she entered the water. Lady Violet Hardy recalled staying in Scotland and borrowing her mother-in-law's antique Victorian costume to cool off in the loch; she dived in only to be instantly dragged to the bottom by saturated yards of fabric – 'I thought I was never coming to the surface!' An energetic woman who felt like plunging into the water needed far more additional strength than her male counterpart, just to prevail against the inert weight of all those garments.

Women who tried to wear more streamlined swimwear paid a price: in 1913 Mrs Lanning of Atlantic City, New Jersey, wearing a short purple bathing dress, was set upon by a mob of two hundred men, pelted with sand and beaten unconscious. 'An extreme slit on one side of the skirt is what started the trouble,' reported the local paper. Perhaps her assailants had been listening to Cardinal John Farley, visiting the city that day, who denounced the latest women's fashions: 'The diaphanous gown and slit skirt are products of the devil's industry,' he ranted. Mrs Lanning was rescued by lifeguards, but the crowd followed her to hospital 'to get another glimpse at the suit', and waited menacingly outside until she was discharged.

Mrs Lanning, 'as she appeared to the mob that beat
her because of the daring cut of her bathing costume'.
South Bend News-Times, 12 September 1913

Women mountaineers were few, but fearless. Elizabeth Le
Blond was a pioneering Irishwoman who in 1907 became the
first president of the Ladies' Alpine Club. Photographs show
her making ascents though deep snow, wearing a fashionably
full-sleeved blouse and tie, a perky hat and a full-length skirt.
However, this was a pose, done for the picture, and to avoid
causing offence. Once the camera was out of the way, Lizzy
removed the awkward garment – and simply replaced it with a
much shorter one.

Though women were steadily encroaching onto the hallowed fields and pitches once reserved for their brothers, progress brought with it new tensions. Sporty women had to cope with the constant dilemma of how to compete without offending, while continuing to look feminine and not dowdy or 'manly'.

It could be tricky, especially in a sport like fencing. *The Gentlewoman's Book of Sports* (1892) gently pointed out that female fencers were likely to be disadvantaged if they wore high-heeled shoes in the salle d'armes. Female cricketers were also advised – in an age when a woman without a chocolate-boxy hat was regarded as having forsaken the human race – to pin theirs on securely. When the Original English Lady Cricketers teams first played in 1890 they were a public and press sensation – but nearly all the coverage dwelt on the decency of their costumes and a slightly prurient concern about the damage that might be caused by a blow on the breast from a cricket ball. Where sport was concerned, the playing field remained very far from level.

By the end of the century gymnastics and organised games were finally on the curriculum in many girls' schools, thanks to the advocacy of physical education pioneers like Martina Bergman-Osterberg and her pupil Rhoda Anstey. For both of them, callisthenics were incompatible with corsetry and petticoats. Osterberg insisted that her students wore form-less, below-the-knee frocks over blouses, with stockings and flat shoes. Anstey, a dedicated vegetarian who supported dress reform and always wore a djibbah (a kind of caftan), was equally committed to cold baths and women's eman-cipation. In 1897 she started her own college of physical training, where young women clad in gymslips practised lacrosse, netball and folk dancing. Despite their inelegance, the increasing popularity of gymnastics began, inexorably, to make the hourglass figure look like a throwback.

But bicycles were the game changer, after a safe version with a steerable front wheel was invented and commercialised. The 'iron steed' craze started in the mid-1890s. And when women took to the bicycle, the result was controversy on an international scale. For many the bicycle came to represent forbidden fruit, making it possible for young women from the bourgeoisie and upper classes to get out of the home, to neglect their domestic duties, their piano practice and their prayers. And its popularity among women made many men feel uncomfortable, and vulnerable. 'She is upon us, the Emancipated Woman,' wrote one panicked commentator in 1894, observing the proliferation of female bicyclists hurtling unchaperoned along thoroughfares and country lanes, wearing rampageous gender-defying trousers. Back in the 1850s many men like him had exhaled with relief when Mrs Bloomer and her 'bifurcated garments' were ridiculed off the streets. But here they were again! 'The flying females who pedal down the roads to-day, is only Bloomerism with a difference.'

Despite her own stature in a male-dominated profession, Dr Arabella Kenealy was opposed to the woman on wheels:

> [She] has sacrificed the elusive aura of womanliness. Though still good-looking, 'the haze, the elusiveness, the subtle suggestion of the face are gone'. Indeed, she is acquiring a 'bicycle face', that is, 'the face of muscular tension'.

A Wordsworthian nymph should not have a 'bicycle face'. And bicycles not only bust up a woman's poetic, womanly aura: they threatened her purity. The belief that motherhood was a woman's prime function was so embedded that there was public concern – from women too – that the activity would damage her reproductive organs. Dr Kenealy was motivated more by eugenic improvement of the race than by feminism, when she pronounced, 'It is the birthright of the babies that [she] and her fellow athletes are squandering.'

The president of the American Women's Rescue League, Charlotte Odlum Smith, was equally outspoken: 'The saddle is a fruitful source of injury. Bicycle riding is ruining the health of tens of thousands of women in this country, incidentally involving the physical welfare of generations yet unborn.' Many like her were dismayed at the necessity for women to straddle the machine. Was it from fear that an innocent female might accidentally be sexually penetrated? If so, this was unspoken. In 1896 the *New York Journal* printed her lengthy denunciation of the sport, entitled 'Is the Bicycle an Aid to Immorality?' Mrs Odlum Smith expressed a neurotic level of anxiety about the sexual connotations of bicycling; she argued that women who took it up became, literally, fast. They were on the slippery slope to ruin because the bicycle code of etiquette didn't conform to the normal rules and, released from strict chaperonage, they would fall into bad company. Young men could be cheeky with impunity, approaching female cyclists and offering to 'inflate their tyres'. Even worse, men on bicycles set snares for virtuous lady cyclists and lured them into 'immorality' – an 'awful traffic in human souls'. Mrs Odlum Smith also deplored the ostentatious dress worn by the 'bicycle flirts', designed to display their figures advantageously. She cannot have been happy to see her diatribe illustrated with a portrait of the curvaceous actress and model May Dunbar, who had jump-started her career by posing astride a bicycle for none less than Charles Dana Gibson. The Gibson Girl endorsement fatally undermined attempts to discourage such reckless gallivanting.

Nevertheless, there remained the vexed question of what to wear. Mounted on a bicycle, a woman was more publicly conspicuous than on foot. Should one wear a corset to look one's best? Though some tried pedalling in a full-length skirt, this was fraught with hazard, with petticoats catching in the spokes. Exposure to bright sunlight demanded hats, veils and parasols, which produced other perils.

Enter the rational dressers, led, as ever, by the dauntless Lady Florence Harberton in knickerbockers, gaiters and a collar and tie. She and her bifurcated sisters braved considerable hostility. Dorothy Peel was distressed to witness two ladies dismounting from their bicycles in front of her village church, revealing that they were wearing bloomers. 'Several boys threw stones at them, encouraged by their mothers who thought it a right and proper way to treat such shameless hussies.' On the morning of 7 October 1899 Lady Harberton herself buttoned up her knickerbockers and set out for a health-giving bicycle ride around the Surrey lanes. At lunchtime, feeling hungry, she walked into the Hautboy Hotel in Ockham, whose landlady, Mrs Mary Sprague, took one look at her and declared, 'No, not in that dress. I don't permit people to come into my house in that dress.' Lunchless but undeterred, Lady Harberton took Mrs Sprague to court, which – though the case was dismissed – attracted welcome publicity for her cause.

For a young woman growing up in the 1890s the freedoms offered by the 'new safety bicycle' seemed intoxicating. Edith Chaplin, later the Marchioness of Londonderry, remembered the thrill of possessing a bicycle with Dunlop pneumatic tyres:

My sister and I frequently escaped out of bounds and went much farther afield than would either have been approved or permitted. 'Young ladies' never could go out alone without a chaperon, even together, in the early 'nineties.

Now chaperones just couldn't keep up! By the late 1890s the velocipedes were so fashionable that a house party guest was often pressed to 'bring your bicycle'; Edith and her friends had the time of their lives doing unladylike wheelie stunts around the fountains and flower beds. On one occasion the twenty-year-old was chased by policemen and nearly arrested for pedalling furiously home from Battersea Park to St James's after a society dinner without lights. For a well-bred debutante, breaking the rules didn't get more exciting than this.

By the century's end the *pédaleuse* had come of age – whether wearing artfully disguised culottes that preserved her womanly aura, or in full-blown 'rationals'. Technology had facilitated liberation. 'The woman bicyclist has come to stay,' pronounced a Kansas newspaper running a fashion feature on 'bicycle gowns'. And 'no-legs' woman's days were numbered. For many on both sides of the Atlantic it felt like freewheeling to freedom.

'The advent of the bicycle ... entirely altered the whole outlook of one's life,' remembered Lady Clodagh Anson in her memoirs; while in 1896 the American women's rights activist Susan B. Anthony commented, 'Let me tell you what I think of bicycling. I think it has done more to emancipate women than anything else in the world. I stand and rejoice every time I see a woman ride by on a wheel.'

The bicycle brought about irreversible changes to women's dress. Laces were looser, limbs freer. But the backlash was quick to follow. Hard on the heels of the new independence came new restrictions, as the style police (this one in *New York World*, 1895) issued a blacklist of bicycle fashion faux-pas:

Don't be a fright.
Don't wear loud-hued leggings.
Don't cultivate a 'bicycle face'.
Don't wear clothes that don't fit.
Don't let your golden hair be hanging down your back.
Don't ignore the laws of the road because you are a woman.

Bicycles had ratcheted up liberation for women by several notches. But while horizons expanded, so too did commercial opportunities, public visibility and bodily exposure.

A new age of freedom was coming – with terms and conditions attached.

The Tatler

Vol. XXXVI. No. 466.
London, June 1, 1910.

REGISTERED AT THE GENERAL
POST OFFICE AS A NEWSPAPER

Sixpence

LADY DIANA MANNERS AS AN ARCHER

Lady Diana is one of the three beautiful daughters of the Duke and Duchess of Rutland. The above photograph, which has never before been published, shows Lady Diana as an archer, a pastime in which she excels

'Lady Diana Manners as an Archer', *Tatler*, 1 June 1910

3

New Century

Diana

Greek – everything must be Greek. I must draw a bow and have a crescent in my hair, draperies, sandalled or bare feet.

Lady Diana Manners was the youngest child of the Duchess of Rutland, the 'greenery-yallery' beauty with a passion for all things classical. The duchess's free-thinking romanticism spilled into the conduct of her marriage, and her daughter, born in 1892, was probably fathered not by the duke but by a dashingly handsome socialite politician and womaniser named Harry Cust. Beauty was Diana's inheritance. However, as an adolescent she saw herself as stocky and overweight: 'Christ, I am so fat! If only I could even feel like Artemis ... [but] I'm more like Diana of the moon; round, white, slow, lazy and generally like an unappetising blancmange.' At fourteen she started 'banting' to lose the excess pounds, secretly bought a bottle of peroxide to lighten her fluffy hair, which she frantically backcombed to thicken it, and filched her sister's illicit rouge to heighten her complexion.

By the time she was presented at court in 1910, Diana Manners was a Professional Beauty, and her name was rarely out of the society columns. That summer the *Tatler* featured her on their cover. She was not yet eighteen years old. With her perfect profile, hair swept back beneath a bandeau, her arms extended into the motions of the archer, she needed no embellishment. Diana – the goddess of the hunt, of the moon and chastity – is portrayed with sculptural simplicity. In contrast to the manufactured, heavily structured, claustrophobic image of a mature Lillie Langtry in the 1880s, there is a naturalness and youthfulness to this portrait. The complexity and multiplicity of Victorian undergarments appear to be reduced. True, it seems this is still the 'no-legs, no-feet' era. But the body of a *real* woman appears visible beneath the clothes. The picture gives off a breath of fresh air: an outdoor activity, a wide-open posture, and an almost casual *déshabille* indicated by the minimally buttoned blouse. Not a single frill or flounce interrupts its comfortable fit, and it has roomy, three-quarter-length sleeves, seemingly designed not to get in the way of movement. Diana is hatless. The formality of the full Victorian cover-up has given way, here, to a light-touch, breezy but statuesque posture, with creamy wrists, throat and neck emerging from carefree clothes. Her expression and pose speak of youth, vigour, liberty and independence, while her columnar skirt in a rough-textured and rumpled fabric and lack of jewellery, seem to stand outside fashion, communicating a neglectful attitude to finery and externals.

And yet – this is a layered image. 'Lady Diana Manners as an Archer' is a consciously publicity-seeking portrayal. It tells the world that her ladyship is playing at being Greek. The misty foliage behind her is a two-dimensional backdrop; she is part of a charade, characteristic of the Edwardian era. Dressing-up boxes and costume were all the rage. Impersonating Artemis, Cleopatra or the Queen of Sheba was much more fun than being one's boring self; and for the circles in which she moved no fancy-dress ball was complete without a stage-struck Lady Diana extravagantly borne in by turbaned slaves or arrayed as a Florentine Renaissance princess and mounted on a circus horse.

Artemis the archer: just one of her many disguises. For this is the artifice that conceals art. The 'no make-up look' – as every woman knows whose mascara clogs, or who applies her foundation on a winter morning in poor light – is hard to achieve. Appearing dewy and natural takes stealth and sleight of hand, conducted in the secrecy of the boudoir. Though this is a long way from the exposure still to come, the *Tatler* picture is printed on the cover of a high-profile society publication, and Diana's photographer has lit, posed and styled his subject with a calculating and flattering eye. The Greek goddess with her bow and quiver certainly owes much of her lissom beauty to a combination of shapely underwear, face powder and clever hairdressing. Emancipation was skin deep.

It was 1910. At the time this picture was published, activism by the Women's Social and Political Union (WSPU) was at its height. Under the leadership of Emmeline Pankhurst, the movement campaigning for women's suffrage had reached boiling point. Militant suffragettes were angrily breaking the law by smashing windows, starting fires and locking themselves to London's railings. Those imprisoned resorted to hunger strikes, and were force-fed by their captors; a direct action group withdrew tax payments until they were granted political representation. That same year, at a suffragette march that came to be known as Black Friday, women protesters were barbarically assaulted by police, who asserted menacingly sexual violence on them.*

---

* Over a hundred years later, there is still live debate about police misogyny and attacks on women.

Meanwhile Diana and her cousin Angie responded to the political crisis with playful mockery. On a weekend visit to Angie's family home in Hampshire, the naughty pair dressed up as suffragettes, climbed on top of a gazebo and merrily hurled biscuit boxes down onto the high-society guests beneath.

And so the sunlit Edwardian era headed into eclipse.

———

What lies beneath the surface of 'Lady Diana Manners as an Archer'? The infrastructure of the lady of 1910 has changed. Though there are still many hooks, clasps and buttons to negotiate, they have become faster and easier. Would a goddess have worn a corset? It's hard to tell, but probably her rounded, nicely uplifted bust and narrow waist owe their shapeliness to something more supportive and substantial than a pair of simple cotton combinations. Straight-fronted stays were out. But it is possible that Diana was an early adopter of the bra – known then as a bust supporter or, by its French inventor Madame Herminie Cadolle, a 'soutien-gorge'. Mme Cadolle had introduced this innovation onto the underwear scene in 1889, as one half of a two-piece corset. By the early twentieth century you could buy the top half separately; it was often heavily boned and buckled. Just a few years later New York manufacturers jumped on board with the brassière, which soon became popular with stylish ladies.

The brassière was a novelty well-judged to appeal to women who were starting to relish sexy, chiffony lingerie, in contrast to the woolly austerity undergarments worn by their mothers. Lucy Duff Gordon had led the way, and word was spreading about satin petticoats, muslin, silk and chiffon chemises. Such garments caused some to tremble with shock; in particular, black lace underwear crossed a line – Victorian associations with death and widowhood made black a transgressive but sexy colour – and it's stayed that way.* Nevertheless, generally speaking, this is still the era of cotton combinations: front-fastening, lace-trimmed, below the knee with button access; and on top of this, a long petticoat. In Diana's case, we can't be sure. She is far too ladylike to be specific about knickers.

At barely eighteen years old, Diana has a svelte body, which can perhaps be attributed to her conscientious banting. 'I don't suppose there is any more beautiful thing in the world than she naked to the waist,' her husband-to-be, Duff Cooper, would reflect during their engagement. Cooper was to become her ardent suitor, and remained in romantic pursuit of her throughout the First World War. The conflict sent the rules of chaperonage into freefall, and though Diana preserved her virginity until their marriage after the war, her biographer makes it very clear that she was adventurous, generous with her beauty, and that middle-class inhibitions were not for her. In her own three-volume autobiography, there are enough clues to show that Diana Manners was a woman of 'normal' vanity, who craved compliments (known by her set as 'dewdrops'). In this light, and knowing that she had a tendency to undress, it's safe to assume that the disrobed Diana would have been conscientiously groomed and *soignée*. Admittedly, it's hard to be sure that she depilated her armpits, for some considered that since sleeveless dresses were obviously indecent, underarms could never be on show. With most fashions covering the skin, de-furring was not a consideration. It is also improbable that she removed the hair from her legs or pubic area – despite the

---

* The 1999 cult teen movie *Ten Things I Hate about You* includes a memorable scene in which Bianca (played by Larisa Oleynik) makes a sensational discovery in her sister Kat's knicker drawer: 'Aha! Black panties!' 'What does that tell us?' asks Cameron. 'She wants to have sex someday, that's what,' responds Kat. My younger daughter tells me, 'The film influenced my entire generation's choice of underwear.'

fact that art, pin-ups and pornography of the time demonstrate that pubic hair was not thought acceptable, and was nearly always scrupulously expurgated.

But Diana was at no risk of public exposure. She loved the water, but even among the more daring like her, swimsuits were still cover-up garments that came halfway down the thigh, so there was no chance of being embarrassed by escaping pubic hairs.* A ghostly whiteness of complexion was part of Diana's unique appeal, so the Archer's virginal body is as milky and luminescent as if she had lived all her life at the bottom of an ocean where the sun's rays cannot penetrate.

In 1919 she and Duff Cooper married. War had ended, waists were out of fashion, and hemlines had risen. Society photographers captured the bride as she left St Margaret's Westminster, swathed in a sheath-like, unwaisted, serpentine pale gold lamé dress draped with lace, ending four or five inches above floor level: she has become the 'ankles woman'. The honeymooners headed for Italy, and stayed in Villa Cimbrone, an enchanted palazzo adorned with classical statuary situated on a vertiginous clifftop overlooking the Amalfi coast. Drunk with the scent of roses and draughts of vino bianco they watched the sun set into the darkening sea. 'Diana's clothes fell from her and she stood by me naked as a statue but whiter and lovelier far. This was perhaps the most beautiful moment of all.'

She is entrancing. But she has been born into an era when the transitions of fashion are gaining momentum. For a public beauty like Lady Diana, the bar was being raised ever higher. The baring of previously unseen areas of the female body

---

* Despite her bohemian tendencies, Diana Manners does not fall into the category of turn-of-the-century 'neo-Pagans' such as the Olivier sisters, who unashamedly skinny-dipped in rivers whenever possible.

offered the freedom to swim, to shoot arrows from a bow, to run and jump, to capture men's hearts and fortunes. But exposure was also relentless and unforgiving. It left women raw and vulnerable. If Diana was to get the dewdrops she craved, the backcombing, the touching-up and the banting could never be relaxed.

There is something haunting about bygone beauty. I encountered Lady Diana Cooper more than once in the 1970s, when she was widowed and over eighty. Old age had not deterred her from a lifetime of unrelenting efforts to stay mesmerising. The Edwardian beauty remained striking in a dazzling purple trouser suit and matching peaked beret, clutching Doggie, her adored chihuahua. For parties she wore a dramatic black and white ostrich feather-trimmed hat, by which she could be identified across a crowded room. It shaded, but did not obscure, the dazzling pallor of her face, which by then had taken on the pristine appearance of a showpiece cake, veneered with a stucco of icing now starting to disintegrate into a mosaic of tiny cracks. The powder heaped up in drifts on the crevices channelled across her once radiant skin, while behind the hypnotic wafting of feather fronds the goddess's eyes stared through: pale blue, ice cold and fascinating.

Austerity

Despite Duff and Diana's happiness,* their marriage was resisted every inch of the way by the Duchess of Rutland. Duff

---

* From Lady Diana Cooper's entry in the *Oxford Dictionary of National Biography*: 'It was a marriage which never staled. Diana had many who loved her and Duff was frequently unfaithful; but for each the relationship with the other remained the most important thing in their lives.'

lacked connections and money; he was feckless. Diana was extraordinarily beautiful and could do better. For matrimony and physical loveliness remained interdependent.

'Marriage must inevitably remain the chief end and object of the Gentlewoman in Society,' wrote the journalist and novelist Lady Violet Greville. She proceeded to explain a mother's duty. It behoved every mamma who cared for her daughter's future to urge her on through the crush of London's ballrooms, and to accept every invitation that might bring her into contact with what Diana Cooper's set called the 'eligibles'. Lady Greville reminded her readers that for every 'eligible', there were dozens of competitors trying to snare him: beautiful 'Georgina' was hovering nearby, wearing an irresistible pink dress calculated to show off 'the statuesque curves of her limbs' while playing tennis, and attract the male prey. Other rivals like 'Louisa' might conquer him by displaying her loveliness on horseback. 'The wary mother knows this, and grudges no expense of tailor-made gowns, bewitching hats, or neat walking-boots, with fascinating tea-gowns *ad libitum*.'

In other words – for the debutante class – skimping on appearance is a false economy. Lady Greville's comments place shopping at the heart of what it means to be a woman: money can buy lacy gowns and big hats trimmed with flowers and feathers; frills and flounces can buy a husband who will look after you for life. Pretty clothes were not just for keeping warm, nor even just for status, pleasure or fashion. They were an investment, a vital down payment on future security. No mother should endure the spectacle of her daughter losing out – 'fading away hopelessly day by day, knowing that they are destined to future poverty and heart-sickening disappointment'. It was a question of 'invest or die': 'The epoch of woman's brightest beauty lasts only ten years – from twenty to thirty.' This is the flip side of the woman who, rouged and dressed in her tawdry finery, sets out her sexual stall on the Haymarket or the Mayfair side streets. The line between propriety and prostitution was a fine one. The perennial skirmishes about bodily exposure and cosmetic enhancement, about taste and vulgarity, femininity and androgyny, were and would remain moral in essence. But they were also about simply surviving.

Meanwhile, the life prospects for a young woman without beauty, money or an ambitious mamma were bleak – particularly afflicting the swathe of society which comprised the genteel middle classes. This worst-case scenario is described with despairing realism in George Gissing's 1893 novel *The Odd Women*, which tells the awful story of the Madden sisters. Their mother has died; their father believes that 'women, old or young, should never have to think about money'. He then dies too, leaving them unprovided for. Fifteen years later Gissing re-introduces us to the sisters, who have lost hope of employment and are reduced to near penury. Alice Madden is now thirty-five:

> [She] tended to corpulence, the result of sedentary life; she had round shoulders and very short legs. Her face would not have been disagreeable but for its spoilt complexion ... Her cheeks were loose, puffy, and permanently of the hue which is produced by cold; her forehead generally had a few pimples; her shapeless chin lost itself in two or three fleshy fissures.

Virginia Madden is two years younger, but – 'She was rapidly ageing; her lax lips grew laxer ... her eyes sank into deeper hollows; wrinkles extended their network; the flesh of her neck wore away.'

The two elder Miss Maddens are clearly disqualified from the race. But their sister, black-haired, bright-eyed Monica, is still young. At twenty-one she, ironically, makes her living working behind the counter in a draper's shop. Instead of *buying* the lovely silks and ribbons that will help to get her a husband and home, she is selling them. She is paid just six shillings a week. Atrocious hours, under-nourishment and prolonged standing have brought Monica to the verge of physical collapse. Nevertheless, she was the sisters' one hope. She would redeem the family, as she was pretty, and 'sure to marry': 'She knew herself good-looking. Men had followed her in the street and tried to make her acquaintance.'

Unluckily, though, the creepy man who first stalks her and then marries her makes her deeply unhappy, and she dies in childbirth. The spinster sisters, however, survive and start a school.

The Odd Women exposes the merciless world of the beauty trap, and demonstrates that work – even in the 'genteel' arenas of retail, nursing or clerical – was for failures. It was a temporary, ill-paid interlude before a woman's 'real' occupation – that of marriage and motherhood – got under way. And the mindset of the gentlewoman would remain fundamentally fixated on wifehood for decades to come.

In 1910 the Board of Trade published a survey into the spending of wage-earning women. One of their analyses took the case of an anonymous invoice typist living at home with her parent in London – and it shows that this young woman would have found it impossible to compete with the women of fashion so pitied by Lady Violet Greville. Though a total of £5 9s 2d (8 per cent) from her yearly income of £66 18s was spent on dress and toiletries, the breakdown shows she was far from extravagant.* The largest sums were twenty-one shillings spent on a coat, and 8s 11d on a pair of walking boots. She bought no new skirts or dresses but paid 4 shillings to have an old one dyed, and spent 7s 5d on fabric to sew a blouse. In one year a similar sum went towards shampoo, soap, toothpaste and hairdressing. Most of the rest was spent on ready-made underwear:

	s	d
2 flannel petticoats	10	
Underbodices	1	5½
Corsets	2	0
2 pairs knickers	8	9
2 chemises	8	9
Stockings	2	1½
Undervests	1	1½

It's an austerity list, with bewitching hats and fascinating tea-gowns strictly off limits for this working woman, who above all needs a hard-wearing wardrobe. Corsets appear to be non-negotiable. However, the invoice typist has spent sixpence on 'braid for skirt', threepence on a 'neckbow' and eightpence-halfpenny on 'frilling'. Whoever she is, she's surely trying her heartbreaking best, by shopping for frilling and bows, to also purchase a little favourable attention.

---

* This typist's earnings are at the upper end of the scale for women; few earned more than £1 a week. At the turn of the century more than half of all male clerks were earning over £100 a year, while all of their female counterparts were earning substantially less than that.

Fluttering, flirting and a pretty blouse might buy an impoverished young woman what she craved: a husband and home. Robert Roberts, a writer who grew up in working-class Lancashire, remembered that women of the Edwardian era 'with their graceful hair styles, sweeping gowns, narrow waists and curving forms ... seem to have held more feminine allure then than at any time since'. But when it came to the shawled housewives living in the cramped cobbled streets of his home town of Salford, Roberts conceded that others saw them differently:

> ... the many women broken and aged with childbearing well before their own youth was done. They remember the spoiled complexions, the mouths full of rotten teeth, the varicose veins, the ignorance of simple hygiene, the intelligence stifled and the endless battle merely to keep clean.

What had beauty bought them? Drudgery, backwardness, the destruction of health and hope. Quite aside from the belief that their political and legal rights were being denied, it is little surprise that some women felt that militant feminism was the only way forward.

Young Ladyhood

> It feels sad to be a woman. Men seem to have so much more choice as to what they are intended for.

It was March 1913. Vera Brittain was nineteen when she wrote this, marooned in the respectable Derbyshire town of Buxton, struggling with what she later described as 'provincial young-ladyhood'.

That same month Parliament passed what became known as the Cat and Mouse Act. It was framed to deal with suffragettes who had been jailed for militant protests, and who had gone on hunger strike to attract attention to the Votes for Women cause. The suffragette Kitty Marion, who was force-fed no fewer than 232 times, described the brutality of this procedure:

> I was suffocating and in my involuntary struggle for breath, I raised myself up to my feet and gasped, 'take the tube out' in spite of which they poured food down which mostly came back up ... From the waist up I experienced every pain imaginable.

By 1913, force-feeding suffragettes had become politically unacceptable. Instead, under the terms of the new Act, a woman was allowed to refuse food until she became dangerously weak, then released and allowed to recover. As soon as she re-offended, she would be re-arrested and the whole process would begin again. A woman's body had become a gladiatorial arena: a site for tyranny and coercion.

Twenty years later, in *Testament of Youth* (1933), Vera Brittain published her reflections on her early life. Her memoir served to exorcise many bitter experiences of the First World War, but also to anatomise her own formation as a committed feminist. The suffragette movement was the distant but noisy backdrop to her youth, during which she fought a constant battle against her parents' view that women were the subservient sex. And a palpable anger – particularly at the sartorial demands made on women – runs through its early chapters.

Throughout her childhood and adolescence, in rain or shine, Vera was encased from neck to foot in black woolly underwear and elaborate clothing, which screened every inch of her body. In 1912 Vera's diligent Mamma kitted her out as a Derbyshire debutante in white satin and pearls, and sent her off with a dance card to see how many eligibles she could snare before the evening was out. For the next two years provincial young-ladyhood held her in its reductive grip. She paid calls, played bridge, assisted with charity bazaars and dressed by the rules.

Vera pleaded to be sent to college. Her father, a commercial paper manufacturer, happily paid for his pretty daughter to have piano lessons, which would increase her value in the marriage marketplace. But Mr Brittain adamantly refused to spend another penny on his daughter's education. Driven by determination, she gained an exhibition to Somerville College, Oxford. 'How *can* you send your daughter to college, Mrs Brittain!' protested a lady acquaintance. 'Don't you want her *ever* to get married?'

Some educated women appeared able to withstand the pressure to be fashionable. They were dubbed 'petticoat pioneers', and 'bluestockings'. Though the latter term had an honourable lineage (it had first been used to describe a salon of enlightened eighteenth-century intellectuals) it was now used with a derisive tone. '[They are] for the most part of the unlovely type known as "Intellectual", that masculine, wisp-haired, tailor-made monstrosity that wants a vote and will not be happy till it gets it,' wrote a contributor to the *Illustrated London News*. Column inches were devoted to airing similar attitudes:

A womanly woman is man's ideal ... If you want to crown your life with the greatest of all happiness – a man's love – don't let him know that you are over-clever.

The appearance of the average Bluestocking is against her. She has a habit of affecting pince-nez ...

Such hostility was, as usual, about men's fear of a land-grab by clever women, for knowledge is power. At the same time, the dress reform movement (described in the previous chapter) was pushing anxiety about gender to new levels, and the 'mannish' garb of some women seemed transgressive and deviant. Not just to men. Here, the American author of a manual for girls gives her view:

> The greatest charm of a girl is her femininity. Nothing is more to be deprecated than the aping of mannishness ... I have in my mind now a girl who affects masculine attire just as far as she can. She wears her hair short, and over it slouches a soft felt hat that she takes off and puts on just as her brother does. It is needless to say that she attracts ridicule wherever she goes ... People wish to deal either with a man or a woman, never with a caricature of either.

Defined by her aggression, mannishness and unkempt appearance, clever feminists – then as now* – frightened men who still wanted the upper hand. 'Beauty and the lust for learning have yet to be allied,' wrote Max Beerbohm in his 1911 bestseller, *Zuleika Dobson – or an Oxford Love Story*, a preposterous fantasy with a famously melodramatic climax. Zuleika is a dazzling beauty (*not* a student); she swoops into Oxford and ravishes the hearts of its entire male undergraduate population, who hurl themselves *en masse* into a watery grave in the Isis for love of her. Whatever else the message of Beerbohm's elegant Edwardian fable may have been, it implies that he saw feminine loveliness as being in short supply in the cloisters of academe.

This extravaganza is thrown into sharp relief by the story

---

* A 2005 survey reported a 40 per cent drop in a woman's marital prospects for every increase of 16 points in her IQ. Ten years later, the *Personality and Social Psychology Bulletin* reported on a study showing that though men claimed to be attracted to smart women, tests showed that they were *less* attracted to women cleverer than themselves, when they actually had to interact with them.

of Enid Starkie, a clever young Irishwoman who in 1915 also gained a scholarship to Somerville College, to read modern languages. Enid was born in Dublin in 1897, the eldest of six children. The Starkie parents were good Catholics. William Starkie, a scholar and civil servant, was a paterfamilias in the Victorian mould. Enid's graceful young mother, May, who had married at the age of twenty, dedicated herself wholeheartedly to being her husband's housebound Angel. 'She saw herself not as a separate human being, but only as his wife.' Accordingly, May Starkie's attention to her appearance was a fundamental feature of her marriage, and of family life:

> [She was] the prettiest mother any children could have; she looked just as if she had stepped out of a story book ...
>
> At 6 o'clock punctually she always left us to go to change into a dinner frock so as to be ready in the drawing-room to receive my father when he came home from the office. I have frequently heard her say that no man would continue to love a woman unless she received him, when he got back from work, dressed in clothes never used for work, as neat as if she had just been taken out of a band-box. Coming into her drawing-room he was to forget that there was outside a world of sweat and toil.

May Starkie's fairy-tale bloom was the real thing. 'She used to say that only actresses used cosmetics, that no lady did, neither did a lady shave her arm-pits, for no lady wore sleeveless frocks.' Nevertheless, she spared no expense in dressing beautifully, and appearing at all times the lavish hostess. But it was a façade, and the Starkies lived beyond their means.

'She was the prettiest mother any children could have.'
May Starkie, aged twenty, around 1896

May required her daughters to conform, as she did, to ladylike standards. Looming over Enid's early years was the constant stipulation to appear a 'Lady's Child' – a status which involved a range of restrictions. There was a correct way for the Lady's Child to wash and dry her hands and nails, pushing the cuticle back with the towel as she did so. Enid and her sisters were dressed by their mother like dolls in long, frilled, picturesque Kate Greenaway-style dresses which tripped them up and tore.

Gentility also required them to wear navy-blue silk veils attached to their hats. Mrs Starkie had absorbed a belief that no parent need endure having ugly children, and that having beautiful children was achievable through diligent effort, so every morning the little girls were put through the torture of having the shape of their noses 'improved', by means of a bent hairpin clipped over their nostrils. Enid pulled hers off at the earliest opportunity. 'We sometimes felt that my mother cared more about our personal appearance and our manners than she did about our happiness and our moral standards.'

Ladylike activities were encouraged. Dressed in their best, Enid and her sisters were in attendance handing cakes to the guests playing croquet at their mother's garden parties. The gardener grew magnificent chrysanthemums. In 1909, when Enid was twelve, Mrs Starkie invited her guests to see the flowers and charged them a fee in aid of the Women's National Anti-Suffrage League, which had been founded in England the year before. The cakes were iced with the anti-suffrage colours: pink, black and white.

> Small child that I was, my feminist instincts were outraged and I protested to my mother. She answered that she saw no reason why a woman should need a vote, since she could always influence public affairs through her husband, that she had in this way more power than she could ever hope to achieve with suffrage.

The Starkie sisters were educated by governesses until they were adolescent. Once Enid did get to school, her mother continued to hold sway over her, barring her from playing hockey because she believed running thickened the ankles. Lack of love and parental oppression coated in conventionality damaged Enid; in her teens self-doubt, and a feeling of being different, crystallised around her appearance. Everything about it seemed wrong. Mrs Starkie still controlled her clothes, and increasingly

Enid hated the pseudo-feminine dresses she was forced to wear. Her hair would never do what it was told, and then there were the pimples which, despite rigorously scrubbing at them with a loofah as her mother advised, continued to erupt in fresh clusters. Enid's acceptance by Oxford University felt like a deliverance.

But her escape from the confines of home life coincided with a different calamity. Her father turned out to be deep in debt. Penury stalked her student years, and yet again coalesced around her outward trappings. The dresses she wore became threadbare; when new ones were needed she improvised them from remnants bought at sales. Undergarments bore the brunt of the new economic regime, a cause of shame and misery, with knickers in critically short supply. And yet when, at the end of term, she returned home to Dublin, it was to hurtful accusations by her mother that she was failing to keep up appearances: 'I was accused of turning into a blue-stocking, into a dowdy English intellectual woman who thought herself above female vanity.'

The rows worsened. All around her women seemed to be pushing against the boundaries, yet Mrs Starkie was against change. For example, she rigidly opposed women using cosmetics: 'She used to declare that these aids to beauty were resorted to only by chorus girls or women of doubtful morals.' One evening over dinner the issue exploded. Mrs Starkie insisted that Enid's fellow students would never be 'well-bred ladies' unless the college principal prohibited them from wearing make-up. Enid indignantly protested that it was not the job of any principal to control the students' personal liberty. 'The argument ended in a violent quarrel. My mother clinched the matter by declaring that I had been altered for the worst by Oxford.'

Nevertheless, three years at university brought Enid Starkie a kind of freedom she had hardly dared dream of. And all pretence of gentility was finally ended with a symbolic act of rejection: she cut her hair short. For her mother, it would be the last straw, but Enid too had reached her limits.

Abundance of hair – one of the key markers of femininity – was yet another facet of women's lives that crushed and oppressed. And it peaked in the early 1900s. Coiled, plaited, frizzed, pleated, puffed, stuffed, steamed and padded, garnished with *postiches*, feathers, tortoiseshell and amber pins, some Edwardian ladies' crowning glories reached a point where they were almost unrecognisable as hair. Caring for these coiffures, too, was laborious and sometimes dangerous: rather than wash such large quantities of hair, women resorted to 'dry', but highly flammable, cleansing agents, and several women caught fire and died.

Enid Starkie was among the trailblazers when she cut her hair; part of a backlash which found expression among pioneering bohemians and New Women – like the children's author Edith Nesbit who, in 1884, had already joyfully braved ridicule and scandal: 'I have *cut my hair off*!!!!!! I retain the fringe but at the back it is short like a boy's ... It is *deliciously* comfortable.' Nesbit didn't seem to have endured any consequences, but Enid Starkie's short haircut caused mayhem. Her mother abused and denounced her. Enough was enough. Enid made up her mind to pursue her studies in Paris. She was awarded a scholarship which covered her debts and the fare with a few pounds left over; then she said goodbye to her family and set out. 'I was on my way alone and I was full of hope.'

The time had come to break with ladylike values for ever.

———

Femininity was changing.

Grace, and ripe, fecund womanliness had given the Victorian home its meaning. With their beautiful aura, wondrous hair and blooming curves, matrons and mothers like May Starkie had held aloft an ideal of domesticity, health and virtue. Meanwhile the empire was ruled over for decades by one elderly matriarch, a mother of nine and grandmother to forty-nine, in prolonged mourning for her dear departed consort. At Queen Victoria's funeral in 1901 the London streets were massed with a sea of pale faces under black hats, gathered to bid farewell to the old monarch. But as a new century dawned ladyhood, fecundity and the womanly aura were under threat. It was time for some fresh young blood.

Enter the flapper. This young woman pre-dates her Scott Fitzgerald-style descendant by more than twenty years, and her origins are even earlier. Though she did not adopt the term, Eliza Linton's 'Girl of the Period' – the 'creature who dyes her hair and paints her face ... whose sole idea of life is fun' – was an 1860s blueprint. For the later Victorians, the word 'flapper' meant prostitute. Though by the early twentieth century a flapper was no longer a fallen woman, the taint of immorality hung over her, and in class-obsessed Britain she didn't qualify when it came to being 'ladylike' – she was more likely to be a shopgirl or a typist. True, in pre-war days she didn't cut her hair, and you could tell a flapper by her pigtails. Nevertheless she was defined by her daring clothes, her nubile effrontery, her youthful stylishness. 'A flapper,' explained *The Times* in 1908, 'is a young lady who has not yet been promoted to long frocks and the wearing of her hair "up".' She was the Lolita of her day, doe-eyed and dewy. There was something demure, disobedient and disturbingly sexual about her, and she made her matronly mother look passé. The flapper had evolved her own pleasure-seeking, bicycle-riding culture. She posed a threat, and as such she was belittled. Correspondence columns in provincial papers were targeted by members of the public who found flappers intolerable, like one who wrote to the *Aberdeen Evening Express* in 1914 complaining of their immodesty. He'd seen them wearing their low-cut blouses and slit hobble skirts that showed their ankles, with 'a glimpse of stocking'.*

They were also made-up – 'Where could she have obtained that bloom of roses on her soft cheek? Perchance from the chemists?' And if she has nothing better to do, 'another very innocent amusement of hers is the art of "making eyes" at any prepossessing stranger who may be passing by'. In other words, she is giddy and wanton. The *Yorkshire Evening Post* reported a reader's alarm at the behaviour of modern girls:

> When their hair is put up and their frocks tightened round the hips the modern minxes are ready for the fray – confident, brazen young hussies, who must startle their male friends by their freedom of speech. I suppose it is a development of modern education.

Flappers were observed cultivating a sexy, asymmetrical slouch, hips to the fore (a posture still adopted by many fashion models today). The *Birmingham Daily Gazette* (April 1914) commented on the flapper phenomenon with misgivings:

> The newest girl is the flapper ... She has short skirts, gay hosiery, walking boots, and tramples upon Victorian traditions with positive glee. She loves chocolates and risky jokes ...
> She will find her true place when the strong man appears to teach her the law of love and the joy of obedience.

---

* Looking back to the turn of the century, Cole Porter made that shocking glimpse famous in his 1934 lyric to 'Anything Goes'.

'The Flapper Walk is the latest craze ... of the modern maiden's
whimsical ways.' Illustration in the *Sketch*, 7 December 1910

But the younger generation was about more than chocolates
and colourful stockings. In the new century's early years wom-
en's lives were swirling with modernity. Vogues and fads flared
up, burned brightly and expired. 1902 saw the emergence of
the Bloomsbury group. The new dance, brought in by wealthy
South Americans, was the tango; dancers were dressed in clinging gowns that revealed the wearer's body; and the corsetry
manufacturers denounced the corsetless women whose busts
were observed to bounce in time to the music. A new silhouette
was evolving, sinuous, svelte and goddess-like. Sexuality was
near the surface, and liaisons ignited at the new *thés dansants*.
Proust and the Post-Impressionists were bringing a spirit of
experimentation to the arts, and Freud's ideas were circulating.
In Britain women were now around 30 per cent of the workforce. Meanwhile, ladies of leisure held onto their hats as they
were whisked along at breakneck speed in the passenger seats
of open-topped automobiles. It felt good to be out in the world.
Though the suffragettes continued to rage and to march, the
prevailing mood remained feminine. Fashion was like a cocktail, with couture houses espousing everything from split skirts
to sheaths, aesthetic tunics and the *jupe-culotte*. The extremes

of fashion displayed by ultra-elegant and willowy mannequins were starting to push at the limits of how women dressed – what Quentin Bell, echoing Thorstein Veblen, would label 'conspicuous outrage'. Around 1908 Paul Poiret introduced the hobble skirt, whose crippling hemlines hampered all movement, and enforced a mincing, 'feminine' gait on its wearers. The hobble, short-lived as it was, not only restricted women's mobility but also caused the death of women who stumbled into canals or into the path of oncoming traffic. It was no coincidence, surely, that this freakish fashion launched when the suffrage movement was at its height.

At this time, film technology was progressing fast; cinema would prove one of the biggest single influences on how women saw themselves in the modern world. In 1895 the Lumière brothers became the effective founders of the modern movie, when they demonstrated the first commercial *cinématographe* in Paris; by 1908 there were over eight thousand 'nickelodeons' across the USA, and by 1910 twenty-six million American people were paying to be entertained, weekly, in these perma-nent film theatres.

Black Beauty

In February 1915 a woman in her late forties named Sarah Walker headed to downtown Indianapolis for her favourite Saturday afternoon entertainment, an hour or two watching melodramas at the nickelodeon, price: one dime. But that day the rules had changed, and the ticket agent bluntly informed her that as she was 'colored' the price of admission had risen to twenty-five cents.

Mrs Walker was not going to take this lying down. She straightaway enlisted the aid of her attorney, who put in a claim for $100 in damages against the management of the Isis Theater to compensate his 'clean, sober, neat and orderly client' who had been subjected to racial prejudice in a public place. Unfortunately, history does not relate the outcome of the proceedings, but the incident shines a revealing light on Sarah Walker, who by this time was more generally known and revered under her professional name of Madam C. J. Walker.

Madam Walker was the daughter of formerly enslaved people. She was born Sarah Breedlove in Louisiana in 1867, two years after slavery in the USA was abolished. The environment in which she grew up did not encourage Black women to think themselves attractive. Long, straight hair was the default preference, and the Gibson Girl remained America's supreme standard of beauty. The few products available for Black women (Kink-No-More, Straightine, Wonderful Face Bleach) claimed to eradicate or 'soften' their racial identity, while mimicking the white woman.*

Sarah married at the age of fourteen. Five years later she was widowed and left with a small daughter to raise on the proceeds of her work as a laundress – an onerous job which at that time was performed almost exclusively by Black women. This was also, despite emancipatory legislation, an era when lynchings, murders and racist terrorism were at an all-time high.

Driven by the need to better herself and her daughter, Sarah undertook a programme of self-improvement. In the early years of the twentieth century she settled in St Louis, Missouri, went to night school, helped in her community and remarried. But the improvement didn't extend to her appearance; to her dismay, her hair had begun to fall out, and there seemed to be no remedy.

---

* It would take a hundred years for the politically inspired slogan 'Black is Beautiful' – often attached to stars like Marsha Hunt or activists like Angela Davis and Kathleen Cleaver, with their Afro halos of hair – to create profound beauty changes.

Annie Turnbo Malone's name was and is synonymous with hair products for Black women. Like Sarah, Annie was also the daughter of formerly enslaved people. She was orphaned, but had the fortune to be educated and discover a passion not only for chemistry but for haircare. Around 1900 she began to manufacture her Wonderful Hair Grower; it met with such success that she was soon able to expand her small business, and start to promote her products through door-to-door agents. By 1918 she would make enough money to open – with great fanfare – Poro College in St Louis, a factory, social hub and centre for cosmetology whose professed aim was 'to contribute to the economic betterment of "Race Women"'. It incorporated thirty-one beauty parlours, a soda fountain, elevators and a roof garden.

Meanwhile, still stricken with hair problems, Sarah Walker took steps to ameliorate her situation. She tried the Wonderful Hair Grower, and for a while worked with Annie Malone's sales force. But Annie's concoctions were failing to make her hair regrow, and Sarah, ashamed and despondent, turned to God for guidance. 'He answered my prayer.'

The recipe for her own miraculous scalp treatment was, Sarah claimed, revealed to her in a dream in 1903; its origins appeared to come from her African ancestors and soon her hair was growing back with renewed vigour. Smart and proud, Sarah could see that this was an opportunity not to miss: as Annie Malone was demonstrating, hairdressing and the sale of hair products could be a route out of poverty.

Annie Malone and Sarah Walker were to become fierce rivals, with Annie accusing Sarah of pirating such products as her Wonderful Hair Grower. Undeterred, in 1906 Sarah launched her own business in Denver, Colorado – the Madam C. J. Walker Manufacturing Company – selling Pomade, Glossine, Vegetable Shampoo, Temple Grower and Tetter Salve, all tailored to the needs of African American women. Just like

Annie Malone's, the company took off. Later she too opened beauty schools and beauty parlours, employing hundreds of Black women.

In 1914, Sarah addressed the National Negro Business League:

'I had to make my own living and my own opportunity,' she recounted to hearty applause. 'But I made it. That is why I want to say to every Negro woman present, don't sit down and wait for the opportunities to come, but you have to get up and make them!'

Eventually, their companies would bring both Annie Malone and Sarah Walker undreamed-of prosperity, and would also give African American women across the USA a transformative sense of identity. 'The Key to Beauty, Success and Happiness is a Good Appearance' was Sarah Walker's advertising slogan. These women's economic success and independence blazed like a beacon of freedom, a release from their enslaved past. Wealthy, philanthropic, political, socially active, religious, feminist, Madam Walker never forgot her early struggles, and prioritised the welfare of her people; she used her money and her increasing celebrity to support the early campaigns against lynching and to promote racial justice. Annie Malone by 1924 was worth $14 million. Her benevolence too was widespread: she used the proceeds of her business to fund scholarships and support educational and children's charities run by the Black community. Their examples, as they stepped resolutely into the moneyed middle classes, encouraged other Black women to feel that they could have rights, a profession and a political presence, while through their hair and beauty products, these two entrepreneurs gave their customers a boost to their self-esteem.

———

Mamie Garvin Fields was another indomitable woman with a righteous passion for her race and family, and a good head for business. In time, Mamie's intelligence, dignity and energy would earn her a deserved place among the many honoured citizens of her home town, Charleston, South Carolina.

She lived for almost a hundred years, and her life story – told with grace, guts and humour as oral history to her granddaughter Karen Fields – is full of vivid references to the fashions of her young days at the turn of the twentieth century: to aprons, underwear, hats and hair.

Mamie's father was a carpenter; her mother, a homemaker and mother of eight. Pervading Mamie's memoir is 'colourism' – a heightened awareness of the gradations of skin colour. In general, this prejudice has privileged those with lighter complexions over those with darker skins. According to Mamie, even the local high school for African Americans favoured the lighter-skinned children:

> It was easy for sister Hattie to go, because she had light skin … if you were black, you couldn't get school honors, no matter how well you studied.

As a child Mamie was taught dressmaking by her mother. But while she acquired skills in hemming and embroidery, she also learnt about growing up Black in South Carolina. When they were both at high school, Hattie was apprenticed to a dressmaker, Miss Bryant, who was mixed-race – 'She was very fair – you couldn't tell her from white.' Miss Bryant was very clear: 'Never a Black child would she have in her workroom.' But one day a wealthy family, the Coplestons, ordered an extensive trousseau for their daughter. It was an important job and Miss Bryant needed help with the necessary embroidery.

Hattie told her that Mamie was skilled at handwork, and she soon found herself taking on all the complicated fancywork that nobody else could do.

> Especially I was to make ball trimming* to put on certain dresses ...
>   Those ball trimmings were something I will never forget. You had to wrap silk thread around to make a ball of the thread, turn the ball, wrap it the other way, get it tight, clip it, very tedious after awhile ... I made every colour of ball trimming, until I almost dropped. I bet I made a thousand of them.

But when Mamie set out to ball-trim her own dress, Miss Bryant was outraged.

> 'What! No, you can't make a dress with ball trimmings on it. No, ma'am. How dare you?' On and on like that, and 'The white people would take their work away from me if they found coloured people wearing those dresses.' Humpf!

Mamie paid no attention. She knew that, living in a divided society, she would never cross paths with anyone in the same dress:

> Charleston had two segregations. White people said, 'You're a n—r. You can't go to this place and you can't wear that dress.' You were that 'n—r' no matter what complexion you were.

At the age of seventeen, Mamie packed her trunk and headed upstate to Claflin, a Methodist teacher training college in Orangeburg. In 1908 she got her teaching qualification. That was

---

* Lengths of decorative braid with tiny pom-poms attached at regular intervals.

followed by a post in a school in Charleston County. However, she was by now engaged to be married to her childhood sweetheart Bob Fields, and when her godmother proposed taking her up to Boston for the summer with the prospect of better earnings to buy her own trousseau, she readily agreed.

Mamie settled into the Black neighbourhood of Roxbury, and for a season she and her friend Myrtle worked as sewing machinists in a downtown factory. 'The first thing our supervisor put me on was sleeves, nothing but sleeves. Sleeves to what, I didn't know.' Production-line work paid four times what she could earn teaching, and soon, in a spirit of entrepreneurship, she, Myrtle and another young woman named Ellestine decided to set up their own little after-hours business, copying designs from *Vogue*, made to measure for the fashion-conscious women of Roxbury. They publicised their enterprise by pinning up cut-outs from the magazine in Ellestine's bedroom window, to spread the word 'that we were stylish girls who knew all about clothes . . . and soon we had more business than we knew what to do with . . . I was making more money than I ever had in my life.'

But it wasn't just about the money. Mamie's new clientele taught her how women dress – women like Sister Green, who came into the workroom one day to order a frock.

[She] was one of those fat church sisters, the kind who wear a lot of perfume, a lot of jewelry, great big hats, and of course the latest style, whatever that happens to be.

Well naturally she wanted a style she saw in one of our pictures, with a long, narrow body and fitted long sleeves, just the thing she needn't wear.

Mamie and the girls measured Sister Green all over, and it was quickly obvious that wherever the dress pattern said 'in' it would have to go out, and wherever it said 'narrow' it would have to go wide; but never mind: as far as Sister Green was concerned, she was going to look like a *Vogue* model. The girls pinned and pinched, expanded and altered, in trepidation all the time that they would be blamed for making her look like a balloon. Then Mamie looked at the overall effect and realised they had to get better buttons – '"You know, those common buttons we got at first won't do," I said.' So they added some deluxe buttons and it made all the difference.

> When we finally pulled the drape from the mirror the day she came to get the dress, she looked at herself for a long, long time. Then all of a sudden she began to smile, turn around, pat her hair, primp, *pleased as could be.*
>
> Hallelujah! She liked it.

Sister Green was an object lesson for Mamie: it had never occurred to this ample, over-the-top woman, as she stood in front of the mirror, that her reflection revealed anything but the last word in elegance. Her belief that she looked completely wonderful eclipsed not only the facts of her figure, it succeeded in convincing all her church ladies that they wanted to look like her too. Mamie's business boomed. For the fact was, the dress was a work of art, and this well-upholstered pillar of the church *did* look wonderful in it.

Mamie found out that self-belief, and smart buttons, can prevail in unlikely circumstances. Truly, it was a lesson for life.

Mamie married Bob and they settled back in Charleston, where they had both grown up. For Mamie, dressing properly had always been about dignity: about holding your head up high, and telling the world that a Black woman was owed the same respect as a white woman. Though her family had been freedmen for three generations, slavery was still too close for comfort. So when you were out and about the community needed to know that you weren't anybody's chattel.

> If you see a Negro woman in the street wearing an apron, that says something. If she has her hair rolled up or her house slippers on, then that says something too.

Her cousin Lala always said, 'Dress. You never know.' So it was worse than embarrassing for Mamie when, in a hurry one morning, Bob asked her to drop him off at work, and she heedlessly popped on a coat over her nightgown to drive him downtown. Unfortunately, on the way back another driver collided with her Model T Ford. 'BAM, a wreck; and out of this wreck comes a white man. Good Lord!' Total humiliation. There was nothing for it but to climb out of the car, trying to hold up her nightgown with her hands through her coat pockets. Nobody spoke until the police arrived, after which poor Mamie was herded off in her slippers and flimsy gown to a swanky lawyer's office. Mamie was used to speaking up for herself. But this occasion was the exception that proved the rule.

> There's no way in the world you can stand up for yourself in your houseshoes – just as you can't get respect in your apron. And that was Lala's point when she drilled into us, 'Dress. You never know.'

Quite unexpectedly, the story had a happy ending for Mamie. The white driver (who had caused the accident) turned out to come from Vermont. In other words, he was 'a damn Yankee', for whom Charleston's law-enforcers had no time. And the lawyers settled with him to pay everybody involved a hundred dollars.

It wasn't long after this that Mamie Garvin Fields got to hear of Madam C. J. Walker and her incredible way with hair. The word was out that it was transformative for Black women, who could now straighten their hair. Not only that, but everyone was talking about Madam Walker because she was a millionaire. Everyone who could copied her in hopes of striking gold; and soon Annie Malone's Poro system was also filtering through. Mamie's friendly neighbour, also called Mamie, had learned about it through a well-travelled woman who had taken the Poro course 'up north'. The two Mamies got straight to work with oils, pomades and herbal rinses – 'Oh, my, didn't we have fun working on each other's heads ... They worked, too.' And soon that same entrepreneurial impulse had the Mamies setting up their stall under a tree in a busy Black neighbourhood and charging the women fifty cents apiece to anoint and dress their hair, 'and a dollar if we rolled the hair on papers'. Before long Bob was able to build his wife her own hairdressing salon in their downstairs bedroom.

Mamie's love affair with fashion and hairdressing is edifying; it tells one educated woman's story of growing up Black in segregated America, and of just how much, for her, appearances mattered. No surprise, then, that the garments covering her skin, and the hairstyles adorning it, assumed heightened importance.

One steamy summer evening in the 1920s, Mamie and hundreds of others crowded into Mount Zion Church in Glebe Street. All Charleston, it seemed, had come out to hear the writer, speaker and campaigner Mary Church Terrell give a lecture about the Modern Woman. The audience were elbow-to-elbow in the pews and on the balconies, and the flicking fans barely moved the humid air around the church's packed interior. Mrs Terrell, the daughter of freed former enslaved people, had graduated in Classics, travelled and studied in Europe, and had become fluent in three languages, which she then taught at Wilberforce College, Ohio; and from the turn of the twentieth century she became a social activist, focussing on Black women's empowerment.

No wonder Mamie's community turned out in force to be inspired by what she had to say in her ringing voice about modern women, and to hear her message of equality, organisation and social betterment. However her head-turning appearance did not comply with any stereotypical notion of a women's rights crusader: 'Oh, my, when I saw her walk onto that podium in her pink evening dress and long white gloves, with her beautifully done hair, she *was* that Modern Woman.'

The Modern Woman was a breathtaking role model; the personification of elegance in her stylish gown – feminine, groomed and chic. This was walking proof to Mamie and everyone in church that day, that a Black woman could be the embodiment of emancipation: educated, outspoken, powerful – and fashionable.

Purple, Green and White

Mamie Garvin was a hairdresser, and, to her, beautifully done hair mattered. But the days of those ornate Edwardian dos which had so oppressed Enid Starkie and Edith Nesbit were numbered.

The new century took a deep breath and got off to a fresh start.

A bell rang inside my head ... The time had come for women to have their hair short.

In 1901 the hairdresser Antoine Cierplikowski had left his native Poland for Paris and established a salon which quickly took the fashion lead. Shockingly chic, Antoine's bobs were (literally) at the cutting edge of modernism: 'This new automobile in which women sat open to the winds, these new women with careers, this busy life. And these clinging clothes, which demanded small, neat heads, not great masses of hair.' Antoine was *'dans le vent'*.

The American dancer Irene Castle incarnated this look.

Irene Castle: '[Her] boyish impression was counterbalanced by an extreme femininity'

From 1911 Irene (with her English husband Vernon) brought jazz dancing to thrilled audiences on both sides of the Atlantic. Lucy Duff Gordon, who was invited to design her dance dresses, described Irene as 'the first of the moderns'. And her liberated, elfin appeal made her the same kind of trendsetter as the model Twiggy over fifty years later. Everyone wanted to be like her: 'Her sleek, bobbed head ... set a new standard which other women imitated,' recalled Lucile.

> It started in New York and spread to Europe, and soon the coiffeurs were working double time cutting off curls and chignons, doing away with hideous pads and atrocious side-combs, and turning out a procession of other sleek, bobbed heads to follow in the wake of Irene Vernon Castle.

Cecil Beaton photographed her in beguiling motion, and his description captures her breezy attraction: 'The primary effect that she created was one of an exquisite grace combined with an extraordinary boyish youthfulness. There was something terrifically healthy and clean about her.' Healthy and clean – but also thin. The nimble-footed Mrs Castle didn't carry a spare ounce of flesh.

The equation of health with weight loss is something new, and set to gather momentum in the twentieth century. For this was also a time of innovation in science. The old, terrifying Victorian epidemics of cholera and typhoid, which had cut so many off in their prime, were being defeated by modern hygiene and sanitation. People were living longer lives. Developments in contraception, such as the manufacture of vulcanised rubber diaphragms and condoms, meant smaller families, and the rounded maternal figure started to seem less desirable. Meanwhile women's increased participation in sport, and in the workplace, contributed to the preference for lissomness over bulk. Doctors were recommending that life expectancy could be improved by better nutrition and exercise, while authors of advice manuals were starting to dedicate chapters to topics like 'Those Extra Pounds', and 'Is Candy-Eating Harmful for Girls?' A woman of eleven stone two no longer looked clever or chic.

In 1909 Lucile ordained that her bosomy, bottomy, voluptuously dreamy 'goddesses' were to dispense with their wasp-waisted corsets. The new look was slender, straight up and down, and tall: five feet seven inches and over. By 1912 *la ligne étroite* was starting to make well-endowed women look like barrels by comparison, and the pressure was on them – and others – to shed their surplus flesh. A short woman couldn't increase her height, but she could reduce her waistline. She could diet. Modification was the name of the game. And already in the early years of the century another shift started to occur – in the world of medicine – as doctors found themselves dealing with an increased caseload of eating disorders.

Angular, slinky and sexy: these were the opening salvos of the jazz age. Fashion's brittle, feverish patterns were rearranging themselves like a cubist canvas by Picasso. And as the European war approached, nerves were frayed by a female insurgency which seemed to threaten disruption and conflict on the home front. Booted and brazen, young, slender and cropped: between them the flapper, the celebrity and the suffragette were rocking society's moorings.

———

From 1905 the Women's Social and Political Union took militant action to publicise their cause. Here were women acting in a way that contradicted everything that their sex was supposed to be. Hatchets, chemicals, knives and bombs replaced sweet, soft smiles. Frills, fluff and lace concealed violent weapons. In the years leading up to the First World War the WSPU undertook a campaign of arson, hunger strikes and window-smashing; and 1913–14 saw a wave of iconoclasm.

In April 1913 three WSPU activists were arrested for breaking the glass over thirteen paintings in the collection of Manchester Art Gallery. They included works by the male artists G. F. Watts, Arthur Hacker, Frederick Leighton and Dante Gabriel Rossetti – soft-hued, idealised images of unclothed heroines like Francesca da Rimini, the naked nymph Syrinx, the dewy-skinned priestess Hero, and a heavy-lidded Venus *en déshabille*.

A year later, following the arrest of Emmeline Pankhurst, twenty-five-year-old Mary Richardson smuggled a meat chopper into the National Gallery in Trafalgar Square, where she hacked and slashed one of the most famous female bottoms in art – that of Velázquez's *Rokeby Venus*. At the time, Richardson stated, 'I have tried to destroy the picture of the most beautiful woman in mythological history as a protest against the Government for destroying Mrs Pankhurst, who is the most beautiful character in modern history.' But forty years later she told a journalist, 'I didn't like the way men visitors gaped at it all day long.'

WSPU activists did not limit their iconoclasm to depictions of nude women; they ripped and hatcheted portraits and religious images too. But though there may be an element of hindsight, it's hard to avoid viewing their attempts to destroy idealised depictions of naked women as something more than an angry call for the vote; such assaults can justifiably be seen as part of a wider feminist outlook: a protest against men's objectification of women in both art and life.*

Like bluestockings, suffragists and suffragettes† suffered from an image problem. Their political demands placed them on a collision course with men, marriage, motherhood and the home. They had, it seemed, sacrificed their sacred auras by turning their collective backs on everything feminine and lovely. Caricatures portrayed the 'shrieking sisterhood' as masculinised harridans and hags.

'Suffragettes who have never been kissed',
portrayed on a 1900 postcard

---

* The topic is interestingly discussed in Helen Scott, '"Their Campaign of Wanton Attacks": Suffragette Iconoclasm in British Museums and Galleries during 1914' (2016).

† To distinguish: suffragists were an assortment of groups who had been campaigning for votes for women since the mid-nineteenth century. Largely middle class, in 1897 they coalesced under the leadership of Millicent Fawcett to form the National Union of Women's Suffrage Societies. They believed in a non-violent, incremental approach. The suffragettes came under the banner of the Women's Social and Political Union, which was started by Emmeline Pankhurst in 1903; it attracted more working-class women, and differed from the suffragists in believing that persuasion had failed. Instead, the WSPU advocated militant tactics, and adopted the motto 'Deeds not Words'.

There were many – women as well as men – who resisted women's suffrage, in the belief that the vote was unnecessary, and that sex equality would harm a gender relationship ordained by God and nature. The Pankhursts and their movement soon realised that, to succeed, they had to avoid falling into the trap of appearing unfeminine. 'The suffragette of today is dainty and precise in her dress,' the organisation's newspaper *Votes for Women* told its readers. In public at least, she had to get her aura back.

With this in mind, a branding exercise took place. In 1908 Emmeline Pethick-Lawrence, editor of *Votes for Women*, introduced the idea of the suffragette colours: purple for dignity, green for hope and white for purity. This tricolour was designed to foster *esprit de corps*, promote the movement's identity and give the public an opportunity to express solidarity. Pethick-Lawrence wrote, 'Be guided by the colours in your choice of dress ... If every individual in this union would do her part, the colours would become the reigning fashion.' At the biggest ever WSPU demonstration, in June 1908, three hundred thousand women rallied to the cause dressed in white with green and purple trimmings.

But more than this, the WSPU's leaders were working hard to steer perceptions of the campaign away from the tweedy spinster in hobnailed boots, and towards a more palatable image of femininity that would not alienate the public. And what could be more feminine than shopping? Retail therapy and the suffrage movement may seem an unlikely alliance, but these women knew what they were doing, and big department stores like Derry & Toms and Liberty were approached to collaborate. Thus, in May 1909, the campaign laid on a twelve-day Women's Exhibition in a Knightsbridge hall, decorated with flags and banners in the suffragette colours. In reality this was a fund-raising bazaar, complete with stalls selling dainty, decorative merchandise close to a woman's heart: household items, craft objects and preserves, scarves, white-purple-and-green striped ribbons and trinkets, bags, baby clothes, embroidered hosiery and ornaments. And, conspicuously, millinery.

Millinery for protests. A 1911 advertisement by the department store Derry & Toms: 'During the next few days we shall be exhibiting in our windows hats and toques made in the colours of the various organisations in connection with the Woman Suffrage movement. This should prove to be a unique opportunity for purchasing suitable millinery for the great procession of June 17'

Statement hats were a particularly eye-catching aspect of the suffragettes' regalia. It's very striking, looking at photographs of WSPU marches from this time, that the protesters appear as smartly hatted fashionistas, topped off with floral, feathered confections like wedding cakes. To these extravagant hats were added feather boas, jewellery and fox-fur muffs (convenient, since most women's garments lacked pockets, for concealing small hammers or axes). In her autobiography, Viscountess Rhondda tells how her aunt, Janetta Boyd, who was elegantly turned out, with soft curly hair and of a saintly demeanour, walked down Oxford Street carrying a hammer wrapped in a brown paper parcel:

> Opposite the windows of D. H. Evans she stopped, and, murmuring to herself, 'Whatsoever thy hand findeth to do, do it with all thy might,' upped with the hammer and splintered the window ... Crash crash went the hammer. Each time she struck she murmured the same text. Finally the policeman came up and arrested her.

As soon as she was let out on bail, Aunt Janetta went straight back to D. H. Evans and purchased a hat – 'to make up for any inconvenience to which her action might have put them'.

It also seems that the suffragettes wore lipstick.* Having opened the first department store make-up counter, Selfridges (founded in 1908) spotted a niche, and targeted their advertising accordingly:

> Fashionable young women are flocking to the store for delicate tea dresses and that most powerful symbol of female emancipation: red lipstick. As the first department store to sell lipstick,

---

*   American suffragettes were also make-up pioneers. Elizabeth Arden, herself a dedicated feminist who marched for women's rights, supplied lipsticks to demonstrators as a sign of solidarity.

powder and rouge, Selfridges is leading the way for the country's suffragettes.

A powerful endorsement!

Mrs Pankhurst and her three daughters were public figures, admired for their beauty; and she herself went in for particularly ostentatious millinery. This was about height, impact and the visibility of the suffragette colours. But it was also about keeping femininity alive by looking charming, frivolous, impractical and unthreatening. Suffragettes chose big hats as political propaganda – to appear unpolitical.

As for the Exhibition – it raised £5,000 for the cause of Votes for Women.

Legs-Woman

Soon after the outbreak of the First World War the ardent suffragist Lady Castlereagh, whose husband had already been sent to France, was having lunch in her Park Lane mansion with the editor of a national newspaper.

> He said to me that he would like to make a bet with me. I asked the purport. 'Well, Lady Castlereagh,' he said, 'it is this. I will bet you five pounds that at the end of the war there will be no Suffragettes. War will teach women the impossibility of their demands and the absurdity of their claims.'
>
> I immediately accepted the bet.

In August 1914 Mrs Pankhurst and her allies called a truce, exhorting their supporters to reject violence, and patriotically to support the government in every possible way. This would prove a winning card. The politicians who in February 1918 would pass the Representation of the People Act, giving the vote to property-owning women over thirty, did so partly because after four years of war the last thing they wanted was a return to militancy on their doorstep – the events of the 1917 Russian revolution offered a fearsome precedent – but also partly in recognition of the vital role played by women wartime workers in factories, farms, hospitals and transport. Lady Castlereagh was confident that women could do 'men's work', and from 1914 her energy and conviction were diverted from the suffrage movement to the deployment of women into war work, particularly agriculture. In 1915 she founded the Women's Legion; more than forty thousand women volunteers joined. By 1918 80 per cent of the labour in Britain would be undertaken by women.

Not everyone was persuaded; prejudice was built in. How could women work on the land? They did not know one end of a cow from the other. As for adopting practical workwear, this was against God's law: 'The woman shall not wear that which pertaineth unto a man, neither shall a man put on a woman's garment: for all that do so are abomination unto the Lord thy God.' Trousers, traditionally worn by men, represented power. A woman who put on trousers was masquerading as a man, wearing his armour and invading his fortress.

But how could a 'no-legs' woman in a long skirt do hoeing, pitchforking and milking? How could she scale a ladder? Trousers were issued to the female workforce, but they were problematic. The overalls worn by women window-cleaners in Manchester filling in for men absent at the front caused a street commotion, with the women subjected to catcalls. One of them told a journalist that 'the first man who insults us when we are up the ladder will have his ardour dampened by a bucket of dirty water'. It wasn't just men who objected to women wearing trousers. Some women regarded them as indecent and embarrassing – 'the fellers would laugh'. But for work, skirts were a hazard, and in 1916 four women working at a Clydeside munitions plant were threatened with dismissal for *refusing* to don trousers. After initial hesitations the experiment proved a great success – though note that in most cases the problematic upper-thigh area was concealed by aprons or tunics. Nevertheless, the new plus-legs comfort was addictive and, in some cases, landgirls were now defying the rules by keeping their dungarees on, and refusing to change back into 'ordinary feminine dress' at the end of a day's ploughing or hoeing.

But feminine norms had to be seen to be maintained. Lady Castlereagh stressed that even when they were spreading manure or cutting cabbages, the landgirls' womanly aura remained intact:

> In case it should be thought that the women engaged on this work were unfeminine and that only ugly ones or those of masculine build were workers, I hasten to add that ... they [were] lovely girls, and never have I seen a happier or healthier lot at work.

A few months before the end of the war, Lady Castlereagh headed a massed procession of women war workers to Buckingham Palace. Her recollection of this momentous ceremony is dominated by the participants' bifurcated outfits: landgirls in brown corduroy breeches, and 'munitionettes' in a range of plus-legs workwear from trousers to scarlet overalls to dungarees.

The feminine myth, and the notion that women's legs were indecent, was now visibly under attack. *Vogue* commented:

> Most of us have always longed to wear 'em, anyway, and now that the war has sent so many women into employments where trousers

are the chosen costume, it is doubtful if we will ever consent to give them up.

The legs woman had arrived. Trousers were liberating. They were comfortable. But the mirror in which women saw themselves was still a male one – and it was standing on the sidelines, laughing, catcalling and shouting abuse.

———

Just occasionally, a woman in trousers was unreservedly cheered and applauded. Aida Overton Walker had been as comfortable in male attire, role-playing her late husband, as she had been in female. During the First World War Vesta Tilley, 'the queen of the vaudeville stage', was at the height of her fame, immaculately kitted out as a dapper military man or a Tommy with a kit-bag. Born Matilda Powles into a theatrical family, Tilley had first stepped before the footlights in 1869, at the age of five. She was just eight when, having romped through most of the female repertoire as 'The Great Little Tilley', she came to the conclusion 'that female costume was rather a drag': 'I felt that I could express myself better if I were dressed as a boy.'

Luckily, Tilley's father took a cooperative view, and suggested that she might like to wear boy's clothes for one of her numbers. He bought her a miniature evening dress suit, and the realisation swiftly followed that her real talent lay in mimicking a man. Her reputation grew, through song-and-dance acts comically satirising the affected fin-de-siècle male swells and dandies, and mocking fashionable 'mashers' and 'toffs' like 'Burlington Bertie', while also mischievously targeting women's devious and flighty ways.

Vesta Tilley as Burlington Bertie

It was surely no coincidence that a cross-dressing female entertainer was able to reach the top of her profession at a time when women were starting to mutiny against traditional stereotypes. The 'New Women' and the rational dressers in their knickerbockers had already pushed against traditional gender lines, while the suffragettes were mustering their troops and the farmgirls wielded their pitchforks. Now, under the footlights' neutralising glare, Vesta Tilley was able to go the whole way. Barely seven stone, she was tiny, chirpy and unthreatening; when she visited America one of the New York critics described her as 'a delicate piece of Dresden china'. It took her an hour to make up and do the necessary work to redefine her body, making it lie flat and straight under her fitted waistcoats. Her wig was a work of art, under which she braided her own long hair (she refused to cut it) so that it lay close to her head. Her singing voice was rich and raunchy; she had a captivating swagger about her.

Though Tilley's admirers were of both sexes, the greater part of her fan base was made up of women. Every day she was deluged with piles of adulatory mail – 'varying from an impassioned declaration of undying love to a request for an autograph, or a photograph, or a simple flower, or a piece of ribbon I had worn'. One young female fan took on the role of 'groupie'. Over ten years she adoringly followed Vesta Tilley from theatre to theatre as she crossed the country. Another female fan sent flowers to every dressing room she occupied on one of her six American tours. Nobody can know whether for these audience members this was a sexual attraction. Perhaps the debonair, androgynous youth with a monocle, twirling his cane in tailored flannels and a straw boater represented a romantic, staged version of masculinity: unaggressive and unsexual, transgressive in trousers – but ultimately safe.* But I find it equally likely that it was precisely Tilley's witty charm and androgyny that explains the intensity of such crushes, and which made her an object of heated desire by women – permissible because, although female, she appeared unimpeachably as a man. As for her own off-stage leanings, Vesta Tilley spoke with contentment of her 'forty years of supremely happy married life'. Her marriage to the entertainment entrepreneur Walter de Frece was a give-and-take partnership which saw a wife become, through her talent, the highest-earning woman in Britain, until the day came when de Frece requested

---

* This is the version laid out by Professor Elaine Aston in 'Male Impersonation in the Music Hall: The Case of Vesta Tilley' (1988).

her to step down from her less than respectable career to enable him to pursue his political ambitions.

Vesta Tilley's farewell tour was a runaway success, at the end of which she was given a forty-minute standing ovation and presented with a tribute signed by two million fans. The leading actress Ellen Terry spoke with emotion of the stage genius of an era:

> 'You are the creature of a paradox. On the stage you have always played the manly part. Now, seeming to assume the gentler function, your business is to be the unobtrusive influence of your husband in … public life.'
> I broke down and wept as the curtain descended for the last time.

She had something to cry about. For it was 1919, and the world wasn't yet ready for a member of parliament whose wife wore the trousers.

———

A year earlier, with the war still grinding on, twenty-year-old Kathleen Hale had enlisted to be a carter in the Land Army. She knew nothing about carthorses, but was accepted, and issued with baggy breeches, a khaki overall and puttees. 'It was not a time for dainty living,' she recalled. After a summer of harvesting, and an autumn of ploughing and muck-spreading, Kathleen wrapped herself in sacks and warmed her frozen feet by plunging them into the steaming manure heap.

She was bohemian at heart, a rebel, at home with improvisation and unconventionality. Her headmistress described her as 'the naughtiest child she had ever had to deal with'. That independence of spirit would characterise her for life. At the age of seventeen she uprooted herself from her stunted background and enrolled in the Art Department of Reading University College. With her academic cap and gown, pince-nez and upswept hairdo, she was now every inch the bluestocking. But Kathleen's hair was slippery and abundant, and refused to stay in place; she walked around leaving a trail of scattered hairpins. 'This was intolerable.' She took a pair of scissors and cut the whole lot short, with a blunt fringe, only to be summoned by the authorities and informed that her appearance was unsatisfactory, and that she must leave the college. Brave and direct, she tackled the reproach head-on: she had not cut off her morals with her hair. 'There was a paralysed silence [and] it was never referred to again.'

Kathleen's time at Reading coincided with the war. The Royal Flying Corps were billeted in the neighbouring building, but female students were forbidden to fraternise with them. Kathleen now began to reflect on the burning question of female charm. Did she possess that mysterious quality? Plagued with nagging doubts, she talked to a friend – 'We had no notion whether we were attractive or downright ugly'. They agreed that the only way to confirm whether their looks passed muster was to give the public the opportunity to judge. So having lightly powdered their noses, they made their way to a well-frequented café in the city centre, sat down at a table amid the throng of shoppers, businesspeople and Flying Corps officers, and waited to be noticed. And waited. 'We sat there for an eternity ... growing more and more tense, and shedding any allure we might have had in our anxiety to please. Eventually we trailed back to college, burdened by our miserable future.'

But Kathleen Hale was not yet reconciled to becoming a reject, a 'fading wallflower at the dance of life'. It must be possible to rectify her perceived physical defects: 'My chest was too flat perhaps? Certainly my rump was too obtrusive.'

Her eye fell upon an advertisement. The Venus Carnis Institute in London's Oxford Street guaranteed the development of a beautiful bosom, and printed glowing testimonials from a host of satisfied customers. Kathleen sent off money she could ill afford from her scanty allowance, only to be deluged with fraudulent packages. A nightmare ensued as the company pressured her by every post, only finally withdrawing when she threatened them with legal action.

But what about her bottom? 'I was still obsessed by what I thought was my oversized rump.' Undeterred, she made an appointment with a corsetière whose publicity promised remedial effects: 'I was stripped, measured and viewed from all angles, and I remember the verdict, "Yes, Moddom, you do, just a trifle, (in tactful *sotto voce*) escape."' Before long she was in possession of a 'pink glory . . . equipped with laces, buckles, hooks, suspenders, flaps, and mice-and-man traps'. The apparatus was so intimidating and unyielding that she couldn't countenance wearing it. For some weeks it sat accusingly in its tissue-paper-lined box, a reprimand to vanity. At last she furtively took the whole thing out into a field, and shoved it into the bowels of a hedge.

As she grew up, Kathleen was learning by trial and error how to come to terms not only with an unruly attitude, but also with an unruly body. The Victorian scaffolding that once supported a woman's wayward flesh had now seemed rusty and ready for the reject heap. But that left Kathleen herself, complete with all her bodily insecurities: her flat chest and her big bottom. She knew, too, that her looks did not match up to the preferred gold standard of 'heart-shaped faces, tiny mouths and plucked eyebrows'.

The following year, 1917, Kathleen went to live in London and pursue her vocation as an artist. Everything was new and stimulating. Gas lamps glimmered in the beautiful Georgian squares, and open-topped double-decker omnibuses plied the thoroughfares. Travelling on the Underground, she had a revelation. The carriage was packed with seated commuters, all men, each one screened behind his evening newspaper. The doors opened and, in a synchronised movement, every single man lowered his paper and unapologetically stared at her as she boarded the train.

Finally, it seemed, she had passed the charm test: 'I was, after all, attractive.'

―――――――

Clad in dingy dungarees halfway up a ladder clutching a pail of soapy water, in corduroys pulling cabbages, or in breeches with her feet stuck in a manure heap, women were learning to shape-shift. But – amid the far worse mud, vermin and stink of the trenches – this was not how thousands of soldiers wanted to picture their womenfolk.

A postcard from the Front, addressing a wife – or maybe a sweetheart: 'A message of cheer to someone dear'

For four long, traumatic years the fighting men endured unimaginable horrors while nurturing a vision of home, and – in countless cases – the women keeping its fires burning. Dug-outs were decorated not just with pin-ups, but with pictures of wives, mothers, sisters and sweethearts. Ribbons and buttons were their talismans, worn close to the heart. At the height of the conflict more than eight million homesick letters and postcards were posted each week by soldiers serving on the Western Front – 'The touch of your hand, your breath on my cheek ... the cadence of your voice.' Memories like this sustained many of them, though sometimes they were more tangible: on opening a parcel from his wife, Billy Wightman caught a waft of her scent:

> Some of the tissue paper must have been used for wrapping up something pretty of yours for it smelt so sweetly of your perfume you use. Oh how far away it seemed but how sweetly reminiscent of your dainty self.

Other similar letters extolled 'Mother' as the Angel in the House, and many of the correspondents urged their womenfolk not to tax their delicate constitutions by working, to stay at home and preserve their domestic mystique. Their missives are permeated with nostalgia for the irrecoverable, sunlit life they had left behind.

But when the surviving remnants of the war limped home, the world they found was not as they remembered it. The wives and sweethearts were no longer sitting by the hearth. The doors were swinging open, and they'd abandoned their posts.

The First World War was pivotal for women in so many ways. When it ended, for those who had fought so hard for it, there was a welcome bonanza in the form of the Representation of the People Act, even though it only enfranchised two in five adult women. Along with tight-laced stays, the grip of puritanical morality was loosening, and some more daring young women tentatively lit cigarettes, and felt permitted to surreptitiously add a dab of rouge to their cheeks, or a tiny touch of pinkened salve to their lips, without fear of attack. During the war, an estimated two million women had replaced men in employment. All over the country women had been liberated from mills and servants' halls and stepped in to fill the shortage of bus drivers, garage hands and factory workers. Dressed in their dungarees, with their hair cropped or scarved and money jingling in their pockets, they had a taste of freedom.

But now, the returning soldiers needed work and homes. It was generally held that the women should give the jobs back to the boys, and most of them did so uncomplainingly. The death toll of men also had a seismic effect on marital behaviour. In 1917 seventeen-year-old Rosamund Essex had listened as the senior mistress at Bournemouth High School for Girls announced to the assembled sixth form: 'I have come to tell you a terrible fact. Only one out of ten of you girls can ever hope to marry ... It is a statistical fact. Nearly all the men who might have married you have been killed.' There would not be enough men to go round, and Rosamund would be just one among the nearly two million women who, following the war's dreadful slaughter, would never marry.* For single women, the stakes were raised after 1918. Getting a husband still meant status, security, economic maintenance, social respect and children – not to mention the entrancing, if often illusory, prospect of true love.

The era of the boudoir and the ballroom was slowly slipping

---

* See Virginia Nicholson, *Singled Out: How Two Million Women Survived Without Men after the First World War* (2007).

into history. The combat zones were now the public dance hall, the workplace and the common spaces where women competed for survival.

For, as marriage opportunities diminished, so women's visibility increased.

Celluloid and Paraffin

Most modern women now went to work until they married, and the job market made different demands on a woman's wardrobe and toilette. You couldn't wear a tea gown on the omnibus – but a tailor-made skirt and jacket looked professional, businesslike and, well, less feminine.

The jacket prompts a digression on pockets – as the women's version, unlike its male counterpart, sadly lacked them. Pockets had been cancelled from the female wardrobe a hundred years earlier, when their 'line' was considered to interfere with the fashion for flowing gowns. Yet again, the demands of femininity ran counter to a woman's actual needs. Pockets are political. While men could keep their essentials – money, keys, documents, even weapons – safely and privately on their person, women (dependents) were left with absurd reticules that barely contained a handkerchief, or chatelaines which put all her belongings on display. In 1904 the American family magazine *The Youth's Companion* entertained its readers by lamenting 'the darkness of a pocketless age', and conjuring up an encounter between a lady and her dressmaker:

'Pocket!' she gasps.

'A good deep one,' I say, with assurance, ignoring her evident consternation ... I see dismay creep into her face ...

'O, Mrs B—,' she laments, 'it will spoil the set! There can't be

any style to a skirt with a pocket in it. I never heard of such a thing.
It'll pull it all out of shape, and—'

The pocket battle has yet to be won; there were no pockets in
Hillary Clinton's pantsuits.

————————

But the daily commute turned the tables in a different way.
New technologies were causing the visual realm of femininity to
expand. Twenty years earlier, a lady's domain had been the confines of her drawing room or her dressing room. If she ventured
out, it was accompanied, on horseback or in a carriage. Already,
bicycles had changed that narrative; and the internal combus-
tion engine was changing it faster. Distant destinations were
becoming closer, long journeys shorter. The street, identified in
the Victorian era as the haunt of disreputable females, was rapidly – and confusingly – becoming a thoroughfare where fashion
and beauty were on public display as never before. And where
once a woman's face was flatteringly blurred and camouflaged
by the soft glow of a candle or the incandescence of gaslight, the
new technology of electricity was blindingly unforgiving. From
1879, electric street lighting was being introduced in England;
but it was not until after the First World War that homes started
to be electrified on a large scale. The brightening of life did
nothing for older beauties, and even debutantes found the glare
in Buckingham Palace, after electricity was installed there in the
1880s, too relentless. Manufacturers of face powder now began
to consider how successfully their products lived up to the blaze
coming from the 'electroliers' suspended from the ceilings of
society mansions. By the same token, electric light bulb manufacturers marketed their products for bourgeois white women:
comfortably off homemakers, who were encouraged to think of

their lamps as beauty aids. Meanwhile, the beauty advisers urged their readers to think more about how electric lighting affected their appearance when wearing make-up: 'Try out the several different shades under electric light,' wrote Antoinette Donnelly in the *Chicago Tribune*. 'For the great majority, eye shadow should be confined to use only under electric lighting.'

Fewer homes were now without mirrors – but just as Alice discovered when she stepped through the looking-glass, the mirror's version of the world appeared distorted, and very different from expectations. Dirt, wrinkles, sags, spots and blemishes were all regularly and brutally revealed in the reflection provided by those chilly, silvery truth-tellers – so coldly reliable and cruel, yet so indispensable to every lady's electrically lit dressing room (their three facets giving new, uncanny perspectives on a lady's left and right profile).

De-professionalised photography performed a similar unforgiving function. By the end of the war, portable cameras carrying rolls of celluloid film were on the market for anyone to buy; Eastman Kodak spun the legend, 'You push the button, we do the rest.' The camera – 'which cannot lie' – was often thought to be objective and infallible in representing appearances, in a way that no portraitist could ever be. Today, particularly if we are no longer young, we are familiar with the slightly unsettling shock that comes with seeing ourselves as the lens sees us. But in the early twentieth century visual self-scrutiny was not taken for granted in the way it is today.

The revolution was cinema. Early experiments in filming and projecting were evolving into a viable movie industry, with 'animated pictures' developing into fully fledged – albeit black-and-white and silent – feature films. Idols would never be the same again. Though the war put economic pressure on entertainment venues, the immense popularity of film stars like Mary Pickford, Gladys Cooper, Betty Balfour, Ivy Close and

Theda Bara caused twenty-one million cinema tickets to be sold in Britain in 1917; in the USA the African American actress Evelyn Preer's outstanding appearances in nineteen silent films made her a star.

Mary Pickford, aka 'Blondilocks', and Evelyn Preer, one of the first celebrity Black actresses

In these fanciful, silent, monochrome dramas, played out with explanatory intertitles, the audience luxuriated in extravagant character portrayals. The picture-palace films were often projected against a white wall rather than a screen, and the image was small by today's standards – just four or five feet high – but for audiences to see a close-up of a face magnified on this scale was unprecedented. Film, widely distributed and widely seen, was setting the beauty bar ever higher, and a woman's world was becoming bigger and brighter. For actors used to stage make-up, it was back to square one. With their imperfections hugely enlarged, colour distorted and the film lighting illuminating every flaw, the procedure was hit and miss. For example, red lipstick photographed black. Theda Bara was one actress who appears to have overdone the eyeliner – nevertheless, it was to become her trademark, along with a sumptuous wardrobe selected to enhance her on-screen *femme fatale* image.

Thousands of young women sat in the threepenny seats and marvelled at the new moving imagery in awe and envy; filmed representations were changing women's aspirations and reframing their fantasies. Gladys Cooper's chic beauty, with a signature single string of pearls, was copied by the masses. By 1915 tiny Mary Pickford had become America's sweetheart and the first real world-famous movie star, with a working-class fan base, for playing the winsome, childlike ingénue. Role models like her were getting younger. For a twenty-first-century equivalent think Ariana Grande, a teen idol since childhood, with her girly ponytail plus cute bunny ears, and 371 million Instagram followers. Pickford was 'Blondilocks', 'the girl with the curls'. Her ringlets were adored; as was the lovable way the corners of her eyes wrinkled when she smiled. In 1916 Pickford was earning $500,000 a year, and a movie magazine industry had mushroomed on the strength of her fame, bringing yet more images of those wayward ringlets into American and British homes. Twenty-four years old at the height of her celebrity, her flapper charm put a premium on the flawlessness of youth and raised the beauty stakes for anyone over thirty.

Money and adoration were heaped on the screen goddesses, with their seemingly artless charm, rosebud mouths and magical, flickering, larger-than-life allure. These were the early days, but here – if you had the talent and looks – was a new way to carve out a career and play out a celluloid fairy tale in which, in the final shot, the beauteous heroine walks into the sunset of matrimonial heaven with Mr Right.

More than ever before, women led their lives in the public eye; and more than ever before, their faces, necks, chests, ankles, arms and hands were seeing the light of day. The corset had been dumped in the hedge, and a woman's bosom and rump were freed from their restraints – while, for Miss Average, the mirage of Miss Perfect was ever more tantalisingly within view.

———

As the spell is lifted, Miranda (in Shakespeare's *The Tempest*) awakes and sees the beings around her with innocent eyes:

> Oh, wonder!
> How many goodly creatures are there here!
> How beauteous mankind is! O brave new world,
> That has such people in't!

In the early decades of the century, breakthroughs by pioneering scientists offered a glimpse of loveliness for all, seeming to promise, through corrective magic, a brave new world of beauty.

Surgeons were seeking ways to banish ugliness and restore youth. With this panacea in their sights, reconstruction, repair and renovation were at the cutting edge of medical progress. The first surgeon to perform a facelift appears to have been the German Eugen Holländer in 1901, when (according to him) a Polish aristocrat used her 'feminine persuasion' to talk him into tightening up her face by removing specific sections of skin. Apparently, the patient was happy with the result. Five years later Dr Erich Lexer continued this pioneering work, by making incisions around the hairline of an actress to 'correct' her wrinkled forehead.

Techniques in plastic surgery and anaesthesia had been progressing over many years, and they became life-changing during
the First World War when Sir Harold Gillies famously used his
skill to restore the faces of soldiers disfigured by their injuries
at the front. Now, it seemed as if the same magic staff could
be waved over protruding noses and ears, sagging eyelids and
double chins.

> If soldiers whose faces had been torn away by bursting shell on the
> battlefield could come back into an almost normal life with new
> faces created by the wizardry of the new science of plastic surgery,
> why couldn't women whose faces had been ravaged by nothing
> more explosive than the hand of the years find again the firm clear
> contours of youth?

So wrote Max Thorek, another of the pioneering surgeons
in this field. And then maybe everyone could be like Mary
Pickford or Gladys Cooper.

For if you wanted to look like a screen goddess, a string of
pearls and a dab of lipstick weren't enough. And there was
genuine heartache for the plain, the past-it, the asymmetrical
or the under-endowed who didn't measure up.

Sonia Keppel (author of the memoir *Edwardian Daughter*
[1958]) gives a child's-eye view of the aspiring beauties of her
day padding out their less-than-adequate bosoms with handkerchiefs, while she herself struggled to live up to adult expectations.
Sonia's teeth stuck out like pegs on a washing line, and a special-
ised dentist was employed to barricade them painfully into place
with hooks, bars and rubber bands; by the age of fifteen they
were straighter, but her nose, which had grown alarmingly, was
now a worse source of misery. Violet, her sister, cruelly told her
she looked like a banana; Sonia sought a second opinion from

an attractive young man, a friend of Violet's: '[I asked] him if he considered my nose looked Jewish. His answer further depressed me: "Oh! No, my dear. Not Jewish. Merely Plantagenet."' The Keppel nose was *not* cutely turned up. It was long, curved in the wrong direction, and reacted violently to embarrassment by blazing red. This problem was discussed, in Sonia's hearing, by her parents, with her mother advocating having the offending feature broken and re-set, but her father resisted. Nose-worry dominated Sonia's years up to adulthood, as she realised that she would have to compete for attention with 'sparkling eyes ... curly hair ... tiny *retroussé* noses'. Fancy-dress disguises provided respite; dressed as a man, her nose looked less inappropriately large. Sonia made her debut at the end of the war: 'Rouge and lipsalve were not used by debutantes in 1918, but fashion decreed a universally white powdered nose to which I eagerly subscribed, reducing my own prominent organ to a leprous hue.'

An unassertive nose and a beautiful bosom might seem unreachably lovely, all the more so as advancing years took their toll. In 1906 (under the headline 'The Cult of Comeliness') the *Daily Mirror* told its female readers that one might tell a woman's age from her nose. Regular tapping, rolling, pressing and sponging could delay the inevitable. Rosewater, vinegar, oatmeal and coal-tar soap helped, and the nose could be effectively whitened with almond oil, then dusted with boracic acid powder. But the *Mirror's* beauty expert lamented that only very fortunate women were able to retain their pretty noses past middle age.

Help, however, was at hand:

Creases, furrows, and wrinkles manifest themselves not only in older people, but sometimes also very early in young persons. In order to render these less conspicuous, ladies usually employ powder or paint ... Perfect filling up of the hollows, moreover, can be obtained by paraffin injections.

These comments were made by Dr Edmund Saalfeld, in *Lectures on Cosmetic Treatment – A Manual for Practitioners*, published in 1910. As a German professional working in the same field, Dr Saalfeld was probably referencing the Vienna-based surgeon Dr Robert Gersuny, who in 1899 had begun experimenting with an inert form of paraffin wax, which he injected as a filler for cosmetic use, publishing a report on it in 1903. He explained that the heated-up wax turned semi-liquid, but gradually solidified as it cooled, whereupon it could be shaped or modelled. Gersuny tried out his new technique on patients dissatisfied with their noses. Success!

The paraffin injection method soon became popular in Britain. The *Daily Mirror* told female readers to stop worrying about their noses: 'Medical skill has reached such a height nowadays that the injection of paraffin-wax under the nose can work a transformation.' Soon a steady stream of women despondent about their appearance began to seek out surgeons willing to straighten, smooth or streamline their features with the new wonder substance. One of these was Gladys Deacon.

Gladys was among the great fascinators of her age. In 1902 she was just twenty-one years old, and worshipped for her huge blue eyes and unusual, hypnotic beauty, which seemed to many onlookers to derive from some Olympian deity – Psyche, Minerva or Venus. Born to American parents, she spent most of her life in Europe, where she attracted the admiration of writers and artists from Proust to Rodin, Monet to Colette. Gladys was an *über*-buccaneer. From an early age, she had set her heart on catching the heart and hand of the world's most eligible bachelor (as seen through American eyes), the Duke of Marlborough – an ambition she would eventually achieve. In 1902, however, Gladys was in Paris: wealthy, unmarried and underemployed. A friend described her as 'content to lie for hours on her bed, happy in loving her own beauty, contemplating it'. But her serenity was disturbed when she examined her nose. Somehow, it wasn't right. Instead of running straight from brow to tip, the bridge hollowed out into a dip. Like Lady Diana Manners, Gladys longed to look Greek, and wondered whether there was anything she could do to achieve those perfect classical lines. Twenty years earlier, this would have been a daydream. But with the advent of plastic surgery, dreams were starting to come true. Gladys travelled to Rome where, among the abundance of marble goddesses on display at the Museo delle Terme, she sought out the most beautiful and analysed their features. Back in France she took the irrevocable step – it was simple. Wielding his loaded syringe, the surgeon deftly introduced the liquid paraffin into the small concavity at the top of her nose, between the eyes; then, as it slowly solidified, sculpted the substance to the desired shape.

'She traversed Europe like a meteor in a flash of dazzling beauty.' Gladys Spencer-Churchill (née Deacon), Duchess of Marlborough, c. 1910

Things went wrong very quickly. On 14 February 1903 the *Boston Globe* printed a photograph of Gladys in profile, headlined:

DEATH OR PERMANENT DISFIGUREMENT.
*Penalty Miss Gladys Deacon may pay for operation
intended to improve the lines of her nose.*

Biarritz, France.

Miss Gladys Deacon ... is ill here as the result of the unsuccessful subcutaneous injection of paraffine [*sic*] last fall in an effort to improve the lines of her nose ...

The operation was apparently very successful, but a little later necrosis of the nose bones appeared and now the beautiful American is seriously ill.

Necrosis is a progressive disease and unless checked promptly is usually fatal. It may result in permanently disfiguring Miss Deacon, if it does not kill her.

Society all over the continent has heard the news with a great horror, in which there is mingled a deep and sincere pity.

Gladys didn't die. But the paraffin under her skin soon dispersed and slipped. Battered and botched as she was, she would survive to become the Duchess of Marlborough. But she started to dye her hair yellow and used more lipstick than was acceptable. 'Isn't it awful?' commented one old friend. 'She looked deplorable – not a lady. It made me v. sad.' Still, the 'fine eyes' continued to shine out from her jarred and ravaged visage. And the duke, who had been stuck in a deeply unhappy marriage with Consuelo Vanderbilt, still admired her. On Gladys's wedding day in 1921, the press were out in force. As a cine camera whirred, the bride was bewildered and cagey: 'Oh,' she asked, 'is that a cinema? I didn't know. I shall come out frightful.'

––––––––

Complications following paraffin injections had gone unnoticed, because often they did not appear until five or ten years after the operation. But by this time practitioners were producing reports of disastrous physical results to patients who had had facial procedures. The wax wandered, hardened and clumped, producing abnormal, knotty lumps under the skin. Accounts proliferated – like these, in an American advice manual for girls published in 1910, whose author had interviewed a German chemist employed by a beauty parlour:

> [A] girl came in one day, and the 'Doctor' injected some paraffin into the skin of her nose to change its shape. 'No one knows what happened,' said the German, 'whether a vein was struck or what, but the girl had the most dreadful looking nose that you could imagine. It was all black and swollen and was in a terrible condition. The girl was in agony ...'
>
> He told me, too, of a young opera singer. Thinking that she would have a few lines in her face filled up, she went to this 'Doctor's' parlor. After the work was done, she had red bumps instead of faint lines, and, of course, she had to leave the stage.

There were accounts of patients suffering from ulcers, embolisms and infections; such reactions were described as 'paraffinomas'. Sometimes, blindness resulted; or death. After 1914, in Europe and America, fewer interventions using paraffin were carried out, and beauty salons took increasing care as to how they advertised their wares. By 1931 Madame Sterling of Regent Street was promising 'Facial wrinkles eradicated in one visit ... No knife, X-ray or paraffin injections used.'

Twenty years after Gladys Deacon's operation Jacob Epstein made a bronze bust of her, which revealed a sad deterioration: her jaw protruded. The wax filler had caused her skin to detach and drop down, giving the impression of jowls. Friends observed that her cheeks were puffy, that she was scarred, with a crooked mouth and distorted features. Her skin had coarsened and she sought the shadows.

Gladys was forty-two.

———

Paraffin got a deservedly bad press. But when it came to repelling the ravages of time, women were not easily deterred. In the early years of the twentieth century, techniques of plastic surgery were making headway, and in 1907 the first American text for practitioners was written by Dr Charles Miller. Miller was searching for materials for body augmentations. He experimented with rubber and gutta percha,* while others (like his contemporary, the American plastic surgeon Dr Vilray Blair) tried celluloid, metal and ivory. Miller was denounced as a quack by doctors who didn't want their reputations sullied by connection with the dubious practice of face-lifting. His Chicago practice was renowned for removing wrinkles, correcting ears and even creating dimples. But his manual was progressive in its descriptions of facial suturing and incision technique. Miller developed his expertise, and some years later (1924) he published an update addressed, with blunt candour, to his fellow surgeons:

---

* The word normally refers to the rubber-like substance derived from the Malaysian '*getah*', or gutta percha tree.

Women may spend thousands having the skin treated. Every kind of treatment has been tried by women to check the sagging of the skin. Massage is useless or harmful, drugs, lights, heat, cold, 'skinning', it matters not what is tried, one or all are impotent, the only effective way to restore youthful contour is by cutting out the slack.

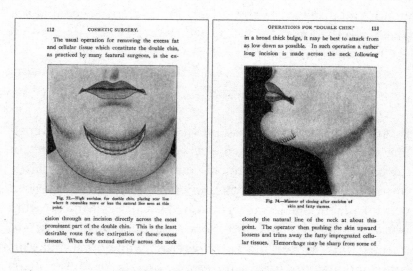

Cutting out the slack. Dr Charles Miller's *Cosmetic Surgery: The Correction of Featural Imperfections* was published in 1907. Its success would result in a later edition, 1924, with improved illustrations

Dr Miller was also perfectly straight with his readers in warning them against certain types of client. There were the vain, demanding neurotics. Then there were the ageing women who wanted to reignite the ardour of their marriage, but who were determined to keep the surgery secret from their husbands, despite the fact they were paying for it. And then there were the Professional Beauties. 'These women in America must retain youth ... Signs of maturity in women must go.' But the older they were, the worse the risk of bad scarring.

> Women who otherwise would be retired from public appearance will accept as a choice scars, which they must subsequently hide with cosmetics.

Over a hundred years ago, Dr Miller paints a familiar picture of these sadly mutilated celebrities.

During the war, when restorative plastic surgery was making headlines, cosmetic surgery was doing good business, albeit less openly. At this time surgeons largely confined themselves to procedures which reduced or reconstructed. Subtracting from the body – 'cutting out the slack' – is easier than adding to it. As women became more active and bore fewer children, the direction of travel, aesthetically, was towards smaller breasts, thus surgery to reduce breast size was becoming widespread. Operations to augment the body's various features were still rare, though attempts had been made as early as the 1880s, using fatty deposits from other parts of the body as filler. In the decades after 1915, following the paraffin wax saga, the search continued for a suitable substance with which to supplement nature's shortcomings. Medical historians write in general terms about the disastrous operations undertaken:

> A huge plethora of materials was used ... The list of these materials was limited only by the extent of man's imagination. During this time the following materials were used: ivory balls, glass balls, vegetable oils, mineral oil, lanolin, beeswax, shellac, silk fabric, epoxy resin, ground rubber, ox cartilage, sponges, sacs, rubber, goat's milk ... and glazier's putty ...

The outcome with each of these materials was similar – chronic inflammation with foreign body granulomas.

Medically, cosmetic surgery was still regarded as barely legitimate. For the women undergoing them, these procedures were veiled in shame and secrecy, and it is not easy to find accounts by women having cosmetic interventions. The diarists and memoirists of the time happily open up about make-up and underwear, but accounts of operations and their results seem to have been taboo. We are left to imagine the distress in individual cases, as desperate women suffered the nightmarish results of unregulated surgery. Or we have to rely on gossip and second-hand observations, like Lady Cynthia Asquith writing in her diary on 8 September 1917 that 'Maud [Cunard] is very amusing about Oreste, the great beauty specialist to whose hands she has now entrusted her face'.

Lady Cynthia was thirty, while the society hostess Maud Cunard (often known as Emerald) was forty-five. But Oreste (surely the pseudonym of a charlatan) – who was he?

LADIES!!!

DR ORESTE THE QUALIFIED FACE
SPECIALIST OF PARIS,

is in London, during the War, and will give free advice for the complexion.

His personal methods for positively building up shrunken muscles, removing lines and double chin, rejuvenating and beautifying the features.

For money order of 30/- a 'Complete Treatment', with instructions, is sent. These four Preparations applied at home will correct all imperfections, and improve and conserve the Natural Beauty and Contours of Youth.

Where Lady Cunard was concerned, it was all a bit unclear. Cynthia Asquith was puzzled, but noticed that her friend was starting to get 'that curious pneumatic look which doctored faces acquire.' What Oreste's 'personal methods' were, was anyone's guess. 'He takes in women's upper lips and reefs in their double chins,' she observed.

Certainly, though women didn't want to admit to visiting the great doctor, his services seem to have been in competitive demand among the more mature. Maud Cunard appears to have had a discreet word with her friend Ava Astor,* who was also in her forties. Maud recommended Oreste's methods – of which Ava professed astonished ignorance. So at the earliest opportunity Maud took the doctor aside, and begged him to treat her friend:

> 'I want her so much to come to you – but she won't.' Oreste flamed with fury and said: 'If Mrs Astor – whose face I have made for the last twenty years – denies me, I shall deny her.'

Oreste exacted a terrible revenge. He denied Mrs Astor any further treatment, and she was forced to take to her bed for two weeks till he gave in. Is this story extreme? Lady Cynthia mocks the middle-aged Ava Astor's clandestine dependence on her beauty doctor, and literal inability to leave her room and face the world without the aid of his magic touch.

But perhaps it was a sign of the times. The spotlight was on women as never before, and the emphasis was on youth.

––––––––

* The American heiress Ava Astor (née Willing) married the business magnate John Jacob Astor in 1891. Their divorce in 1909 left her with a $10 million settlement; she remarried to Lord Ribblesdale in 1919, and was known as a prominent London socialite.

The contradictions and controversies surrounding the topic of cosmetic surgery are illuminated by the story of Suzanne Noël, the first female plastic surgeon in the world.

> To think that this is a face into which one is so casually cutting . . . and that this elegant incision will be so decisive, is pretty emotional. The surgeon always gets that little flutter of anxiety which comes with this kind of intervention – but at the same time, I feel huge gratitude to the woman who, full of quiet trust, has laid down on the operating table before me, and placed the fate of her beauty in my hands.

Noël was describing performing a facelift in her book *La Chirurgie Esthetique: Son Rôle Social* (1926), by which time she was known not only as a pioneer in her field, but also as a dedicated and forward-thinking feminist. Today, for a woman to perform facelifts on another woman may seem incompatible with opposing the patriarchy. Suzanne Noël, however, took a different view. A brief run-through of her life story, a century ago, may help to explain why.

Suzanne Gros was born into a bourgeois family in Laon,* in northern France, and prepared for her inevitable future role as a wife and mother by learning embroidery, the painting of miniatures and all the usual *ouvrages de femmes*. Suzanne was blonde, petite and pretty, but from the start she was also exceptionally bright and independent. At the age of eighteen she married Henry Pertat, a clever doctor nine years her senior, and moved to Paris; Henry's specialty was dermatology. It was at this point, in 1900, that Suzanne stepped off the female conveyor belt by deciding to go to university, and in 1905 she

---

* For a critical and scholarly account of Suzanne's Noël's life, see Paula J. Martin, *Suzanne Noël: Cosmetic Surgery, Feminism and Beauty in Early Twentieth-Century France* (2014).

obtained a degree in chemistry and natural sciences; it was Henry, surprisingly, who then urged her to study medicine. In 1908, while still a medical student, she gave birth to her only child, a daughter, Jacqueline.

Suzanne now found herself being pulled in too many directions. The child was sickly, and Suzanne had to take time off from her books to care for her. Her marriage suffered, and in 1911 she and Henry separated. Despite these tribulations she was – almost incredibly for a woman – invited in 1913 to sit for the highly competitive exam for a place as an *interne* in one of the elite Paris hospitals. She passed with starring grades. Her existing interest in dermatology (through Henry) now led her to focus on this area of medicine.

But the defining influence on her career had happened the previous year: 'In 1912 one of our greatest artistes returned from America after a triumphant tour,' recalled Suzanne. It was the renowned actress Sarah Bernhardt, now aged fifty. She had been in a motor accident, and though not badly hurt she had consulted a doctor – probably the Chicago-based Dr Miller – who checked her over and then suggested that he could do some work that would make her look younger.

All the newspapers were commenting on how, following an operation on her scalp, she appeared astonishingly youthful. This struck me very forcibly. So I had a go myself, on my own face, using my fingers to squeeze and pull the skin in different areas and in different directions, to correct the furrows. I was amazed at the results.

Wishing to explore further, Suzanne sought out Bernhardt herself:

She welcomed me with great charm, and told me what had been done to her in the United States – but it had no connection with

what, by then, I was hoping to achieve ... The outcome had effectively eliminated the wrinkles on her forehead and taken out her
crows' feet, but had in no way altered the lower portion of her face.

War broke out. Suzanne's dependants now included her
elderly mother, and she had little money. Day and night she
worked tending to the wounded, and in 1916 she learned
invaluable lessons from her medical mentors who were performing reconstructive surgery on the *gueules cassées* – the
men whose faces had been disfigured by war injuries. But
Suzanne's troubles were only just beginning. Henry died, aged
just forty-nine, in 1918. Not long after, she married her fellow
dermatologist André Noël, and the couple were able to enjoy
a short-lived period of stability – only for it to be shattered by
the death, during the Spanish flu epidemic, of little Jacqueline,
aged just thirteen. Suzanne was devastated, and André too was
inconsolable; he descended into a spiral of depression, and in
August 1924 Suzanne was witness as he drowned himself in
the River Seine.

Suzanne now drew on all her extraordinary powers of
resilience to recover from this double tragedy. It was at this
time that she began to direct her energies towards women's
rights. In 1923 she orchestrated a protest against the payment
of taxes by women: if they couldn't vote, why should they
contribute from their earnings?* She blazoned her views to
the world with a lapel button that read *Je veux voter*. She was
also actively working to form a French branch of the American
women's movement dedicated to peace and equality, known

---

*   Despite repeated reintroductions in the French parliament of a bill propos-
ing French women's right to vote, it was blocked by the Senate no fewer than
six times between 1919 and 1936, until Charles de Gaulle eventually granted
them suffrage in 1944.

as the Soroptimists. This would grow into a passion, and over time Suzanne would found Soroptimist branches internationally, including in East Asia, eventually becoming known as the organisation's godmother.

Suzanne Noël performing a facial operation

Despite personal losses that would have flattened a lesser spirit, Suzanne Noël showed that she had fight in her – it never left her, even as she herself had the misfortune to lose her eyesight, much later, at the age of fifty-eight (thankfully, after two years of blindness, it was restored). From 1925 Suzanne ran her own medical practice, specialising in cosmetic surgery, and her ability to do so is testimony to the primary lesson life had taught her: women need to be strong and independent. But reconciling women's empowerment with facelifts? Suzanne's work as a plastic surgeon was a vocation, informed by a democratising impulse and a determination to help women to better themselves; in her mature and most successful years Suzanne would see no contradiction in bringing beauty to women from all classes of society. Her story was far from over.

———————

Beauty was starting to change. It was becoming available to everyone. And now that a woman's world had expanded beyond the drawing room, seeing and being seen meant something different. After four years of wearing the breeches during the First World War, women had to perform a balancing act in their search for a post-war identity and a post-war look. Uncertain territory lay ahead. The signpost back to safety was marked Womanly Aura, Lady's Child, Domestic Angel, Drudge, Provincial Young Lady, Goddess.

But there was another way, and it was marked Suffragette, Bluestocking, Flapper, Worker, Trouser-wearer, Crophead, Rebel, Feminist.

The 1920s were on the horizon.

Freda Dudley Ward: *The Lady in Black and Green* by Sir John Lavery, 1920, and in the late 1920s, photographed by Cecil Beaton

4

Jazz Age

Freda

Mrs Dudley Ward was ... the embodiment of the new conception of allure ... No one had ever looked quite like her before.

Cecil Beaton, the photographer, aesthete and authority on twentieth-century style, was paying tribute to Freda Dudley Ward in *The Glass of Fashion*, his 1954 round-up of 1920s beauties.

Winifred ('Freda') Birkin was the oldest daughter of a wealthy Nottingham industrialist and his American wife. In 1913, at the age of just nineteen, Freda married William Dudley Ward, Liberal MP for Southampton. Mrs Dudley Ward,* as she was generally known, was famous for being fashionable and attractive. In other words, she was what we would now call a celebrity influencer, a woman whose beauty fuelled the media of the day:

---

* Though her husband's family name was Ward, Dudley Ward would become their familiar surname. The common practice of the time was for wives to relinquish not just their surnames but also their forenames on marriage.

Mrs Dudley Ward was wearing a new type of frock, the top being of sapphire-blue panne that moulded closely to her tiny figure ... On the left shoulder she wore a tiny jewelled fob to match her dress. Possibly we shall all be wearing these soon.

This Spring will see a revival of the Tahitian flower hair decoration craze ... It was Mrs Dudley Ward who originally started the vogue with one camellia worn just over her ear.

Mrs Dudley Ward, looking lovely in black with a wide-brimmed hat.

Mrs Dudley Ward, about the most admired of our young married women.

It's the language of *Hello* magazine, transposed to the 1920s.

There are individuals who seem to embody the zeitgeist, and Freda Dudley Ward was one of them. Cecil Beaton tried to define what gave her this special quality, by comparing her to the Professional Beauties like Lillie Langtry and the other statuesque Boadiceas who had dominated society thirty years earlier, in the *belle époque*. But times had changed, and next to those curvaceous ladies, Freda appeared an exquisite shrimp, resembling an undernourished adolescent, tiny and reduced to the essentials. She was all that was modern and boyish. Even her voice was reported as high-pitched and plaintive, with a touch of a Nottinghamshire accent. She wasn't to everyone's taste. The socialite diarist Chips Channon described her as 'whining, dull ... That terrible voice she has made fashionable ... A tiny piping of catchwords and clichés.' But Beaton saw her differently. She had an 'exaggerated feminine allure'. Her huge, startled eyes, pretty red-and-white gingham dresses and pink-and-white complexion completed a look of contemporary femininity: 'Whenever any man was fortunate enough to sit by her, she gave him the impression not only of being more interested in him than in anyone else in the world, but of being in need of his protection as well.'

But there *was* one similarity to Lillie Langtry. In 1918, the Prince of Wales fell for her, though arguably it was he who needed her protection, not the other way round. Edward's taste for modern women may have been a partial revolt against his old-fashioned father. Freda's short hair, smoking habit and visible legs summed up all that King George V – who loathed emancipated women – found abhorrent. Whatever the case, a slavishly adoring on-off relationship began between her and the prince, which continued for more than a decade,* until all other loves would be supplanted in 1934 by 'that woman' – the dazzling American divorcée Wallis Simpson.

But Freda Dudley Ward was ahead of Wallis's game in showing the world a different way to be a woman. She wore her hair in a sleek, snipped shingle. She didn't carry a spare ounce of weight, being all hollows and concavities. Sir John Lavery's 1920 portrait plays on her sinuous neck, prominent clavicles and the perfect symmetry of her features. A gilt sphinx on the armrest of her chair seems to nod to her crisp, enigmatic beauty, and her pearls glitter. She appears poised, almost pert, if not relaxed. Beaton's later representation is composed of geometry and angles: her compact head tilted over the studiedly staccato prop of her shoulder. Uncomfortable, even jagged, the uninterrupted slope of her body extends like that of a basking lizard along the black surface of a highly polished table, and you can

---

* William Dudley Ward initially turned a blind eye on his wife's liaison with the heir to the throne, since a divorce would have damaged his political career. Freda's infidelity was not restricted to her relationship with the future Edward VIII; she also had affairs with the banker Michael Herbert and the American polo player Rodman Wanamaker. The Dudley Ward marriage remained one in name only until their eventual divorce in 1930.

almost hear her structured bangles clank against its glassy surface. A consciously casual, bony, elongated wrist emerges from a pocket in her natty costume, whose grid of checks picks up the graphic theme. If it's plaid or tweed, Freda was trendsetting, wearing a fabric traditionally used for menswear. The image is quintessentially jazz age, with its backdrop of monochrome triangles and quadrilaterals. And, like the random vorticist shapes behind her, Freda is made up of long, straight lines: completely devoid of bosom, hips, waist or bottom. Here, less is more; her power as a beautiful woman plays out a series of contradictions within the image. As Beaton observed, fashionable women of this era looked 'expensively poor'. The minimalism of Freda's garments is offset by the opulence of pearls and jewelled bracelets; while despite the full-face directness and unmistakable lipstick, there is something soft, inviting and dreamy about her gaze. It's fascinatingly at odds with the sexual jut of her pelvis. Androgyny competes here with femininity, modesty with sex appeal. It's a tension also present in the Lavery portrait. Her contemporary, Barbara Cartland, confirmed Beaton's take on Freda: 'She has that air of ... not being strong enough to face the world without [a man's] strength, of being physically weak, yet spiritually courageous. It is irresistible!'

––––––––

Undressing Freda Dudley Ward in the 1920s involves many fewer buttons, hooks and ribbons than it would have a decade earlier. True, in the Lavery portrait she has chosen an elaborately trimmed hat. She is also relatively smothered in layers of copious sleeves and wraps. In the Beaton picture the furbelows have given way to severity and simplicity. Freda's jacket is unstructured, without buttons. If the ensemble she is wearing is not actually a Chanel creation, then it certainly owes much

to the pioneering designer's pared-down aesthetic, which permeated 1920s style. The long, belted tunic or pullover Freda
wears beneath her jacket also ticks the Chanel box. Clothes
like this emphatically did not look good over projecting busts
and bottoms.

Neither the Lavery nor the Beaton portraits reveal Freda's
legs – so we need to be quite clear that this is a story of rising
hemlines. The no-legs woman is outdated. The post-war
woman had ankles. By about 1924 she had also reclaimed the
lower half of her calves, and by 1926 the full extent from foot
to knee might be entirely exposed. Although the trend for knee-
length skirts lasted for a quite brief period (roughly 1925–29),
it meant, temporarily, giving thought to a previously neglected
part of the anatomy: legs.

A century ago, with trousers off limits, legs were visible
year-round, but a white woman's naked skin was still largely
taboo, so stockings were virtually mandatory. Holding up
hosiery was a perennial problem, and each woman had to
decide between garters, elastic bands, suspender belts or
corsets with adjustable clip attachments. The other difficulty was that a fashion leader like Freda wouldn't dream
of wearing cotton – lisle – stockings. She had to be seen
in stockings of gossamer-fine silk, seamed up the back,
and often decorated with knitted patterns at the back of
the ankle known as clocks; they were fashioned to fit, as
silk had little stretch to it. And at the least provocation,
these expensive accessories ripped. For our grandmothers and great-grandmothers, darning stockings was a
routine chore.

And of course, the finer the stockings, the more risk of
making public that unwelcome exhibit: leg hair. Freda was
on display. So it's safe to assume that she would have conscientiously depilated both her underarms and lower legs. To

achieve this, some women still swore by scouring with pumice, which sounds painful. At the other end of the scale, electrolysis was now increasingly, if expensively, available. Most likely, she would have shaved, with the new miniature safety razors marketed to women. But there was also Veet, manufactured in England from 1922, and Ashes of Roses depilatory cream:

> The fastidious woman to-day must have immaculate underarms if she is to be unembarrassed. Sleeveless dresses, the thinnest of silk hose and knee-length skirts make superfluous hair an embarrassment ... Ashes of Roses ... is safe, pleasant, effective and easy to use.

In the Beaton portrait Freda has tweezed and shaped her eyebrows, and she is undisguisedly wearing lipstick. Close scrutiny reveals that she has powdered and rouged. By the 1920s make-up ranges were growing. Beauty parlours also catered for women like Freda. Maybe she got all her beauty needs supplied at a salon such as Pomeroy in Kensington, which sold cosmetics and 'skin food', as well as offering depilatory and facial treatments, manicures and massages. Her dark hair is, we assume, its natural colour, but the gleaming, immaculately crimped Marcel wave that frames her delicate features is the work of an expensive hairdresser.

And what did Freda wear to retain her svelte silhouette? Foundation garments have simplified, for these clothes are unsparingly clingy. This is a laxer, looser age. Lingerie in the 1920s was reduced in bulk and quantity – though by today's standards it was still intricate. A young woman with a slender, linear figure like Freda Dudley Ward could have chosen a garment sometimes known as a teddy. This had the usual button-up crotch, and might have been worn over an elasticated bandeau brassière, designed to suppress curves. The

American feminist writer Susan Brownmiller recalled how her mother repented of her binding days: she was convinced that her breasts had been 'ruined' for ever, because she had followed the fashion for binding them in the 1920s. '"Don't ever bind your breasts," my full-figured mother would say.'

Some women preferred to wear a more elongated but unstructured bust bodice to contain their upper half and reduce wobbles. Many larger and more mature women still opted for corsets, or lighter corselettes, though these were now being redesigned to produce a flattening effect.

Ethel Mannin, author of the memoir *Young in the Twenties* (1971), gives more detail. She and her friends, she explained, opted to wear silk cami-knickers, which were all-in-one undergarments:

> ... they were fussily pretty, with a good deal of lace, and threaded with very narrow ribbon, in pink or blue, called 'baby ribbon' ... The most popular shade for *lingerie*, as we genteelly called underclothes, was pink. It might be vulgar – I seem to remember that the term was 'prostitute pink' – but we liked it.*

Garters also get a mention, 'delicious concoctions of ribbon and rosebuds and lace, sometimes with a dashing touch of feather or marabout, excitingly glimpsed when the knees were crossed'. Freda's lingerie would have belied her austere chic. Pretty, sexy underwear was slowly becoming acceptable, risqué but feminine.

When Freda first met the Prince of Wales she was the mother of two young daughters. Apparently, she was an affectionate

---

* My mother, who grew up in this era, took a snobbish view of any non-white underwear. I remember how scornful she could be if one chose to wear pastel shades – 'Well, darling, if you really *want* to look like a knicker shop in Croydon ...!'

parent, but motherhood seems not to have taken a physical toll. We don't know what dietary lengths she went to, to keep her weight just seven stone, but her figure would remain svelte. Waiflike and nubile, Freda seems to have been regarded – both by the future king and other lovers – as intensely sexy. Edward wrote saying that looking at her photograph by his bed made him feel 'naughty', while Michael Herbert declared his passion for her, 'from the crest of your permanent waves to the soles of your shoes'.

Freda Dudley Ward's image changed the public perception of femininity for white upper- and middle-class women. Her whip-thin sex appeal was exciting, complex, as audacious and modern as a cubist canvas. She was also capable, smart and liberated. Those who knew her reported that she could hold her own in a political discussion, that she was a liberal who preferred conversation to cocktails. By the end of the decade she was among those women who could vote. And yet, essentially, she was a decorative dilettante in the tradition of her class, reliant on rich men to validate her sleek beauty; reliant too on their money to perpetuate the vision – and to pay for hours of expensive maintenance, embellishment and grooming. Her loveliness had always been her calling card and, insofar as Freda is remembered, it is not for her well-documented dedication to charity work.

Freda Dudley Ward remained, all her long life, a fastidious and elegant woman; there was no let-up in the morning beauty routine she had evolved in the 1930s and she exerted herself to ensure her hair and make-up were as perfect as they had been in the days when she had charmed the future king. As her great-niece remembered, 'It was like seeing someone from a different world. She had an overwhelming innate glamour, without being ostentatious. I loved her delicacy, she was ethereal and enchanting.'

Ladies of Leisure

Freda Dudley Ward was a lady of leisure, in a time-honoured mould. During the war she had done her bit by nursing with a Voluntary Aid Detachment; after it ended she supported charitable work, as was expected of the Lady Bountiful. Playing these roles meant being *soignée*, dressing elegantly and socialising. Freda learnt the Charleston, went to nightclubs, gave dances, smoked and had high-profile extramarital affairs.

Assuming you had the financial resources, the key to being a lady of leisure was looking the part. But there was no magic formula. Diana Holman-Hunt's captivatingly comic 'growing-up' memoir, *My Grandmothers and I* (1960), unpacks the 'lady of leisure' myth. It is the story of a clever, naive, rebellious girl whose family has set her on the ideal path to privilege, dainty manners, perfect posture, scented underwear and good hair. But the past – personified by her two grandmothers, one old-school Edwardian, the other a high-minded aesthete – looms large. By both reckonings, Diana falls short of the ideal, as she painfully maps her own route to modern adulthood in the 1920s.

From her country grandmother, Mary Freeman, Diana learnt that ladies spent a lot of time at the dressmaker's, that they deadheaded flowers, knitted and attended lawn tennis parties. They wore Parma violets, *papier poudré* and Pomade Divine. Their personal maids rolled up their silk stockings, ironed their nightdresses and preserved their shoes by slipping padded red velvet hearts into the toes. Little girls learnt from a young age how to be ladies. Their hair was tortured into ringlets, bags were fastened around their fingers overnight to prevent nail-biting, and their shoulders were buckled daily into canvas harnesses designed to prevent bad posture. Diana's harness cut into her flesh. From an early age her body was painfully manipulated and groomed for her inevitable destiny: a curtsey to the king and queen, followed by marriage – and leisure. And Grandmother Freeman explained to her how debutantes maintained their posture in the Throne Room. Young girls from the gentry needed to train for this by walking backwards with a bag of beans on their heads: 'Only a knack – I could do it very well. I hope you won't grow any taller.'

Edith Holman Hunt (the eccentric widow of the celebrated Pre-Raphaelite artist William Holman Hunt) is Diana's London grandmother. Visiting her in Melbury Road, Kensington is very different. Diana describes how – at a safe distance from disapproving scrutiny – there's a moment of intense, guilty joy when she cuts up her horrible controlling body harness and throws it in the fire. But 'Grand H-H' imposes her own Victorian doctrines on the little girl: art, prayer, the life of the mind and female servility are what matter – 'It is a feminine delight to tend the helpless male. The joy I had from darning and mending Holman's clothes.' She also comes from the generation of dowagers whose old-fashioned ideas about female beauty included mouthing the words 'prunes, prudes and prisms' before entering a room, to create a pretty budding pout.* (Diana misunderstands. 'Dear child, I didn't mean you to say it *aloud*!')

In 1928 Diana is aged nearly fifteen. She has bobbed her hair and her absentee father reappears in her life to release her from boarding school, piano lessons and grooming. There's another joyful moment as she strips off her regulation scratchy combinations, though not the elastic bandeau which flattens her bust: she can't quite bring herself to go all the way.

---

* The method was described by Dickens in *Little Dorrit* (1857), where a prim teacher of manners comes in to instruct her: '"You will find it serviceable, in the formation of a demeanour, if you sometimes say to yourself in company – on entering a room, for instance – Papa, potatoes, poultry, prunes and prism."'

On their arrival at Melbury Road, Grand H-H is overjoyed – but as usual Diana's appearance is seen as inadequate. She is growing, she is toothy, her mouth is too wide and her forehead too high. Grand pronounces that the only solution is to remodel her jaw by making her chew bones and drink her Bovril from the spout of a little china teapot. Dismayed, Diana books herself in to see a dodgy dentist – 'I've got too many teeth. I should like to have some out this afternoon. No, they don't *ache*.' A few hours later she staggers home, bleeding copiously and frothing pink foam at the mouth.

With a light touch Diana Holman-Hunt's story questions the materiality and meaninglessness of the lives led by the ladies of leisure. At its centre is the reckless, dashing, defiant Diana, unwilling to be ladylike, but powerless and trapped in the controlling harness of expectations. Similarly, her memoir reminds us of the pitiable and perennial belief that beauty can be constructed – by ringlets and the singeing of split ends, by elastic bandages and dentistry, by chewing bones and drinking from a teapot.

―――――

When Diana Holman-Hunt was a little girl Margaret Haig Mackworth was already a married woman. She was born in 1883. Clever and critical, she had found it dismaying that, despite increasing emancipation, the upcoming generation of women – like Diana – was still being turned out of the same 'leisured lady' mould. Fancy hats, bridge and lawn tennis dominated their waking hours. Little seemed to have improved since her own debutante days twenty years earlier.

Margaret had always felt like a misfit, and at five feet six inches and twelve stone, she was never going to match the increasingly fashionable boyish template: 'One might as well have tried to put a carthorse into a drawing-room as turn me into a young lady.' But there was no escape. Margaret, who in the 1920s became one of Britain's foremost feminists, endured three aimless, useless years on the merry-go-round of the marriage market at the turn of the century. She was bored and loathed it. But at the time, she succumbed stoically, even when her mother insisted she compress her plump flesh into a whalebone corset: 'Oh, how I hated those great, box-like, restraining things!'

In 1908 she secured her 'eligible', and married a dull, fox-hunting landowner named Humphrey Mackworth. Humphrey was easy-going; he even seemed happy enough to let her join the suffragettes, provided he was left to his dogs and horses. But they were incompatible, and the marriage would fizzle out conveniently and amicably in 1923. These experiences of bodily and psychic oppression fed but also freed a spirit and intellect dedicated to speaking out about women's plight.

Two weeks before her wedding Margaret and nearly four hundred other women climbed aboard a train at Cardiff and travelled to London to take part in Women's Sunday – a demonstration by an estimated half a million participants who assembled to demand the vote. From then on she embraced the suffragettes' militant cause; before long she was its leading light in Wales, and within a year of marriage she dumped her corset and never wore it again. In 1910 Margaret Mackworth defied police by harassing the prime minister in his car; in 1913 she set fire to a pillar box and was arrested and jailed, but went on hunger strike and was released after five days.

Margaret was a risk-taking woman of energy and ambition. During the First World War her father, an industrialist and newspaper magnate, employed her as his 'right hand *man*' to run the family businesses, and in due course handed over to her the responsibility for over twenty companies; on his death she would inherit both his wealth and his title.* During the First World War she worked to recruit women to the war effort, while campaigning for the rights of women workers.

In 1920 Lady Rhondda (as she now was) used her money to found the feminist political and literary review *Time and Tide*, and in 1921 she set up the Six Point Group, which promoted key issues of equality for women. She was a prolific journalist and campaigner whose perspective on her generation sheds light on a slice of fast-changing twentieth-century history.

Lady Rhondda's long and provocative essay *Leisured Women*, which was published in 1928,† explores the social shift from Victorian woman to 'modern' woman. It was a commentary on the women of her own class, and on the effect of their increased freedoms since the 1870s. Victorian women had been, as she saw it, largely inward-looking, narrow-minded and focussed on the home. Under-educated, they were preoccupied by trivial health concerns, and even more by matters of personal adornment and physical beauty, which they saw as the

---

*   For a woman to inherit her father's title was, of course, unorthodox. Her father, the first Viscount Rhondda, had no male heir, and the title passed to his daughter through a 'special remainder' issued by the Crown. One of Margaret's earliest battles – which she lost – was to be allowed to take her seat in the House of Lords. Women were barred from the Lords until 1958.
†   This first appeared in the form of a series of six articles published in *Time and Tide* in 1926, under the title 'Women of the Leisured Classes'.

way to attract men sexually, and which absorbed their waking hours. The nineteenth-century woman contributed nothing to the public benefit. And even if she had tried to, she would not have been taken seriously.

Roll forward half a century and conditions for women had been transformed: they were having fewer children, they were better educated and they had increased rights and opportunities. Over the fifty-year period from the 1870s to the 1920s, the number of female university entrants had increased from thirty to fourteen thousand; the number of female doctors from just one to thirteen hundred, and the number of female teachers from near zero to 187,352. The laws had also changed in respect of property, divorce and the vote. 'In political life, in the press, in the schools, women are – if still reluctantly – being listened to, are being taken semi-seriously,' wrote Lady Rhondda.

'So far, so good,' she declared. But fundamentally, attitudes among the better-off in society had barely changed. In a passage that clearly references her own dismal experience after leaving school, she describes how nobody saw anything wrong in a girl drifting until marriage:

> She is ... taught that her duty is to potter about, to learn to do nothing ... to accept her condition as a 'kept' human being as part of doing her duty in that station of life unto which it has pleased God to call her.
> The young woman is taught, explicitly, to place a high importance on dress.

Thus, she was growing up as vain, idle, irresponsible and inward-looking as her mother and grandmothers before her;

lacking culture, confidence and a sense of her own worth. And thus 'she becomes the same kind of creature that the leisured girl of 1870 became; [she] overestimates the sexual side of life – since sex appears to be her sole *raison d'être** [and] spends half her time thinking about her clothes'.

Overall, the essay paints a depressing picture of complacent, trivial-minded, under-employed women across the country, whether unmarried or married. They led futile and meaningless lives: they trimmed hats and embroidered handkerchief cases. They did not read the newspapers or consider the plight of people poorer than themselves. These were the short-skirted, shallow, dance- and cinema-crazy flappers, irresponsible young women who idly took for granted all the rights that Lady Rhondda and her suffragette sisters had battled and suffered for. Their children were educated at boarding school and were insufficiently numerous to occupy them fully. Once married, they passed their afternoons deadheading the dahlias, or spending as much money as they could afford at the dressmaker. As she saw them, these ladies were not fully rounded citizens, they were stunted parasites. This was not how women's emancipation was supposed to look.

Yet their trickle-down influence on our national life was disproportionate. As Lady Rhondda saw it, their narcissism was corrosive, teaching the young to prioritise appearances rather than to serve the society they lived in – 'to value material

---

* To clarify, Lady Rhondda would not – in 1926 – have meant here that such young ladies were obsessed with the sex act as we understand it today; in the context of the 1920s, 'the sexual side of life' had a lesser connotation, implying ardent romancing and amorousness, in all likelihood leading to a betrothal. This generation continued to understand the phrase 'making love' in the way expressed a hundred years earlier by Jane Austen in *Emma*: 'she found her subject cut up – her hand seized – her attention demanded, and Mr Elton actually making violent love to her'.

comfort, personal adornment and social advancement, to judge people upon how they dress ... and since sex is their profession, they put an enormous emphasis on sex ... and on the importance of sexual attraction'.

Lady Rhondda's condemnation of fashion and femininity is implacable. Nevertheless, her view is a valuable insight by a leading campaign veteran on how far down the road feminism had travelled. Some of the way, certainly – but there were mountains still to climb. And, from her perspective, progress was constantly held back by dressmaker appointments and sex. Lady Rhondda felt that all she and her movement had fought and suffered for was being betrayed by her class.

The patriarchal status quo prevailed, built on deep-rooted dependence and inertia. Ingrained in the female psyche was the associated necessity of appearing fashionable and desirable: a magnetic force field – formed of feathered hats, hairstyles, lipsticks, trinkets, silk stockings, lacy suspenders and excitingly short skirts – that, as Diana Holman-Hunt found out, few seemed able or willing to dodge. The modern world had flung open the doors of opportunity to women. But it also left many of them powerless, vulnerable, and wondering what to do about their legs.

Handmaids' Tales

Leisured women had the luxury of fussing over their appearance – a luxury that in its turn depended on staff. In the first half of the twentieth century every household from the middle class upwards could afford domestic help, usually live-in. Legions of housemaids, kitchen maids, parlourmaids, cooks, laundry maids and lady's maids were the victims of a cruel beauty-irony, hard-wired into the social system. For the women at the bottom of the heap were the agents of beauty. Through their labour, the ladies they served maintained their gleaming curls, white skin, shiny shoes, elegant apparel and scented boudoirs. They were washed and dried, warmed and aired, fed and watered, tended and mended by an army of 'menials'. Even their pimples were squeezed for them. The work took its toll: the price being coarse hands, aching joints, swollen ankles and sallow skin. Prettiness in 'front-of-house' servants might be valued, but below stairs it was unachievable, irrelevant or a positive disadvantage. As for cosmetics, their use was often a sackable offence. If you were downstairs, beauty was for them, not us.

In 1920, £1 was a good weekly wage for a live-in lady's maid. Out of this she had to buy her uniform, send money to her family and pay for a trip to the picture palace on her once-a-week afternoon off. There, she might sink exhausted into her plushy seat and escape into an intoxicating world of romantic make-believe, peopled with kittenish smoky-eyed flappers swept off their feet by passionate swashbuckling heroes. And then it was back to the sink, the mangle and the ironing board, with just the memory of those jumpy, crackly images to sustain her. Domestic servants could dream on.

My Life in Service by Rosina Harrison, *Below Stairs* by Margaret Powell and Phyllis Greenhow's unpublished and untitled recollection of life in the 1920s* are three extraordinary real-life handmaids' tales: records of what it felt like to be the

---

* *Rose: My Life in Service* by Rosina Harrison was first published in 1975 and republished in 2011 as *The Lady's Maid: My Life in Service*. *Below Stairs* by Margaret Powell first appeared in 1968 and was followed by a number of sequels, including *Climbing the Stairs* and *The Treasure Upstairs*. Phyllis Greenhow's seven-page autobiographical fragment is held in the Burnett Collection of Working-Class Autobiographies at Brunel University.

woman who enabled other women to be womanly – but who was herself barred from the club.

Few working-class families could afford to prioritise their daughters' education. Rosina Harrison was sixteen when, in 1915, it was decided that she could make the grade as a lady's maid if she 'smartened herself up a bit'. That meant learning basic French and fine dressmaking, but the costs of her lessons and apprenticeship were a drain on the family budget. Phyllis Greenhow, the *sixteenth* child of a Wiltshire coal merchant, was sent into service in 1927, at the age of seventeen. Margaret Powell was the daughter of an odd-job man and a charlady, one of seven children, who won a scholarship to her local grammar school.

In 1924, after a long period in training, and in lowly positions, Rosina started her first job as a real lady's maid to Lady Cranborne, wife of the fifth Marquess of Salisbury. Her ladyship had high expectations. Rosina was required to turn her skills as a needlewoman to recreating the latest Chanel or Lanvin designs in her mistress's favourite fabric, *mousseline de soie*, and to hand-sew her underwear, copying the delicately appliquéd silk knickers that she bought on her frequent trips to Paris. It was also Rosina's job to care for all of Lady Cranborne's wardrobe, including shoes, gloves and lace. She was ranked as a superior servant, and could choose her own clothes and minimal jewellery, provided they were modest and unflashy: 'Make-up was not encouraged; indeed later I was rebuked for using lipstick. When ladies and their maids were out together there could never be any mistaking which was which.'

Hierarchies were rigidly upheld. Rosina commented on the curious confidence that connected two women, one of whom occupied her working day caring for the other's most intimate garments. And yet – 'Ladies never exposed their bodies to their maids. I never saw any of my ladies naked, except for Lady Astor, and then only when she was nearing the end of her life ... Dignity at all times and in all places was very much the order of the day.'

Phyllis Greenhow's life in service began in the late 1920s, in a large Kensington townhouse. Here she arrived from her rural village, aged seventeen, to work as lady's maid for 'an autocratic old dear'. Phyllis had to provide her own uniform: two unfashionably long navy blue dresses, plus white aprons. Tending to madame's dressing routine was a test of memory:

> I had to lay out a large clean white handkerchief on the right-hand side of her dressing table. On this, I must arrange masses of hair pins, all in their different lengths and thicknesses. I had to memorise how they went into her hair, and when she put out a hand, be ready to put the right pin into it.

Once madame was dressed, Phyllis spent the morning washing and ironing the satin 'baby ribbons', which were removed from her mistress's knickers and nighties before laundering, and threading them back in; and darning handkerchiefs. When madame returned late Phyllis had to be available to prepare her for bed by brushing out her long white hair, and arranging it in curling pins. Madame also suffered from bowel problems, and Phyllis was expected to help administer her enemas. After six weeks she was dismissed for inexperience.

Margaret Powell's early years as a kitchen maid give a different slant on the domestic story a hundred years ago. Her mother had to borrow money to kit her out with the required dresses, aprons, caps, stockings and shoes, which together cost nearly £2. Thus equipped, she started her live-in job in 1922, in the home of the Reverend Clydesdale and his wife, where the first shock was being told that every trace of her long hair must be entirely hidden from sight under her cap. The effect was utterly unflattering, and so too were the dark blue dresses: 'I thought I looked hideous. Little did I know I was going to look hideous the whole time I worked there, so really it made very little difference starting off like that.'

After a year with the Clydesdales Margaret decided to try her luck in London, and applied for a post with the Cutler family in Thurloe Square, Knightsbridge. In her memoir, Margaret explained that employers judged domestic servants on their virtue as well as their capacity for hard work. Women like Mrs Cutler were afraid that their female servants would be 'flighty', and they scrutinised applicants for signs of flightiness, such as make-up. 'If you used any, or if you had your hair waved, or if you wore coloured silk stockings ... you were flighty, and flighty girls came to bad ends.'

Margaret got the job. It was laborious and exhausting. On her fortnightly evenings off, she and the under-housemaid, Gladys, went to the cinema together. When they did, they talked boyfriends. Never, ever reveal what you do, cautioned Gladys, because men look down on skivvies. Tell them you work in a factory. The objective in every female servant's life was marriage – but Margaret, determined to escape bondage, resolved never to consider marrying anyone in service. And yet, barred as they were from lipstick, pretty hair and fashionable frocks, how were such women supposed to attract any man?

Their fantasies were nourished by fairy-tale films that portrayed broad-shouldered Latin lovers, and sensational magazines packed with film gossip. The male sex symbols of the 1920s were Rudolph Valentino, Cesar Romero, Ramon Novarro.

As Margaret remembered,

Gladys and I were avid readers of those women's magazines of the time; things like *Peg's Paper*, *The Red Circle Magazine*, and the *Red Heart*. Between their pages many a poor and lonely heroine ended up marrying some Rudolph Valentino sort of man, or a Rothschild with loads of money. Of course the girl, in spite of her upbringing, always had a lovely almond-shaped face and beautiful liquid violet eyes, and although Gladys and I hadn't got these attributes, it didn't prevent us from dreaming that we had and that one day our prince would come.

The difference between the woman of leisure and her female servant was not just madame's wealth and her maid's comparative poverty. It wasn't even about their relative social status. Built in to the relationship between mistress and maid was a denial – and an active negation – of the maid's female desires, and of her femininity. The lives of dependent live-in servants like Rosina, Phyllis and Margaret were controlled day and night. A ten o'clock curfew was normal. From the requirement to wear an unflattering uniform and the concealment of hair under caps, to the ban on male 'followers' whose attentions might compromise the morality of the household, women in domestic service were expected to be nuns, but without the spiritual compensations. There were even households where the maids were forbidden to wear artificial silk knickers, because their sexy swishing noise might give 'wrong ideas' to the male servants.

Rosina, Phyllis, Margaret and countless others started in service at an age when many adolescent girls are more preoccupied by their appearance than they will ever be again. But their employers seem to have been merciless, intentionally excluding them from the pretty clothes, the pampering, perks and accessories that come with beauty and self-adornment. Margaret Powell confessed that this rankled, above all when Susan, the daughter of the house, just two years her junior, came tripping into the kitchen. Like Margaret, Susan was tall and fair-haired – but there the resemblance ended:

> She had masses of clothes, a horse to ride, a tennis court to play on ... Everything was done for her, the under-nurse used to brush her hair, her bath was got ready, even the toothpaste used to be laid on the brush ready for her.

On such occasions, camouflaged in a hessian pinafore, her inflamed wrists submerged in hot water and congealed grease, Margaret brooded over the inequality: 'I was another young girl of about her own age ... The contrast was so marked ... And you see she never spoke to me or even noticed me.'

There were more than one million servants in Britain after the First World War. This army of women, mute and invisible, were non-participants in the march of female progress. And if even in their uniforms, scrubbed and sallow, the real beauty of some of these young women shone through, they may have wished it hadn't. At the Cutlers' in Knightsbridge, one of the lowliest servants was Agnes, the under-parlourmaid, a naturally pretty, soft-hearted, starry-eyed girl. Soon after Margaret Powell went to work there, it was discovered that Agnes was pregnant. The worldly-wise Gladys went to the chemist's and bought pills and quinine. Agnes took them, to no avail. She took hot mustard baths. She shifted heavy furniture and jumped off heights, but when her swelling stomach started to show, Mrs Cutler gave her notice to leave at the end of the week. Margaret and Gladys were powerless – but though Agnes wouldn't tell, they suspected who the father was: it was Mrs Cutler's suave, smooth-talking young nephew, who had been seen more than once on the servants' back staircase, and who was doubtless the source of Agnes's unexplained gifts of silk underwear.

As for Margaret, she rose up the servant ladder to become the household cook. But like a prisoner, she remained focussed on the day of release: 'I was determined to get married.' For these working-class women, escape from drudgery via marriage was, if anything, more of an imperative than it was for their 'betters'. But with so few courtship opportunities, an event like a dinner party was a red-letter day.

This was because the guests' chauffeurs were entertained in the servants' hall while the gentry feasted in the dining room:

> You never saw such a fluttering in the dovecote as there used to be on these occasions. There we were, six or seven of us women who hardly ever spoke to a man and whose femininity was so suppressed that we got to be like female eunuchs. We would suddenly realise that we'd got a sex, that we were real females. So noses would be powdered, hair all fripped up, and waists pulled in ... Bosoms were stuck out, and rears stuck out, so if you pulled the waist in, you looked like an hourglass ... And all because of these chauffeurs in their uniforms.

Margaret failed to land a chauffeur. However, in 1931 she escaped from service by marrying a milkman, Albert Powell. Phyllis Greenhow left domestic service after two years, became a nurse, and married. Rosina Harrison was 'partial to the boys' and got engaged. But relationships just weren't compatible with the hard work and long hours required of a lady's maid. She never married. Instead, service would be the ladder to a wider experience: she travelled the world, met the cream of international high society and, as lady's maid to Lady Astor, made herself indispensable to the doyenne of one of the first families in the land.

Fat Worry

Pints of cream and butter. Seven-course dinners. Turbot with hollandaise sauce, saddle of mutton, chocolate mousse and orange compote. From the nineteenth century, cooks like Margaret Powell were employed to serve their upper-class masters and mistresses with a suffocating superabundance of rich food: 'People weren't figure-conscious, nobody thought of dieting. They merrily consumed three-course lunches, and five- or six-course dinners every day, and "hang your figure".'

But times were changing, and this calorie-heavy diet did not help if you wanted to look like Freda Dudley Ward. By the mid-1920s the cover-up days were over. Flattering folds and concealing frills were replaced by tubular clothes, demanding tubular bodies, with legs, arms and chests on view as never before, and freedom to dance, play ping-pong or to plunge head first off a diving board. And if you no longer wished to be confined, like your mother and grandmother, to the drawing room, the new short, revealing fashions left no place to hide. The rigid infrastructure that had for decades concealed and propped up the female frame had been removed, leaving all that bulgy flesh to flop around unsupported. To compete in the marriage marketplace, the 1920s female had to confront her own uncovered body, and take steps to modify and reshape it. She couldn't just appear slim, she had to *be* slim.

The 1920s were heady times, when a new set of dreams began to seem within reach for a generation of women: dreams of political power, of public life, of professional achievement and personal affluence, of creativity, exploration and self-expression. It was time to throw out the corsets. And yet the evidence also shows that the emancipated woman was haunted, more than ever before, by bodily insecurity: nagged at relentlessly and persistently by leg-worry, arm-worry, excess-hair-worry, wrinkle-worry, old-age-worry, but, above all, fat-worry.

The 1920s released a kind of mass panic about weight loss. It is one that we have been living with ever since.

Today, terms like 'body dysmorphia' and 'negative body image' describe the dissatisfaction people (mostly women) feel when they compare their appearance to an unrealistic ideal. A hundred years ago these labels didn't exist, but the feelings certainly did, and so did the unrealistic ideals. Indeed, with magazines bearing imagery of stick-thin mannequins and boyishly flat-busted film stars, they were on the increase. The advice columns in the press tell a story of doubt and the quest for self-improvement, as a few examples demonstrate:

In less than a week three of my best friends have remarked on the increase in my weight ... I dance the Charleston ... but I am much too fat.

I am twenty-six years old, but look thirty-six. My skin is very dry, with many wrinkles round my nose ... I have plenty of black-heads ... and besides all this I am 30lbs overweight.

From what you tell me, dear, I think it would be best to slim all over. Go on the 'bread and butter' diet; it is quite simple to follow.

Even so-called bohemian or artistic milieux weren't exempt from body anxiety – if anything, scrutiny by male artists made matters worse. Nicolette Macnamara grew up in the circle surrounding the macho, womanising painter Augustus John. The backdrop to Nicolette's teenage years was Augustus's parade of stunning models – like the beautiful Kit Dunn, who would appear dressed in a bathing suit for picnics, looking slender and stylish in a '1920s' way. Augustus's daughters Poppet and Vivien were also beauty benchmarks, long-legged with fashionably perpendicular figures. Nicolette and her sister Brigit measured their looks against those of the John girls, and found themselves falling miserably short: 'I was bulging with puppy fat, and the size of my breasts embarrassed me. [I was] five feet two and a half and never grew any taller ... Brigit got fat like me and suffered tortures.' The third sister, Caitlin, was thought by all to be gorgeous: 'a joy to men and a pleasure to herself.' But even in the 'anti-fashion' environment of the artist's studio, 1920s chic prevailed. The girls hated their curves and bound them tightly with elastic, only to be betrayed when they put on swimsuits.

Augustus John's milieu professed liberty, poetry, art and rebellion. But it was skin deep. The young women in his orbit felt vetted and objectified. 'We heard the beauty of women discussed and analysed as a subject of major importance,' remembered Nicolette. Predictions were made, and judgement pronounced on each of them. Brigit's creamy, Renoir-esque qualities were thought winning, if unfashionable – she would marry a farmer, have babies and bake bread. Caitlin's sumptuous beauty and vitality would ensure she married a duke (though she actually married the penurious poet Dylan Thomas). Poppet was the outright winner, for her wonderful figure would surely win her the most coveted husband of all – the golden boy of the age. In this closed coterie of artists and poets, the topic of man-hunting seemed inexhaustible, and getting a husband young was prioritised; if you left it too late you were regarded as a withered bud. But Augustus never predicted a husband for Nicolette, who resigned herself to the prospect of a lonely life.

More typical than Nicolette is her contemporary, the teen-age schoolgirl Jean Lucey Pratt, who started out in 1925 to keep a lifetime of diaries that tell the cumulative story of a quietly adventurous spirit. One of Jean's early entries (30 April 1926), made at the age of sixteen, includes a baleful lament for her waistline: 'I wish I wasn't so fat! I've gone up 10lbs again this holiday! It's too sickening for words. Next holiday I must keep myself more in hand. I am now 10st and it simply mustn't be – at school last term I was 9st 4lbs.'*

A couple of months later (8 August) we see Jean in a mood of self-scrutiny, staring at herself in mirrors. 'I wish I was slimmer . . .' In particular she was critical of her large hips, and commented despondently about how 'well covered' she was. On the positive side, she liked her eyes, which were large and blue, and she knew that her mouth was nice. But these assets were offset by 'horrible nails', a poor complexion, and frizzy, beige hair. 'And then I wear glasses – that always puts people off a bit!' Unfortunately this was true. Jean's aunt invited her to the cinema with 'two awfully nice boys', but then unforgivably told them that her niece wore spectacles, at which they started to produce excuses.†

It was the first of many betrayals of hope, for Jean's life was to be tormented by man-disappointments. It's becoming increasingly clear that, self-critical as they are, both Nicolette Macnamara and Jean Pratt see their own appearance through

---

*   130 pounds, or 59 kilograms.
†   A generation of short-sighted girls grew up with the words of the satirist Dorothy Parker ringing in their ears: 'Men seldom make passes / At girls who wear glasses.' (Originally a short verse, published in 1926.)

men's eyes. At the age of fifteen Nicolette's squeamish shame about her body tipped into sheer panic when Augustus John remarked, 'You have interesting lines, Nicolette. I'll draw you in the morning' – which of course meant in the nude. After a sleepless night Nicolette rose at dawn and fled on the first bus back to her mother's house. The offer was never repeated.

––––––––

'The corset was internalised in the form of dieting,' writes fashion historian Valerie Steele.* And – it can be argued – its punitive aspects originated with a religious hatred of sinful gluttony, and the puritanical emphasis on self-denial. The new science of nutrition took a lead, by measuring out our lives in calorie counts. This was a time of bestselling mass market self-help guides offering to divulge the secret of body-size-management.† Cecil Webb-Johnson, a doctor and controversial dietitian, confronted this weighty matter in his short 1923 book, *Why Be Fat?*: 'There is nobody to whom the approach of fat in excess, or corpulence, terrifies so much as a woman who has the reputation of being a beauty ... The fat woman feels that her day is done.'

The overweight woman, he stressed, was 'worse' about snacking on chocolates and cakes, and also far more prone to ridicule than men: 'A fat man is a joke, and a fat woman is two jokes – one on herself and one on her husband.' And he went on to describe her 'normal' diet: a hefty breakfast of sausages, bacon, toast and marmalade; a substantial lunch with pudding;

----

* In *Fashion and Eroticism – Ideals of Feminine Beauty from the Victorian Era to the Jazz Age* (1985).
† The underlying message in many cases was a eugenicist one. As will be discussed later in this chapter, measurable physical improvement was thought to favour racial improvement. See Ina Zweiniger-Bargielowska's essay 'The Culture of the Abdomen: Obesity and Reducing in Britain, circa 1900–1939' (2005).

muffins and plum-cake for tea; and a four-course dinner. To counteract this, Webb-Johnson recommended hill-climbing, rowing and a low-carbohydrate diet.

The message was getting through, and in 1927 'Phillida', the *Daily Mirror*'s beauty reporter, wrote that 'restaurants have become used to banting women. In my favourite teashop our lot is made lighter by some quite delicious iced tea and lemon, rusks, and even cakes, made of non-fattening flour', adding that waiters were now automatically offering lemon juice dressings for salads instead of oil and vinegar. Lucky Strike cigarettes exploited women's fat-worry with an opportunistic promotion: 'Reach for a Lucky instead of a fattening sweet. Thousands are doing it – men keep healthy and fit, women retain a trim figure.'

By 1928 Americans were spending more than $80 million annually on weighing themselves, both in the local drugstore or on their bathroom scales. Americans were thinking about diet before Europe did, and they were counting calories.* Ten years earlier the doctor and journalist Dr Lulu Hunt Peters had written the first diet bestseller, *Diet and Health: With Key to the Calories*. Her simple (and still uncontroversial) message was that you could eat turbot with hollandaise sauce to your heart's content, provided the calories consumed did not exceed the calories burned. Peters adopted a chatty style, and populated her pages with comically named characters like 'Ima Gobbler' and 'Mrs Weyaton'. 'If there is anything comparable to the joy of taking in your clothes, I have not experienced it,'† she told her readers, who bought over a million copies of her book and

---

* The science of calories was understood and recognised by the late nineteenth century. The Germans led the field in the home weighing scale business. They imported the first ones to the USA in 1913. Post-war, America took over the domestic market, and by 1925 the Detecto Scale Company was claiming that their product was used by a million customers.
† The phrase has an echo of 'Nothing tastes as good as skinny feels', the mantra popularised by model Kate Moss in 2009.

made her a medical celebrity. The beauty columnist Antoinette Donnelly was another diet star. 'The national feminine cry is not Votes for Women – but Fatless Figures for Women,' she wrote in 1921, and in the same year published her bestseller *How to Reduce – New Waistlines for Old*: a chirpy volume in which she recommended a regime of celery and sour pickles that would help the inhabitants of 'Fatland' migrate to 'Slimville' –

> All aboard for the Promised Land!
> Chug! Chug! We're off!

'The new fashions [gave] a wonderful stimulus to that branch of charlatanry that involved "anti-fat" products,' wrote Dr Arthur Cramp, an American medical practitioner who made a career out of exposing frauds and quacks. In the 1920s the American market saw intense activity among commercial companies profiting by the slimming craze. Inevitably, the insecurities of young women (like Nicolette Macnamara and Jean Pratt) were seen as a golden opportunity by manufacturers of fraudulent 'anti-fat' products. 'WASH AWAY FAT AND YEARS OF AGE – with La-Mar Reducing soap – no diet or exercising. Be as slim as you wish. Acts like magic.' 'GOOD NEWS for the OVER-STOUT – Send for my FREE BOOK ... you are not required to wear rubber garments, or asked to take poisonous drugs.'

Magazines were deluged with advertisements for bogus 'reduction' cures – like Neutroid tablets that allegedly (but non-sensically) counteracted the yeasts in the gut that produced fat; in reality, their active ingredient was toxic. A weight-reduction chewing-gum sold as Silph contained harmful laxatives and was banned in 1926; while Reducine promised spuriously to slenderize the figure by dissolving fat ('Milady! If you have a single ounce of unwelcome flesh on your figure, here's good news for you').

Other advertisements began to appear for slimming gadgets: vibrating electric bands that pummelled one's flab, treadmills to burn off the calories and studded rubber rollers that were supposed to massage away the excess in just ten minutes. In 1926 the ladies of Mayfair and Fifth Avenue were being instructed in 'physical jerks', secretaries in city offices were taking up lunchtime dance classes, side-stepping and leg-shaking to slim their hips.

Celebrities had their say too of course. The film star Gloria Swanson found meals boring, and was alleged to live off black coffee and green salad – 'Why should anyone want more?' 'Dorothy' wrote to the aptly named Fay Filmer, agony aunt of *Girls' Cinema*, to ask how screen star Norma Talmadge had lost twelve pounds for her role in *Smilin' Through* (1922). But Filmer didn't know; 'I do know of a famous star, however, who is reducing by adhering to a diet consisting merely of milk and potatoes, taken separately, of course.'

When the chorus line in Cole Porter's *Wake Up and Dream* (1929), having subsisted on a diet of orange juice and cigarettes, started repeatedly fainting during rehearsals, its producer C. B. Cochran insisted the girls stoke up on cream soup and bread and cheese. But it was hard to persuade them. Cochran's star, the Austrian-born dancer Tilly Losch, had a passion for Neapolitan ice cream, and chocolate and whipped cream pastries. Losch would endlessly interrogate her friend, the writer Barbara Cartland, about the merits of various diets. Did she recommend the bread and butter diet? How was she to keep track of a diet that required her to eat protein one day and starch the next. And the banana diet? 'Every day bananas, bananas? Oh *no*! ... Oh dear, I do so like my food!'

Goldmines

Bananas, bananas? Oh, *yes*!

From 1925, the headlong rise to fame of the American-born dancer and entertainer Josephine Baker can be partly attributed to her adoption of a skirt made from bawdy bunches of fake bananas that was to become her trademark on-stage costume. That, and little else.

In Paris, the decade following the First World War was a time when artists flocked into the city. It became a bohemian merry-go-round, a mecca for 'free spirits', many of them wealthy Americans. And for a Black minority, France offered its own respite.

Josephine Baker in *La Revue Nègre* at the Folies Bergère, wearing her infamous 'banana skirt', 1926

France was a haven for African Americans like Josephine, who had grown up in the heavily segregated South: the world divided between 'whites only' and 'Blacks', with the ever-present threat of the Klan. In Paris, by contrast, you could share space with white people in bars and bistros; in the theatre, you could sit in the stalls. And yet a sinister strand of racism accompanied this tolerance. Paris, it turned out, was crazy about so-called Black culture. In 1925, the Exposition des Arts Décoratifs presented a show of African statuary which influenced a generation of artists. Jacques-Émile Blanche, Cocteau, Rouault, Picasso and Apollinaire appropriated motifs from tribal art and extolled the 'exotic' and 'natural' attributes of contrasting civilisations. Josephine played into the game: her dance in *La Revue Nègre* was perceived as African, not American – an 'animal' display in which she frenziedly jumped, writhed and emphasised her buttocks. One journalist wrote, 'Josephine Baker, our lives on the banks of the Seine were weary and depressing before you came along. In the eyes of Paris, you are the virgin forest.' Shockingly, he added: 'You bring to us a savage rejuvenation.'

Baker's lithe body and fronds of black hair licked into place against her skull made her fascinating to photographers, and her beauty encircled with clusters of yellow fruit quickly became iconic.* You could buy a doll in a banana skirt; there were Josephine cocktails, and Josephine swimsuits. Alice B. Toklas invented a banana dessert and named it Custard Josephine Baker. Though Baker was herself trying to lighten her skin – vigorously anointing herself with lemon juice – she now lent her name to Bakerskin, a lotion formulated for skin-darkening, as well as to Bakerfix, a hair pomade for lacquering

---

* Beyoncé paid tribute to Josephine Baker by wearing a similar banana skirt at Fashion Rocks in 2006. Rihanna followed suit by wearing a Josephine Baker-inspired gown to the CFDA Fashion Awards in 2014.

those kiss curls. Chic Parisiennes, influenced by her extraordinary talent and sexy jazz age electricity, slicked down their hair and tinted their skin several shades darker, allowing them to act out a version of Blackness, based on colonial fantasy, racist stereotypes and contemporary cultural allusions.

By 1927 Josephine Baker was earning more money than any entertainer in Europe. And she was muse to fashion gurus and artists. But though her popularity in Europe was unbounded, her 1930s 'homecoming' to the USA – where her reviews and reception were blindly racist – would prove disastrous. She returned to France, and became a French citizen on her marriage in 1937. 'Paris is the dance,' she said, 'and I am the dancer.'

Baker remains controversial. Her 'Danse Sauvage' can be seen as conforming to a racial stereotype. But there is another view, that sees Baker as knowingly acknowledging and celebrating her race, sexuality and exceptional, modern beauty, while also creating a new female narrative. Josephine was bisexual, and her near-naked body had a slender-hipped, crop-headed, *jolie laide* androgynous quality. In the early days in New York, there had been romances with other female performers – it's easy to imagine that women in showbusiness would find each other's company more trusting and rewarding than that of the men they encountered. Whatever the case, it appears that they turned to each other as so-called 'lady lovers'. Later, Josephine probably slept with the dancer and musician Mildred Smallwood, with the owner of Bricktop's nightclub Ada 'Bricktop' Smith, with the writer Colette – and others. She was secretive about her relationships with women, but her impulsive, liberal sexuality, and – later in life – her glittery glamour, would increasingly make her a magnet for gay audiences, who loved her transgressively camp act.

Either way, nobody has ever put Black beauty on the map with quite the panache Josephine Baker did.

'What's the name of that *petite nègre* who dances in bananas?'

Mistinguett* was jealous. Looking at the meteoric success of Josephine Baker, she saw her own star on the wane. 'One day, sex will take over,' she prophesied. For the flamboyant chanteuse had in her day been an Olympian of the Parisian stage, reigning queen of the Folies Bergère, idolised for her sexiness, grainy voice, temperamental starriness – and shapely legs. Mistinguett's moment peaked in the early years of the new century, when she had her legs insured for half a million francs, as well as claiming to be the highest paid female entertainer in the world. Legs had been Mistinguett's calling card – but Josephine Baker had so much more to reveal.

The musical theatre boom years of the 1920s created a steady stream of all-singing all-dancing showgirls whose names – Fanny Brice, Barbara Stanwyck, Marilyn Miller, Norma Shearer, Ginger Rogers – were legends in their lifetime, and whose images sold countless magazines. We are entering the age of the monetisation of mass icons.

'Too *too* divine' was the default chic term of the 1920s. Twenty years earlier, goddesses were remote mythological beings who belonged in museums, or – lightly swathed in gossamer drapery – on the canvases of Royal Academicians. But movies, photography and magazines not only democratised divinity, they also made heavenliness hugely profitable.

The Professional Beauties of the *belle époque*, as we have seen, catered to the public appetite for posh pin-ups. High-end couturiers like Lucy Duff Gordon placed beauty at the service of commerce when she realised she could sell haute couture by associating it with real-life 'goddesses'. But as it became

---

*   Mistinguett was the stage name of Jeanne Florentine Bourgeois.

more reproducible, creative fashion photography – using posed mannequins – was beginning to put fashion illustrators out of business. And beauty was becoming a consumer durable. Actor John Powers, who opened the first model agency in New York in 1923, had a down-to-earth view of his function, describing himself as a 'broker in beauty', while his models were 'commodities who must meet certain requirements'. Evelyn Gordine, the principal of the famous modelling school and agency Lucie Clayton (founded in 1928), saw her alumnae in the same light: 'A top model is an infinitely valuable commercial asset.'

In the early decades of the twentieth century, most ladies still ordered their outfits from dressmakers, but inexorably, the fashion business was growing. Over time, it would harness a relationship with celebrity models that would drive it from being a low-key, bespoke shopping experience to becoming a mass-production, billion-dollar, designer-label, corporate phenomenon.* Meanwhile, dress designers were seeking ways to sell their products. You could pay a model. Or you could persuade your own clientele – the upper-crust leisured ladies like Diana Manners or Freda Dudley Ward who bought your dresses – to be walking advertisements, photographed for the social pages as *mannequins du monde*. It worked. As the designer Madeleine Vionnet told one of these *grandes dames*, 'I know that when you go to a dinner there will be three women who see you there who will be at my door on Monday asking for the model you wore.' Then, early in the 1920s, someone in Paris had the bright idea of creating a yearly best-dressed list, and out of rivalry and exclusivity was born an insatiable demand for copycat elegance. The high society icons were born – Daisy Fellowes, Margaret Whigham, Elsie Mendl, the Duchess of Peñaranda, Eugenia Errazuriz, Millicent Rogers,

---

*   Bernard Arnault, founder, chairman and CEO of LVMH Moët Hennessy Louis Vuitton, is currently among the ten richest men in the world.

Rita de Acosta Lydig, Baba d'Erlanger, Lady Iya Abdy, Paula Gellibrand. The newspapers – like social media today – couldn't get enough of these ladies, quoting them, revealing their fashion tips and revelling in the trivia of their everyday lives.

The world was accelerating; the economy was starting to embrace new merchandise like make-up and hair products. Beauty was reaching parts that it hadn't reached before.

Below-stairs workers like Margaret Powell and her friend Gladys, and countless other young women, were spending their afternoons off in picture palaces across the land, and getting their sense of style from the goddesses of the silver screen. By 1925 there were 3,500 picture houses in Britain (in 2022 there were just 1,087!). For the low-income fashion-conscious, the 'flicks' were the equivalent of an accessible weekly catwalk show. 'At the films,' remembered Margaret, 'we too, for a while, could be as sexy as a Clara Bow, or as slinkily seductive as a Pola Negri.' 'Sex appeal' or 'It' were the voguish terms of the day, applied to screen sirens who batted their eyelashes and flaunted their half-clothed bodies with a hint of garter. For their producers, the goddesses were goldmines.

Clara Bow was the original 'It girl' of the 1920s: the most bankable star in Hollywood. According to the producer David O. Selznick, a Clara Bow film could gross $1.5 million – three times the figure any other actress could earn the studio. Clara, who had won a photographic competition for the 'Most Beautiful Girl in the World', appeared in a total of fifty-seven films (forty-six silent and eleven talkies). She exuded sex appeal (and still does), bobbed her hair and struggled with her weight. But for her and so many of the great screen goddesses, their frailties were eclipsed by their legend.

Venus was Clara Bow in flapper guise, in a satin and lace camisole and hennaed kiss-curls, her appealing eyebrows with their descending arc seeming to speak of some heart-catching vulnerability. Clara had survived an impoverished, abusive upbringing to become one of the most highly paid stars of her time – though the studio made three times what they paid her. Or she was Gloria Swanson, another lucrative star from that generation, in a beaded haute couture gown.

Beauties like this spelled pure profit for the men around them. 'You are not born glamorous. Glamour is created.' These were the words of the Polish-born make-up artist Max Factor, who launched an empire and became a millionaire through perfecting cosmetics that dealt with the unforgiving glare of film lighting.

Clara Bow, the 'It' girl, and African American actor, singer and activist Lena Horne

Under his direction Clara Bow's cute cupid-bow lips were made to appear plumper and perter –

To be an actor
See Mr Factor

He'll make your kisser look good...
Hooray for Hollywood –
Hooray for Hollywood!

Max Factor was also responsible for Gloria Swanson's intense make-up and sleek hairstyle, and Pola Negri's lustrous, smoky-eyed allure. His transformative career would encompass the screen appearances of Jean Harlow, Marlene Dietrich, Judy Garland, Greta Garbo. He was also the originator of 'Light Egyptian', a new make-up tone created for the African American singer and film star Lena Horne. When Horne, light-skinned, was cast by MGM in the film *Panama Hattie* (1942), the studio leant on her to play a Latina. When she resisted they sent in make-up artists who tried, unsuccessfully, to 'match' her to the other, darker-skinned members of the cast. It was only Max Factor's new foundation shade that was able to complement Horne's natural complexion.

The 1920s also saw a burgeoning satellite market for fan magazines. Titles like *The Girls' Cinema*, *Screenland*, *Film Fun*, *Photoplay* and *Picture Show* were sold by the thousand to movie-goers who dreamt of looking like their idols. Advertisers jumped in eagerly, using their pages to promote freckle cures, permanent waves, nose adjusters, kiss-proof lipstick, whiter teeth and endless bogus slimming products. For those who needed to economise, there were features such as how to 'Marcel your Hair Yourself at Home in 30 Minutes' and 'Dress Like a Star on an Extra's Income'.

Movies were about buying into the dream: a way to worship at the shrine, to have your own share of the stardust. If you couldn't be *It*, you could make believe. Artifice was in the ascendant, make-up was no longer disguised and a woman who appeared with her face 'in the raw' was beginning to look underdressed.

Femininity was changing. The boundaries were blurring between romance and eroticism. The intangible aura of womanliness – class, feminine virtue and delicacy – was starting to lose its appeal, as the public lapped up more palpable assets: seductive gloss, sexuality and surface glamour. Beauty was not just for princesses and P.B.s; it was within the reach of everyone: 'The little shop-girl, the typist, the middle-class girl of the big towns, the younger and the older Society woman – all, all have the one wish, to be beautiful and well groomed.'

The new freedoms invited everyone to join the party and come as your picture palace heroine, mascara'ed, rouged, glossed and powdered. Jessica Mitford sums up the fantasy and reality of screen goddess magic when she describes how, as a susceptible teenager in the 1920s, she projected her own unformed self onto the leading ladies of the day. In her dreams she was the captivating 'It' girl, Clara Bow; or the enigmatic Swedish beauty Greta Garbo.

> But then, when you catch sight of yourself in the mirror, you realize sadly that while all these people are extremely thin, you are plump and healthy; [and] that while some are exceptionally beautiful and some fascinatingly ugly, you are medium pretty.

Hollywood, the expansion of post-war possibilities for women and cosmetic technology were beginning to make daydreams seem more democratic, and more reachable. If a scruffy, low-income tomboy from Brooklyn could be transformed into an It girl, there was hope for anyone. The huge growth of the beauty market at this time demonstrated the opportunism and greed of the marketing men, in their cynical manipulation of women's insecurities ('You are all *wrong* – our cream will make you all *right*'); but it also represented a triumph of hope.* Sadly, *It* was easier said than done. Not everyone could have a hairdresser, as Clara Bow did, on call eighteen hours a day, tending the most famous red hair in America. Even for movie icons, keeping up the illusion was demanding. What seemed like liberation and opportunity was also exposure to a whole new set of pressures: to be thin, leggy, flat-chested, tanned, cute, kissable, plucked, sexy and, above all, young.

Eternal Youth

The Victorians put up a fence between youth and maturity, with the child – in her short skirts and Alice-in-Wonderland tresses – on one side, and the debutante or married lady – styled, statuesque and floor-length – on the other. This landscape started to change with the appearance of role models like fresh-faced Irene Castle and 'Blondilocks' Mary Pickford, while on the street the coquettish Edwardian flapper fashions ruffled the serenity of these monumental matrons. And yet, when those matrons looked in the mirror, did they sometimes ask themselves, were they monumental – or were they past it? It was noticed that Lady Cunard and Mrs Astor had been sneaking off to get expensive youth-enhancing treatments.

In the wake of the war, nobody wanted to look like a veteran. The 1920s reverberate to the sound of jazz bands, partying to forget. The Charleston craze demanded stamina and a spring in the step, emancipation was in the air, and couturiers like Chanel were designing for immature figures.

---

* In the United States, the number of perfume and cosmetics manufacturers doubled between 1909 and 1929, and the volume of sales increased tenfold.

The premium placed on nubile youthfulness in fashion sent more women than ever in search of ways to turn back the clock. When Diana Mitford married Bryan Guinness in 1929 it was the society wedding of the season. The bride's beauty drew universal admiration, but when her younger sisters, Jessica and Debo, visited the newlyweds at their country home, they were bewildered by Diana's new-found fixation on appearing ageless:

> She had almost given up laughing or frowning, and developed a permanent expression for all occasions not unlike that of Mona Lisa . . . She once unbent to explain to us that if you keep your face in a relaxed and beautiful expression when you are young, you are less likely to suffer the normal ravages of age.

When she got home Jessica tried out the beautiful expression. It got concerned reactions from Nanny – 'What's the matter, darling? Aren't you feeling well?'

The 'resting Mona Lisa face' approach may have worked for some, but there were those, like the American silent actress Fannie Ward, who sought other kinds of help. 'She was the first person we ever heard of who had her face lifted,' remembered Barbara Cartland. Ward, a stage actress, had defied the norms by making her film debut in 1915 at the rather late age of forty-three. In 1926 she opened her own cosmetics shop, The Fountain of Youth, in Paris, and when she died in 1952 the focus of the *New York Times*'s obituary was her tireless devotion 'to appearing perpetually young, an act that made her famous'. At the age of sixty, Ward was said to look thirty. According to the tribute, this 'peppy young flapper' was always ready with an answer to the question 'How do you look so young?'

> Sometimes it was 'proper manipulation of the muscles'; other times the use of a 'Siberian snow face mask.' Now and then she advised

mixing with young people; once she said, 'Marry a young husband,' advice that she herself followed in her second marriage ...

Her good times were subordinated to her lifelong profession of keeping young. She even stamped her pale-blue stationery with golden letters spelling 'eternal youth.'

In 1921 the American writer Gertrude Atherton was sixty-four. Since childhood she had been guided by the example of her mother, a classic Southern belle from New Orleans:

> She made a fetish of her beauty and preserved it in every way she knew how ... She went to bed every night with cold cream on her face an inch deep ... As time passed and her complexion lost its brilliancy she used a good deal of make-up ... But she resented bitterly the passing of youth.

That was the 1860s, a time before there were even beauty parlours. But the young Gertrude internalised her mother's lesson: it might not be possible to go on looking lovely for ever, but there was no harm in trying.

Meanwhile, Gertrude Atherton's talent paved her path to fame as a novelist. By 1920 she had successfully authored nearly forty books. But in her sixties a fog seemed to descend over Gertrude's previously fizzing and agile brain; she was finding it hard to write. One day her weary eye fell on a newspaper article; it described the work being done in the field of 'rejuvenation', by a brilliant Viennese practitioner named Dr Eugen Steinach. Steinach had first conducted hormonal experiments on guinea pigs; this led to further operations on humans – and the results, for both men and women, were astounding.

Apparently, wealthy European women were now flocking to Dr Steinach's Vienna clinic and booking expensive treatments. With mounting excitement Gertrude read that Dr Steinach had a disciple, Dr Harry Benjamin, who was running a practice in New York. She immediately arranged an appointment with Dr Benjamin, who explained that he planned to direct X-rays at her ovaries, stimulating them to produce the life-giving hormones that supplied women with their youthful bloom and zest.* In 1922 Gertrude's treatment began. Within six weeks she was able to report an irresistible surge of energy. 'My brain seemed sparkling with light ... I wrote steadily for four hours.'

The 'Steinach' treatment gave Gertrude the idea for her next, Faustian novel, *Black Oxen* (1923),† written at the peak of the American debate about rejuvenation. For this was the era of Serge Voronoff and his 'monkey glands',‡ a time when science was credited with the incredible and, incidentally, the moment when cosmetic surgery was beginning to take off. The plot revolved around the mystery of the beautiful Countess Zattiany who, when she makes her breathtaking appearance among the audience at a New York opening night, steals the hero's heart: Lee Clavering is mesmerised by the countess's youthful perfection. She exuded intelligence and sex appeal, and above all 'she did not look a day over twenty-eight'. But who was she? And

---

* In the early decades of the twentieth century radium was seen as a panacea. Its toxic effects were not fully recognised until 1925.

† The peculiar title derives from lines by W. B. Yeats in his verse drama *The Countess Cathleen* (1895): 'The years like Great Black Oxen tread the world / And God the herdsman goads them on behind.'

‡ Serge Voronoff was known as the 'monkey gland man'. He became conspicuously fashionable and wealthy in the 1920s through his work in grafting tissue from the testicles of monkeys into the human scrotum – allegedly prolonging life and improving eyesight, memory and sex drive. By the mid-1930s his work had been discredited.

why did she so closely resemble a young beauty who had disappeared from society three decades earlier? The secret is revealed that, of course, this was the same person. Mary Zattiany, as she herself explains, had undergone an X-ray renaissance: 'My skin, as flesh accumulated, grew taut and lines disappeared. My eyes, which had long been dull, had regained something of their old brilliancy.' The heart of the book is their love affair and Clavering's dilemma when he realises that, actually, she is sixty.

On publication *Black Oxen* immediately became number one in the bestseller list. Letters flowed in from female readers asking Gertrude whether the book was true, or just a fairy tale. Could they, too, be rejuvenated? She replied to them all. Dr Benjamin was besieged; his fame spread and he opened new clinics.

Gertrude, meanwhile, was having difficulty extricating herself from her heroine. And in 1935 she confessed to a *New York Times* journalist that she had had what she called 'reactivization' treatment: 'I have seen myself the benefits.' Photographs of Gertrude show her posed in off-the-shoulder gowns, displaying her creamy throat and arms: like her mother, she is playing the belle. But nobody would mistake her for a forty-year-old. 'Miss Atherton appeared in a black satin gown with a feather-trimmed pink satin jacket. Her nails were carmined to match her lips. She wore her straight golden hair in a pompadour.'

To the last, Gertrude Atherton resisted the ageing process. Dr Benjamin prescribed medication to stimulate her pituitary gland, and she also had some sessions with a plastic surgeon who was trialling the surgical implantation of ovarian tissue taken from sheep. Neither worked. Nevertheless most people who encountered Gertrude over the rest of her long life were struck by her vigour and mental agility.

But one person was scathing. This was the celebrated photographer Edward Weston, who in November 1928 came to shoot portraits of her, expecting to meet a charismatic tigress. Weston described the sight that met his eyes; Gertrude appeared as 'a watery, washed up, squat scrubwoman, bursting out of her bespangled evening gown ... Of course she has had her face lifted, tried gland rejuvenation, and I'm sure wants to simulate fifty. This lying about one's age nauseates ... such people only fool themselves.'

In 1948, a few months before she died, aged ninety, Gertrude Atherton wrote to Dr Benjamin – 'I take your hormones regularly as directed.'

———

W. B. Yeats wrote his poetic series *A Woman Young and Old* between 1926 and 1929. The first stanza portrays a contemporary fantasy:

> If I make the lashes dark
> And the eyes more bright
> And the lips more scarlet,
> Or ask if all be right
> From mirror after mirror,
> No vanity's displayed:
> I'm looking for the face I had
> Before the world was made.

But trying to control or stave off the advance of time was, of course, a no-win predicament. Middle-aged women, for example, were no longer seen as over the hill – but they were expected to do everything possible to head off their wrinkles, whereupon people like Edward Weston condemned them: 'mutton dressed as lamb'. Women 'of a certain age' were damned if they submitted to anno domini, but equally damned if they tried to look younger – like Gertrude Atherton helplessly trying to be a Southern belle.

The 1920s was a time of agonising about what was acceptable. The older generation still saw make-up as morally deceptive and the sign of a scarlet woman – like Barbara Cartland's aunts, who tut-tutted at the sight of their niece, powdered and rouged, seemingly walking blindfold into sin. She was 'improper' because she 'painted', they told her. And the devoutly Christian Lady Frances Balfour, presenting her case at a debate held at the London School of Economics in 1924, was even more disapproving:

> The young woman of to-day does everything she can to imitate the courtesan. Her face is a mass of powder. Her red lips are gashed out of human resemblance. The stinking reek of her which comes up as she passes makes me long for a breath of God off the heather!

Lady Violet Greville was another Victorian in mourning for the past: 'The truly natural woman who has abjured cosmetics and paint will endure far longer.' But Lady Violet and Lady Frances were elderly dowagers; such views were passé, and like it or not pillar-box-red lipstick was the new normal.

But shame and scandal still attached to the deployment of other 'unnatural' beautification procedures – like plastic surgery – and few women owned up to it. Could it really be true that the goddess-like Lady Diana Cooper (now aged thirty-four) had had 'a five-angle face-lift', asked the weekly columnist of the *Sphere* in April 1926. How sadly destructive of our illusions. And who was the *Sunday Post* referring to in 1927, when it whispered that 'a famous beauty' who had just undergone 'stringent facial operations, including a "face lift"' was afraid to leave her Mayfair address for fear of meeting an acquaintance? – the blinds being pulled down to make people believe she was not at home.

An almost childish desire to preserve the magic was accompanied by a punitive and puritanical attitude to the follies of wealthy and privileged women. Facelifts were reputed to take twenty years off a woman's age, but they cost upwards of 100 guineas. As one journalist spluttered disapprovingly in his 'Home Notes' column: 'Plenty of fresh air and exercise, plain simple living, and early hours will work far greater miracles than operations for "face lifting".'

But the roll-out of plastic surgery was unstoppable. The surgeon Adalbert Bettman of Portland, Oregon, was triumphant when one of his facelift patients bounded straight off the operating table, fit as a flea: '[She] proceeded immediately to a local department store, where she purchased a new hat suitable to her now youthful appearance, certainly an amusement not indulged in when one is in pain.' In 1920 a forty-nine-year-old Parisian woman travelled to New York for a top-notch American facelift. '[She] has recovered the beauty she had when she was 25,' wrote the *New York Times*'s reporter. 'No wrinkles mar her face, and the contours of her features are as round as twenty years ago. The disadvantage is that she must suppress her sense of humor and emotions, and refrain from smiles, frowns and crying.' Madame X was delighted, however: 'I'm just crazy with joy about it all. But I daren't smile. That would start the wrinkles all over again! I would never have needed an operation if I hadn't gone around laughing and crying over nothing all my life.' The message was clear: be like Mona Lisa, poised and passionless.

It was a two-way traffic. The French surgeon Raymond Passot, who had worked repairing the broken faces of First World War soldiers and now made a good living ironing out the wrinkles of rich Parisiennes, commented on his experience of 1920s plastic surgery tourism:

> Foreigners react according to the temperament of their race: the American, determined, energetic, wilful, climbs the 'table' in a playful mood. Very demanding, she wants a cocktail before, a cocktail after the operation, both of which are possible, and even a cocktail during the operation, which is a ticklish position. She wants a phonograph playing a jazz tune, so that she won't have to think about what is going on.

But more often, cosmetic surgery got a bad press. And it was never worse than in 1928, during the infamous Dujarier case.

Dr Charles Dujarier was a Paris-based surgeon; he had written a classic treatise on the anatomy of the limbs, and was considered to be top in this specialty. In February 1928 he was approached by a pretty young woman named Suzanne Geoffre who had formerly worked as a mannequin for the designer Paul Poiret, but who was now planning to launch her own label. She was engaged to be married, and life was full of promise. Only one shadow darkened Mlle Geoffre's future. Her fiancé loved slender legs, and hers were too fat. She came to Dujarier and begged him to make them thinner, crying 'I will kill myself if I have to keep my fat calves!'

Dujarier was not a cosmetic surgeon; nevertheless he agreed to operate. But he didn't know what he was doing. In the course of the procedure he removed muscle as well as fat, and took away too much skin, so that the wound could not be closed. The limb had to be trussed tightly – 'like a sausage'. Over the next three weeks the flesh on Mlle Geoffre's leg started to turn grey and mortify. It was gangrene, and on 20 March Dr Dujarier told the patient that she had to choose between dying and losing her leg. The distraught Geoffre was at first unpersuadable, and only submitted to the inevitable when her fiancé agreed to a bedside marriage. This was performed, and the following morning her leg was amputated.

As soon as she had recovered sufficiently the couple took Dr Dujarier to court. The lawyer for Madame Le Guen (as she now was) needed to show that his client was a frivolous woman, but one who had acted in earnest in her choice of surgeon: and he proceeded to argue that cosmetic surgery was evidence of 'a woman or a man's vanity, their desire to follow a trend'. The risky tactic paid off, and a year after these dreadful events the Tribunal de Paris awarded the Le Guens 200,000 francs in damages.

But the court's ruling was not just an indictment of the surgeon. The ruling drew a distinction between 'necessary ... beneficial' surgical interventions and an operation carried out solely with the aesthetic aim of correcting a part of the body seen as imperfect. As such it was also an indictment of cosmetic surgery conducted for beauty purposes, and following the Dujarier case the Paris courts issued a ban (short-lived) on such procedures.

Much debate ensued in French medical circles about the legitimacy or otherwise of *la chirurgie esthetique*. But the pioneering plastic surgeon Dr Suzanne Noël (see Chapter 3) had little to contribute. For one thing, she spent much of this period in America, and for another, she had already had her say in a monograph on the subject, published in 1926. Suzanne was a confirmed feminist whose views were coloured by her personal experience; at the age of fifty, with her practice now established and with an international reputation, she had no doubts about the benefits of her branch of the medical profession. And as proof she provided case histories – like this one, about a forty-six-year-old woman I will call Madame Moulin.

Madame Moulin had been a comfortably off lady of leisure; she had done what society expected of her, but her husband ran into debt and abandoned her and their child. She had no skills, but eventually secured a job in a restaurant. After working there for a year her manager called her in, told her she was looking tired and stale, and sent her on indefinite unpaid leave. Today this would be described as ageist constructive dismissal, for it was clear she would not be asked to return.

A friend took the distressed Madame Moulin to see Suzanne Noël.

The following day I performed the first of her operations. I operated rather low, in front of the earlobe, to tighten the lower part of her face. Afterwards, [Madame Moulin] could not believe her eyes, as so much had been done. She left for vacation, confident in the future ... Upon her return, I operated at the base of her hairline in order to raise the nasal labial folds, whose sagging had given her a sad and tired look. The same day of the operation she saw her manager; her operation was bandaged and hidden by her hair and under her hat. Their amazement was obvious and [Madame Moulin's] happiness was immense when her manager said to her, 'The vacation has suited you very well, you look like the picture of health ... when will you be returning?' She came imme-diately to tell me the good news and embracing my hands, and crying, she said, 'I hold the hands that took ten years off my age.'

This was a world in which the economic odds were stacked against the wrinkly, the faded and the female, especially those in public-facing jobs. Another of Suzanne's case histories tells the story of sixty-year-old 'Madame Vidal'. Madame Vidal, an erstwhile beauty, came to Suzanne in despair, having been fired by her employer at a small luxury goods company, due to her fading looks. She had put in countless job applications, only to be told 'We'll let you know'. She never heard back.

I agreed to undertake the rejuvenation of her appearance ... I dis-covered how desperately she needed my immediate help on the day I removed her stitches. [Madame Vidal] fainted and admitted that she had not eaten for 48 hours! I served her lunch and encouraged her all I could. The next day she was able to find work ...

I have operated on her three times in two months. Since then, she is able to make a living as easily as she had in the past 15 years ... I still frequently see her, and she has gained an extraor-dinarily young demeanour, and a feeling of security in having taken on life's difficulties. This is truly the best compensation any surgeon could receive.

Suzanne Noël knew what it was like to suffer poverty, hardship and sex discrimination. 'One must remember that,

in 1924, women had no political rights, no personal freedom whatsoever,' she would recall many years later. Most
of Suzanne's patients were in their forties. Once she was
off the table, the patient was invited to re-style her hair;
and there was tea and cake. Suzanne would often perform
operations unpaid, and she tried to protect her patients from
post-operative shame.

For her, the fact that – in a discriminatory society – older
and uglier women were financially disadvantaged was sufficient
motive, but she was also strongly influenced by psychological
considerations, and compassion. 'Those who are operated on
always benefit from the intervention,' she wrote. Suzanne's passion for justice made her a believer in women's right to beauty,
and she was indignant at the prejudice they encountered when
they confessed to their yearning to stay young: 'It is the same
as with our right to vote. Nowhere did women meet with such
headstrong resistance.' She knew that appearance was not just
about vanity, it was about money, status, dignity and the power
balance in an unjust world, and she owned the skills that could
help compensate for ingrained discrimination.

For Suzanne Noël facelifts were the reinstatement of the
power balance between the sexes, and of gender equality.
Facelifts *were* feminism.

Winning the Beauty Race

And feminism was going to need all the resolve and staying
power it could muster, in the face of a sexism increasingly
manifest across modern society. More and more, as women
stepped outside the confines of home, the superficialities of their
appearance were displayed under a harsh spotlight.

America was the driving force. The competitive beauty parades started by circus entrepreneurs like P. T. Barnum were starting to gain traction, and as early as 1903 the bodybuilder Bernarr Adolphus Macfadden* from Missouri had promoted an international contest where entrants competed to win £200 each for being 'the most perfectly developed man and most beautifully proportioned woman on Earth'. The British final took place in November that year, with five women (*and* five men) displaying themselves, mounted on green baize-covered ginger-beer boxes on the stage of Leeds Town Hall in front of an audience two thousand strong. Though the contest was gender-inclusive, the Leeds organiser commented that 'the ladies were the principal attraction'. Tape measures were wielded, and judgement took place. The winner, twenty-year-old Miss Annie Oxley from Sheffield, wore a vaguely classical robe with a sash, and her precise measurements were duly recorded: 'Height, 5ft 4¼ in., weight 126 lb., neck 12½ in., biceps (flexed) 10⅝ in., forearm, 9½ in., calf 14 in., bust 36½ in., and waist 26 in.' Annie attributed her fine figure to her love of exercise, and recommended walking, swimming and jumping, as well as the use of the chest expander, a combination which had caused her to gain an inch round the chest and three inches on her hips. Early in 1904 Annie was sent to New York to participate in the final of the international competition, where she came fourth.

By the 1920s beauty competitions were an entrenched feature of public hype. The *Chicago Daily Tribune* sponsored a weight-loss competition in 1920. In 1921 a consortium of businesses and newspapers sponsored the first Miss America pageant, held in Atlantic City, New Jersey and watched on the Boardwalk by a hundred thousand spectators. The judges awarded points

---

* Macfadden apparently changed his name from Bernard to Bernarr because he thought it sounded more manly and ferocious, like a roaring lion!

for each physical feature, and the Miss America title was won by sixteen-year-old Margaret Gorman, wearing a sea-green chiffon and sequinned dress, who took home a trophy for 'The Most Beautiful Bathing Girl in America'.

African American women and anyone over the age of twenty-four were excluded from beauty pageants. In Britain a high-minded approach was taken by the organisers of a 1924 competition to find the 'Modern Venus' – a woman whose body measurements matched those of the Venus de Milo in the Louvre. There were thousands of entries. Time for more tape measures. The winner, Miss Stella Pierres, told the *Daily Sketch* that she had moulded her body to the sculpture's statistics by playing hockey and swimming.

Newspapers increased circulation by mounting beauty free-for-alls with big money prizes. Over the summer months of 1928 the *Sunday Mirror* invited entrants to send in beach photographs for readers to judge their '£2,000 Bathing Beauty Contest'. The newspaper ran full-page photo features of blithe belles in bathing suits frolicking on the sand – like Miss Bobbie Dawson of St Leonards perched on a rock playing a banjo, or Miss Iris Greenwood of Wimbledon provocatively twirling a parasol.

The Pathé News archive contains striking footage of one of the early beauty contests. The Beauties of Brighton, aka 'Dainty Dimpled Damsels', was staged on the seafront in 1929, a spectacle in which a crocodile of local belles was filmed parading on the seafront in their best dresses, in front of an audience of men in suits: the judges. Some of these are shown having a feel of the competitors' silk-clad calves as they sit laughing and smiling, cross-legged above the promenade.

It seemed like good clean fun. But in reality, the name of the game was objectification. A twentieth-century Venus was evaluated differently from her mother or grandmother who grew up in the Victorian era. Nineteenth-century loveliness had been suffused with a sacred aura:

> Her beauty was a godly grace;
> The mystery of loveliness,
> Which made an altar of her face ...*

Beauty in the Victorian era was loaded with moral freight. The patriarchy, preachers, pundits and beauty advisers recognised white hands, carefully coiffed hair and innocent cornflower blue eyes as signs of truth, purity, virtue, Christian conduct and social status. Externals – even the shape of one's skull, as the adherents of phrenology believed – were seen as indicators of such inner character traits as sublimity, benevolence and conjugality (small wonder that this habitual mindset also confirmed a bias against perceived 'difference', for example that darker skin signified inferiority).

Thirty years later, the modern Venuses and the Dainty Dimpled Damsels lining up to be measured, were doing something new by removing their concealing garments in public and allowing themselves to be pawed by the judges. The sacredness had gone. Instead, they were like merchandise in a window display, waiting to be purchased. The beauty contest mentality seemed to be entering the gender transaction. Robert Roberts, who grew up in 1920s Salford, remembered men taking their pick in the dance hall, as though it were a shop: 'Generally, men lined one side of the hall, women the other. A male made

---

* From Coventry Patmore, *The Angel in the House.*

his choice, crossed over, took a girl with the minimum of ceremony from in among and slid into rhythm.'

The marketplace mindset was becoming rooted in society, at a time when the 'science' of eugenics was also gaining widespread acceptance. In the first decades of the twentieth century, eugenics, first explained by Francis Galton (see Chapter 2) was popularised by a number of well-known exponents, including Marie Stopes, H. G. Wells, George Bernard Shaw and Winston Churchill, who believed that selective breeding could eradicate undesirable human traits, and bring about a fitter, purer, more beautiful race. Thus, more attractive people should be encouraged to reproduce.

Great efforts were made to confer credibility on the eugenic theory. For example, Miss Carrie Gilmore examined the records of the Southwestern State Normal School of Pennsylvania (not far from Pittsburgh) and enlisted a group of 'disinterested judges' to grade, retrospectively, the facial appearance of the girls in the class of 1902 and give them marks out of 100. The results were then related to their life outcomes. Had the prettiest ones married? It turned out that, yes, they had. And among the less pretty, fewer had found a life partner.

Albert Edward Wiggam was another indefatigable eugenicist, who started his quest to get to the heart of beauty by visiting as many art galleries as possible. Having done so, he decided that the ideal of ancient Greek faces and physiques transcended all others; it followed that they were superior. Wiggam then set out to establish that ugly people were inferior. He stationed himself at the Port of New York, where immigrants were processed as they entered the United States:

Examine these women as they are unloaded at Ellis Island. I have
studied thousands of them ... Scarcely one in hundreds would be
called beautiful. They are broad-hipped, short, stout-legged with
big feet; broad-backed, flat-chested with necks like a prize fighter
and with faces expressionless and devoid of beauty.

For Wiggam, the implications were clear. A tidal wave of
stout-legged women was entering the country, and having
three babies for every one produced by the 'beautiful women
of the old American stocks'. America would be infiltrated
by 'the lackadaisical, the thriftless and the ne'er-do-wells'.
Eugenicists like Albert Wiggam took the view that beauty was
a signifier of moral worth, and he noted that attractiveness
always seemed allied to human excellence. 'Good-looking
people are better morally, on the average, than ugly people.'
In this, the eugenicists were like the Victorians. Both
admired the alleged Christian virtues of a white woman with
a straight nose, and that special daintiness that comes from
an indoor life spent pouring tea into porcelain teacups. Both
were fundamentally patriarchal. But they differed in that
the eugenicists stressed a utilitarian/political view of human
beauty. Wiggam wrote with urgency about heredity, and
the need to educate handsome young men to marry beautiful wives, thereby breeding beautiful children and infusing
society with nobility and virtue. Beauty contests, bonny
baby shows and fitter family competitions all chimed with
his view of society. By extension, the eugenics movement
believed that inferior, ugly, deformed or insane people should
be discouraged or prevented from reproducing. Above all,
beautiful women had a responsibility to build a great race:
'This improvement of life, the perfecting of the babe at her
breast, is woman's supreme duty ... At last her new freedom

has given her the opportunity to make *her natural passion her political platform.*'

Looking good was already a question of identity and economic survival for many women, involving effort and expenditure. Now it was also seen by some as a stern national duty, with an expectation of bringing up generations of Grecian-nosed, fair-skinned, superior children: a master race.*

––––––––––

The eugenics movement was hugely popular, and few doubts about it were raised until the 1930s. But under the onward march of twentieth-century thought, the 'beauty burden' was reconfiguring.

In his study *Beauty in History* (1988) the academic Arthur Marwick explains the change from a traditional evaluation of beauty to a 'modern' notion. To summarise: the Victorians tended to see people who possessed beauty as being also the possessors of righteousness. Being beautiful denoted being good. By extension, an ugly person might be assumed to be evil and corrupt. As the twentieth century advanced, the idea of beauty was stripped of its moral and spiritual content. People continued to be judged by their looks. But beauty was becoming an autonomous characteristic. Though it comes with essential baggage, beauty is a stand-alone physical attribute. And what is that baggage? In the modern era we tend to regard beautiful people as owning sex appeal

––––––––––

* This was national policy in Nazi Germany. Many people with congenital disabilities were sterilised, or euthanised. Huge numbers of women died from complications associated with surgery. In the USA between 1907 and 1939 more than thirty thousand people were sterilised under eugenic programmes, without their consent. Today, advances in genetic coding and engineering mean that the ethical debate has far from elapsed.

and success. Marwick's explanation shows how autonomous beauty has been pushed up the aspirational agenda to the unsustainable height it has now scaled, from which beauty imagery dominates us on all sides, and at all times. We'd have to be blind to ignore the blitz of beauty on our screens and billboards.

In the 1920s that imagery could not dominate as it can today. Many white, middle-class women still spent a large portion of their time in the home, with their porcelain teacups. Many of those homes still had no electric light. Large-scale urbanisation was still in the future and international travel was for a tiny elite. The quality of photographic reproduction was inferior, and colour printing was embryonic. Film screens had introduced the black-and-white close-up, but talking cinema and Technicolor would not go mainstream till the 1930s. There was no television or digital media.

In the 1920s the impact of modernisation on women's self-image had barely begun.

Prunella Stack, aged about twenty. An illustration
from her memoir *Movement is Life*, 1973

5

Modern Girls

Prunella

Twenty years old, with a typically English beauty of golden curls, wild-rose complexion and clear, grey-blue eyes, she is physical perfection from her head to her toes.

Prunella Stack was born in India, just before war was declared in August 1914. Her father, a captain in the Gurkha Rifles, returned promptly to fight in France; his wife Mollie set sail for Plymouth with their baby daughter. But by the time they arrived, Captain Stack had been numbered among the early statistics of the slaughter on the Western Front. Mollie, the young widow, had to rethink her future.

She wiped away her tears and proceeded to do so with energy and vision. When Mollie Stack started teaching exercise classes in the 1920s, she introduced a messianic message: 'My dream is a world where the women are so beautiful that they are an inspiration rather than a temptation.' Her bold concept was to take sex out of the beauty transaction, and she saw her daughter Prunella as perfect raw material for this vision – one which she promoted with determination. In 1928 she persuaded *The Times* to publish a photograph of Prunella wielding a discus; this was followed by a series of articles in the *Daily Express*, headed 'How I Train My Daughter' – 'Prunella is one hundred percent alive. She is fourteen years old ... Our goal is the body beautiful' – and Mollie went on to describe mother and daughter's morning routine. It was a spartan discipline: they both sprang out of bed at 6:45, plunged their faces in cold water, disinfected their mouths, opened the windows and exercised for half an hour to gramophone music, then took a cold bath and went for a run with the dog, followed at 8:45 by a nutritious breakfast. Prunella swam, rode, climbed trees, dived, surfed and practised Greek dancing. 'I suffered the usual emotional upsets of adolescence,' she recalled many years later, '[but] worry about a podgy figure was not one of them.'

In March 1930 Mollie Stack launched the Women's League of Health and Beauty. In mid-June that year she arranged displays of dancing and exercise in Hyde Park and at the Royal Albert Hall:

> The arena ... was filled last night by 300 young women who were swinging their graceful bodies to the tune of 'Little Brown Jug', and who afterwards walked round and round with a free and easy stride, singing 'Tipperary'. They wore white sleeveless blouses, short black knickers, and neither shoes nor stockings ...

reported the *Sunday Times*, acknowledging, in its reference to those scanty garments, how far women's release had come. By 1934 the League had over thirty thousand members. Membership was 2s 6d, and every session cost sixpence. This brought it within the range of working women.

From the outset, Prunella was the poster girl for the League; at the age of nineteen she featured in the *Daily Mail* as 'the most physically perfect girl in the world'. But in 1935 the indomitable

Mollie died of cancer at the age of fifty, and Prunella found herself – at twenty-one – fronting a rapidly growing, women-only organisation with more than 130,000 members.

Only twenty years earlier the no-legs woman had been the norm. Now, the conventions have been deftly upended – for nothing could look less indecent than the smiling ranks of 'health and beauty' ladies in their black knickers. Breezes caress their skin, and sunshine warms it. Limbs are released from their prisons, freed to swing, to curve, to windmill, bend and extend. 'Movement is life' had been Mollie Stack's declaration. In minimal blouses and satin pants, the League women's bodies were astonishingly visible, yet unequivocally virtuous. And in Prunella they had a beautiful role model to aspire to.

In 1930 an exposed female was still a novelty. The League offered safety in numbers to a woman who wanted to divest herself of superfluous garments, and hop, leap, kick, dance and shimmy, unconstrained and in public. But in fact there was nothing unconstrained about it. Film footage of the massed ranks of members demonstrating their routines in the arena at Wembley shows a perfectly drilled and synchronised spectacle; to the accompaniment of a brass band playing the tune of 'Jeepers, Creepers', five thousand seemingly identical, slim-hipped, white-skinned and small-waisted women in uniform lie on the grass doing rhythmically choreographed leg extensions and tummy crunches, then precision push-ups. The effect is mechanical. The band plays 'Land of Hope and Glory' as five thousand flaming lanterns are simultaneously raised in the air. 'The lights shine out on the perfection of British womanhood,' proclaims the commentator. 'To *them* belongs the future!'

Physical flawlessness belonged with the concept of a winning nation. This was the time when the Bund Deutscher Mädel in der Hitler-Jugend (the League of German Girls in the Hitler Youth) was in the ascendancy in the Third Reich. The philosophy of the Women's League was also eugenicist, being founded on the notion of 'racial health'; but unlike the German version, membership was never compulsory.

Probably a fairer comparison would be with the cinematic chorus lines choreographed by Hollywood dance director Busby Berkeley: human kaleidoscopes created by the unwavering geometry of dozens of perfectly depilated female legs, smooth white arms and plumed headdresses. Berkeley's specialty was directing commodified showgirls: anonymous ranks of female beauty, so robotic, artificial and depersonalised that they weren't even sexy.

In *Dames*, Busby Berkeley created complex geometrical tableaux using interchangeable female bodies

Prunella herself was not immune to Hollywood, and confessed to being a fan of the tap dance stars Fred Astaire and Ginger Rogers. But she was careful to control the League's image. In an essay on the Women's League of Health and Beauty, the historian Jill Julius Matthews has written:

> Through an ethic of desexualised fun, the League was able to appropriate to itself some of the glamour of the increasingly popular world of film, while at the same time maintaining, or rather, creating a new standard of respectable femininity for modern business girls and young housewives.

By the 1930s the milky-skinned, demure princess ideal was looking passé, likewise the mother/Madonna. Modern princesses climbed rocks, skied, swam lengths and touched their toes twenty times before breakfast. Modern Madonnas were lean and svelte from top to toe. Mollie Stack proudly claimed that she had given birth quickly and painlessly, and speedily regained her figure. 'The modern girl no longer regards wife-and-motherhood as her only career,' she wrote.

Today, the idea that the body can be reshaped and beautified if only we can train it into submission is a familiar one. Prunella Stack's fresh-faced, gleaming, girl-next-door loveliness belongs to a different era from ours, but was the result of the same willingness to submit to a strict diet and exercise discipline: her regime was cold baths, cartwheels, twenty-mile hikes and always leaving the table a little hungry, though without being self-denying: 'I have drunk what I chose and enjoyed my cigarettes.'

Out on the parade ground, with Prunella's army of smiling, semi-undressed athletes, there was no room for spare pounds or ounces. Bosomy, billowy ladies who enjoyed a cream tea were left on the sidelines, to be replaced by a new ideal of victoriously healthy beauty. And anyone who doubted the potential of that ideal to bring about happy endings had only to look at Prunella Stack.

'It's a marriage made in heaven,' declared the plummy voice of Pathé's reporter. On 15 October 1938 Prunella walked up the aisle of Glasgow Cathedral to join her bridegroom, Lord David Douglas-Hamilton, a clean-cut, outdoorsy boxer, mountaineer, pilot and the youngest son of the Duke of Hamilton. Outside on the street a crowd of thousands (mostly women) was held back by police as they jostled to catch sight of the radiantly smiling bride in parchment velvet and lilies-of-the-valley. It was a potent moment, a mix of romance and patriotism. 'She is one of Britain's most photographed girls ... And now – these two are married, the acknowledged leaders of a new and fitter Britain!'

———

Prunella chose the ecstatic photograph of herself on tiptoe, reaching for the stars, to illustrate her memoir, *Movement is Life* (1973). It was probably taken around 1934, the year before Mollie died, when she was barely twenty. Undressing the image of a woman who is already almost entirely undressed may seem superfluous. But Prunella's choice of leotard requires a comment. Satiny and cut to fit, its puckered side seam catches the light with a compelling gleam. It's unmistakably 'for best'; something about it seems to have originated in a movie-star wardrobe, as if she couldn't resist a hint of forbidden allure. 'Nothing more exquisite could be imagined than her beauty and her glamour,' effused one journalist, 'beyond the dreams of Hollywood.'

And it's also worth noting the modesty of the design around the hips. Like a 1930s bathing dress, this garment hugs the upper thighs, and it embraces but skims over the pubic area ('inspiration not temptation ...'). The emphasis is on youth. Taut and springy, Prunella's body doesn't need any buttressing; the extended, thrown-back pose, and the entire absence of excess fat streamlines what little there is of bosom into an overall graceful linearity. It's an image which strives to banish sexual overtones. Few, I guess, would make it their back-of-the-locker-door pin-up of choice and much about the picture – devoid of any suggestive background – is intangibly but palpably virginal. This portrait of Prunella works hard to encode a message of immaculate sublimity: a modern, sexless, healthy, smoothly hairless, pre-pubescent 'angel' perhaps? And yet – it's hard to look at the arched torso, flung-back head, closed eyes and outstretched arms, and not associate it with a moment of overwhelming erotic abandon.

Prunella liked to look spontaneous. For David Douglas-Hamilton her unembellished glow was part of the attraction. At their first meeting he glanced at her fingernails while shaking her hand, and remarked, 'I'm glad you don't paint them. I hate artificiality.' 'Her lovely complexion is free from the usual cosmetics,' observed one interviewer. The photographer, however, hasn't left beauty to chance. Artfully lit and modelled, this picture of Prunella's body appears touched up, and her face may also have had some cosmetic assistance – a little mascara maybe? And she surely had a Gillette Milady in her bathroom, in order to achieve those shimmering calves.

Prunella Stack would die in 2010, aged ninety-six. Towards the end of her memoir Prunella included another photograph, of herself and her small grandchild playing together in the garden. She is still dressed in the League's black knickers and white top, arms raised, leaping above a daisy-strewn lawn. Her muscles are almost as tight, her waist as small and her stomach as flat as they had been forty years earlier. Looking this leggy and lissom at nearly sixty takes dedication; and a lifetime's commitment to the cause of health, beauty and slimness.

Prunella with her granddaughter Saba, c. 1970s

'Youth is glorious,' wrote Mollie Stack: 'In her heart-of-hearts, this slim-through-look is instinctively and quite rightly desired by every normal woman.' But was it normal to spend a lifetime holding maturity at bay? Was it normal to resist the slackening of muscles, the thickening of contours, and to determine a woman's value primarily by her youthful appearance? Through the League, through their life's work, Mollie and Prunella Stack set the beauty bar higher than it had ever been set before. It's still rising.

Exposure

In 1924, Rebecca West wrote: 'I am an old-fashioned feminist ... When those of our army whose voices are inclined to tell us that the day of sex-antagonism is over and henceforth we have only to advance hand in hand with the male, I do not believe it.' Her scepticism was justified.

With pay far from equal, the imposition of a marriage bar in many professional sectors, and power still firmly in the male camp, there were many battles still to be fought, and there was an explosion of lobbying groups who all worked to support women's equality.* In the 1930s more women were competing in athletics events, including the Olympics. In 1934 English women cricketers travelled to Brisbane where they beat their Australian counterparts in the first women's Test match, and from 1930 the Serpentine in London had been opened to mixed bathing. The Women's League of

---

* For example, the Six Point Group, set up by Lady Rhondda in 1921 to promote key issues of equality for women; the Open Door Council, established 1926, which campaigned for the removal of legislation that restricted women working in industries such as mining; the National Women Citizen's Association, founded in 1917, to encourage women to engage socially and politically; the Soroptimist movement, an international support network for professional women started in America in 1921; St Joan's Social and Political Alliance – a Catholic organisation named after Joan of Arc – which from 1918 promoted political representation and social and economic equality for women; the National Spinsters Pensions Association, founded in 1935 to reduce the age of pension eligibility for unmarried women; the British Federation of Business and Professional Women, a campaigning body set up in 1933 to gain equal rights, pay and compensation for women in the workplace; and the Electrical Association for Women, a feminist and educational body started in 1924 by Caroline Haslett, who saw electricity in the home as offering extraordinary potential for liberating women from domesticity.

Health and Beauty had a high level of public visibility.

Women's bodies were on display, with onlookers positively invited to enjoy the unfamiliar spectacle of an abundance of toned female flesh. But as the doors of opportunity swung open, a cage descended. Physical freedom came with strings attached. Women were placed on view to perform, to be admired, criticised and judged.

In the last year of his life the pioneer sexual psychologist Havelock Ellis (d. 1939) reflected on what he saw as a new freedom: 'I cannot see now a girl walking along the street with her free air, her unswathed limbs, her gay and scanty raiment, without being conscious of a thrill of joy in the presence of a symbol of life that in my youth was unknown.' But others were enraged by the sight of a woman's limbs – especially if they were swathed in trousers.

During the First World War the wearing of trousers by women had been tolerated and even encouraged, because it had practical value. In the post-war period, trouser-wearing evolved in tandem with women's rights and freedoms, the two seeming to be interconnected. The male opponents of trousers were correspondingly vocal. One woman who owned a pair of beach pyjamas was told by her father, 'Don't go out in those, and – if you go out – don't come back.' 'A Mere Man' wrote to the *Eastbourne Gazette*, deeply dismayed to hear that women in 'pyjama suits' had been attending religious services – 'Can a woman in a pyjama suit be in a proper frame of mind to take part in religious worship?' And the fiancé of a young woman was told by her father, when he asked permission to marry her: 'Yes – but you'd better get her out of those trousers, or you'll never be boss in your own house.' Shops might refuse to serve the female trouser-wearer, and she could be sent home from work.

There was also concern about gender identity. The Hollywood star Marlene Dietrich made androgyny fashionable and sexy, but also inflamed anxieties (for some) by wearing a full tuxedo, top hat and pants for her role in *Morocco* (1930). Those in the know were aware that, with Dietrich, 'anything goes'. For other women, fed up with old-fashioned frilly femininity, male attire was a refuge from the sex war. If your gender identity or sexual orientation didn't happen to be orthodox, 'mannish' dress could help to define it – causing a visiting Frenchman in London to be scandalised by the sight that met his eyes in Piccadilly: 'strange creatures half masculine, half feminine – men's trousers, women's hips, high heels, and hands in their pockets'.

Clothes and haircuts spoke the language of sexuality.

In 1928 Radclyffe Hall, author of *The Well of Loneliness*, stood trial on the grounds that her book, which portrayed love between women, was an obscene libel. At this time, the author was forty-eight years old, and was renowned in the literary world not just for her courageous fiction, but also for her audacious dress sense.

Radclyffe Hall* had inherited wealth. Her money released her, and made it easier for her to choose her own identity. In 1920 she was an early adopter of the shingle. True, Radclyffe Hall did not forsake skirts; trousers were still more of a violation of the social codes than she was prepared to commit in public, though she wore riding breeches in the country. But

----

* Known to her friends as John, or Johnnie, Radclyffe Hall was the pen name of Marguerite Radclyffe-Hall, author of eight novels which explore her own sense of being a social outsider.

in every other respect she went for a conspicuously masculine style, choosing a man's brocade smoking jacket for work wear, collars and ties, and teaming her tweeds with gartered socks and clumpy lace-ups. For special occasions she wore tricorn hats, swaggering velvet capes over tuxedo jackets, white shirt fronts with bow ties or cravats, and her signature monocle. She smoked heavily. This ultra-modern look was not calculated to blend in with the men she saw around her. Radclyffe Hall chose her outfits from Nathan's, the theatrical costumier's, emerging with a fashion-conscious, slightly decadent iteration of the camp *fin-de-siècle* dandy with his green carnation and purple velvet. Her Prince Charming staginess gave off similar messages of a love that still dared not speak its name.

The word 'lesbian' was uncommon in the 1930s, and Radclyffe Hall did not use it to describe herself, or her sexuality. She adopted the terminology used by Havelock Ellis, who had started publishing his studies on sexual psychology from the late nineteenth century onward; she would have described herself as an active 'congenital invert', bearing 'some approximation to the masculine attitude and temperament'. Ellis also put a name to her counterpart, the 'pseudo invert' – a 'womanly woman' who 'seem[s] to possess a genuine, though not precisely sexual, preference for women over men'. In Radclyffe Hall's case, this would have been her devoted lover Una Troubridge, who also cut her hair short and often dressed in a masculinised fashion, though less extreme.

It was hard, if you were a woman who desired women, to communicate that desire to them. But clothes, and hair too, were a medium as eloquent as words; you wrote your sexuality, and your desire, on your body – with an Eton crop and a collar and tie. A simplification, maybe. Today it may not seem necessary to mediate lesbian identity, or preferences, through masculine iconography. But a hundred years ago ideas of sexuality were profoundly embedded in ideas of gendered appearance. Switching from one to another was a potent, if coded, statement.

In the 1920s and 30s Radclyffe Hall and Una Troubridge gathered around them an exuberant crowd who shared their style sense – like the novelist Naomi Jacob and her girlfriend Olivia Etherington-Smith, and the accomplished fencing champion 'Toupie' Lowther, a wartime ambulance driver who loved to tell the story of how she had been stopped by officials on the Franco-Italian border and questioned whether she was masquerading as a man. So on the return journey she wore a skirt, only to be arrested for being disguised as a woman! The artist Romaine Brooks sometimes put in an impressive appearance with her lover, the American poet Natalie Barney. They rode motorcycles, smoked jewelled pipes and danced to jazz. Radclyffe Hall herself wrote all day, talked and partied all night.

In this bohemian social whirl, 'Sapphism' was for some just another life-enhancing eccentricity. If you wanted to call yourself Dickie, Jo or Billie, wear double-breasted jackets, wing collars and short hair, nobody felt threatened.

In November 1928 crowds gathered outside Bow Street Magistrates' Court. Radclyffe Hall's appearance was dramatic. She wore a Spanish riding hat and a leather coat with astrakhan collar and cuffs. *The Well of Loneliness* – which today could be seen as guilty of little more than some rather hot kissing – was reviled for 'acts of the most horrible, unnatural and disgusting obscenity', and taken away for all copies to be destroyed as an 'obscene libel'.

Radclyffe Hall, photographed in 1928

Of course banning the novel guaranteed that it would be publicised and discussed as widely as possible. Radclyffe Hall became, in her conspicuous attire, her shingled hair and her jewelled tie pins, the public and political face of lesbianism.

Western culture in the mid-twentieth century was built on an entrenched assumption. That the genders should be clothed distinctively was regarded as a law of nature, causing ideas of gender to be inextricably identified with, on the one hand, trousers, and on the other, frocks. Virginia Woolf wrote (in *Orlando*, 1928): 'In every human being a vacillation from one sex to the other takes place, and often it is only the clothes that keep the male or female likeness, while underneath the sex is the very opposite of what is above.' This clothes-fallacy could be cruel.

Laura Dillon, born in 1915 into a privileged and vaguely aristocratic family, began life biologically and anatomically female. Dillon's mother died when he* was a baby; his bereaved father rejected him. He grew up in Folkestone with his maiden aunts and a nanny, but was uncomfortable with the femininity he felt was being imposed on him, and even as a child refused to wear 'girly' clothes. Instead he envied his brother's boyish activities as well as his appearance: 'One morning we were being dressed to go to the barber when I inadvisedly said: "I want my hair cut like Bobby's." Nanny only laughed and said: "Don't be silly, you can't, you're a little girl and he's a little boy."'

Dillon had no male adult in his life, and no vocabulary to describe the deeply rooted conviction that he was a different gender from that which his body declared. As a young woman his only means of expressing that conviction was through clothes. Thus, as he grew up he rejected – as far as was possible – the shapely fashions of the 1930s. Instead he cut his hair short and adopted figure-disguising masculine attire on his top half, plus a skirt and heavy, flat footwear. Trousers still seemed a step too far.

In 1934 Laura Dillon went to the all-female Society of Oxford Home-Students (now St Anne's College) to read Classics. There he took up rowing, a sport which was generally considered inappropriate for women and, in 1937, having proved his excellence by gaining a rowing blue, was elected president of the Oxford University Women's Boat Club. In this capacity he set out to improve the women's uniform. This meant he could row in a white vest and blue shorts with impunity.

---

* To respect Michael Dillon's own articulation of his gender, I have referred to him using masculine pronouns throughout.

In the garden at Folkestone: Laura Dillon, right, then
studying at Oxford University, with his brother Robert

But outside his rowing career, Dillon was despondent,
unable to endure a life of ambiguity, yet equally reluctant to
buy into the demands of femaleness. Oxford had tolerated a
certain level of eccentricity, but back in Folkestone the public
weren't so broad-minded. In his daily life he was harassed by
passers-by who commented on his enigmatic appearance – 'Is
that a man or a woman?' – or remarked with surprise, 'Oh,
I thought that was a man ...' when he rose from a café seat,
revealing his skirted lower half. Dillon had no way to describe
what was amiss. In an uncomprehending world, the misery
was unremitting – 'I was to reach the nadir of mental suffering,' he remembered later. 'I developed a "poker face" to it all,
but underneath was sheer agony of spirit.' It was by luck that,
in his twenties, he discovered one doctor who could prescribe

hormone tablets, a second who performed a double mastec-
tomy, and a third able and willing to undertake the series of
thirteen complex operations that would finally, in 1949, give
him the external genitals of a man. Not for another ten years
would the term transsexual* come into medical usage.

Laura Dillon's appearance posed a threat to universal expectations about how women should be and look, challenging the
stereotypical premise that they were frilly and docile. But his
decision to change gender poses a more fundamental question
about how we define femaleness. For Dillon, it wasn't enough
to reject feminine attire. The outward projections that appeared
to define his destiny could be cast aside, but rejecting skirts
was insufficient to define his sense of self. Instead, confirming
the gender he knew himself to be demanded full bodily reassignment, and massively interventionist surgery. From then on,
Laura became Michael. Dillon's case history – the first of its
kind – begs an important question to women too: must we be
defined by the clothes we wear, and the style we adopt? Dresses,
lipstick, curls, curves and finery are not what make us female.
And if they don't, surely any woman should be free to cut her
hair short, disport herself in trousers, Chelsea boots, or jackets
and ties, if that is her choice. Michael Dillon felt fulfilled in his
gender only when his bodily changes conformed to maleness.
The rest was just decoration, trimmings.

Dillon's life, though short, would continue to take unusual
turns. After the war he trained as a doctor, while undergoing
the series of operations that would confirm the inner conviction
that he was male. In 1952 he joined the Merchant Navy and
set forth on a life of travels; after which he settled in India and
was ordained as a Buddhist monk. The years of gender uniform

---

*   The term transgender is now more commonly used, but there is continuing
debate and controversy about definitions and distinctions. Neither was diagnosed or in use in the 1930s, but 'transsexual' was the earlier term.

were over as he shaved his head and donned the simple, long, maroon-coloured, unisex robe that denoted his philosophical rejection of all material things, a statement which could not be clearer. We are not our hair. We are not our clothes. We are our selves.

———

The British clergy were finding it difficult to endure some women's fashion choices. In 1935 the Reverend Harold Harley, vicar of Sedgley in Worcestershire, told his flock that he would refuse Holy Communion to women wearing lipstick; 'also that girls attending service with bare legs will be asked to leave the church'. Harley had a tortuous rationale for this:*

> I consider that the girl who thrusts her unclothed flesh ... before the close attention ... of the male sex is doing a cattish trick.
>
> The male mind being what it is, is bound to be diverted from God, and if it be said 'Well, then, I don't think much of the male mind,' then my answer would be, 'It is as God made it.'
>
> Woman was given those fair limbs and that fair skin just so that she might attract man's attention, but she was to attract him so that she might help him on his way through life and not hinder him.

The Reverend Braley of Durham was also deeply concerned about the 'modern girls' who wore shorts for hiking, and backless evening gowns. He blamed the false worship of athleticism:

———

* Nearly ninety years later the Reverend Harley's tirade was echoed in April 2022 by a row over claims made by Tory MPs (reported in a newspaper article in the *Mail on Sunday*) that the MP Angela Rayner, then Deputy Leader of the Opposition, had deliberately tried to distract Prime Minister Boris Johnson by crossing and uncrossing her legs in Parliament.

'I ask, is it advisable for the future mothers of this world with their muscles trained like a man's? Is it good for the nation to have a lot of women who want to play football?'*

Whether in church or on the pitch, modern girls were spending more time in public spaces. But the new freedoms in dress were as oppressive as they were liberating, for there was no shortage of angry old onlookers to lecture the ladies on their proper role. A few years later, during a warm spell in August 1933, and under the heading 'The Cult of the Demi-Nude', the *Eastbourne Gazette* published a letter from a townsman outraged by the indecent spectacle that met his eyes in Terminus Road, of a tall, attractive woman wearing a large sunhat. This man had a good look, then described in great detail the sight he preferred not to see:

> Her back was bare to the waist; her neck was bare to the chest; her breast was emphasised by the drawing in of her upper garment; her eyebrows were pencilled half-way up her forehead; her lips were carmined; her arms were bare; so were her feet, except for a pair of low shoes; her legs were covered with a pair of pyjamas; she smoked a cigarette and she carried a toy dog. Frankly, she ought to have been arrested for indecent exposure directly she stepped into the public street.

The same Eastbourner then described the horrors that he encountered on the town beach – 'a butcher's shop of human carcases ... When I saw two white girls sunbathing with a coloured man I wondered if the public cult of the semi-nude could go any further!'

---

* This account also carries a nice irony since the Lionesses, England women's national football team, gave the national mood a jet-propelled boost by winning the UEFA Women's Championship in 2022 and reaching the final of the FIFA Women's World Cup the following year.

Mockery of provincial narrow-mindedness is easy. But anger was widespread, and the press carried regular reports of the evils of exposure. Semi-dressed Brits on Channel beaches even made headlines in the French press: 'The Englishwoman when on holiday at the seaside shows herself as Nature made her,' commented a reporter visiting Bournemouth in the hot summer of 1933. 'She lies about voluptuously, presenting to the sun, now her back, now her front, and exposing as much skin as possible.'

———

'In the summer of 1932 Mrs Corrigan took us for a cruise of the Mediterranean,' recalled Daphne Fielding, the former Marchioness of Bath, in her memoirs. Laura Mae Corrigan was a wealthy American hostess who, since her arrival in London in 1919, had presided over a sector of socialites from whom she drew her guest list. The company on board the *Argosy* could be loosely defined as bright young things: aristocrats and privileged politicos.

> For the next six weeks we lived in bathing dresses all day. Diving from the decks of the yacht and aquaplaning behind a fast speed-boat, putting clothes on only to go ashore and for dinner. Those days at sea were devoted to fanatical sun-worship, and we all vied with each other to see whose skin would go the deepest brown.

The suntan was – and is – a way of reinventing the body. It was a creation by high-caste white-skinned people who aspired to refashion their whiteness. It was and is complex, elitist, expensive, hard work, unhealthy and a triumph of conspicuous consumption.

From the late nineteenth century until the 1920s, the French Riviera had been a magnet for rich people seeking sunshine (and tuberculosis cures) in the winter warmth of Nice and Cannes. The summer was thought to be too scorching to remain, so on 1 May the hotels all closed. That changed in 1921 when the wealthy couple Gerald and Sara Murphy took flight from New York and, with their coterie of classy cosmopolitans, landed like a flock of seabirds on the Côte d'Azur. Picasso, Man Ray, Scott and Zelda Fitzgerald and Cole Porter came to visit. The expatriate Americans and their friends swam in the sea and picnicked on the sand; the summer sun burned their skin, and Sara Murphy wore her pearls on the beach at Cap d'Antibes as she believed its rays enhanced their lustre.

In *Tender is the Night* (1934), Fitzgerald based his heroine Nicole Diver on Sara:* 'Her bathing suit was pulled off her shoulders and her back, a ruddy, orange brown, set off by a string of creamy pearls, shone in the sun. Her face was hard and lovely and pitiful.' Tanned legs, backs and arms began to look up-to-date – telling the world you were cultured, fashionable and rich enough not only to afford holidays on the French Riviera or the Venice Lido, but also an array of suitably adapted cosmetic products: coconut oil, brush-on tanning powders and the like. A tan also demonstrated that you were not spending fifty weeks of the year working in the twilight zone of a factory. Lady Dorothé Plunket whispered to her friend Barbara Cartland that she topped up her tan in the winter by applying diluted iodine to her skin. The Duchess of Peñaranda dazzled in a white dress that contrasted with her deeply sunburned throat and giant white pearls; 'she

---

* The topic of early twentieth-century suntanning is fascinatingly discussed in Susan L. Keller's essay 'The Riviera's Golden Boy: Fitzgerald, Cosmopolitan Tanning, and Racial Commodities in *Tender is the Night*' (2010).

wore sunburn stockings with white satin shoes,' recalled
Cecil Beaton. Elizabeth Arden and Helena Rubinstein sold
oils and lotions to aid the browning process. Coco Chanel
placed the seal of approval on the suntan when she was photographed bronzing her face on a Normandy beach; later a
picture appeared of the deeply tanned designer on board the
Duke of Westminster's yacht. For Chanel, the shimmer of
diamonds and pearls was complemented by the deep colour
of a sun-kissed skin. 'I think she invented sunbathing,' commented a friend. 'At that time she invented everything.' By the
1930s, English-rose pallor was looking anaemic and pasty.
Sanatoriums that advocated 'ultraviolet cures' benefitted from
a clientele also seeking to brown their bodies on sunbeds. And
the sunray motif was the design hit of the decade, adopted on
powder compacts, garden gates and cinema screens. The new
heliophiles threw their veils aside in favour of vitamin D and
replaced their parasols with beach pyjamas, while manufacturers found a new niche market in plastic sunglasses. Sun
was glorious, sun was healthy, sun was life. Everyone wanted
to be a golden girl.

The higher echelons of white society no longer wanted to be
white. It was a radical moment for pale-skinned beauty when
Daphne Fielding, the Murphys and a host of duchesses, dames
and other socialites began to roast, toast and baste their bodies
till they deepened to the tint of old leather.

Being tanned *comme il faut* was yet another hard-to-acquire
luxury that spoke of choice, of leisure and of wealth.

Depression

The 1930s saw the growth of social research groups. One of these – Mass Observation – was launched early in 1937 by three idealistic young men who saw it as an anthropological initiative, democratic and reconstructive in its aims. Ordinary members of the public were recruited to record their everyday lives, by filling in questionnaires, submitting their diaries and responding to surveys. One topic was 'Personal Appearance'; the public contributions to this directive offer a revealing record – a snapshot – of how British women saw themselves at this moment in history.

On a rainy day in March 1937 twenty-six-year-old housewife Grace Hickling from Olton in Warwickshire was carrying a heavy basket of shopping home. She walked, to save the bus fare:

> I passed a local hairdresser's, the door opened and out came an immaculately dressed, 'permed', manicured, young woman who got into a super-limousine and drove off. My 'feelings' were a momentary feeling of shame at being seen walking along with a heavily laden basket at 4.30 p.m. ... looking (I imagined) rather like a charwoman; secondly a feeling of resentment ('I'm much better looking than she and have a much better figure, why shouldn't I be able to afford smart clothes &c').

The brief encounter between the limousine lady and Mrs Hickling has a timeless quality. Haven't we all been there? But for Hope Sykes, an independent-minded Cornish shopkeeper, the whole topic was irrelevant:

> I devote no expense and very little time and trouble to my appearance ... A bathroom and running hot water would make things easier ...

I don't use cosmetics because I have always lived in the country and have a good complexion. Besides I mostly wear breeches or shorts, and even in a skirt I look so boyish that make-up would look out of place ...

Shampoo my hair about twice a year and wash it on the rare occasions when I have a bath ... Never have it waved or permed.

Another of the respondents, twenty-two-year-old Sylvia Terry-Smith, agonised about how she looked:

The chief reason for bothering about looks, is, of course, the sex factor ... I often honestly long for a holiday away from this furious competition of looking more attractive than the next woman, a holiday when I can go around with no make up and old comfortable clothes ...

Even so, I know myself that if there is an attractive male around or a young woman, I must rouge myself almost against my will to look at least presentable.

At sixty-six, a widow from Blackheath, Nora Corfe, felt that she was out of the running, though she held sternly conservative views:

I'm content to be neatly dressed, hair dressed to suit my age. I hate to spend time on the art of dressing, unless going among well-groomed folk ... I like my own sex to look natural and to dress and do their hair accordingly. I loathe bare legs and bare backs.

Women in the public eye had other things to worry about, like Dorothy Brant, a Conservative organiser from Hampshire, who was concerned for her professional reputation:

Should I be with working class women who cannot afford to dress well I shall not make them feel uncomfortable by my appearance ... To dress 'down' to a person or audience creates a bad impression and in many cases is looked upon as an insult. My clothes must not be 'flighty' as many of the older women would consider me lacking in a sense of responsibility and be suspicious of my capabilities.

As a general rule when moving to a new constituency I wear tailored coats and skirts with rather severe hats. Once my committees have gained confidence in me and know me I then begin to wear rather more daring millinery without serious effect to my position.

There's something endearing about Miss Brant suppressing her taste in flighty hats – until the time's right!

And for Margaret Hedges from Lytham St Annes in Lancashire, appearance took the highest priority:

I devote 75% of my pocket money on clothes and such articles as will improve my appearance ... I spend approximately 3/- per week on cosmetics ... I think nothing of spending ¾ of an hour on my face before going out to the pictures and would think I was rushed if I had to manage it in less.

For many ordinary women, standards of grooming continued to be an obsessive source of anxiety: about being judged, about self-respect, about norms of femininity, about attracting men, and about cost. The observations of these 1930s women are also a salutary reminder of how preoccupied they were with the dos and don'ts, the hows and how-not-tos of make-up, at a time when spending on cosmetics advertising had reached the unprecedented peak of over £1 million a year. In all these respects the Mass Observers provide a welcome reality check, unburdened by the freight of hindsight.

Every so often someone's autobiography also penetrates the layers of the past like a geological probe, emerging with the strata of history undiluted and intact. One woman whose writings possess this quality is the diarist Jean Lucey Pratt,* who appeared as an overweight teenager in the last chapter, tormented by her unkempt fingernails and off-putting spectacles. Now in her twenties, she is agonising about whether she is marriageable, and her appearance worries jump from the page:

Sunday, 10 May 1931
I vowed I would die a spinster rather than walk from the altar with a man shorter than myself.

Thursday, 14 June 1934
I am angry and bitterly ashamed with myself ... I have let myself slip, am getting fat and not paying enough attention to my clothes.

Friday, 22 July 1938
I want ... 'to be rescued from virginity'. Feel myself growing flabbier and flabbier.

---

* Pratt, born in 1909, kept diaries from the age of fifteen. Many of them were submitted to the Mass Observation project, but a selection spanning her life have more recently been edited by Simon Garfield and published under the title *A Notable Woman: The Romantic Journals of Jean Lucey Pratt* (2015).

Tuesday, 21 March 1939
[Filled] with humiliation that I am still a virgin. It is preposterous. I am not flat-chested ... I have, I know, an exceptionally attractive body.

(Jean would finally be 'rescued', at the age of thirty-one, from her burdensome virginity; but marriage continued to elude her.)

The three short volumes of Phyllis Willmott's life have the same immediacy, and are also pervaded with a heightened awareness of clothes and physical appearance. In *A Green Girl* (1983) we meet Phyllis Noble – as she then was – in the 1930s: the daughter of a jobbing builder and a housewife, growing up in a run-down terraced house in Lewisham. At the age of eleven Phyllis gained a scholarship to a grammar school in Greenwich.

There, her red-haired friend Anita was the first of the group to encounter puberty. In the gym changing rooms, stripped to her underwear, it was clear that her breasts were starting to develop – this was in a time before manufacturers introduced the 'training bra'; girls wore a vest until their breasts grew sufficiently to fill an adult bra. Phyllis lagged behind – but soon she too started to feel an ominous sensitivity in that area.

Eager to find out what lay ahead, I asked Anita if I could see her breasts. On our way home after school one day we went into the public lavatories at Lewisham ... Anita's breasts looked delectable, rather like little party blancmanges each topped with a bright pink cherry.

Phyllis longed for hers to look the same. '"If you want them to grow you need to rub and pull them like this," [Anita] said, sending a shiver of delight through me as she acted on her words.' After that the girls stopped off regularly at the public

WCs: 'We took off our tunics and pulled up our blouses to work on the enjoyable task of breast development.'

As Phyllis grew from girl to woman the example of her own mother – now in her mid-forties – loomed always in front of her. Jenny Noble had been lovely, bright-eyed and handsome. But three children, money worries and endless drudgery had caused her looks to deteriorate beyond recall. Phyllis portrays Jenny as a woman confined to the kitchen, slopping around in slippers, legs bulging with varicose veins; she went barelegged rather than risk laddering an expensive pair of stockings. During the day a turban anchored the waves of her perm – to be replaced at bedtime with an unsightly pink hairnet. Her false teeth were removed, and her gums and sunken jowls made her appear like a hag. 'Poor old M.,' wrote Phyllis in her diary. 'She hasn't had much of a life.' And yet this existence, in which beauty was part of the bargain, to be exchanged for corrosive domesticity, looked inescapable.

———

These were the years of the worldwide economic slump that followed the Wall Street Crash in 1929. Among the many women to whom beauty, and the benefits it brought, were now becoming unaffordable luxuries was Helen Forrester.* When Helen was twelve her father lost his job and became bankrupt. The Forrester family, previously moneyed and privileged, was forced to leave their comfortable home in the south-west of England. They moved to Liverpool, where they lived in a tiny terraced house stinking of 'neglect and malnutrition'. Helen would never forget catching sight of herself reflected in a dress shop window:

———

*   The pen name of June Huband.

Coming towards me, amid the well-dressed shoppers, was an appa-
rition. A very thin thing draped in an indescribably dirty woollen
garment which flapped hopelessly, hair which hung in rat's tails
over a wraithlike face, thin legs partially encased in black stockings torn at the knees and gaping at the thighs, flapping, broken
canvas covering the feet. I slowed down nervously, and then stared
with dawning horror.

The Forresters were all perpetually hungry, while Helen's
dirt-ingrained cuticles betrayed the hours spent cooking,
scrubbing pots and laying fires. Her mother, Lavinia, was
another has-been beauty who had lost her looks along with
the bankruptcy; her teeth fell out, her figure suffered from
a diet of white bread, and her lovely legs, once sheathed
in fine silk, were now 'horrible with varicose veins'. She
was lavishly unsubtle with hair dye, lipstick and eye make-
up, but face cream and hand cream were unattainable
luxuries.

With difficulty, Helen persuaded her parents to let her
attend night school and learn the clerical skills which were the
only route out of drudgery and penury – apart from marriage:

Girls did not look for careers – they worked until they got married.
If a woman was not loved and cherished by a man, she must be
hopelessly ugly or there must be something else wrong with her.

Romance featured in her adolescent imagination; the novels she
read all ended with a kiss, but something told her there had to
be more than that. Men hung around outside the picture palaces waiting for the girls to come out, but Helen never got so
much as a wink. She had never been kissed. Was it because of
her height, her cheap clothes, her glasses, or her acne – a result
of economising on soap? Despite her pride, it got her down.

Helen tells a story of relentless, miserable poverty: the kind that humiliates and de-feminises; of wearing out shoe leather to save bus fares, of tattered underwear held together with safety pins, rags recycled to serve as sanitary towels, of hosiery mended and re-mended. New stockings cost a prohibitive ninepence a pair – '[they] were my single biggest expense'. Being fashionable was a distant dream. At a time when smart women spent money on having their hair cropped and permanently waved, Helen still pulled hers back into a bun. In debt to her mother and the pawnbroker, she scraped together an outfit for the office Christmas party, but nobody asked her to dance. 'You'll have to stop looking like a frozen rabbit,' was Lavinia Forrester's feedback. 'Men don't like plain girls – and girls who look both plain and dull never get anywhere. You must smile – look gay.'

But what was there to look gay about?

Helen Forrester's harrowing memoirs of youthful deprivation, *Twopence to Cross the Mersey* (1974), *By the Waters of Liverpool* (1981) and *Liverpool Miss* (1982), paint a picture which rang true to the many readers who loved them. Femininity was incompatible with the grinding poverty she described. If you wanted a good job, a better income, promotion, dates, boyfriends or a husband you had to invest in looking attractive. But that meant an unaffordable outlay on hair, make-up and clothes in order to recoup later. Just as in the metropolitan cafés and dance halls, Depression-era Liverpool was a world where a woman's worth and value was measured in time and money spent on maintenance. And there was the question of self-respect. Helen describes the predicament with agonising clarity:

There was no one to whom I could confide my shy desire to look chic, to ... become a normal middle-class girl again, groomed and cared for. Even the working-class girls who lived round me knew how to take care of their hair and their skin ...

But I had no money for hairpins ... and now no money for make-up or lunches or even stockings ... And I still owed Mother the pound she had lent me for [my] coat.

Keep Young and Beautiful

Though Hollywood took a hit in the Great Depression, movies now entered a golden age. Even in times of austerity cinema-goers found the price of their weekly ticket to fantasy-land. In this context extreme glow and glamour – the beauty epitomised by the great cinema legends – flourished.

The transition to talkies was now complete. Pre-Hays Code* Hollywood producers cast leading actresses, like Jean Harlow, who smouldered. The camera loved Harlow's sultry sexiness, her satin-clad bottom, creamy skin and above all her phosphorescent coiffure. She was the 'blonde bomb-shell', and by 1932 sales of peroxide in America had risen by 35 per cent. Harlow was a natural brunette, who dyed her hair palest platinum using a combination of ammonia, peroxide, laundry detergent and household bleach, which, when mixed, created a noxious gas. This cocktail of chemicals badly damaged her hair and was rumoured to have caused her premature death from kidney failure at the age of twenty-six – a cautionary tale which has a ring of victim-blaming about it.

---

* The Hays Code (named after Will H. Hays, President of the Motion Picture Producers and Distributors of America) was a clean-up-the-movies initiative which laid down guidelines as to what was acceptable to be shown on public screens. These were introduced in 1930, but weren't rigidly enforced until 1934.

The blonde was assertively sexy: a devil not a doll. She was fast, brassy, easy, a good-time girl. In the wake of Anita Loos's comic flapper-lit bestseller *Gentlemen Prefer Blondes* (1925), the perception was reinforced – it's still a slur today – that blondes were airheaded, gold-digging bimbos.

Either way, the aspiration to look like a film star collided with real-life expense, health risks and disapproval. Hollywood's fantasy world penalised glamour-seeking fans and stars alike. Jean Harlow's hairdresser put in hours to maintain her hair's sensational shimmer, and Harlow herself admitted that it was high-maintenance – 'Every little speck of dust or grime appears on the surface as clearly as it would on a white dress or coat.' She shampooed nightly.

The screen was unforgiving. 'I've got to hide those freckles,' Joan Crawford told Max Factor, and make-up departments were kept busy covering uneven pigmentation with pancake foundation. There was a belief that eyebrows were more expressive the thinner they were, so tweezers and razors were deployed to eliminate them completely; the pain could be alleviated with ether, and the brows pencilled in afterwards. Under the lights, angles were more flattering than curves – so leading ladies were required to keep their weight down.

Margaret Mitchell's bestselling novel *Gone with the Wind* was published in 1936. Before the film adaptation of Mitchell's Civil War epic was even made, its heroine – and hero – were set to become idolised emblems of femininity and masculinity. In the novel, Scarlett O'Hara is magnolia-skinned and green-eyed, with a seventeen-inch waist and 'well matured' breasts. And she is young (just sixteen when the story starts). Her first encounter with the hero is a meeting of opposites:

Her eyes fell on a stranger, standing alone in the hall, staring at her in a cool impertinent way that brought her up sharply with a mingled feeling of feminine pleasure that she had attracted a man and an embarrassed sensation that her dress was too low in the bosom. He looked quite old, at least thirty-five. He was a tall man and powerfully built. Scarlett thought she had never seen a man with such wide shoulders, so heavy with muscles . . .

From the outset Mitchell makes it clear that her protagonists are sexually irresistible to one other. And in the screen roles of Scarlett and Rhett, the petite British actor Vivien Leigh and her well-built American co-star Clark Gable mirrored the diehard orthodoxies of manly and womanly beauty of the time.

Scientific debate continues about why older, larger men are more attractive to women, but even today society tends to close ranks around the cliché that a woman must be younger, shorter, poorer and weaker than her man. From his craggy forehead to his immense hands ('I could tear you to pieces with them') Gable's Rhett Butler oozes masculinity. He rescues Scarlett from the burning city as it collapses around them. He seizes her in his steel arms and carries her effortlessly to the bedroom. Where Scarlett is little, frilly, passionate and childishly impulsive – in other words, feminine – Rhett is tall, rich, a rough diamond, dominating and grown-up – in other words, manly. And when times get tough, Scarlett fashions an outfit from a set of velvet curtains, hopes her chapped hands won't give her away and sets out to beg three hundred dollars from Rhett, knowing she has just one commodity left to sell: her charm.

Through this all-American fable, *Gone with the Wind* upheld the time-honoured model of sex relationships: that for a woman to be attractive in men's eyes she must stay young. But eternal youth is obviously not feasible, and our society is still struggling to find an acceptable model in which a desirable woman can also be a mature woman.

————

The novel and the film of *Gone with the Wind* not only stereotype gender relationships – they are also deeply problematic in their depiction of race.* The most controversial portrayal was that of Mammy, played by Hattie McDaniel.

Vivien Leigh as Scarlett O'Hara and Hattie McDaniel as Mammy in *Gone with the Wind*, 1939

————

* In 2020 the American streaming platform HBO MAX removed the film from their library after Hollywood writer/director John Ridley criticised them for giving access to a movie that glorified slavery. It was later reinstated, accompanied by a disclaimer and video footage discussing the film's context and legacy.

McDaniel, in her performance as the loyal but enslaved maid, forever adjusting Scarlett's neckline or giving her an audacious ticking-off, made film history as the first person of colour to win an Academy Award – for Best Supporting Actress in 1939. But her exceptional talent was exhibited within the constraints of a pernicious travesty.

The 'Mammy' caricature may have taken root in the American imagination just before the Civil War, when the (white) abolitionist Harriet Beecher Stowe created Aunt Chloe, wife to the eponymous hero of her best-selling novel *Uncle Tom's Cabin* (1852): 'A round, black, shining face is hers ... Her whole plump countenance beams with satisfaction and contentment from under her well-starched checked turban.'

In a concise critique of how of this myth became implanted in American culture, Dr David Pilgrim explains that in slave-owning societies the young Black women were routinely subjected to their masters' sexual desires. It was against this background that the Mammy was constructed (by whites) – who, with the aim of de-eroticising her, portrayed her as a generic Black female, plump and of mature years. 'The implicit assumption was this: no reasonable white man would choose a fat, elderly black woman.' Mammy was a fabrication. In reality, house servants were usually thin from lack of nourishment, and young – because 90 per cent of enslaved women did not live beyond the age of fifty.

But unlike her real-life counterparts, Mammy had staying power. In film, on TV and radio, on detergents, drinks, pancake mixes and breakfast cereal packets, her glossy visage beamed forth the unambiguous message: 'I'm wholesome, nourishing, trusty and safe.'

————

Just in case the message wasn't getting through, the hit musical movie *Roman Scandals* (1933, starring the white vaudeville actor Eddie Cantor) also spelled it out. The whimsical plot takes the protagonist, an Oklahoma delivery boy named Eddie, back in time to ancient Rome, where he is sold in a slave market. The film's biggest, staggeringly unacceptable set piece, choreographed by Busby Berkeley, has Eddie in a tunic and blackface, prancing around as a bevy of platinum blonde Roman damsels are having a pampering day in the marble-columned spa, complete with powder puffs, steam baths – and Black handmaidens to massage their legs.

The bathhouse setting offers plenty of opportunity for shots of all the ladies in semi-undress, and the catchy lyrics unashamedly list the ways in which a woman must groom and prettify herself in order to become desirable:

> Keep young and beautiful
> It's your duty to be beautiful,
> Keep young and beautiful
> If you want to be loved!
>
> If you're wise exercise all the fat off
> Take it off, off o' here, off o' there –
> When you're seen anywhere with your hat off
> Have a permanent wave in your hair!
>
> Each wrinkle in your skin
> Rub it out and rub a dimple in –
> Keep young and beautiful
> If you want to be loved!
>
> Take care of all those charms
> And you'll always be in someone's arms –

Keep young and beautiful
If you want to be loved!

– and much more of the same.

The number is a romp, albeit one that comes across as irredeemably offensive today – principally for its glib racism, but also for its invidious presumption that slimming, cosmetics, spa treatments and freedom from wrinkles are the only way to true love. Insulting, out-of-date nonsense, maybe. But the opulent choreography also pushes the notion that women are so many frothy erotic products in sequinned bras and blonde wigs, can-can'ing past on an endless conveyor belt; the name of the game is all-singing, all-dancing commodification. Meanwhile, the cutesy lyrics thinly mask a tenacious narrative – and one as prevalent as it was fifty years earlier – that female youth and beauty were a fair exchange for male protection, and that getting a man was not for slackers.

A Demanding Life

Gone were the days when a woman with a spotty back, a droopy bust or cellulite on her thighs could, as it were, sweep the mess under the carpet. The protective veils, cloaks and floor-length dresses of the nineteenth century, and its deceiving substructures of corsetry that built the illusion of wished-for femininity were gone. But with them was gone a woman's hiding place.

In 1930 a British woman of twenty-one could vote. She could drive a car, study to be a lawyer, stand for Parliament. For many, life may have seemed to be brimming over with opportunities to become equal with men – in government, in hospitals and laboratories, in Fleet Street; in the air, on the water, on mountaintops, on the tennis court or golf course. The captive was released, striding with new confidence in a direction of her own choosing, reaching her arms towards the light. But what if those arms, or worse still armpits, were hairy? What if the ankles were fat or the knees bony? Generations of women had grown up saturated with the notion that it was their duty to appear desirable in the eyes of men – 'if you want to be loved'. Here was a momentous task that had to be faced. But not faced alone, for an army of beauty professionals, salespeople, captains of commerce, therapists, scientists, medics and meddlers were at hand to counsel, to attend to a woman's needs – and to sell their products.

Most notoriously high-maintenance was Edward VIII's mistress Wallis Simpson. According to the hairdresser Antoine Cierplikowski, an entire room of her suite in Cannes was dedicated to her personal beauty salon. Dressing and grooming was, for her, a business – 'It is, though most people do not realise it, a demanding life.' Reporting on a dinner party in 1936 Chips Channon noted how chic Wallis was looking: 'smothered in rubies ... and has been on a fish diet for four days'. She had taken her own diktat – 'You can never be too rich or too thin' – to heart. 'That woman' also had her hair fully dressed three times a day: in the morning to complement her choice of hat, in the afternoon to attend the races or some other function, and in the evening ornamented for dinner. The freedom of the modern woman was an illusion, for each session took at least half an hour. The socialite and fashionista Daisy Fellowes often had her hair re-set ten times a day. Lady Mendl, comparatively undemanding, merely required her hair – silvered with age – to be restyled once a day, but the challenge for Antoine was to find her a flattering tint, which he did in a spirit of experimentation by first dyeing the coat of his white Borzoi hound with a hint of lilac-blue. On Lady Mendl the colour proved sensational.

The upper-class wardrobe was intensely time- and effort-consuming. Though the splendour of the great Edwardian house parties had diminished by the 1930s, the diarist James Lees-Milne complained about the incessant changing of clothes still deemed necessary at weekend gatherings:

> We ... first assembled in breakfast clothes at 9 o'clock. We changed for church at 11. We changed for luncheon at 1.30. Those of us who went for an afternoon stroll in Windsor Park changed at 3. We certainly changed for tea at 5. Thereafter I do not think we changed again until the dressing gong went at 8. Then we changed to some tune, the women into long trailing gowns, and the men into tails and white ties. Some of us therefore put on six different garments that day as a matter of custom, not vanity.

Royal occasions made exceptional demands. Following the abdication of Edward VIII, his brother George VI was crowned on 12 May 1937, and Antoine and his team were yet again indispensable:

> I went to London with a staff of sixty-five people. We were men and women, hairdressers, shampooers, manicurists, pedicurists, masseuses ...
>
> All the preceding day until midnight we spent on the foundation work of the Coronation hair-combs, the shampooing, the cutting, the dyeing, the waving. Then at three in the morning

we reopened, and the peeresses came in to be hairdressed for the final ceremony of the morning . . .

That night my assistant and I coiffed four hundred ladies at a rate of twenty dollars a head.

Beauty parlours had long clustered in the privileged, high-priced neighbourhood of London's Bond Street. But by the mid-1930s demand had risen; such services were democratising and could be found, equipped with permanent waving machines and beauty culture appliances, from Skegness to Southampton. In America, between 1920 and 1930 the number of beauty parlours rose from five thousand to forty thousand. Some offered an 'electric horse', upon which clients were invited to bounce up and down wearing rubber corsets and a bathing suit to help them lose pounds. Housewives and business girls could make appointments to have their eyebrows arched, or have a manicure conducted in a chichi mirror-glass and marble interior. 'Your finger tips will excite the envy of your friends,' boasted one establishment. And in 1930 *Woman and Beauty* was launched – a monthly magazine whose pages were crammed with features on how to stay young-looking, how to diet, and advertisements for must-have beauty aids.

Far from simplifying life, technologies and science were now deluging women with complex choices. In 1918, at the end of the war, just two new cosmetics lines had been introduced onto the market; twenty years later that number had increased to nearly forty. Almay, Wella, Maybelline, Revlon, Clairol, Max Factor and Tangee were just some of the names that launched in the 1930s. Unfamiliar colours, unconventional adornments, gadgets and products were appearing in the lady's dressing room. Face packs arrived on the scene from the early 1920s; you could buy them in mud, or 'lemon and magnesia'. False eyelashes were slow to catch on; the first patent had been taken out in 1911, but by 1933 socialite Patrick Balfour was spotting them at dinner parties. Ready-mades were available and more convenient, but many women preferred to have extension lashes glued on one by one by their beauty specialist. 'The whole operation takes about four hours – an ordeal which a man would shrink from,' reported a columnist in the *Leicester Evening Mail*. It was important not to cry or they might become detached. Eyelash curlers were patented in 1931, and the same year iridescent eye shadow was in the shops, along with Max Factor's Super-Indelible lipstick. By mid-decade women could buy waterproof cosmetics and lipstick stencils. Fingernails had all the shock of the new. One Bond Street manicurist offered to lacquer them in green and elaborately paint over them with staves of music from the latest Hollywood musical hits; cost, 10s 6d. Margaret Whigham claimed to be the first debutante to wear luminous pearl-coloured nail varnish.

Most innovative of all was La Crème Ramey, launched in 1933 by Tho Radia in Paris, who sold it on the claim that their product, which contained thorium and radium, would eliminate fat and remove wrinkles. Radium was believed to be a kind of 'liquid sunshine'.* The launch advert gave the impression that Tho Radia would make one glow in the dark!

---

* See Lucy Jane Santos, *Half Lives: The Unlikely History of Radium* (2020), which explores the uncanny story of this unpredictable element.

Advertisement for the Radiante corset, launched in 1937

How did anyone ever think a radioactive corset was a good idea? By the 1930s awareness of the damaging properties of radium was growing, in reaction to several notorious cases of death and poisoning. Nevertheless, in 1937 Silhouette manufactured and marketed the Radiante corset: it was 'slenderising' and the beneficial effects of small amounts of radium added to the elasticised material from which it was made would, it was claimed, cause its wearers to feel rejuvenated. Fortunately, perhaps, the outbreak of war put a stop to its distribution.

The foundation garment industry was in flux. Sport, dancing and the fashion for flat, boyish figures were problematic. Manufacturers panicked and abused the 'evils of the no-corset fad'. Corsetry companies needed to steer fashion in a new direction, and by the 1930s womanly curves were firmly back in, with underwear styles echoing the clinging bias-cut forms of Vionnet's svelte silhouettes. The manufacturers breathed a collective sigh of relief as their sales figures improved.

But perhaps most commercial of all was the war against fat. The slimming craze showed no sign of abating – ironically, as the Depression era was a time of extreme poverty and, for many, hunger. The grandmother of author Sabrina Strings* was among the thousands of African Americans who migrated from the southern states of the USA at that time, in search of a better life. For her, it was hard to understand how, in the presence of such abundance, white Californian women should be refusing food. 'All of the white women she was meeting were on diets. And she had lived through a time when simply being able to have food was a triumph ... So this was something she just could not wrap her mind around,' recalled Sabrina.

Then as now, diet books were best-sellers. Sali Löbel, author of *Glamour and How to Achieve It* (1938), promised her readers their heart's desire if they followed her directions, which involved walking along a raised plank with a bowl on your head, a weight-loss diet of salad and hard biscuits, and always wearing a hairnet at night.

The manufacturers of the hugely popular patent medicine Bile Beans continued to spend £60,000 a year promoting their gelatine-coated pills which promised to 'Keep you Healthy, Happy & Slim', exploiting women's desperation to hold on to vanishing youth. A court later ruled that their product was

---

* In her book *Fearing the Black Body: The Racial Origins of Fat Phobia* (2019), Strings argues that white Western women's obsession with being slim is rooted in racist attitudes fostered at the time of the slave trade. '[Europeans] think that Black people are overly sensuous. They love sex. They love food. And as a result they are chock-full of venereal diseases, and they are overweight. So from this we have the seedlings of our current aesthetic system, which suggests that white, slender bodies, especially women's bodies, are valuable. But fat bodies, and especially fat Black bodies are worth denigration.' 'Sabrina Strings Explains How "Fatphobia" is rooted in Racism', YouTube, 1 April 2001.

fraudulent. Weight-loss dieting was heading into the danger zone. 'It was almost a madness,' recalled Barbara Cartland:

> Women who were nothing but skin and bone talked animatedly of taking off another pound. Every other woman was on a diet, sweating baths of all kinds were crowded, reducing pills ranged from mild aperients to dangerous, and in some cases fatal, drugs ...
>
> It was not only the idle classes who were stupid enough to 'slim', the shop girls and factory hands took it up too. Girls collapsed at their work and were found to be suffering from acute malnutrition and anaemia.

Alarming stories abounded in the press. In 1930 the *Daily Mirror* warned that thousands of women were becoming 'nervy', weak and vulnerable to infections – and in 1936 their front page ran the headline, 'Women who deliberately stint themselves of food ... increase their chances of having [tuberculosis] in a serious form.' The word anorexia did not feature, but from this time the newspapers increased their sensationalist coverage of starvation stories – like that of twenty-six-year-old Phyllis Anna Chadwick from Cheshire, who was gripped by the fear of becoming fat. She refused food, took tablets and came down to a weight of 4 stone 11 pounds. A few months later she slipped into a coma and died. 'She brought on her own death,' blasted the *Mirror*. 'Slimming had killed her.'

None of this deterred the same newspaper from running advertisements for Silf obesity tablets – 'All your unwieldy and unhealthy poundage vanishes as does the dew of the morn before the rising sun.' And maybe these were the tablets taken by Beccy, in a tragedy recounted by her younger cousin Letitia Simpson. Letitia grew up as the daughter of a London publican, and in later life wrote a memoir of her interwar childhood, which includes the awful cautionary tale of her cousin, 'a most beautiful girl, about twenty years old':

> How proud she was of her slim figure, and boasted to Mum about the little pills she had been taking, as she existed on a diet of lettuce and tomatoes. 'You should take some of these, Auntie Bib, darling, they're wonderful for losing weight.'

'Auntie Bib' (Letitia's mother) was comfortable with her figure, and had no intention of taking anything, but – having declined a meal – Beccy set off home, insisting on leaving her aunt a box of the wonder-working pills. A few days later, as she was opening up the bar, Bib came upon the pills and discovered to her horror that they had hatched, and were alive, crawling with maggots. She immediately telephoned Beccy's mother:

> 'Don't let Beccy take any more of those pills for slimming.' There was a long silence on the line. 'Maggie, are you there' she asked urgently, impatiently. 'It's too late,' her voice trembled, 'she's dangerously ill in hospital.'

It seems Beccy died soon after.

For certain, the rapidly changing landscape of beauty was bringing a rush of untried and untested products onto the market. Lash Lure was the cause of another fatality. The mascara contained p-phenylenediamine, which caused blisters, ulcers and abscesses. Miss Norris, an American socialite, blackened her eyelashes with Lash Lure. It destroyed her corneas and she went blind, and another woman who used it died. Hair removal could also have disastrous results. An American woman, ulcerated and scarred by Koremlu, a sodium sulphide depilatory which contained thallium acetate, wrote: 'There was nothing to live for. The mischief done to my face and arms will last forever. I wish I could go to sleep and never wake up again.'

Gouraud's Oriental Cream was advertised as a 'magic beautifier'. But it included a mercury compound which not only produced smoky dark rings on a woman's neck and around her eyes, but also blackened her gums and caused her teeth to loosen. Hair dyes were particularly risky. One hairdresser raised his concerns in a terrifying warning addressed to colleagues in the industry who would not wish to be taken to court for negligence:

> First of all there appear small pimples, or pustules, and these are accompanied by intolerable itchings, followed by a kind of eczema; the skin is violet red, inflamed, damp and oozing ... The forehead is often burnt and blistered, and the neck is covered with red patches ... Violent headaches and shiverings are also felt, and in chronic cases, the legs and feet become swollen.

Partly as a result of this, the Pharmacy and Poisons Act was passed by the British government in 1933, though it did not come into effect until 1939, while America passed the Food, Drug and Cosmetic Act in 1938.

Hairdressing technology could also be fearsome in its effects, with permanent waves being particularly culpable. The medical populariser James Harpole* described a typical case history in his newspaper column. In 1936 a woman came to his consulting room. Her head had been burnt while she was having her hair permed, and she had an unsightly bald scar-patch on her hairline.

---

* The surgeon, novelist and broadcaster J. Johnston Abraham used a pseudonym because at that time doctors were barred from using their real names if they appeared in any way to be self-advertising.

She was in acute distress about it ... She had lost her sparkle. Her interest in life seemed gone. I sent her to a cosmetic surgeon, who very skilfully excised the bald patch and drew a circle of new hair into position to cover the defect.

Some months later she came to see me.

I hardly recognised her ... She had got rid of her obsession, she had recovered her poise.

She told me she was going to be married in a month.

Mr Willi

This neat happy ending also serves as the re-entry point to the brave new world of cosmetic, or aesthetic, surgery. Face-doctoring had been around since the late nineteenth century – witness the botched paraffin-wax work done on poor Gladys Deacon's nose – and had gained momentum following Sir Harold Gillies's pioneering work on disfigured soldiers during and after the First World War. Post-war, and in the 1920s, Dr Suzanne Noël had been carving out an unprecedented career in *chirurgie esthetique*. Now, in the run-up to a second global conflict, more women than ever were seeking the help of the scalpel. Discretion and subterfuge surrounded this controversial sector, and not all the endings were happy. When fifty-one-year-old Lizzie Rigby from Nuneaton put her head in her gas oven after botched facial surgery left her disfigured, she left a pathetic note: 'I look at least ten years older. Everybody used to say Miss to me; now it is definitely Madam.' The coroner commented, 'This woman ... could not grow old gracefully and accept quietly the ravages of time.' He told the inquest that Mrs Rigby was in denial about her real age and noted, 'It is a tragedy of vanity.' Nearly as tragic was the awful case of a naive young woman who went to see Dr Henry Schireson in Chicago, and asked him to treat a burn on her shoulder. Schireson was a charlatan. He had been jailed for practising without a licence, and advertised himself as surgeon-beautician to Greta Garbo, Lady Diana Manners, Mary Pickford and the late Queen Marie of Rumania – none of whom had never heard of him. He talked the young woman into having her legs straightened, and took her off to an orthopaedic hospital, where he sawed through both her tibias. The consequent gangrene nearly ended her life, before a genuine surgeon stepped in and performed a double amputation to save her.

But how many women could dodge the trap that society laid for them? Our moralists have always condemned vanity. And yet they themselves are responsible for creating the conditions in which, for women, 'improving on nature' was (and is) an inescapable survival strategy. James Harpole was emphatic: 'To appear young is a necessity in modern life.'

You did whatever it took.

––––––––––

The surgeon's skills were manifold. Suturing techniques had been developed to ensure that no stitch holes were visible, and scars were concealed. Noses could be re-contoured, ageing eyelids could be tightened, ears flattened, reduced or tidied up, facial wrinkles rectified, eyebrows re-grafted, lips tattooed permanently red, bald patches covered, moles and blemishes removed. Add-on beauty was for sale. The Lewisham housewife Jenny Noble, with her sunken jowls, her dentures and worn looks, would not have been able to afford such treatments, but her wealthier counterparts no longer needed to resign themselves to becoming old women in their forties.

At this time Charles Henri Willi was probably the best-known aesthetic surgery practitioner in Britain. And unlike his contemporary James Harpole, no legal controls prevented him from advertising his practice in Hampstead, London – which he named the Hystogen Institute. This was because he had absolutely no medical qualifications.

Charles Willi was born in Switzerland, of humble origins; at some point in his youth, according to his biographer,* he became fixated on acquiring money, and realised that women could best serve this ambition. Professionally, Willi was an autodidact who appears to have learnt his impressive surgical skills by observation; he was prodigiously energetic, fanatically punctual and a social climber with few real friends. He was also driven by an insuperable ego, with a rooted conviction that he was right about everything, and given to pronouncing 'I am the tops.' As a husband Willi was a tyrant, who never forgave his wife for failing to bear him a son. He came to London in 1910 and remained until 1960.

The loophole which permitted Willi to promote his business, provided he did not *wilfully* pass himself off as a physician or surgeon, also allowed him to operate as a plastic surgeon. But his activities were limited: he could only undertake operations – like filling, facelifts and rhinoplasties – that required *local* anaesthetic, with the patient fully conscious. Any anaesthetist who assisted an unlicensed practitioner by administering general anaesthetic would have been struck off; Willi could not, therefore, attempt operations such as breast reduction. But his practice was intensively promoted, and there was no shortage of takers; clearly, his interventions were meeting a huge demand. Thus over fifty years Mr Willi carried out over fifteen thousand

---

* The American journalist James Ludovici was the author of a short life of Willi: *Cosmetic Scalpel: The Life of Charles Willi, Beauty-surgeon* (1981).

cosmetic procedures, and amassed over £1 million, though he was not a doctor.

In 1930 the glamorous travel writer Rosita Forbes plugged Willi's work unconditionally in the pages of the *Tatler*: 'Until I met Mr Willi, I was resigned to waking up one morning somewhere between my fortieth and fiftieth birthdays and finding myself old. Now I know that so long as Mr Willi lives I shan't be old at all,' she wrote. Explaining that the treatment left no mark, lasted a lifetime, and cost barely more than a new dress, Forbes professed herself a complete convert: 'Don't hesitate. You wouldn't wear last year's hats, so why wear last year's wrinkles?'

Another admirer, Elisabeth Margetson, was so enthusiastic about her transformative treatment that she published a book, entitled *Living Canvas: A Romance of Aesthetic Surgery* (1936), with the aim of promoting Mr Willi's practice by sharing her personal story. The youth myth had cast its spell on her. The short book was written out of the conviction that an ageing face was an ailing face, which could only be cured by surgery. It was the declaration of a new belief that ageing is not a natural process but a pathological condition to be combated and corrected. But it is easy to sympathise. She too, like Suzanne Noël's clients and so many others, was just trying to survive in an environment rife with prejudice against the wrinkles and spreading hips of mature women.

Living Canvas gives away little about Elisabeth's own background. Probably she was born around the turn of the century. Writing was her talent, which she turned to popular romantic fiction, but she was also an ambitious journalist who saw herself as a professional woman. Her book starts with a sad tale: the story of Elisabeth's very dear friend, who, since she doesn't name her, we'll call Dorothea. Dorothea was a woman in her late thirties who was employed in a high-profile post in the fashion industry. She loved her job and had given her life to it. One day Dorothea returned home in great distress. She had been dismissed 'because the manager had decided that she looked too old to continue in her work and would not do justice to *him* among *his* clientele' (my italics). Powerless and inconsolable, Dorothea retreated into herself: 'She took her dismissal pitiably to heart; she lost all hope and retired to the country to live a miserable and lonely life on her small savings.'

Dorothea's experience stood as an awful warning to Elisabeth.

> I resolved then and there that [Dorothea's] fate should never be mine ... I told myself, I would not be baulked by ageing looks.
>
> From that day I began to study the science of beauty preservation and culture with deadly seriousness ... Every pound that could be squeezed from a limited income was devoted to creams, massage, astringents, beauty masks and facial treatments. I studied my diet, took lots of exercise.

But things started to go wrong. Elisabeth fell ill. The story hints at 'a great sorrow'; she seems to have had a chequered marital history. In her mid-thirties, Elisabeth's face began to sag, and wrinkles started to appear. She sensed a palpable hostility coming from her employers, and became convinced that her fading looks were the cause of it. 'I [turned] my face away, panic in my heart.' One day, lunching with another friend, she learnt that this woman was not, like herself, approaching forty years old, but actually fifty-five, and was on her way that very afternoon to get a top-up facelift. That was how Elisabeth met Charles Willi.

The remainder of Elisabeth Margetson's book reads like a pure testimonial of thanks to the great man who in little over an hour had given her a new face. She stepped into his surgery. Novocaine was administered. Then with skilful fingers Willi plied his diathermic knife or radio-needle that cauterised as it cut, and dressings were administered. Fat, removed from her eye-bags, was injected into her facial wrinkles, the analgesic ethyl chloride was sprayed onto her skin, and she could sense the surgeon's gloved hands moulding and manipulating her contours.

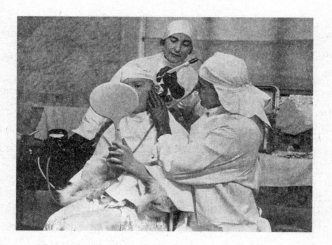

Charles Willi carrying out facial surgery in 1932

Then I was handed a mirror ...

I gazed ... gasped ... gazed again ... The face of my youth looked back at me, clean-jawed, smooth-cheeked, bright-eyed youth ... The transformation was so complete that I nearly burst into tears with happiness.

Elisabeth took ten days off work. Then she got a new permanent wave, a new outfit, and walked back into her office buoyant with joy and confidence. 'That terrible unbelief in oneself that can do so much damage to the soul [was] a thing of the past.' She had rediscovered herself – and that self was young, not ageing.

Soon, she started to talk to female friends about her experience, and discovered that many of them had considered having defects corrected through plastic surgery, but were deterred by the attitude of their husbands: husbands who, she pointed out, had originally married them because they were young and beautiful, but who were now reluctant to seem tactless by referring to their middle-aged wives' loss of bloom. Other husbands, they told her, were puritanical about the idea of meddling with nature. But nature, insisted Elisabeth Margetson, was a lost cause in the modern age. 'The whole of the life we are forced to lead to-day is "unnatural" ... We must go to modern science to relieve modern troubles.'

Her argument can be justified. 'Unnatural' is a subjective concept, charged with a moral load. Since the dawn of time humans have decorated, modified and adorned themselves. Ancient Egyptian women outlined their eyes with mineral pastes; the Romans dyed their hair, as did the Elizabethans. The Chinese practised foot-binding for more than eight centuries, and many West African tribes have used skin scarification as a rite of passage. Eighteenth-century women wore wigs and nineteenth-century women sought to reshape their bodies by tight-lacing, while by the twentieth century it was no longer unacceptable to deceive and misrepresent through the use of make-up, painted onto the 'living canvas' of the face.

Is surgery in a different class? Why do we distinguish a radio-needle from a make-up brush? And if we do, at what point do we draw the line? It's a topic that continues to be hotly debated, but by the 1930s a line had certainly been crossed. Where whalebone once fashioned anatomical realities, a woman's body had become increasingly malleable: the raw material of the male vision. 'The plastic surgeon is undoubtedly the greatest of all contemporary artists,' claimed Charles Willi. '*He* cannot exhibit or sell *his* work to be immortalised by fame. Nevertheless, *his* genius is tacitly appreciated by each patient' (my italics). Stand aside Renoir, Rodin, Matisse, Modigliani! The male gaze has subdued female flesh and remade femininity according to its own vision.

Fifty years earlier 'Dorothea' would not have been fired from her job by her male boss because she looked old; Elisabeth Margetson would not have been overwhelmed with panic and paranoia in her mid-thirties because the men she worked with made her feel she was withering. For, of course, two middle-class women like Dorothea and Elisabeth would not have been working. They would have been ladies of leisure: feeding the canary, attending sessions at their dressmaker, pouring tea into porcelain teacups. The patriarchal pact, by which women stayed indoors looking decorous, had been broken by an advancing army of emancipated, independent and would-be economically productive women. But it appeared that the patriarchy still held the winning card.

Elisabeth, and thousands of other women, submitted voluntarily to Charles Willi's diathermic knife, never registering any regrets and delighting in their rejuvenated faces. Looking back from the distance of nearly a century, their willingness is easier to understand. Women's self-image was – and remains – refracted through centuries of oppression; feminism was still a new movement, and the concept of sexism was as yet largely unformulated. History and hindsight shine a different light on the Hystogen Institute. In this context, the invasive snipping, shaving and dissecting of women's faces by men like Charles Henri Willi could be construed less as artistic genius, and more as society's – specifically men's – fear of the older woman.

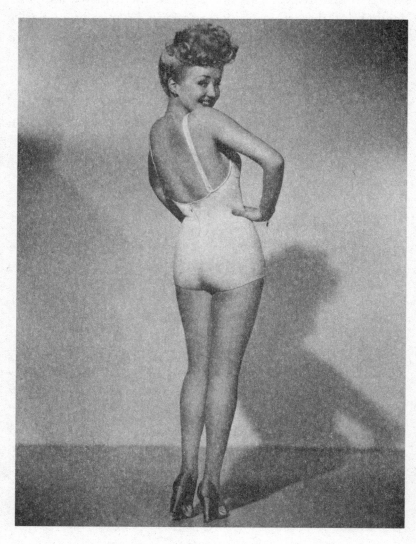

Betty Grable, in the famous publicity photograph
taken by Frank Powolny for the movie *Pin-Up Girl*, 1944

6

Beauty is a Duty

Betty

The movie star and wartime icon Betty Grable was all
about legs.

It was a numbers game. Betty measured thirty-eight inches
from her bottom to the floor. Her thighs measured nineteen
and a half inches round, and her calves thirteen inches. Ankles:
seven. Famously, Twentieth Century-Fox paid Lloyd's of London
to insure Grable's legs for $1 million – a publicity stunt that
guaranteed mass coverage – and when her stockings were auc-
tioned off to raise money for the war effort, the winning bidder
paid $110,000. The Grable legs were also immortalised by
being imprinted in cement set into the sidewalk on Hollywood
Boulevard, and in 1943 *Life* magazine ran a five-page photo
feature headlined 'Betty Grable's Legs' – showing a 'day-in-the-
life' of the star's shapely limbs viewed from every angle:

Here the legs are shown as she prepares morning shower at
home ...

Going to studio in the morning, Betty steps into roadster ...

In her dressing-room ... Betty pulls on black mesh stockings for a scene that will feature the legs ...

Photographs from the *Life* feature, 7 June 1943

With Betty Grable, the 'no-legs' era was consigned to history. We have travelled a long way from the coquettish glimpse of a boot peeping from under a riding habit that George Augustus Sala found so erotic back in 1858, or the shock effect of women in knickerbockers on bicycles in the 1890s. The previous century had left legs largely to the imagination – or art. Who knew what was really concealed under those surging layers of fabric? Grable's highly desirable legs set the standard for her time. By 1940, whether beautiful or bandy, stumpy or shapely, women's legs were out of their time-honoured closet and on display. And that meant taking care of them. As reported by Pathé News, the gymnasiums were full of women working on limb loveliness. 'Girls, it seems that after you've helped to win the war, you'll still have another battle on your hands: legs and things!' declared the male commentator over footage of some glamorous women in high heels having their calves machine-massaged; 'Thigh no more, ladies,' was another typical voiceover comment. For no matter how much or how little of a woman's legs was revealed, it seems men's eyes all swivelled in the same direction. For many heterosexual men, a woman's leg has something tantalising and intensely sexual about it.*

Improbably silky, sleek and shapely, the pair of legs now uncovered for the delight of millions of servicemen and cinema-goers in the 1940s are an artefact well suited to the machine age: frictionless, streamlined, hairless and perfect.

Betty Grable's leg appeal was disseminated and discussed. In 1943 the *Washington Evening Star* saw it as a sign of the times: 'Legs are running riot again in Hollywood. Something to do with the war, I believe.' *Life* delved a little deeper: 'Betty Grable's legs have not attained fame by being unusual. They are The Great Average American Legs: straight, perfectly rounded and shaped, but withal judged by the same standards as millions of others.' *Time* scrutinised them critically: 'Even her intensively publicized legs ... cannot compare in symmetry to Dietrich's.' In an interview Betty offered her own assessment:

> I can act a little, sing a little, dance a little. But I can't do any one of them as well as a dozen other girls I know. Maybe it's the legs – and the fact that I can do all those three things well enough to get by ...
>
> They are fine for pushing the foot pedals in my car!

Time agreed. 'Her talents are unremarkable. Unlike some other movie stars, she can lay no claims to sultry beauty or mysterious glamor ... Her peach-cheeked, pearl-blonde good looks add up to mere candy-box prettiness.' Ordinariness was part of Grable's secret. As was timing. Her movies were formulaic. But her pop-ularity during the war soared because, as *Time* commented, 'the pert, sexy, but basically "nice" girl that Betty plays on the

---

* In this context, for anyone of the post-war generation, it's hard not to imme-diately summon up the image of the poster for *The Graduate* (1967) starring Dustin Hoffman and Anne Bancroft, showing Hoffman hypnotised by the sight of Bancroft's shapely, semi-stockinged leg extended across the foreground.

screen is young American womanhood at its best'. From a GI to a stenographer, she was somebody everybody could aspire to have, or to be: a patriotic American dream that really might come true. There was little talk of her prowess as an actress. This was a dream of long pinky-white limbs, bottle-blonde curls and a confectionery smile, produced from the mass unconscious of a century that had fallen in love with women who looked, sang and danced like mechanical dolls.

Frank Powolny's iconic picture, first released in 1943, 'launched a million dreams'. Powolny was chief stills photographer at Twentieth Century-Fox and, over forty years, was responsible for hundreds of their most compelling cheesecake pictures. From December 1941, and the Japanese attack on Pearl Harbor, the world seemed to be engulfed by war, and America, like Britain, became focussed on the fight. The image of Grable decorated jeeps and boats; it was plastered across the noses of fighter planes, stuck to the marks used for army recruits' target practice and in the pages of the official GI magazine *Yank,* but above all in the knapsacks and wallets, and thumb-tacked to the barrack walls and locker doors of five million American servicemen. One US veteran later told her:

> There we were out in those damn dirty trenches. Machine guns firing. Bombs dropping all around us. We would be exhausted, frightened, confused and sometimes hopeless about our situation. When suddenly someone would pull your picture out of his wallet. Or we'd see a decal of you on a plane and then we'd *know* what we were fighting for.

British reactions to Grable seem to have been more mixed, ranging from highbrow revulsion at her 'hideously painted lips' to the genial relish of a thirty-eight-year-old gunner: '[She's] cheerful and vulgar – cheer you up after a bad spell of duty.' The boys may have been 'batty about Betty', but her female fans were almost as besotted: 'How could a young girl not want to look like that?' said one.

Director David Lean summed it up, commenting on the impossible competition his own movies encountered when up against Betty Grable's brand of Hollywood glam: 'Life is very drab. I see their point.'

Love her or loathe her, American idol or downmarket imported sweetie, dressed in her white swimsuit and high heels, the Betty Grable pin-up has become an emblem of a time in history when men endured danger and hardship far from home, to protect and preserve an ideal of womanhood.

The Hollywood goddesses of the 1940s were, of course, created by and for men. The film industry propagandised civilians and services, at home and abroad, British and American, with images of glamourised everyday women. And when soldiers' resolve to win the war needed a boost it was Betty Grable's image that helped stiffen it.

———

Betty was born in 1916 in St Louis, Missouri, and pushed before the public by an ambitious mother who showed her little affection, but who had no qualms about putting her small daughter on display. At the age of thirteen she was enrolled in stage school. She learnt to play the saxophone, to sing and dance. She played a string of B-movie roles. Then she landed the lead in *Down Argentine Way* (1940) and emerged from the movie a star. Soon she was the highest-paid name in Hollywood, and under the patronage of producer Darryl F. Zanuck took top billing in nearly thirty subsequent movies.

Betty Grable's personality is elusive. The image has eclipsed the woman behind it. Journalists who interviewed her portrayed her as friendly and perky, but also shy and uptight: 'nervous as a cat. She wasn't sure her dress was right, so she went back to her room – and changed it, three times. She was worried to death about how her hair looked.' Betty had her share of love drama and heartache with a series of leading men; both her marriages failed; she drank, smoked heavily and gambled. Her daughter Jessica revealed to one biographer that her mother had vulnerabilities which she didn't show, on or off-screen:

> She had so much pain, so much hurt – and so much naiveté. Even though she had been an actress and everything, she didn't know how to express herself ... her life wasn't real. She was never allowed to be a little girl.

The picture emerges of a hard-working, professional, over-controlling but well-intentioned woman who had lost her way, riddled with faults and weighed down by wealth and stardom. Betty's intense privacy runs counter to her public presentation as a sexy sweetie-pie with a curvy silhouette and a 'Welcome in, boys!' smile.

Powolny's picture is so comprehensively iconic that attempting to deconstruct the shiny high heels or the white bathing costume seems diminishing and reductive. His own version of events was simple: he lit the shot; she tried on several swimsuits and the white one was best. Walking away she glanced over her shoulder – it looked good so he asked her to do it again, shot it, 'and that was that'. But it was a publicity still – and as such Betty would have been under contract to look her best. So, exposed though she is, layers of artifice remain between viewer and woman. What the GIs were lusting after – and they probably knew it – was a brightly lit fiction. The celebrated legs show no trace of a hair or blemish; we can guess that Powolny or his assistant has burnished and polished them with a paintbrush back in the studio. And as the eye travels down, it's arrested by the sight of the slenderest of bracelets encircling Betty's right ankle. Anklets are symbolic, though their meaning has faded. Worn on the right ankle, they might denote that the wearer was unmarried, and seeking a relationship. My mother (who, like Betty Grable, was born in 1916) disapproved of anklets: she saw them as tarty, and sexually suggestive. That interpretation seems to have been a wide one, and whoever commissioned Powolny's photograph would not have released it publicly without an awareness that the bracelet could add to the overall titillation of the image. Her vertiginously heeled pumps, too, contribute to its showy exhibitionism.

The swimsuit tells its own 'corset' story. What can be seen of the bra shows that it's cantilevered, while a close look reveals that the back has a zipper. Together they do a careful job of cinching in, structuring, controlling and uplifting Betty's abundant curves – for by the 1940s fashion had definitively rejected the inter-war flat-as-a-pancake body shape.

I have found no evidence that Betty Grable had cosmetic surgery – but her face and hair were as manufactured as her body. Her close friend, the hair stylist Mike Levitt, told an interviewer that Grable's real hair was kinky and unattractive, and that her updos were often concocted from false switches. A few years later Grable talked to Lydia Lane, beauty columnist of the *Los Angeles Times*, about how she composed her cutesy, kittenish look. Lipstick was key – and though the photograph is black and white her mouth is clearly defined with a strong colour. 'I love lipsticks,' she told Lane. 'I must have hundreds of them.' And she happily disclosed – no surprises here – that though she had started out a blonde, her hair had darkened, causing her to experiment with a series of dyed shades. 'I've had mine every color, even black.' How often did she shampoo it, enquired Lane. '"Oh, I wash it once a week under the shower," Betty confided.

"I do everything myself, even my make up."' Thus the heavy-duty mascara, pencilled eyebrows and peachy cheeks would appear to have been the star's self-created work of art. As for her figure, Grable confessed – helping herself to a slice of coconut custard pie – that she always put herself on a diet in the ten-day run-up to a new movie role: 'My weight just seems to melt away.'

Late in life, in a rare moment of candour, Grable opened up to Mike Levitt about her sensitivity to criticism. Levitt was with her when they both overheard a passing woman commenting on the ageing star's deteriorating looks: 'She sure doesn't look the way she used to, does she?' It would have been gratifying, she told him, to be able to turn round and respond – 'Well who the fuck does look the way they used to?'

'And she said, "Am I supposed to walk around the rest of my life with my hand on my hip, looking over my shoulder?"'

Die Führerin

'Unlike the Nazi frau, the Englishwoman has a leg worth fighting for,' declared the writer of a 1941 article entitled 'Stockings, Cosmetics and You'.

Whether or not they felt proud of their legs, women had little choice in the matter. From knee to ankle, they were now on view – yet another part of the body to worry about. And that in turn meant a high level of stocking stress.

Before the war, any white woman who could afford to wore silk. Increased leg exposure since the previous war meant that without her stockings she felt undressed. When the Blitz started, some reacted by bulk-buying silk stockings. On the rare occasions when a consignment was rumoured to appear, queues started to form in the early hours of the morning. But silk soon became unavailable (it was required for parachute manufacture), and with a shortfall in the production of rayon stockings, many women resorted to socks or leg-staining products, some home-made, others commercial. Coffee, onion skins, wet sand, gravy browning and even potassium permanganate were used. A sister or friend was enlisted to draw the obligatory seam up the back with eyebrow pencil. Shop-bought options – 'bottled stockings' – included Silktona, which advertised its leg make-up as giving bare legs 'the elegance of sheer silk'.

In wartime Liverpool Helen Forrester had an office job. As an employee, you did what you were told, but you also wore what your boss told you to wear. The female employees could not afford stockings, so went without, shaved their legs and did their best to disguise them with stain or make-up. Helen's exposed skin suffered in cold weather. But her manager, Mr Fox, issued an edict: the reputation of the company was at stake, and the women were to wear stockings – 'Bare legs are not respectable, you know that.' Hostilities now broke out. Next morning two of the girls outrageously turned up in slacks, whereupon Mr Fox called the girls into his office and threatened to fire them. The girls brazened it out and threatened to quit en masse. Eventually a truce was called. There would be no further objections to them going barelegged, but slacks were a step too far and would not be tolerated.

––––––

Hitler himself never issued an edict on women's appearance.

There's evidence that he was enthralled by stylish, glamorous women, including film stars like Marlene Dietrich and Greta Garbo. According to his secretary, 'all the women met their Führer with carefully painted lips'. But his partialities contrasted strongly with his party's line on women's appearance.

The chic, short-haired, Americanised cultural scene of Berlin under the Weimar Republic, with its gender ambiguity, androgyny and vampish female artificiality, was dismissed as decadent and debauched. An ideal of beauty – of Aryan *volk*, unspoiled by ugliness – underlay Hitlerism. Prudery prevailed. Traditionalism was back. Officially, Hitler purported to be single and celibate, while unofficially conducting relationships with a number of attractive and younger women; his British biographer records that he preferred 'girls he could dominate, who would be obedient playthings but not get in the way'. But the official face of fascism upheld the mother figure, pure and uncontaminated by cosmetics. From broad-hipped hausfrau making babies for the Third Reich to sexy lipsticked glamour girl – the Nazi leadership benefitted on both female fronts.

The hausfrau had a bureaucracy dedicated to her welfare and repute. NS-Frauenschaft, the women's wing of the Nazi Party, played a significant role in supporting the propaganda machine and instructing the female population in the domestic arts. From 1933 its 'Führerin' was Frau Gertrud Scholtz-Klink. Though not close to Hitler himself, Scholtz-Klink was powerful, and in the know about Nazi terror tactics, including those against women; for example she supported eugenic movements that advocated the compulsory sterilisation of women who were thought to be unfit for motherhood.

By the late 1930s Nazi hardliners had constructed a new, ideal German femininity, composed from peasant skirts, aprons, blouses and blonde hair. Hitler also gave his approval to strictly standardised uniforms, with prescribed skirt lengths and badges to indicate rank, to be worn by the various women's and girls' groups. The Nazi programme outlawed nail varnish, plucked eyebrows and dyed hair as un-German. Hair was to be kept neat and tidy. Powder and rouge, it emphasised, were superfluous, since such women possessed the inner glow of health.

In dress and demeanour, blonde, blue-eyed and fertile,

Scholtz-Klink conformed to the ideal. In public she was often to be seen in a folksy dirndl with her hair in Gretchen braids. She had had six children (two of whom died). She was a true believer, and such was her stern irreproachability that she became known as the 'perfect Nazi woman'.

Insofar as German women were wedded to *Kinder*, *Küche* and *Kirche*, they also conformed to that mystical image of womanhood so adored by Victorian patriarchs, the Angel in the House. But retiring Victorian damsels they were not. German women still enjoyed trying out new hairstyles, or copying the latest international fashions. German women's magazines also continued to promote French couture alongside the hair dyes and complexion creams used by Hollywood stars.

Constant vigilance against such corrupting influences was essential. So women were encouraged to participate in sport and gymnastics. In 1935 *Time* magazine reported on the Nazi party Congress held at Nürnberg, attended by nearly a million people. 'I EXALT WOMEN!' thundered Adolf Hitler from his podium. Frau Scholtz-Klink had assembled fifty thousand female supporters:

> [They] hailed Herr Hitler with bursts of wild, ecstatic cheering which kept up for the whole 45 minutes that he addressed them in his happiest mood . . .
>
> 'I exalt women . . . We deny the Liberal-Jew-Bolshevik theory of "women's equality" because it dishonors them! A woman, if she understands her mission rightly, will say to a man, 'You preserve our people from danger and I shall give you children." (Cries of '*Ja*! *Ja*! *Heil Hitler*!')

Gertrud Scholtz-Klink's first visit to England was in 1936. Her fact-finding mission provided ghoulish fascination for British journalists and column inches for their readers. In 1939 the she-Nazi returned. This time it was at the invitation of the Women's League of Health and Beauty.*

Chapter 5 explored the League's ethos of healthy beauty and dedication to the cause of slim shapeliness under the leadership of Mollie Stack and, following her death, of her daughter Prunella. In March 1939 the meeting took place between Hitler's perfect woman and the *Daily Mail*'s 'physically perfect' Prunella Douglas-Hamilton (née Stack).

It helps to explain some background. In 1937 Prunella had been invited to join the board of the National Fitness Council, so she too was representing her nation. In her autobiography she makes no mention of her meeting with the Führerin – nevertheless she issued the invitation with her eyes open. In 1938 Prunella had travelled in Austria and Germany, where she had encountered Nazi demonstrations and accompanied League members to Hamburg, where they had been invited by Kraft durch Freude† ('Strength through Joy') to contribute a choreographed routine – 'The League performed twice, their neat black-and-white uniforms contrasting with ... the generous build of the blonde German girls.'

There, Prunella was introduced to Heinrich Himmler ('[he had] a handshake like a wet fish'), who at this time was spearheading the persecution of the Jews. As winter approached the pitiless Nazi machine was moving into a new, terrifying gear. Back in England Prunella must have been aware of the events of 9–10 November 1938, for *Kristallnacht* ('the night of the broken glass') – a pogrom in which around thirty thousand Jewish men

---

* The visit is the subject of a forensic piece of scholarship, 'Peace at any Price: The Visit of Nazi Women's Leader Gertrud Scholtz-Klink to London in March 1939 and the Response of British Women Activists', by Professor Julie Gottlieb and Professor Matthew Stibbe (both of Sheffield Hallam University), published in *Women's History Review* in 2016.

† The Nazis ran Kraft durch Freude as a tourist and propaganda operation. By 1939, approaching twenty-five million people had participated in KdF-run leisure programmes, including keep-fit, cruises, carnivals and concerts.

were arrested and taken to concentration camps, and hundreds were killed – was widely reported in the British press.

Despite this, from late 1938 plans went ahead for the Führerin's trip to London. The publicly given reason for the visit was 'to study social conditions'. But though the invitation to Frau Scholtz-Klink was evidently a return match, there is no evidence that Prunella sympathised with Nazi aims. 'The full horror of the Nazi regime, with its accompanying concentration camps and secret police, was not yet understood by the majority of Britons,' she wrote in her autobiography. 'Total rejection of Hitler's word had not yet taken place.' Nor that of his female counterpart, it would seem.

On 7 March 1939, when the flight carrying Hitler's most prominent henchwoman landed from Berlin the press were waiting at Croydon aerodrome to greet her. Frau Scholtz-Klink, they reported, had chosen low heels, a severe halo-shaped hat, a white blouse and a neat navy-blue skirt and coat 'which hid her swastika badge'. 'Her face is freckled and her eyebrows are unplucked.' Bearing the colourful bouquet with which she had been presented, she stepped into a car and was carried off to the German Embassy. That evening she dined at Claridge's, at the invitation of Prunella, her husband and their friends from the conservative Anglo-German Fellowship. The Führerin wore a high-necked brocade evening gown, with her hair dressed in a coronet of plaits. 'She prefers a shiny nose to wearing make-up.'

So far, so lacking in glamour.

The following day Frau Scholtz-Klink visited the headquarters of the Women's League of Health and Beauty in Great Portland Street. There Hitler's perfect woman joined perfect Prunella for a smiling photocall, and over the next two days she made the rounds of girls' schools and hospitals. On the final day of her London visit there was a small anti-fascist protest by members of the Women's Committee for Peace and Democracy, who made their way to the German Embassy bearing placards with the message 'Clear Out Schultz-Klink' (*sic*). That evening Prunella made a radio broadcast to Germany, in German, calling on both nations to share a common belief in the importance of physical fitness.

March 1939: the *Daily Mirror* reports on Gertrud Scholtz-Klink's arrival at Croydon airport, and with Prunella Douglas-Hamilton on her visit to the headquarters of the Women's League of Health and Beauty

When Prunella wrote her autobiography in 1973, she would have been entitled to shudder retrospectively at encounters that had happened thirty-five years earlier, just as she was entitled to edit them out of her life story. It is hard to tell how susceptible she was at the time to the aim of physical perfectibility propagated by the Nazis, and which she and her League seemed to share.

Prunella firmly believed that her mother's vision of health and beauty could, indirectly, combat evil in the world; peace and cooperation were fundamental to the League's vision. But she must have realised, as she travelled in Europe and witnessed the infiltration of Nazism into every facet of people's lives, that the mass pursuit of physical perfection had the potential for cruel and terrible dehumanisation. Did she reflect on those gargantuan, highly choreographed spectacles arranged by the League that she represented, held – like Nazi rallies – in colossal arenas, and dramatised with flaming torches? Those displays were organised with parade-ground precision. The ideals of health and beauty, it seemed, could too easily be co-opted in the service of a regimented totalitarianism, with the reduction of individuals into insignificance. And Nazism brought with it too the fearful prospect of the relentless destruction of all those perceived as non-beautiful. Beauty could *be* evil.

On 8 March 1939, when the beaming, leggy Prunella Douglas-Hamilton, in vest and satin knickers, welcomed Gertrud Scholtz-Klink to the League's headquarters, did she writhe a little when Hitler's delegate stepped forward, with her scraped-back hair, stompy shoes and discreet dark costume? Did she draw comparisons? Did she avoid all the awkward questions which the press and protest surrounding the long-planned visit must have prompted? And with war on the horizon, did these two 'perfect women' share notes on how to build up the physique of a winning nation – or on how to suppress dissenters?

A week later, on 15 March, the *Wehrmacht* marched, in perfect formation, into Prague.

War and Wardrobes

A journey to Mussolini's Italy was planned. It was the spring of 1935 and my great-aunt Virginia Woolf* and her husband Leonard decided to travel through Germany. Leonard had a contact in the Foreign Office who had advised them to steer clear of Nazi demonstrations. But Virginia made light of it: 'We're just off motoring to Rome,' she wrote to a friend, 'and as we go through Germany, and as Leonard's nose is so long and hooked, we rather suspect that we shall be flayed alive.'

They knew the risks. Leonard, though Jewish, wanted to see the Third Reich for himself; both he and Virginia were among the many British opponents of fascism who anticipated another world war. It wasn't pleasant, and in Bonn they encountered Nazism at fever pitch. That sunny May morning the Woolfs' car slowed to a crawl between mile-long parades of delirious swastika-waving Germans and armed stormtroopers shouting 'Heil Hitler! Heil Hitler!' Strung over the street were banners declaring 'The Jew is our enemy'. 'Nerves rather frayed,' recorded Virginia, which was probably an understatement since Leonard had cautioned her to self-edit her diary until they crossed the border. Such direct experience of Nazism could only have served to make world peace seem ever more fragile, while the sight of frantic crowds and marching soldiers in shiny knee-high black boots must have fed into Virginia's writings about the approaching war.

---

* Just one generation separates me from my namesake (she died fourteen years before I was born). Woolf was my father Quentin Bell's aunt. He knew her well, and was her first biographer: *Virginia Woolf*, *Vols 1* and *2* (1972). My mother, Anne Olivier Bell, edited the five volumes of *The Diary of Virginia Woolf*. Critics and scholars refer to her as 'Woolf', but for me that jars. Both her principal biographers use 'Virginia', and as one knew her and the other didn't, I'll follow their lead. I was thirteen when my great-uncle died and to me he'll always be 'Leonard'.

Those notes were expanding into the long essay which would become *Three Guineas* (1938): an extended outburst of dismay and accusation against tyranny and patriarchy that asked the question, how can war be prevented? In it Virginia also explored the symbolism of dress – with much to say about men, women, their wardrobes and war – while developing her feminist vision. *Three Guineas* proposed to its readers that the Victorian male hegemony, with all its exclusion, oppression and love of power, was paralleled by the ugly tyranny of fascism; the evil of dictators was rooted, she declared, in the evil of the patriarchy. In other words, though she is clear that women were collusive, war could not happen without the innate aggression of masculinity. And in one of the book's most persuasive passages, Virginia explains how the wearing of ostentatious clothes confers unassailable public status on 'our fathers and brothers':

> Your clothes . . . make us gape with astonishment. How many, how splendid, how extremely ornate they are – the clothes worn by the educated man in his public capacity! Now you dress in violet; a jewelled crucifix swings on your breast; now your shoulders are covered with lace; now furred with ermine; now slung with many linked chains set with precious stones. Now you wear wigs on your heads; rows of graduated curls descend to your necks. Now your hats are boat-shaped, or cocked; now they mount in cones of black fur; now they are made of brass and scuttle shaped; now plumes of red, now of blue hair surmount them . . . After the comparative simplicity of your dress at home, the splendour of your public attire is dazzling.

Clothes wield power, and they intimidate. When I watched the funeral procession of Queen Elizabeth II in September 2022 I was struck by the contrast between countless men marching in grandiose colourful fancy dress and the women beside them walking in black obscurity, shaded with hats and cloaked in veils. Likewise, the new king's coronation robes dazzled: scarlet, gold and white. Men's military apparel, every badge and button, symbolises male prestige and affirms male authority and glory. But the men's grand clothes are not for the battlefield. They are there, as Virginia says, 'in order to impress the beholder with the majesty of military office, partly in order through their vanity to induce young men to become soldiers'. The competitiveness, ostentation and expense of such garments therefore contributed to the negative dispositions which led to war.

Virginia pursues her theme; the centuries of women observing public and military glamour from the sidelines, she says, are passing. Since biblical times women have been subordinate – required, as St Paul tells his followers, to veil themselves in acceptance of men's mastery over them. But now, she says, in the twentieth century, women have joined the procession. The day may even dawn when they can wear a judge's wig, speak from a pulpit dressed in a purple vest, or even decorate their chests with silver lace, carry swords at their sides and adopt shiny headgear in the shape of plumed coal-scuttles. (Nobody at this time foresaw female conscription into the armed forces, which would be introduced just three years later.)

But wouldn't such an alliance and an identification with men simply corrupt, and provide evidence that women had capitulated? Certainly, women bearing swords was no way to prevent war. Instead, *Three Guineas* urges 'the daughters of educated men' to reject such complicity, to split off from the male establishment, to group themselves under the banner of 'outsiders' and experiment with new ways of thinking about life, society and politics. They should eschew ostentatious pageantry – 'in which only one sex takes an active part' – and the symbols of prestige: those medals, badges, ribbons and the like. The male markers of superiority are pernicious, with their 'obvious effect ... to constrict, to stereotype and to destroy'.

> Here, as so often, the example of the Fascist States is at hand to instruct us – for if we have no example of what we wish to be, we have, what is perhaps equally valuable, a daily and illuminating example of what we do not wish to be. With the example then, that they give us of the power of medals, symbols [and] orders ... to hypnotise the human mind it must be our aim not to submit ourselves to such hypnotism.

And in that passage, she was surely recalling driving with her Jewish husband past the frenzied Nazi faithful and the goose-stepping stormtroopers of Bonn. The vision was ever-present: the figure of a man –

> His body ... is tightly cased in a uniform. Upon the breast of that uniform are sewn several medals and other mystic symbols. His hand is upon a sword. He is called in German and Italian Führer or Duce; in our own language Tyrant or Dictator. And behind him lie ruined houses and dead bodies – men, women and children.

Three Guineas came out in 1938. The following year, war was declared. In September 1940 Virginia's short article 'Thoughts on Peace in an Air Raid' was published. Here again, she explored the symbolism of regalia and embellishments. Men's destructive impulses were in part motivated by the love of such trappings – 'To earn undying honour and glory by shooting total strangers, and to come home with my breast covered with medals and decorations, that was the summit of my hope.' As Virginia saw it, women had to oppose male hate, and men's thoughtless ambition, through the healing power of their creativity. Only in that way could they bring about peace and freedom.

But male aggression and the desire to dominate was also sustained by women's conditioning, by their need to appear attractive. And Virginia uses an arresting image to illuminate the sexual/economic trade-off which lies at the heart of so many human interractions, and to demonstrate the ways in which men and women alike are subjugated: prisoners of a 'subconscious Hitlerism', which oppresses humanity:

> It is the desire for aggression; the desire to dominate and enslave. Even in the darkness we can see that made visible. We can see shop windows blazing; and women gazing; painted women; dressed-up women; women with crimson lips and crimson fingernails. They are slaves who are trying to enslave. If we could free ourselves from slavery we should free men from tyranny. Hitlers are bred by slaves.

As for her own relationship with her appearance, Virginia was perpetually tormented by insecurity. Her forays into fashion were uncertain. As a young woman at the turn of the century, though slender and classically beautiful, she had been devastated by her older half-brother's criticisms. He made her feel like a social failure, lacking a good hairdresser and a good dressmaker. Wearing stays was such an ordeal that she could not even bear to name them in her diary.

In 1919 she admitted, 'I am resigned to my station among the badly dressed,' and for the rest of her life an onlooker's gaze could be torture. Child-free and intellectual, Virginia felt like a misfit, detached from mainstream constructions of the feminine or motherly woman. She doubted her beauty, and she struggled to find clothes that suited her – 'To be fitted, to come into a room wearing a new dress – still frightens me,' she wrote, while the writer Vita Sackville-West described her as being dressed 'quite atrociously'. And yet Virginia and the idea of female appearance are inseparable – countless people who have never read a word by her know what she looked like. (She herself has become an instance of female commodification; you can buy a Virginia Woolf T-shirt, a Virginia Woolf tote bag, a Virginia Woolf fridge magnet, a Virginia Woolf doll.)

Countless people who have never read a word by her know what she looked like. Virginia Stephen photographed by George Beresford, 1902

But I believe Virginia's clothes-angst was central to her recognition of fashion's primacy in our lives. As she explained in
Orlando (1928), clothes – far from being the 'vain trifles' that
they seem – are fundamental to identity. We become what we
wear. In *The Waves* (1931), she dazzlingly merges the body, and
clothes, of a woman on a train being admired by a man – 'I see
him lower his paper. He smiles at my reflection in the tunnel.
My body instantly of its own accord puts forth a frill under
his gaze.'

Her observations on how people choose to present themselves
are profound, and ahead of her time. My great-aunt knew that
clothes and appearances were among the foundation stones of
the human psyche. Her vision was rooted in the everyday. The
creative soul took sustenance from elegant shops, from 'the
everchanging and turning world of gloves and shoes and stuffs'.

For myself, I'm strongly drawn to her recognition that fripperies and finery can teach us about human nature – but I'm
drawn even more by her insight that 'trivial' female concerns
are judged inferior to 'heroic' male concerns like war and battle.
Virginia knew that this judgement was biased and untrue.

Mascara Magic

By 1939 feminism and fashion had, together, changed many
women's lives. But in mid-twentieth-century Britain Monica
Baldwin was suffering from clothes-angst. Her story* provides an extraordinary reveal of the feminine landscape at the
beginning of the Second World War. The perspective she gives
is unique and valuable, because for twenty-eight years she had

---

* Monica told it in her bestselling memoir *I Leap Over the Wall* (1949). She
had grown up in privileged circles: her great-uncle Stanley Baldwin served three
terms as Conservative Prime Minister, 1923–4, 1924–9 and 1935–7.

been completely shielded from the rapid shape-shifts of the twentieth century.

This historical 'fossil' was born in 1893. Just a few months before the start of the 1914–18 conflict, aged twenty-one, she entered an enclosed order of Augustinian canonesses, and took the veil of a nun. Behind her, she left a world of curvaceous Gibson Girls, iron-clad in corsets, with abundant, piled-high tresses, milky-skinned faces virtually free of cosmetics, and only the glimpse of an ankle to show they had legs.

For the next three decades Monica's own appearance conformed to a set of rules laid down in the Middle Ages. Nothing could be seen of her body apart from hands and face, the latter enfolded in a starched cambric wimple to the chin. As the world around her collapsed, and was rebuilt, only to unravel again with disastrous consequences, Monica in her religious enclave was oblivious – not only to the international meltdown, but to Hollywood, lace lingerie, bobs and Marcel waves, backless evening dresses, nail polish and mascara. She had never been to a talkie. She saw no men.

On 26 October 1941, at the age of forty-eight, Monica left the convent for ever. 'I was,' she wrote, 'no more fitted to be a nun than to be an acrobat.' And at a moment when everyday life was in turmoil, she re-entered the world. 'Culture shock' best describes her reaction to it.

Freda, Monica's sister, helped to turn her into a modern woman: 'She brought with her ... a suitcase containing the clothes into which I was to change before finally going forth into the world.' The first trauma was the underwear. Freda handed her 'a wisp of gossamer,' announcing, 'Here's your foundation garment.' The neck-high camisoles and ample drawers from Monica's Edwardian adolescence were to be replaced with 'cobwebby' cami-knickers. Next, Freda had to reassure her that her 'naked' legs would not look conspicuous in transparent stockings. But there was one final horror: '"This," said my sister cheerfully, "is a brassière."'

Women, it seemed, now wore undergarments fashioned deliberately to emphasise their breasts as individual entities rather than squishing them together into an amorphous, unidentifiable blob. For Monica, this monstrous indecency contradicted the assumptions of a lifetime.

Freda then supplied her sister with a hat, a nondescript dress and shoes with such precariously high heels that she found it difficult to balance.

So much for her own appearance. But encountering real-life women in 1941 left Monica distraught: '[They] appeared to belong to a different civilization. They had narrow faces, high cheek-bones, wide, heavily-painted mouths and slanting eyes ... And most of them had terrible, claw-like, purple-painted nails.' It was awful. Even middle-class women dyed their hair and reddened their mouths. They went hatless, their jacket shoulders were aggressively padded and their skirts were short. At the same time they were 'alarmingly competent'. Modern women drove cars, travelled and played sport. 'I began to feel dizzy and bemused ... What kind of a world, really, was this to which I had returned?'

As the war progressed Monica tried to find her niche. She got a job as assistant matron at a hostel for female munitions workers in Lancashire. But she had little in common with the majority of the occupants – 'Most of them belong to what are called the working classes.' And as for the sight of their made-up faces, their tight slacks, and their bare legs ... 'I could hardly endure to look at them.'

Betty Grable had a lot to answer for, as did a neighbouring GI camp, whose inmates were the cause of much of the young women's giggling, flirtatious behaviour. Monica discovered that these working women modelled themselves on their favourite 'Hollywood cuties': '"Cutie" ... a terrible word for a terrible thing.'

More culture shock was to come. Monica next took up a placement with the British Army Canteen Service, where she was employed to peel potatoes with other kitchen skivvies who started each day with a copious breakfast, consumed in curlers, followed by a dash back to their flea-infested quarters – 'Here they removed the curlers from their hair, anointed their faces with skin-cream, rouge, powder, mascara, lipstick and what-not and came forth so resplendent as to be hardly recognizable.'

In Monica's youth resplendent looks had been the preserve of the upper crust who were blessed with blue eyes, curly hair and a peachy complexion. Now, she concluded (regretfully) that – thanks to dyes and cosmetics – they were within easy reach of everyone.

In 1941, women of all classes had an increased sense of self-worth. They walked taller, on higher heels – but more than ever they were bewitched by their reflection in the mirror of men's eyes. The GI Romeos still required their Juliets to look the part. Cinema, technology and the vagaries of war were the agents of change in a high-stakes world. But as Monica found out, high heels could be treacherous. And the ex-nun's reactions serve as a vivid reminder that the balancing act was as challenging as ever.

———

The years 1939–45 saw Britain come under a command economy, in which civilians and the military, men and women, did what their masters told them to do. Following orders from the largely male government,* our grandmothers and great-grandmothers carried gas masks and sewed blackout curtains, recycled paper, bathed in five inches of water with a line on the bath to show the fill-up limit, improvised sanitary towels and eked out their rations. They took in evacuees, nursed the wounded, grew crops and packed parachutes. They fought, suffered, dared – and died. And every morning, when they got up, they adapted their appearance to what was available, and to what was deemed feminine, for the sake of victory, all in obedience to the demands of a nation at war.

From its outbreak the pressure was on to maintain feminine standards. 'It would be [a] calamity if war turned us into a nation of frights and slovens,' *Vogue* told its readers in September 1939, less than a fortnight after war was declared.

The government worked with the media and the manufacturers of clothing and beauty products to propagandise women, with one pre-eminent message: Beauty was a Duty. 'Put your Best Face Forward,' Yardley told its customers. 'We must remember that the slightest hint of a drooping spirit yields a point to the enemy.' The *Daily Mirror*, meanwhile, stressed how vital it was to be 'a thing of beauty in a world where ugliness has raised its standard': 'Remember that every frock, every hat, every banner of colour a woman wears is making a memory for someone – especially for some man.'

But in June 1941 this task became a whole lot harder: Hugh Dalton, President of the Board of Trade, announced that, in order to prevent waste of resources, clothes would henceforth be rationed. Dalton appointed Sir Thomas Barlow, a man in his sixties, to oversee dress regulations, and Barlow in his turn created a bureaucracy which issued a deluge of directives, such as –

---

* Out of the 615 MPs elected in 1935, just nine of them were women.

Women's and maids' dresses and blouses are to be simplified ...
The number of buttons, seams and pleats, and the amount of
ruching and gauging are strictly limited; no braid, embroidery or
lace is to be used.*

The days of impulse buys were over, and the make-do-and-
mend era had begun.

Within the year the Board of Trade introduced its 'utility'
scheme, which applied to a range of goods including clothing,
and soon became synonymous with pared-down affordability.
The Board did its best to involve talented designers in this latest
economy drive. But in their new tight, skimpily pleated skirts
and single-breasted jackets with minimal buttons, many women
had to make brave efforts to think of themselves as stylish.

———

Looking like a cutie was getting harder as the war ground
on, and resources grew scanter. But, as Monica Baldwin had
noticed, that didn't deter young working-class women from
trying. Many wartime Cinderellas boosted their self-respect by
doubling up as fairy godmother, enacting transformation scenes
with the last of their lipstick and a touch of mascara magic. One
of these was Doris Scorer.

Doris was a Londoner by birth. When war broke out she was
seventeen, employed as a lowly machinist in a dress factory.
Blessed with a sunny temperament and a taste for fashion, the
life suited her – but it came to an end in the winter of 1940
when she and her widowed mother surfaced one morning from
their Blitz-time public air-raid shelter, aching and longing for

---

* Men were not exempt. Trouser turn-ups, zip fasteners and double-breasted
suits were banned, and boys under the age of fourteen were prohibited from
wearing long trousers.

a cup of tea, to discover that their Islington home had been
bombed. They were allowed briefly into the unsafe building
to collect necessities (and the cat), and Mother telegraphed her
sister Elsie in Wolverton, Buckinghamshire, to tell her they were
homeless. 'Come to us at once,' replied Elsie.

Relocated, Doris found new employment in another dress
factory, and life 'settled down to some semblance of order'.
Then the blow fell.

By 1941 the British government faced a controversial decision. The army desperately needed more men – men who
were already needed to work in the factories. The Minister of
Labour, Ernest Bevin, conceded that the only way to make up
the shortfall was to compel women – like Doris – who were
regarded as 'mobile' to step into the men's shoes by undertak-
ing 'essential' work. At the end of that year registration began.
Conscription would over time affect the lives of every available
woman in the country between the ages of eighteen and fifty, by
directing them into the services, transport, nursing, agriculture
and essential industry.

Doris signed up for a job at the Wolverton Works, where she
would be trained to repair damaged aircraft. A month later she
donned her boiler suit, tied a headscarf round her shoulder-
length hair to keep it out of harm's way and set out, 'ready to
win the war'.

Like many other women's war memoirs, Doris's short book
tells a story of broadening horizons. As well as turmoil, loss,
friendships and, ultimately, love and marriage, the Second
World War was bringing women like her a new kind of equality. Doris's record bears witness to the unstoppable advance
of women like her, as they encroached ever further into zones
previously preserved for men: in her case, the aircraft factory.
Yet the fashion-conscious slant she brings to her experiences is
also timelessly representative.

Day one at the works saw Doris with a cohort of women of varied ages who had applied to learn mechanical and engineering jobs:

> We came in all shapes and sizes, the boiler suits showing off our slim figures to advantage, or the more portly, older ones to disadvantage, our rear portions flattered, or perhaps unflattered, by the tight trousers. At least we were brightening up many of the middle-aged men we worked with.

Overalls and twelve-hour shifts didn't deter Doris and her friends from the prospect of a Friday-night dance. Even if the women were busy on the nuts and bolts of an aircraft till eight in the evening, they came to work prepared. With no time to go home and get ready, the trick was to put your hair in curlers in the morning, anchoring them under your headscarf, wear stockings under your boiler suit for speed, and carry a paper bag containing your dress and shoes into work. As the clock struck eight it was time for the transformation scene: a rapid retreat to the Ladies to sponge off the day's grime, curlers out and hair brushed. Then make-up: in the 1940s mascara was sold in solid cakes in a small plastic box; a little spit loosened the colourant so that it could coat the applicator brush. Next, red lipstick. Shake your dress out of its paper bag, discard your overalls, slip your silky toes into their high heels and add the final touch: an artificial flower, or a diamanté clip. Metamorphosed, the girls fluttered out like butterflies from their chrysalises, to the wonderment of their male colleagues. The idea that a painted woman was a harlot was hard to dispel: 'Bet there's not a virgin amongst yer,' one of them was heard commenting.

'Glamour was all the rage for us girls,' recalled Doris, who felt herself to be more sophisticated than the Buckinghamshire bumpkins: 'I had been wooed by the London shops, who in turn were influenced by films and American fashion.' Doris's own dream was to look like movie star Rita Hayworth.

But while the shortages of wartime intensified women's cravings for pretty stuff, it was regarded as unpatriotic to use up scarce resources. Chapter 15 of Doris's story is headed 'Frippery and "Fings"'. She learnt all kinds of dodges. Little scraps of aluminium were scavenged from the works and refashioned into brooches or pendants. You could make a sparkly belt by folding and plaiting the cellophane wrappers from cigarette packets. 'Make-do make-up' was the order of the day – 'Our one aim in life seemed to concern our faces and hair.' Sugar water was used as a substitute for wave-set to stiffen their curls, and a touch of Vaseline on the eyelids made one look irresistible – 'or so we thought'. Shoe polish was a chancy substitute for mascara, and starch could be used instead of face.powder. Lipstick was crucial: the aim was to resemble Lana Turner, Rita Hayworth, Veronica Lake – or Betty Grable. A lipstick's final days could be prolonged by adding warmed almond oil, or by melting it in an egg cup over hot water, and when you finally ran out, beetroot would stain your lips almost as well. Doris and her friends styled their hair into pageboys or peek-a-boos to resemble their favourite screen goddesses.

Wartime also forced a rethink on the underwear prudes. Moralising about whether your petticoat was showing, or getting censorious about skirt lengths seemed gratuitous when raw materials were in short supply and the priority was winning the war. These days you just had to laugh, or cry, when issued with your hard-wearing underpants – often known as 'passion killers' – in khaki, navy or black, stamped with the royal cypher and date of manufacture. Dorothy Brewer from south London recalled that the day she joined the ATS (the Auxiliary Territorial Service), the corporal in charge handed out all the necessities to the rookies, including brass-button cleaner, shoe brushes, stockings, pants, one-size-fits-all foundations and a khaki sewing kit, before announcing: 'Here's your brassière ... Make it fit before morning parade tomorrow.'

Across the country, women were learning to sew their own bras and 'directoire' knickers (bloomer-style, with elastic top and bottom) from parachute silk or knit them from remnants of wool – but elastic was hard to come by and quickly lost its efficacy over frequent washes. Knickers had a tendency to collapse unexpectedly, due to elastic or button failure. Accounts of this catastrophe, which seems often to have been greeted with wolf-whistles and guffaws, recur with comical frequency in wartime memoirs. Doris was always prepared. She never went anywhere without a small gold safety pin.

Making your own corsetry was beyond the majority of women. Despite the shift away from heavily structured clothing, many women still opted to wear supportive foundation garments. 'Gone are the boyish contours of the '20s,' wrote a journalist for *Picture Post* in March 1940. 'The modern woman is as feminine as she has ever been in history, and she does not propose to allow war to deprive her of her figure at this stage.' A generation had grown up with the embedded idea that a woman wasn't really a woman without her corset; for example, even with the air-raid sirens wailing, Gladys Watkins's father couldn't persuade his daughter to hurry up and get to safety: 'If Mr Hitler's coming,' she called from the top of the stairs, 'I'm not going to meet him without my corsets on!' Women in the services (apart from the Land Army, for some reason) had their corsets provided for them. But civilians were not prioritised. Early in the war a convocation of women's magazine editresses was assembled to put the 'tragic' case of the large women in need of elastic corsets who had written to them in despair; sadly, the rubber shortage made their case hopeless. In 1940 corset production was down by 40 per cent, corset factories were turning over their machinery to the manufacture of parachutes, and the workers were leaving in droves to enlist. As the war dragged on the patience of women trying to prolong the life of their foundation garments by mending them was wearing as thin as the corsets themselves.

Their quality was abysmal: soggy armatures of cardboard and cotton, they failed to hold in anybody's waist, and corset-rage intensified. In June 1944 housewife Hannah Wright from Macclesfield penned a furious letter to the *Daily Express*, in which she issued a challenge to the President of the Board of Trade.

Hugh Dalton was a petulant, difficult, middle-aged, balding old Etonian. Just put yourself in my shoes, Mr Dalton, fumed Mrs Wright: try being a housewife who has to walk a mile to join a queue at the fishmonger's, while trussed up in a cardboard corset, wearing baggy utility stockings and clumpy wooden clogs! 'His corset would have wilted into [a] revolting mass of cotton and cardboard. He would find himself supporting the corset, instead of the corset supporting him.' Shamed, Dalton and his Board caved in, allocated enough extra steel to manufacture an additional 1.75 million corsets and, true to form, appointed nine middle-aged male apparatchiks to spend the summer inspecting and approving designs for the new, stronger models. They would report in November ...

For King and Country

Joining up promised perks like free corsets. But conscription also brought with it progress for women. A future beyond home and family began to seem a reality for many; and though peace seemed far away, a world of work, endeavour, unprecedented freedom and equality with men looked possible.

For most of the conscripts, it was a leap into the unknown. All they had to judge by was externals, so the look of the uniform made a big difference. Again and again women cite uniform as being the key factor in their choice of service. If you were going to serve your country alongside military men, it was worth considering how you measured up to your masters. For, lightly 'feminised' though they were, women's uniforms were unmistakably modelled on those worn by the men. And what appears tough and authoritative when worn by a slim-hipped, broad-shouldered serviceman doesn't produce the same effect in the case of a curvaceous woman. The women in the ATS, for example, were kitted out in a single-breasted belted khaki jacket bulked out with cumbersome pleated pockets which made one look like a badly tied parcel. The headgear was modified, and some of them wore skirts; but apart from that, women's uniforms were indistinguishable from those of men. Collar and tie were universal. 'The uniform is of a drab colour ... the style is not sufficiently becoming,' was the common lament, making the ATS the least sought-after of the services. The blue WAAF (Women's Auxiliary Air Force) uniform, with its pockets and belts, also designed to echo that of the men, had the same unfortunate effect of drawing attention to one's hips and bottom. However the Women's Royal Naval Service was besieged by applicants wishing to join: 'Joining the WRENs was quite the most fashionable war work,' remembered Christian Oldham, who signed up in 1940. '[We] had this nice straight uniform which concealed your worst points.' The twenty-year-old was in love with the flattering double-breasted tailored jacket, slimming skirt and above all with the jaunty tricorn hat that comprised the officers' uniform, as designed by couturier Edward Molyneux. As she put it, 'the effect was a winner'.

Chic or frumpy, uniform had a homogenising effect, though even this was undermined by the ability of wealthier recruits to advertise their privilege by ordering their suits from Harrods or an expensive Regent Street tailor. Many women loved the sense of belonging, almost inviolability, that uniform gave them, while for those from lower-income backgrounds, who had grown up on hand-me-downs, the quality of the clothes elevated them into an unfamiliar world of pride in their appearance. 'I learnt that though you could be proud when you're wearing rags, you can do better when you're smart,' said one.

The uniform of the Women's Land Army (WLA) fell into a special category, however, for farm work was dirty, smelly and could not be performed in skirts. From 1939, seventeen thousand volunteers applied to enrol in the WLA and the Timber Corps, with the exodus from the cities of shop workers, hairdressers, waitresses and typists, into the fields and milking parlours of Suffolk and Shropshire amounting to a culture clash.

It was the usual story. The publicity was attractive, and soon had these young women dreaming of an outdoor life clasping sheaves of corn, cuddling new-born lambs and wearing open-necked shirts and picture hats. The mismatch of expectations was striking. One journalist gave his readers a description of the unsuspecting new recruits: 'They arrive unsuitably shod, unsuitably clad; with four-inch heels and eye-veils. Make-up masks their faces.'

Wilfred Shewell-Cooper, author of the *Land Army Manual*, also issued a solemn warning to the townie volunteers who failed to adapt to rural ways:

Town girls, on the whole use far more make-up than country girls. The WLA volunteer should therefore be prepared to 'tone down' her lips, complexion and nails considerably ... Long nails are quite unsuited to work on a farm, especially when covered with bright crimson nail varnish. The volunteer ... will find, too, that she will get such a healthy colour to her cheeks that rouging will not be necessary!

Shirley Joseph was one of the 'new girls' from a protected background who came down to earth with a crash when she received her kit. She was supplied with dirty green corduroy knee-breeches, a green jersey, rubber boots, and a short over-coat – 'Somehow khaki breeches and what is vulgarly known as the bum-freezer coat do not make for glamour whichever way you look at them, least of all from behind,' she told an inter-viewer. Another landgirl said that the whole ensemble made her feel 'like Humpty Dumpty'.

————

Trousers, in any case, still roused controversy. Barely a gener-ation ago, the man had been a dark, vertical cylinder, while the woman was all colourful curves, but in uniform they were almost indistinguishable. Function was at war with form, for though men dictated that the servicewomen should wear 'male' garments, many of them felt uneasy at the sight of a woman square-bashing in khaki.

Pathé newsreels had a habitual trick of neutralising the shock effect of women doing men's work. Their upbeat reports came accompanied with plummy commentary to reassure the public that the women were not rivals in the male arena, but just a sporting troupe of amateurs. Under the heading 'Jolly Good Fellers', a typical 1942 report shows a group of dungaree-clad 'lumberjills' with saws and axes at work in a Scottish forest. 'Felling trees may harden the muscles, but see what it does for the dimples!' says the jocose male voiceover, behind a shot of a woman beaming at the camera. 'There's a knack, and a great deal of effort in swinging an axe, especially for a girl who's never swung anything heavier than a handbag! Whoever would have thought that among these sturdy log-rollers were a nurse, shop assistant, usherette, teacher?' And so on ...

'Jolly Good Fellers' – women
Timber Corps volunteers

Essentially, the popular belief was that trousers could be worn while doing your patriotic duty, sawing timber or hoeing turnips, but underneath, the girls were still girls. As for wearing trousers after hours, well, it just wasn't ladylike. 'You are *not* going to church dressed like a man!' one landgirl was told.

Ignorance and fear prevailed. Were the trouser-wearers lesbians? One late, golden September afternoon in 1944 Vita Sackville-West was strolling in a Kentish orchard, when an appetising sight met her eyes, of four rosy-cheeked young women sorting apples under a tree. Green jerseys clung to their young figures. Vita's loving description of this melt-in-the-mouth spectacle appeared in a short propagandising book* about the WLA, which demonstrated her love of the land and keen appreciation of young women clad in boots and breeches, and which may well have fed that stereotype. There was also a widespread sense that female farmworkers were immoral. The Ministry of Agriculture's recruiting slogan 'Back to the Land' was mangled by some as 'backs to the land', and the made-up 'townies' were regarded as scarlet sirens from Babylon, luring hapless peasant farmers to their doom.

———

The war garbled people's notions of how women were supposed to be. Were women in uniform warriors or whores, heroines, lesbians, or traitors to their sex? Did you applaud them for doing their patriotic duty, or shame them for quitting their post: hearth and home?

Mixed messages proliferated. In November 1944, a woman with ninepence, buying her copy of *Woman and Home*, was confronted by two gung-ho WAAFs, with lipstick, brass

---

* Vita Sackville-West, *The Women's Land Army* (1944).

buttons and shiny peaked caps, setting out to do their duty for king and country. But the cover strapline also advertised a knitting pattern for a 'Jumper with a Fair-Isle Front (directions inside)'. The lure of feminine pursuits and an appealing hand-knit pullover competed with the freedom and romance of the air force – not to mention all those dashing aircrew!

Woman and Home, November 1944

Or take that quintessentially propagandist wartime movie *Mrs Miniver* (1942), with Kay Miniver played by Greer Garson. The script of this Academy Award-winning picture successfully played off the lady of leisure against the home front heroine, in a story which elevates Mrs Miniver from fragrant, domesticated wife to inspirational woman of destiny. At the start of the film, Mrs Miniver is engaged in the most feminine activity its director could envisage: a shopping trip, from which she returns with a frivolous beribboned hat packed in a lovely stripy box. But war intervenes, and the hat is put away, never to be seen again. Mrs Miniver, however, evolves into a dauntless champion who heroically disarms a wounded German paratrooper.

Common among many men was the fear that women would stray into their territory, appropriate male characteristics and steal their liberties. 'There's no need to go mannish on us just because you're doing a man's job and wearing man's clothes to do it ... Even if you are a lorry-driver, you don't have to look like one,' complained one newspaper contributor, making it clear where he stood on the trespass across gender boundaries: 'Men are notoriously sentimental – it's our women that we're fighting for – but where's the sense in fighting for a woman who can stand on her own feet?'

The world order may have been unravelling, but the stereotypes remained unscathed. Look like Betty Grable. Be a 'cutie' in red lipstick. Wear your hair permed, or swept into luxuriant curled styles with combs and pins. Another journalist described his encounter with a tall, attractive landgirl – an ex-fashion model – whose hair was 'rather blonder than Nature made it': 'She was dungareed, and worked a ten-hour day at what was formerly reckoned a "man's job", [but] she stayed feminine. Very feminine.' Gratifyingly, his investigations showed that women who took on 'masculine' work did not, in fact, become masculinised. On the contrary, 'so far from going synthetic male ... the trouble has been to curb their resolute femininity' – and they continued to have their frivolous foibles, wearing attractive colourful accessories to make themselves look dainty, and making as much effort to pluck their eyebrows as their Hollywood role models. Meanwhile, commanders had completely yielded to the women's demands to be allowed to wear a minimum of make-up: 'Cosmetics are as essential to a woman as a reasonable supply of tobacco is to a man.' It was the wartime recognition that their products were not optional that, as much as anything, established the cosmetics industry on an unshakable footing.

The focus on looking lovely, on keeping up appearances, on 'feminine' trivialities: silk stockings, pretty hats and porcelain teapots were – it seems – reinforced under adversity.

The Second World War maimed and killed. In London alone, more than forty thousand civilians were killed in seventy-one major air raids. Bombs fell directly on civilians' homes not just in the capital, but in Coventry, Birmingham, Liverpool, Hull, Clydebank and many other cities. For those women who suffered its direct impact – and there were thousands of them – the Blitz brought with it death, terror and grief. But even for those it spared, the bombs often tore indiscriminately into their lives, shredding and vandalising the treasured elements that contributed towards their feminine identity. From the contents of her wardrobe to the trinkets and potions on her dressing table, the bombing raids exposed a woman's innermost sanctums, laying bare her mystique for all to see. One might encounter the cross-section of a bathroom, with a towel laid out ready on the tub waiting for its occupant, an assortment of stockings draped in a tree-top, remnants of dresses hooked over broken rafters, someone's best floral hat at the bottom of the garden, buried under wreckage and matchwood.

Buried, but not dead. After the war, consumerism, and with it, femininity, would rise from the ashes.

The Pedestal

Between 1939 and 1945, 25,399 civilian women* were killed or were reported missing (believed to be killed), while 624 British servicewomen died for their country.

In 1997 the authorities decided to commission a memorial commemorating the valiant women of the Second World War. A charity was created, with a judging panel made up of one woman and two men,† whose remit was to choose a sculptor. Their choice fell on John Mills. Born in 1933, Mills was a wartime evacuee whose mother had worked in munitions, and who had himself done national service in the 1950s. They were formative years: 'I had two years learning how to fight, learning how to kill, teaching other people how to kill, for the Queen,' he told an interviewer in 2019, adding: 'I like people, my sport was swimming and diving, [and] my hobby was young ladies.'

Somehow, Mills had to find a way to accommodate a prohibitively unwieldy crowd on the memorial – and then there was the expense to be considered. If the plinth had to carry representations of landgirls, factory workers, clippies, nurses, air raid wardens, the women on the anti-aircraft batteries, the spies, the welders and riveters, the WVS, ATS, WAAFs, WRNs and so on and so on, the budget for the project would rocket! 'It was,' recalled Mills, 'a hell of a big brief!'

The problem seemed irreconcilable, until he had a flash of inspiration. He decided to abandon the attempt to portray human figures, and settle instead for the pedestal alone. 'It took a long while to convince everybody that this was right,' he recollected.

---

*   This figure includes civil defence workers.
†   The members of the judging panel were Dr Judith Collins, Head of Modern Sculpture at the Tate Gallery, Professor Philip King, President of the Royal Academy of Arts, and the sculptor James Butler.

Plinths or pedestals have always had a special place in gender mythology. They are a simple visual device to elevate sculptures of goddesses, queens, Madonnas – and occasionally lesser people – above the heads of their worshippers, so that everyone can see and admire them. Mills's winning design dispenses with the goddesses and Madonnas, and instead privileges the plinth over its hypothetical occupants. 'I came up with this idea when thumbing through the photographs. I saw a photograph of clothes hanging in the entrance to a dance, and you could tell who was in them, so I thought that's the solution to this.'

Thus, the memorial takes the form of a bronze megalith studded with a row of seventeen oddly spooky disembodied uniforms: the clothes and accessories of the servicewomen, factory workers, farm workers and women who worked in hospitals, emergency services and volunteer bodies across the nation between 1939 and 1945, suspended in a featureless void. Even before the memorial was unveiled its design was criticised, particularly by war veterans: 'The jumble sale tat on the memorial is an insult to all who wore uniforms as a symbol of their help in making the world a better place for our, then unborn, children,' objected one. Another complained:

> Don't depict women of the Second World War as a lot of old clothes hanging on hooks! We lived, and breathed, and went through that war as human beings and for those of us still here today, can only feel deeply insulted by this memorial in its present form.

On 9 July 2005 Mills's twenty-three-foot-high monument was unveiled by Queen Elizabeth II. Lady Boothroyd, who spoke at the unveiling, was effusive: 'I love this monument,' she said. Others however, like the art historian and broadcaster Richard Cork, were taken aback by its casual imagery:

> I can't get why that was considered a good way to memorialise the women of WWII, to have empty coats. It doesn't say anything about their contribution and it rather underplays their role. It's very puzzling and quite annoying.

Public reactions remained mixed. Posting on Tripadvisor after her visit in 2016, Jackie from Canada thought it was 'touching and beautifully sculpted', and Bonnie from Texas agreed: 'This monument is one of the most beautiful on Whitehall Street! We gawked at it for quite awhile appreciating the detail and the sentiment!' But when Jill from Edinburgh saw it in 2018 she was 'dumbfounded' – 'commemorating the very brave work of all those supportive women by clothes hanging up on pegs. As my late mother was one of these women I cannot think she would have been impressed. Those women deserved better.'

And an academic from the University of York, Carolyn Dougherty, blogged about it on The F-Word (Contemporary UK Feminism) website: 'The monument to the women of World War II ... commemorates "women", but carefully avoids portraying any actual, physical women ... Dozens of statues in London represent the men of World War II.'

The rebuke carries weight. Male firefighters, tank crews and air crews have all merited dedicated memorials, whose sculptors have delineated and characterised their portrayals. As a result their acts of brutality, their aggressiveness, their masculinity and their weaponry have pride of place on our streets. But in our public spaces, the images and names of the real women who worked, suffered and died for victory are conspicuous only by their absence.

Sculptor John Mills's monument to the women of the Second
World War in Whitehall, London, was unveiled in July 2005

The monument to the women of the Second World War tells us that this is the way men saw women not only back then, but also today. It implies that a woman's outer garments continue to be an acceptable way to define her. It also tells us that men may talk airily about putting the women they admire on pedestals but, when it comes to the point, they just can't bring themselves to do it.

And it's made to last for ever, in solid bronze.

Brigitte Bardot aged nineteen, photographed on the
beach at Cannes during the 1953 film festival

7

New Look

Brigitte

In the early 1950s a new leading lady emerged whose breathtaking, feline beauty captivated men and women alike. Her name was Brigitte Bardot, and at the age of nineteen she appeared modelling a two-piece which took swimwear to a point of no return.

Fashions in beachwear had crawled to a halt during a war that saw European coastlines fortified with barbed wire and concrete blocks. But the post-war clear-up lifted the effective ban on seaside holidays, and beachwear *joie de vivre* made a comeback. The game-changing costume was first seen on screen when Bardot wore it in *The Girl in the Bikini*, a film that was released in France in 1953 (but didn't reach British screens until 1959). Bardot played the beautiful daughter of a humble Greek island lighthouse-keeper; she dived elegantly off cliffs into crystal waters, scampered over rocks and revealed her minimally clad loveliness to the lithe-bodied young hero. It ended with a kiss.

Women had been baring their ribcages to a lesser degree since the early 1940s, but few had dared go lower. The bikini was named after Bikini Atoll, the site of America's well-publicised nuclear tests carried out in July 1946 – and it was intended to be explosive! That year designer Jacques Heim had come up with the appropriately named *Atome*, a scanty version of the two-piece, with proportions just generous enough to cover the wearer's belly button. But it was quickly superseded by Louis Réard's creation, which plummeted below the navel. This design was so minimal that no respectable mannequin would model it for him, and he had to persuade a stripper to give the new bikini its debut. By today's standards, Réard's boned and underwired creation – with its artificially pointy cups, coupled with matching, relatively high-cut, pouchy gathered knickers – looks rather conservative. But at the time the bikini sent shock waves round the world.

No one popularised the bikini as Bardot did. In the summer of 1953 she posed on Cannes beach, strapless and floral, during the Film Festival, her long hair in a tousled, bed-head style; the picture captures the very essence of radiant, carefree youthfulness.

'Ah, Cannes!' remembered Brigitte, 'I was the "starlet-in-waiting", the up-and-coming starlet who went barefoot, the starlet with the tiny bikini and the revealing *décolletés*, the starlet everyone was talking about.'

Bardot was bohemian and like to pose *au naturel*, with a touch of raunchy danger in her sex appeal – very different from that of stars like Betty Grable with her polished glamour. Brigitte's own description tells the story of how she became a semi-naked sun-worshipper in the south of France:

It was at Cap Myrthes near La Croix Valmer that I first discovered the sun, the smell of pines and thyme mixed with orange blossom and eucalyptus, the softness of the air and the warmth of the sand at night when we lay on it, looking at the stars. It was there that I learned to live like a wild child, barefoot, in a bikini, and for the first time allowed my whole body to become tanned. This new way of life suited me perfectly.

Following Bardot's subsequent appearance in *And God Created Woman* (1956), St Tropez and its beaches, now strewn with bikini babes, was on the map. And beachwear designers found themselves in the happy position of having a sparkly new niche product to sell. But international scandal ensued. In Australia any woman seen wearing a bikini on the beach was immediately ordered off; a number of American states banned them, with the National Legion of Decency putting pressure on the Hollywood studios to keep their films bikini-free. In Johannesburg repugnance to skimpy swimwear was expressed by the chairman of the body which oversaw the city's leisure facilities, who declared 'I shall fight tooth and nail to prohibit these disgusting bits of frippery ... It is not good for young people and non-white attendants to see half-naked women romping about.'

Letters of outrage were received by newspaper editors who printed pictures of bikini-wearers. 'Photographs of women in immodest bathing attire show the tendency toward sex exploitation and are not a good thing for the younger generation,' complained Mrs Constance Kemp of Shropshire Women's Institutes. The French actress Danielle Darrieux deplored the new minimalism: 'You go on the beach and see nothing but nudity. I wear a two-piece myself – but not the Bikini.' And American film star Esther Williams (herself an accomplished swimmer and diver) agreed:

Young girls can wear a couple of Dixie cups and a fishing line if they want, but that's not my lady. A bathing suit is the least amount of clothing you are going to wear in public, so you had better give it some thought. A bikini is a thoughtless act.

Catholic countries were particularly prudish. In Spain the police insisted that women wear 'Victorian-style' swimsuits designed to include a skirt. In Italy, Portugal and Belgium, the authorities prohibited two-piece swimsuits on their beaches, issuing high-profile fines to offending women. In Britain, some schools suspended girl pupils who started wearing brightly coloured bikinis for swimming contests. The dress censors were out in force, as seafront cafés refused to serve bikini-wearers and many public swimming baths forbade them. Not for the first or last time, women's bodies were the site of a battle.

Nevertheless, for countless white women the bikini declared the end of alabaster skin, while across racial boundaries it transformed the body agenda and signified the collapse of the final frontier protecting women from the exposure of their tummies. If Betty Grable's sphere of influence was legs, Brigitte's was the midriff. After its appearance on the fashion scene, there was no going back. Never before had anyone ever exposed so much female flesh to so many – yet, for the majority, Brigitte Bardot's loveliness was unattainable. The era of watching, judging, manipulating and measuring, doubting and distrusting had also arrived. For the cruel paradox was that while these minuscule patches of fabric were advertised as the ultimate bodily liberation, their actual effect was the opposite. Women's bodies were becoming ever more visible, ever more commodified, and ever more the site of implacable anxiety. Medical researchers started to alert the profession to the increase in incidence of eating disorders; in the USA cases of anorexia nervosa in females aged fifteen to twenty-four were on course to double between the 1960s and the 1970s.

In addition, the 'freedom' of Bardot's bikini, against the background of 1950s France, was a myth. French women had no access to contraception, and abortion remained illegal there until the late 1970s (Bardot herself being among the many who resorted to an illegal termination). Whether in a crinoline or a bikini, women remained the inheritors of centuries of discrimination – a situation described by the feminist philosopher Simone de Beauvoir in her ground-breaking book *The Second Sex* (1949):

[Woman] is nothing other than what man decides; she is thus called 'the sex', meaning that the male sees her essentially as a sexed being; for him she is sex, so she is it in the absolute. She determines and differentiates herself in relation to man, and he does not in relation to her; she is the inessential in front of the essential. He is the Subject; he is the Absolute. She is the Other.

———

Brigitte Bardot's bikini leaves the spectator with little guesswork to do. The playful strapless top epitomises Riviera chic, while allowing her upper torso to be uninterruptedly tanned. As a celebrity fashion influencer she wore off-the-shoulder boatneck tops so often that commentators dubbed this style the 'Bardot neckline'; her taste for ballerina flats (as against the teetering stilettos of Hollywood goddesses) also felt youthful and full of *joie de vivre*. Here, her body, visible as it is, conforms to the standards of perfection expected in the 1950s, while raising the bar for decades to come. Has anybody ever achieved Bardot's sheer dazzle? She possesses 'killer curves', as well as a tiny waist; some have speculated that it was just twenty inches, creating a faultless hourglass between bust and hips, both at thirty-five inches. For most women, to look this slender would demand sacrifices: no more fries, no more chocolate. Brigitte's limbs are lissom and hair-free, her posture is upright and her radiant skin shows no blemishes or wrinkles. Her hair is wild – but it is also copious and beautiful enough to look effortlessly messy. It is hard to tell whether she is wearing make-up; her glowing features require little definition or improvement, though she has surely had her brows tidied and lashes darkened; later, Bardot would be famed for her smoky eyes, winged eyeliner and pale lipstick.

But back on the beach, her smile is sunny – and the sun smiles back at her.

Titillation

From a distance of over seventy years, the screen pin-ups of the 1950s appear more superhumanly glamorous, glitzy and sexy than ever before or since. And it was in the same year that Brigitte Bardot first appeared in black and white on French cinema screens in *The Girl in the Bikini* that the names of two firmly established leading ladies made *Gentlemen Prefer Blondes* – in Technicolor – one of the highest grossing films of 1953. They were Jane Russell and Marilyn Monroe. But where *gamine*, *bohémienne* Bardot embraced earthy, outdoorsy Mediterranean hedonism, Monroe's allure was rooted in *la dolce vita*: *Gentlemen Prefer Blondes* was all about dissipation and diamonds.

Unusually, it is a film in which both the central characters are women. But it tells a far from feminist story, one in which the aim of ditsy blonde Lorelei Lee (played by Monroe) is to use her sex appeal and gloss to scoop up a millionaire, and with him as many diamonds as possible. Lorelei and her hunk-hungry chum Dorothy (played by luscious brunette Russell) are both improbably perfect. The lipsticked pair have only to sashay across the set, flesh heavily on display, hips forward and breasts pointing skyward, for every male eye to swivel on stalks in their direction.

'Boy, oh boy!' Lorelei (Marilyn Monroe) and Dorothy (Jane Russell) on board the ocean liner to Europe in *Gentlemen Prefer Blondes*, 1953

And on one level, the film playfully upends the patriarchal status quo, with men seen as goofy and powerless. In both the big musical numbers, too, the movie thwarts convention by choreographing depersonalised men in the chorus line. In 'Ain't There Anyone Here for Love?' Dorothy is centre stage, camping it up among a team of genuflecting gymnasts, weirdly clad in flesh-coloured shorts; while Lorelei's smash hit showcases

Monroe in a fuchsia satin evening gown against a backdrop of adoring swains in white tie and tails.

However, *Gentlemen Prefer Blondes* would not pass the Bechdel test;* the story portrays the age-old theme of beautiful women capturing rich men. Bosoms, legs, lipstick and loose morals abound. But within that tradition it hands agency to its radiant and shapely heroines, who are shown manipulating the wealthy but unattractive men who surround them. The story attributes status and prestige – as opposed to purity and virtue – to a woman's physical attributes in a way that feels new and unapologetic. The 1950s beauty icons are of a different breed to the Professional Beauties of fifty years earlier, like the king's mistress Lillie Langtry, with her ambiguous reputation. Admired as she was, Langtry was performing a balancing act when it came to social acceptability. By contrast, in *Gentlemen Prefer Blondes* the heroines are explicitly aspirational. Sexy Lorelei is seen as sympathetic and enchanting, while the carpers and critics (like the po-faced Lady Beekman) are portrayed as ugly losers. And the outcome of the movie cleverly shows us that, though she is never going to rock the boat when it comes to the gender transaction, or threaten anyone with her intellect, Lorelei is far from being as dumb as she looks. Instead, she is street-smart, persuading her future father-in-law that it's as reasonable for a woman to want diamond bracelets – 'the most wonderful things in the world' – as it is for a man to want dollars in the bank. This is about monetising one's assets (for which, read the female body) in return for a step up the socio-economic ladder. Obviously, it's an unfair bargain – but the ending is pure happy Hollywood.

---

* The test, the principles of which were set out in a 1985 comic strip by cartoonist Alison Bechdel, is a measure of the representation of women in fiction. A work passes the test if it has at least two female characters who talk to each other about topics other than men.

Lorelei Lee had several real-life counterparts. Some said Anita Loos's original character was based on the diamond-loving vaudeville actress Lilian Lorraine, while others made the claim for 'everyone's favourite gold-digger', the socialite Peggy Hopkins Joyce, who married six times and was described as 'alimoniously rich'. A more recent member of this club was Pamela Churchill Harriman, whose knack for attracting millionaires deserves a short detour. Pamela's husbands and lovers gave her diamond earrings, real estate, Renoirs, Rolls-Royces and even respectability. In return, Pamela gave these men something they wanted. Sex, yes. But what else?

Pamela was posh; coming from the gilded Digby dynasty counted for a lot. Horsey, well-covered and red-headed as a teenage debutante, she had a certain pushy class confidence. A contemporary described her as 'terribly sexy and very obvious; she was plump and so bosomy we called her "the dairy maid". She wore high heels and tossed her bottom around; she was known as hot stuff.' Pamela's first husband was Randolph Churchill, son of Britain's wartime prime minister. His absence, his debt, and her infidelities, contributed to the break-up of their marriage.

'For nearly twenty years,' writes one of her biographers,* 'she lived as a courtesan ... She used many talents, only one of which was her sexuality, to charm and hold a man of wealth for years on end.' The affluent contenders included Gianni Agnelli, head of Fiat and the richest man in Italy; Aly Khan,

---

* For this section I have largely referred to Sally Bedell Smith's biography, *Reflected Glory: The Life of Pamela Churchill Harriman* (1996). A *New York Times* review of 10 November 1996 praised Smith's book: 'The biographer's dislike for her subject boils on the page, but she is too honest to disguise the grudging admiration that goes with it. The Pamela Harriman she paints is both monstrous and magnificent.'

playboy son of the Aga Khan III; star crooner Frank Sinatra; the Greek shipping tycoon Stavros Niarchos; Leland Hayward, one of the most powerful names in Hollywood production; and the railroad heir and politician Averell Harriman. There were numerous others.

Undoubtedly, Pamela pampered herself. In an era of sun worship, she protected her delicate skin from its rays with a parasol. She didn't take drugs, kept her head when drinking and preferred early nights. For half a dozen years from 1954 she was mistress to Baron Élie de Rothschild, inheritor of his family's banking dynasty – a period which overlapped with her affairs with several other men. She would have liked to marry Élie, but his wife wasn't having it. But Pamela didn't give up. As mistress to a millionaire, looking the part was her full-time job. She was now in her mid-thirties. With middle age approaching she spent hours caring for her face and figure, having massages and manicures. Pamela was super-high maintenance. She learnt the art of the perfect *maquillage*, while the care of her auburn hair was delegated to Alexandre, coiffeur to the Duchess of Windsor and Princess Grace of Monaco, who visited her in person once a day to give it a camomile rinse and dress it in a soft bouffant style. When Pamela travelled, she brought with her a multitude of cases containing her jewellery and her beauty apparatus: bottle after bottle of nail lacquer and perfume, jar after jar of face cream and hair pomade. It was said that ahead of any prestigious social occasion she would take to her bed for three days, where she would rest, and drink only water and lemon juice in order to appear at her incomparable best.

'Hot stuff': Pamela Churchill Harriman

Pamela ordered up to twenty dresses a year from Dior, via a vendeuse, Eliane Martin, who attended once a week for fittings. Her yearly budget for clothes approached £7,000. 'She had very nice legs,' Mlle Martin recalled, 'but the bad thing was her waist. She had good shoulders, and maybe I shouldn't say this, she had beautiful breasts, probably the best I ever saw in my life.'

The cumulative effect was dazzling to many. But Pamela's principal object was to dazzle Élie, and it worked. All Parisian society knew that he was besotted with her – for not only did she dress and drink lemon juice to please him, she fed him his favourite meals, laughed at his jokes, chatted when he wanted to be amused, refrained when he preferred silence, and took trouble to learn about Rothschild tastes and preferences, from modern art to wine vintages to eighteenth-century decor. She was a calming presence, who listened, flattered, never challenged, and worked hard to make herself indispensable, including in the bedroom. Élie apparently told a friend, 'I like a woman who is quiet in bed – a woman who is lovely to wake up to. Pam was that.' She was sexy. Her admission that, for her, 'the bed part is less important than all the rest', seems to imply that she herself did not make sexual demands. But if her behaviour outside the bedroom is anything to go by, it seems safe to assume that she put on an equally smiling and eager act with her lovers: a polished performance that would have ignited any man's desire to be desired.

Pamela got what she wanted too: diamonds, and the admiration that came with them. But she never nagged or pestered. She possessed the skill of an experienced geisha or courtesan, and in one form or another she deployed it with all the men who loved her.

Pamela Harriman appears to have put looks first: above friendships, above family. And being the highest-rated arm candy in society was as much a route to prestige as being a film star or a princess. Pamela played to her strengths, in a world where men had the power and the wealth. Disregarding old-fashioned morals, she used her magnetic 'feminine' skills to manipulate the traditional sex transaction to her advantage. From her radiantly cared-for complexion to her Dior dresses; from her buoyant bosom to her compliant sexuality, Pamela Harriman was the living projection of a male fantasy. And it appeared that that was something they were more than willing to spend a *lot* of money on.

Pulp Fiction

Pamela Harriman's expenditure on couture dresses made her a favourite at Paris's right bank salons. But by the 1950s designers like Dior and Balmain needed more than the *grandes dames* of society to showcase their collections.

In the late 1940s and early 50s the mannequin's star was in the ascendant. Generally, photographic couture models stood bolt upright, without a hint of sexual suggestiveness. Frozen, carefully lit studio shots were still the norm; but with improved camera technology – Leica, flashbulbs, the Rolleiflex – fashion photography was becoming more adventurous, and Richard Avedon's fluent, stirring pictures were starting to shift the way magazines and their readers perceived haute couture. Clothes rationing stopped in 1949, the ready-to-wear industry started to boom, and the end of paper rationing in 1950 meant more magazine features, and more gloss. The readers of *Vogue*, *Harper's Bazaar*, *Woman*, *Tatler* and *The Lady* had an insatiable appetite for the images of enchanting, unruffled ladies in pearls and court shoes with hourglass figures which dominated their covers. And post-war, photographic models suddenly found there was as much work as they wanted.

My mother was a keen follower of fashion through the pages of *Vogue*, and I was introduced at the age of four or five to the enthralling imagery contained within its gleaming pages. She and I lingered joyfully over the photographs of these unattainably slender yet spectacularly proportioned women in their swishing gowns, swagger coats, stiletto-heeled shoes and picture hats with veils. And my mother found a name that seemed to suit these perfectly attired goddesses – to me, they were always the 'Swanky Ladies'.

In 1947, Christian Dior had galvanised the fashion world. Flawless, expensive and romantic, his New Look was a man's eye view of femininity, deliberately promoting women as the fragile flowers of a bygone age: eighteenth-century aristocratic heroines whose bosoms heaved, and whose tight-laced waists caused them to faint and flutter, while enveloped in oceans of surging petticoats. The New Look was controversial. Many women couldn't wait to put the khaki days of wartime behind them. And yet – war had offered women so many freedoms, and these padded confections seemed to be a visible intent to turn the clock back on emancipation.

But my mother and I loved them. The Swanky Ladies – arching their perfect eyebrows as they stepped, wearing their New Look outfits, from their perfect Rolls-Royces – told a romantic story about how women could be: like Pamela Harriman, with her beautiful breasts, so 'lovely to wake up to'. Dior's vision was uncompromisingly dreamy and feminine.

One of Dior's Swanky Ladies was Jean Dawnay. *Model Girl* (1956), Jean's jaunty memoir of days spent primping and posing for cameras and on catwalks, opens a window onto the everyday lives of fashion models like her, and also onto the hazards and demands of a punishing and precarious career – including some insights on the workarounds they deployed to maintain the illusion:

> Most models have figure faults, but they know all the tricks of the trade to camouflage them. If a girl has a very small bust, she wears falsies ... If a model's back curves in too much below the waist, pads are used to fill it out, and they are occasionally used on the hips to give a more rounded effect.

Normally, Jean preferred the term 'mannequin'; even in the late 1950s the word 'model' was often a euphemism for hooker. But mannequin was pejorative too. It originally meant 'dummy', or lay-figure: a wooden doll with articulated joints, used by artists to experiment with poses. Later it came to refer to life-size dressmakers' and tailors' dummies made of wood or wickerwork. A mannequin was, in Jean Dawnay's words, a 'stuffed dummy': an inanimate, speechless doll made to simulate perfected femininity,* but who prostitutes her body by displaying the couturier's wares. '[She was] a new kind of working woman,' writes Professor Caroline Evans: 'a figure freighted with ambiguity and contradiction. She wore fashionable clothes for money rather than love and thereby brought the oldest profession and the newest into uncomfortable proximity.'† Either way, the word 'mannequin' was used to signal contempt for something flimsy, artificial and rather sordid.

At the age of twenty-two Jean paid 5 guineas to enrol in a London model training school. To her horror, she immediately encountered what appeared to be an insuperable setback:

> We were all measured on our first day and I learnt that a model must be between 5 ft 6 inches and 5 ft 9 inches tall without shoes, have hips between 35 inches and 36 inches, bust 34 inches to 36 inches, and waist 21 inches to 24 inches.

But, disastrously, 'I was only 5 ft 5¾ inches.'

Size mattered; this factor was of fetishistic significance. But Jean had what it took: natural elegance, an eighteen-inch waist, plus what her daughter later described as 'a very English post-war look', so she simply stretched the truth – and herself – by adding an extra quarter inch. And beautiful women have

---

* The cultural fantasy of woman as doll/automaton/gynoid, particularly in science fiction (a genre generally created by and preferred by men), has staying power. The Pygmalion myth springs to mind, as does Fritz Lang's *Metropolis* (1927), *The Stepford Wives* (novel, 1972; films 1975 and 2004), *Her* (2013) and *Ex Machina* (2014). Wikipedia lists thirty-seven films and thirty-four TV shows in which versions of fembots appear, from replicants to cyborgs, androids to bionic women, synths to sexbots. From 2010 AI technology has brought actual sex robots onto the market, with skin that the makers claim feels lifelike, warmed orifices – and a choice of customisable personalities.

† Caroline Evans, *The Mechanical Smile* (2013), is a history of the early mannequins.

always had takers. The professional model could monetise her appearance in the way that, for example, a secretary monetised her typing speed. But the similarity ended there. For a model, any shortcomings in her height, her bust, her teeth or her nose felt like personal failures. Jean's career would take her to the topmost ateliers of Paris, but modelling was not a money tree, and if the raw material of beauty was insufficient, you could forget the catwalk as a career.

The upfront expenses were crippling. To begin with, it cost Jean 60 guineas, paid in instalments, to have her prominent front teeth fixed. She also had an unsightly facial scar, dating back to a childhood accident. With the use of a pioneering needle technique, the scar was almost completely removed – at a price – leaving only the faintest trace. 'Now it hardly ever shows under my make-up and in the few photographs in which it appears, they just touch it out.' Jean's contemporary, queen of models Barbara Goalen, had a more challenging difficulty to overcome, in the shape of her prominent nose. '[It] cast bad shadows in photographs and had to be made more photogenic by means of plastic surgery — quite a big decision to take for the sake of one's career. As it turned out it was a wonderful investment.' Not all were so lucky. 'One very lovely model had to have the operation four times and her nose is still not right.'

Every model had to be skilled in using make-up, and supply their own. Jean divulged some tricks of the trade, such as using a lipstick with tints of blue, that showed up as clear red under studio lights, or painting the inner rims of her lids with white theatrical paint, to give a wide-eyed effect.

There were other expenses: hairdos, jewellery, hats, bags, gloves, shoes and stockings. 'I had vaguely imagined that the photographer produced everything when one was photographed ... I soon discovered how wrong I was.' She was always in debt, and always in a hurry, which meant taxis, and yet more debt.

Then there were the auditions – 'real slave markets'. Describing the casting process, Jean betrays the casually antisemitic mindset of her day, though her recollections also conjure up associations with the repulsive manoeuvres of more recent producers and directors:

> Eventually we would be called into a small office one by one and interviewed by a fat man smoking a cigar with a name like Stinkinstein. He asked you to walk up and down, smile, turn, sit down, stand up, show your profile and any moment you felt he would say: 'Now show your legs.' These auditions were always horrible experiences.

The photographer was king. If he (it was always *he*) asked you for a toothpaste smile, you obliged – 'you were being paid for it'. When he told you to 'throw your bust out', you threw it.

Being super-slim was essential, as pictures were unforgiving. Hard work went into this. Jean Dawnay swore by a low-starch, high-protein diet – 'steaks and salads' – started each day with a glass of hot water and lemon juice, and counselled aspiring models to get out in the countryside and go for bracing walks. The gym was not at this time part of a model's daily routine, nor were frequent visits to beauty salons. Whatever her regime, there was not a visible spare ounce of subcutaneous fat clinging to Jean Dawnay's sculpted shoulders!

New Look dresses not only needed pronounced curves but also (as Jean explained) a tiny waist – and this was generally attributable not to nature, but to the *guipière*, or 'waspie', which cinched it in – and constricted the breath – just as it had done for the fashionable ladies of the 1870s. In *Model Girl* Jean tells how she modelled a tight 'bust-crushing ... waist-pinching' gold lace-covered ballgown for a particularly exacting photographer. The gown had been fitted on a model whose waist was an inch smaller than hers, and after four hours posing in it, she passed out. It took her a while to come round, 'but only when my dress had been undone'.

Posture, too, took effort. A model had to learn the art of turning. She had to learn not to slump or fold her arms, how to carry an umbrella, gloves and a handbag, what to do with her hands, her hips, her buttocks, her tummy, her expression and her smile – and all the while looking natural, nonchalant and poised.

The result was fantasy made real. Here, the untouchable image of Victorian femininity – the Angel beloved by poets and parsons – is reincarnated as an elevated, decorous deity. As one model remembered later, 'We couldn't have looked sexy. It wouldn't have been allowed. We were Belgravia ladies.'

The 'look' of Swanky Ladies like Jean Dawnay was a fiction. The exquisite woman posing on the page, or preening on the catwalk, is a confection, an artwork, an illusion. She has been plucked, painted, polished, camouflaged and corrected, until – like the scar on her cheek, erased by surgery – all ugliness has been eliminated, leaving only the ghost of that childhood insult to beauty.

For the aspirational world of the fashion model was one in which nothing less than unattainable, flawless, all-over perfection would do.

———

She never reads a book, and buys two 3-shilling monthly woman's magazines and ... never bothers to read anything but the fashion articles ... 'I'd love to get a pair of those new corsets that make you have a small waist, and I'd pad my coat basques like in *Vogue*.'

The diarist Nella Last, aged sixty-seven, from Barrow-in-Furness, was quoting her friend and neighbour Mrs Howson, a woman of a similar age, who Nella pityingly criticises for her slavish fixation on the glossies, and her 'insistence on perfection'. Later, she points out that despite Mrs Howson's exactly matching accessories, her clothes fitted her badly and she foolishly economised on her foundation garments: 'She even buys the cheapest girdle or corset.'

Nella was all for economy. She saw fashion magazines as a waste of money, and did her own dressmaking. And it was her love of a bargain that took her one Saturday morning in June 1952 to the market in Barrow-in-Furness town centre, hoping to pick up some cheap chintz to run up a dress. Ironically, that day, she found herself ambushed by a highly coloured magazine stall. Maybe she could find something there to tempt her increasingly morose husband? 'I saw rows of *Life in the Future, Tales of Thrills and Horror, True Love Stories*, etc. I've often said lightly "My breath stopped", but felt it true this morning. I never imagined such sexy, pornographic pictures and captions.'

The lurid illustrative artworks displayed hideous caricatures of the Swanky Ladies. Nella leafed through one or two, before replacing them in disgust. Then she stood transfixed, watching two down-at-heel teenage boys, slack-mouthed and pimply, poring over the porn.

The cover of *Spicy Detective Stories*

One of them was unable to take his eyes off the images which she had cast aside, and which showed a woman with exaggeratedly long legs visible up to the buttocks, a voluptuous bust, heavily made-up eyes and a mane of unruly hair, wielding a revolver. The caption read, 'If *you* don't talk, my gat does, big boy'.

'I felt slightly sick to see his tongue licking his loose lips and hear his little snicker.' Times had changed, reflected Nella sadly, as the stallholder snarlingly warned the boys off, telling them, 'If you want one, buy one.' And she commented: 'How they got past the censors who ban books is a mystery.'

For sure, this was not subtle stuff. Pulp fiction* was cheap, and designed to sell in large quantities – mainly to young white males. The stories sold on their covers, lavishly illustrated with pneumatic, wasp-waisted blondes in erotic predicaments: lashed to boards as spiky space-age machinery descended from above, trussed up and abducted by Black men in jungles, grasped by the hair and menaced with swords, or roped up and held at knife point. (The narrative had not moved on from the wish-fulfilment fairy tale depicted by John Everett Millais eighty years earlier, in which a naked damsel in distress tied to a tree is rescued by Sir Lancelot – or whoever it was – in full armour.) Less often, the covers depicted aggressive villainesses brandishing guns. Women were either defenceless captives or dominatrixes, and in both cases they were – like the *Vogue* mannequins – improbably curvaceous, gleaming with lipstick, and white.

Each age has its partialities, where female body shape is concerned. It's revealing, seventy years later – when we are inured and habituated to imagery showing glamorised, highly coloured, leggy women with perky breasts – to encounter these pulp pin-ups, to gauge their shock effect on women like Nella Last, and to get a picture of what they represent in terms of male 'requirements'.

Very big breasts denoted voluptuous sex. An inheritance of men's wartime longings for maternal safety and erotic intimacy, they now typified the desirable contours of the 1950s. And the gleaming, plasticised representations that so horrified Nella

---

* Pulp fiction took its name from the cheap grade of paper on which the magazines were produced. The sensational covers – key to selling the product – were printed on higher-quality paper, in colour.

were far from being the only highly sexualised imagery now legally available to the pimply teenagers of Barrow-in-Furness, if they wanted it. After the Second World War, there was a rapid growth of 'girlie' imagery which measured a woman's worth by her bra size: 1953 saw the launch of *Playboy* magazine, which sold itself to urban sophisticates on a winning combination of topless glamour photoshoots and high culture. The magazine ran features and fiction by writers such as Jack Kerouac and Alberto Moravia, alongside alluring, heavily retouched centre-folds of Playmates baring gravity-defying breasts.

The first of these was Marilyn Monroe, photographed by Tom Kelley. Meanwhile, from the late 1940s calendar companies were cashing in, with seductive pin-ups for sale ranging from the coyly 'artistic', to the blatantly sexy. With narcissism imposed on them – and face values prioritised – a generation of baby boomers was growing up disproportionately conscious of body shape, body image – and breasts. In the early 1950s the lingerie industry anticipated a profitable decade ahead; 'training' bras were now available in AAA and AA sizes for very flat girls and teenagers, who were – it seems – being trained to be precociously sexually alluring to men.

The writer Nora Ephron puts this into words better than anyone, in her article 'A Few Words About Breasts', which looks back on her flat-chested teenage years in the 1950s. In adolescence, Nora felt desperately the need to demonstrate that – despite her outspokenness, boyishness and scabby knees – she *was* a girl. 'As soft and pink as a nursery. And nothing would do that for me, I felt, but breasts.' Daily, she sat in the bathtub silently urging them to grow – 'They didn't.'

Nora was thin, dark-haired and tall. She started out with a 28AA bra. The situation failed to improve. 'I knew that no one would ever want to marry me. I had no breasts. I would never have breasts.' She splashed cold water on her ribcage, took up sleeping on her back, and bought a Mark Eden Bust Developer,* but eventually caved in and started to wear padded bras on her skinny torso. 'Breast-worship' intervened in her friendships and, later, her love relationships. 'I always minded.' Twenty years later, in the era of 'bra-burning' feminism, Nora Ephron tried to explain how hard it was to shake off the legacy of growing up in the 1950s: 'with rigid stereotypical sex roles, the insistence that men be men and dress like men and women be women and dress like women, the intolerance of androgyny – and I cannot shake it, cannot shake my feelings of inadequacy.'

They went too deep.

The Female Fairy Tale

'There's a reason why 40, 50, and 60 don't look the way they used to, and it's not because of feminism or better living through exercise,' Nora Ephron told O, *The Oprah Magazine*. 'It's because of hair dye. In the 1950s, only 7 percent of American women dyed their hair.'

There was a prevailing sense that going blonde – like wearing black – was fine for film stars, but borderline immoral for you and me. It would take a breakthrough in dye production, and sophisticated advertising, to remove the stigma and permit women to feel good about colouring their hair. When Clairol launched their one-step home colour treatment in 1956, it took advantage of the reservations their customers still felt about taking that step, with the slogan, 'Does she or doesn't she? Only her hairdresser knows for sure.' But by 1962 the product would

---

* This product – a spring-loaded muscle exerciser – was advertised as miraculously adding inches to the bustline; it sold by the thousand. But after a long drawn-out legal battle the promoters were found guilty of fraud and put out of business.

become sufficiently acceptable for the advertisers to shout, 'If I've only one life, let me live it as a blonde!' from the rooftops. The line apparently caused the grandmother of second-wave feminism, Betty Friedan, to go the whole way with Clairol's latest flagship product, Lady Clairol, in the summer she published *The Feminine Mystique* (1962).

So what had been happening to feminism? The suffragette generation was getting old, and could look back with satisfaction not only on political rights gained, but also on a degree of welfare reform and economic opportunity. Younger women – like novelist and journalist Marghanita Laski, writing in 1952, in her mid-thirties – felt that there was nothing left to fight for: 'I was born too late for the battle . . . Rights for women, so far as my generation is concerned, is a dead issue.'

Laski was wrong. Feminism wasn't dead, but it was evolving. Ahead of Betty Friedan, European feminists like Edith Summerskill, Judith Hubback, Alva Myrdal and Viola Klein firmly and politely put the case for women who, as wives and mothers, felt their education was being wasted. They examined the housewife's work/life balance and explained that married women still had much to contribute in the workplace. And, in the cold war era, there were feminist activists – like Dora Russell – who believed that their main contribution was to the cause of peace. Dora, an idealist and a brilliant student of philosophy and politics, believed passionately that hope for the future lay primarily with women.* But she despaired of the younger generation's absorption with materialism. She could feel nothing in common with

---

* In 1958 Dora set out in a battered second-hand charabanc with a band of like-minded idealists on a mission to make common cause with women in countries behind the Iron Curtain. The sides of the bus were blazoned with banners reading 'Women of All Lands Want Peace'.

the made-up, stiletto-heeled fashion princesses to be seen on the streets, aping Marilyn Monroe, with their contorted hourglass bodies and 'dressing up like film stars'. Did the younger generation only care about plucked eyebrows and nail polish? When she was just twenty-six Dora travelled to Russia and met the Marxist activist Alexandra Kollontai, the most prominent woman in the Soviet Union, a powerful Bolshevik and advocate for her sex. Kollontai appeared to her everything a woman should be: elegant, tasteful – 'yet new clothes and style were the last things that could then be considered'. Clad in coarse undyed linen, she exuded dignity and simplicity. As Dora saw it, Russian women like this were the antithesis of the fake, poised, beauty-queen blondes so adulated in the West. 'When you think,' she wrote sadly to a campaigning colleague, 'of the lovely intelligent faces of Russian women and their devotion, and compare it with the false values our women seem to have.'

In the 1950s the women's movement still had a mountain to climb. But it was more necessary than ever.

In English suburbia, Mary Evans (later a respected social scientist) explored the essentials of femininity in her book *A Good School: Life at a Girls' Grammar School in the 1950s* (1991). It's a story of the imminent, all-out generation war, yet it demonstrates, too, how little had changed.

Mary, born in 1946, attended a girls-only school in Brentwood, Essex from 1957. At this school there was a rule that skirts could not be beyond the length at which the hem touched the floor when the wearer was kneeling.* Mirrors, jewellery, coloured underwear and high heels were banned.

---

* In 1972, the teachers at my own school finally relented, after the sixth-form girls presented a petition pleading to be allowed to wear trousers. Recently, I discovered that the same school now stipulates trousers for all students, and no longer permits any female students to wear skirts.

But the girls' actual bodies were a locus of contradictions. On the one hand, they were told that interest in appearance was mere vanity. In their sternly unglamorous blouses, sturdy round-toed shoes and ankle socks their teachers were the irreproachable embodiments of virtue; they lived in a dowdy world where you had a bath once a week, and in which your Gor-Ray box-pleated tweed skirt was 'made to last' for ten years. But Mary and her friends saw things differently:

> We knew, and we strongly suspected that [the teachers] knew, that being physically attractive mattered. Indeed, physical attraction and appeal did not just matter, it was going to be central to our experiences and our very circumstances after we left school.

Mary and her peer group were primarily preoccupied with how to be 'attractive, very attractive or stunningly and irresistibly attractive'.

What were the metrics of success?

Girls prayed that they would not grow tall, dreading the fiendish fate that would then befall them, of towering over their dancing partners, not to mention the destruction of any hopes they might nurture, of becoming an air hostess or a ballerina: archetypically feminine professions in which the stipulated maximum height was five feet three inches for a dancer, and five feet five inches for an air hostess.

Being slim was also imperative: 'Here morality took a truly firm hand. Being tall could always be explained by an unlucky chance of nature ... But being fat was all your own fault.' Fat girls were at the bottom of the school's popularity pile.

But here again, adults were inconsistent: with the years of wartime rationing still vivid in their memories, they stressed that any girl who didn't eat every last suety carbohydrate on her plate was a selfish fusspot. The pounds piled on, and – since those were the days when daily PE lessons were compulsory – plump pupils had nowhere to hide: 'Fat girls were mocked and they were laughed at.' For them, the changing rooms represented torture chambers.*

Clearly, you also had to be white: 'We never thought any other possibility existed.' In 1950s Britain the rare appearance of an Indian woman in a saree made headlines when India, captained by Vinoo Mankad, played England in the 1952 Test match at Lord's:

> HOW THE MANKADS BRIGHTEN LORD'S
>
> Vinoo Mankad['s] ... wife and two children lent vivacity to the stand for Indian visitors. Mrs Mankad wore the most exquisite of many fine saris, a gauzy petunia and gold affair. She had a diamond stud in her nose and gold-decorated pins in her dark hair.

The implication was that Mrs Mankad was a special case. But for Mary Evans and her peer group, appearance was supposed not to matter.

At this time mass consumption of fashion, cosmetics, bath and hair products was rocketing. The production of the UK beauty industry more than doubled between 1938 and 1950. Its value (estimated in dollars) had risen from $26 million to $58 million; while in the USA, in the same period, it more than tripled – from $148 million to $560 million. Cosmetics companies were spending nearly 80 per cent of their budgets on promotion. Though they were banned, no schoolgirl was without her mirror and her compact. '[We] spent our lunch hour practising the art of fixing false eyelashes,' remembered

---

* My own school memories of a few years later confirm this. Communal changing rooms and showers were a daily humiliation for self-conscious pubescent girls, made worse by a gym teacher who stood sentinel by the entrance to the shower room, urging us on with intrusive pawings.

Mary, describing the group-think of her schoolgirl circle. Alongside mathematics and English literature, she and her contemporaries learnt to put narcissism, and attracting men, at the heart of who they were.

––––––––

Roberta Cowell didn't learn any of the how-to-be-a-woman lessons until she was in her thirties – and that was because she started life as a male. Cowell was born in 1918, and during her* life as a man was a successful racing driver, as well as a Spitfire pilot during the war. Cowell could hardly have chosen activities that spoke more of male power, control and authority. True, many women could and did drive cars at this time, but men's position behind the wheel was invariably the default when both were present, while 'women drivers'† were frequently dismissed as incompetent and unsafe. Cowell, witty, attractive and fickle, was quite the cavalier – she liked pretty girls, and she didn't mind how many there were.

But in 1941 she married; and though she and her wife had two children all was not well:

> Superficially, my life seemed full; actually it was pointless and empty ... Later I was made to realise clearly that this pattern was a frantic effort to show the world at large how masculine and assertive I could be. It was an attempt to make up for what I knew, deep down inside me though not consciously: my nature was essentially feminine and in some way my world was out of joint.

––––––––

* As in the case history of Michael Dillon, I have respected Roberta Cowell's own articulation of her gender, by referring to her throughout using feminine pronouns.
† Nobody seems to have found it necessary to specify the converse, via the terms 'men drivers' or 'male drivers'.

She and her wife separated. Around 1950 Cowell met Michael Dillon, whose earlier obstacles and times of distress were outlined in Chapter 5. Dillon had transitioned in 1944, with ensuing surgery, carried out in secrecy. The meeting was transformative, for by this time Cowell had decided that a gender confirmation operation was imperative. After many hindrances along the way, this was successfully carried out – as far as is known, the first occasion on which a British person had undergone male-to-female sex reassignment surgery – and in 1951 Robert became Roberta.

Roberta's commentary on how she then learned about the externals of becoming a woman is fascinating, for like most men she saw women from the driver's seat. The projection on her windscreen showed a lipsticked blonde lady, slim and shapely, poised and groomed.

According to her autobiography,* Roberta followed up her gender confirmation operation with facial surgery. Some time later, heavily made-up and equipped with a new *retroussé* nose, a new hat and hairdo, she set out to make her public debut:

> I saw two men coming towards me. I kept on, doggedly resisting a wild impulse to put my head down and flee. As we passed, both men gave me a searching glance. My heart seemed to stop completely. Then one man said to the other, in a low but distinct voice, 'Definitely, yes.'
>
> I realised, with a sudden glow of pleasure, that my appearance was acceptable.

---

* *Roberta Cowell's Story* (1954) is not a reliable source. Liz Hodgkinson, author of a biography of Michael Dillon (*From a Girl to a Man*, 1989), knew Cowell, and reports that 'much of what she put out about herself was fantasy'. Nevertheless the assumptions and prejudices that emerge from Cowell's memoir tell their own story.

Validated by male desire, Roberta could now embrace her new identity.

She did so with alacrity, devoting her days to 'educating myself in the minutiae of being a woman': 'I became absorbed in the details of correct dressing and deportment, of beauty treatment and of hairdressing.' Her bodily measurements had altered; with the help of hormones her bust had grown and her waist had slenderised. Her voice rose in pitch, and she had to remind herself to keep it soft, and to silence all her old army blasphemies. Just as it had for Michael Dillon, women's clothing now became symbolic for her; but whereas Dillon saw dresses and high heels as signs of captivity, for Roberta Cowell they represented 'my new and happy life'. She particularly relished the opportunity to wear bright colours, and to shine out against a gathering of monochrome men. But skin care was a minefield. Did you apply powder direct, or on top of foundation? Experts disagreed. The contradictions multiplied: use face packs, don't use face packs; put cream on at night, don't put cream on at night. Learning to put her hair in pin curls took for ever, and when, in her new identity, Roberta received her first invitation to a dinner party, it took her six whole hours to get ready. Slowly she learned 'to move gracefully' – but when were you supposed to wear gloves? When were you supposed to sit down? She discovered that it was ungainly to go upstairs two at a time and inappropriate to stand warming her bottom before the fire. The available photographs present an appealing bouncy-haired blonde, wide-eyed and strongly made-up, with a sensual mouth: an echo of Marilyn Monroe perhaps?

Roberta Cowell

Roberta's character started to metamorphose along with her body. Her 'drive', she noticed, was diminishing, while her once phlegmatic temperament changed to one more soft and capricious; tears came easily. She started to read romantic fiction, suppressed her in-depth knowledge of car mechanics (rather than humiliate her new men friends), and taught herself to appear dim-witted, if a good listener.

But the paramount lesson was one that embraced Roberta's own life experience. There was no cosmetic concern that could not be remedied by the magic wand of a fairy-godmother doctor:

> I earnestly believe that there is no such thing as a plain or ugly
> woman; there are only women who do not know how to make the
> best of themselves ... Even if a woman's face is actually malformed
> it can be vastly improved by modern surgery.

The black eyes, bruises, scars and stitches had all been worth-
while. With her own reshaped mouth and brand-new nose,
Roberta felt she could face the world as a woman.

Roberta Cowell's book ends with a Cinderella transformation scene, as she was whisked off to her first ball. 'That night,
for the first time, I was going to be dancing in a brilliantly
lighted room, with a large number of people.' Ahead of the
great occasion she had a massage, and carefully selected her
dress and shoes for the dance, before applying her eyeliner
and lipstick. But Roberta, who had competed in Grands Prix
and successfully crash-landed a Spitfire in enemy territory, was
trembling with nerves. A final glance in the mirror to check
all was correct. 'In a few moments the dream of your life will
be coming true. No jerkiness, hands flowing from the wrist,
perfect poise.'

Roberta was a woman. She had made the transformation,
and it was for life, not just till midnight. But she had also
bought into the stereotype, in every little detail. This was some
time in the early 1950s: an era before second-wave feminism,
before gender-identity awareness, before there was any under-
standing of non-binary individuals. In that moment, in perfect,
poised conformity with the female fairy tale, Roberta Cowell
found happiness.

The band is playing. 'I am myself,' she says, as she smooths
her dyed-blonde curls and steps daintily onto the dance floor.

'[The] men gave me a searching glance. My heart seemed to stop completely.'

How could any woman ever match up to the projections, which now deluged her on such a scale, of male fantasy? John Berger's now famous comment (in *Ways of Seeing*, 1972) that 'Men look at women. Women watch themselves being looked at' is a distillation of his earlier discourse, in which he explains the pressures on women: 'A woman must continually watch herself. She is almost continually accompanied by her own image of herself.' This image was a phantom, a male projection, with the reality lost in translation.

> Whilst she is walking across a room or whilst she is weeping at the death of her father, she can scarcely avoid envisaging herself walking or weeping. From earliest childhood she has been taught and persuaded to survey herself continually.

Margaret Atwood puts it even better: 'You are a woman with a man inside watching a woman. You are your own voyeur.'

The male gaze – that pervasive, macho, heterosexual perspective which treated women as sexual exhibits on display for their pleasure – was comprehensively reinforced and internalised in the mid-twentieth century. By 1960, when Betty Friedan was writing *The Feminine Mystique* (1963), she was able to observe, despairingly, that American women 'could desire no greater destiny than to glory in their own femininity'. The female imagery of this era was confirmation of a dehumanising cycle, by which men objectified women and women sought to be objectified because that was what men wanted. It was inescapably omnipresent. Everywhere, the sellers confronted the buyers. Everywhere, women were ambushed by beauteous blondes. As they walked to work, travelled home on the train, queued at the fishmonger's, strolled on the promenade or met their date at the cinema, their eyes met those of other women: bolder, brighter, bustier women, with slenderer waists and redder lips. These images of perfection flaunted themselves across the full range of society: from pubs to hairdressing salons, on public transport and in the newspaper, in shops and picture palaces, from advertisement hoardings and illustrations, photo-features and covers, in colour and black and white, the women smiled back. The starlets and socialites, the models and celebrities appeared to rejoice in the visibility of their gleaming limbs, their blemish-free skin and buoyant breasts. All of them were white, and under five foot six. They had more perfect teeth, longer lashes, glossier hair, prettier noses. Compared to the onlookers they had better romances, a better social life, better families, better food and better material possessions; so they were happier too.

Television ownership was rocketing; the decade saw TV licence figures rise from 382,000 to 10,554,000: a twenty-sevenfold increase; in the USA, between 1950 and 1959, there was a 77 per cent increase in TV ownership. Television technology brought female legs and lipstick into the corner of every living room. Albeit in black and white, up to nine million viewers watched *Sunday Night at the London Palladium*, where the Tiller Girls – a dozen or more matching marionettes, smiling in their sparkly swimsuits – performed sexy synchronised high-kick routines to a big band soundtrack. Weeknight sitcoms included Lucille Ball's gorgeous-but-goofy redheaded heroine in *I Love Lucy*; then there were the British game shows and talent shows like *Double Your Money*, *What's My Line?*, *Opportunity Knocks* and *Take Your Pick*, hosted by effervescent middle-aged men with the cutesy assistance of well-coiffed and deliriously happy female 'hostesses'.

In the commercial breaks slim blondes sat in the passenger seats of fast cars, while radiantly smiling women with perfect teeth placed crunchy biscuits in front of their grateful children or envied their neighbours' whiter-than-white washing. Sexy females with lovely hair draped their bosoms over cars and beverages. The prototype was ubiquitous, as embedded in a woman's consciousness as her own reflection in the mirror.

In the enveloping plush of the movie theatre, yet more ash-blonde Technicolor beauties with peachy complexions and perfect legs danced in formation or flashed their diamonds under the spotlight. These goddesses were the ultimate screen legends – like Grace Kelly, Sophia Loren, Elizabeth Taylor, Diana Dors, Natalie Wood and Doris Day. The leading ladies were, as one contemporary described them, 'radiant with success and confidence'. Hollywood's leading cinematographer, John Alton, persuasively argued that everyday women should look to the aesthetic principles of film lighting in order to 'beautilluminate' their complexions and look their best on the street, in the workplace and at home. 'Remember, love at first sight is love at first light.' Sure enough, in the final frame, the perfectly lit movie heroines were clasped in the embrace of tall, sexy, square-jawed male leads: Marlon Brando, James Stewart or Gary Cooper.

And then, in 1959, the BBC televised Miss World.

Vital Statistics

The early beauty pageants had been amateurish circus-style events. In the mid-twentieth century they proliferated and professionalised, and by the early 1950s every British seaside resort from Bognor to Blackpool had its own bathing beauty contest in the local dance hall, or by the local lido. Supported by sponsorship, the contests became a familiar feature of the British summer holiday, attracting crowds of spectators to see the local lovely crowned by the mayor, often followed by her ride through the streets in a Cinderella coach. Prizes were in the region of £50.

'I just can't believe it's all happening to me,' shop assistant Pat Wilkinson breathlessly told the *Yorkshire Evening Post* when her 'blue eyes ... disarming smile' and 34"–23"–37" figure won her the title Beauty Queen of Yorkshire 1949. The mania for measurements had seized beauty commentators – as if female perfection was a matter of mathematical conformity, that could be robotically replicated – and a post-war winner needed to be smaller overall than the winner of a generation earlier. There were strict rules about aids to the girls' appearance. The swimsuits worn for the contests had to be free of boning, wiring or artificial padding of any sort, and there was a nurse at hand to check.

'Vital statistics' (implying something mandatory and formulaic about the precise curvature of a woman's body) were also embedded in the philosophy of the Miss World contest, launched in 1951. This was the year when Eric Morley, under the banner of the Festival of Britain, inaugurated an international contest with a £1,000 prize for the winner. Morley wanted to introduce some 'razzamatazz' to the rather worthy cultural festival. But more than that, he wanted to boost the commercial interests of his employers, the Mecca organisation, by promoting a British winner. And about prizewinning qualities he was very specific. The ideal Miss World was 5' 5" tall. Weight: 8 stone 10lb to 9 stone 6lb. Waist: 22"–24"; hips: 35"–36"; bust: 36"–37". 'No more, no less.' Morley made no mention of her skin colour, but inevitably, she would be white.

Her legs had to be perfectly shaped whether they were seen from the back or the front, all the way up ... and naturally, she would have to have a lovely face and good teeth ...

In a nutshell, as long as we had the correct *basic* material we could turn the girl into the *perfect* material for the international contests, including the Miss World competition.

In other words, a Miss World could be created, formulated, like a plastic product.

Originally, Morley branded his brainchild the Festival Bikini-Girl. Unprecedentedly, entrants were asked to wear the scandalous new two-piece swimsuits. But as things turned out, the 1951 Miss World contest was – for its creator – the realisation of male fantasy on an alarming scale:

When I first saw the bikinis which some of the girls were going to wear I had to take not only a big gulp but a big grip on myself ...

It was not until I saw all the contestants together in their tiny two-piece costumes that I realised [my] decision might have been a big mistake. All the girls were attractive, some of them were highly voluptuous and when they were seen en-masse they provided an almost overwhelming picture.

Miss 'World' operated racial apartheid; it didn't include any contestants of colour,* and it was a Swedish beauty queen, Kiki Håkonsson who was crowned and took home the £1,000 prize. '[She] filled a bikini more perfectly than anyone I have seen, before or since,' recalled Morley. Miss World was judged such a huge success that it should become annual. But it was also decided that bikinis were too extreme. Audiences weren't ready for such high-octane erotic impact, and in succeeding contests

---

* Five years later, in 1956, a contest was established to find Miss South Africa. Only white females were permitted to enter.

one-piece swimsuits would be the rule. The same would apply in the US, at their annual Miss Universe competition (founded 1952). Nonetheless, a few years later the press in Lahore reported that, at the specific request of the president's wife, Pakistan – the only nation who might have fielded a non-white candidate for the title – would not be participating:

> The decision to abandon the beauty contest was taken on an appeal by the Begum Nahid Iskander Mirza, yesterday asking the [Pageant Association of Pakistan] to bow to the growing public demand and abandon the beauty contest.

The British press was more specific: 'Religious leaders ... had complained that the contest would disgrace Pakistan in the eyes of the Moslem world.' Pakistani public demand may have had a point.

Short of actual nudity, women's public undress had now pretty much peaked. In ensuing years, the televised Miss World event continued to attract record viewing figures (in 1967, nearly 24 million UK viewers tuned in to see Miss Peru win her title) – which, in 1970, would make it an ideal platform for feminists to stage a highly visible protest against the semi-naked contestants' objectification.*

The increasing visibility and publicity surrounding beauty queens, models and film stars set the bar impossibly high for ordinary women. As icons like Kiki Håkonsson, Marilyn Monroe and Brigitte Bardot were awarded society's accolades,

---

* In November 1970 members of the Women's Liberation movement infiltrated the audience for the live TV broadcast of Miss World in the Royal Albert Hall and stopped the show by unleashing banners and hurling flour bombs.

it was getting harder to dismiss the 'beauty' as superficial, degraded or negligible. And statistics were becoming ever more vital. Bit by bit, the noose of feminine beauty was tightening its grip, ratcheting up insecurities, exposing vanities and vulnerabilities, and feeding a cycle of conformity, anxiety, dependency and embarrassment. In her book *Femininity* (1984) the author Susan Brownmiller, who was a teenager in this period, used her own experience of puberty to explore the trap of post-war femininity. It was during one summer vacation that darker, coarser hairs made their first appearance on her legs. Brownmiller was prepared for it, and she was excited. This was a glamorous all-American rite of passage, and there was something sexy about it. Now she was a grown up. Now she could wear nylon stockings: 'I purloined a razor and hurriedly shaved the emergent fuzz off my legs as fast as it appeared – even faster, so entranced was I with this grownup rite of passage ... Now I could be a pinup girl, Betty Grable.' But the glamour wore off as fast as the stubble reappeared on her legs. '[It] ceased to be an exciting ritual of glamour and became a time-consuming, repetitive chore very similar to housework.' There seemed to be no escape. And the hypocrisy of the procedure nagged at her. '[The hair] had a perfect biological right to be there.'

Time for some sisterly advice. These were boom years for the beauty books. Countless well-meaning authors took up their pens to advise young women how to make the best of themselves: *Everyday Grooming, Glamour Secrets, Individually Yours: A Guide to Your Personal Beauty and Charm* and *Susan, be Smooth! – A Handbook of Good Grooming for Girls*. Almost exclusively, such books were written by women.

The need had now become pressing to maintain and groom previously unseen areas of the female body. Constance

Moore's book *The Way to Beauty* (1955) was dictatorial. Readers were commanded to touch their toes twelve times before breakfast and to avoid frown lines by cultivating 'a serene and happy outlook'. There were so many things to remember. Steer clear of lacy bras – every woman needs support, so make sure your bosom is held up with *strong* fabric. If you are fat, try to choose clothes that make you look thinner, and if you are thin, choose clothes that give a broadening effect. Try the banana and milk diet – 'you can lose four pounds by this method' – or the liquid weekend diet: 'two days with nothing but liquids'. Another advice-merchant, Veronica Dengel, author of *Can I Hold my Beauty?* (1946), was clear that bodily functions were linked to loveliness: 'Unless you establish a regular schedule of bowel elimination, you cannot hope to have shiny hair.'

One of the bossiest of advice manuals came from the pen of Eleanore King Kalmus. She started life in North Dakota, and became a B-movie talkie actress. Her also-ran film career opened the door to a supply of celebrity connections, through whom she reinvented herself as a beauty consultant to the stars, and in 1953 published the 'secrets of some of the world's most beautiful women', under the momentous title *Glorify Yourself.*

The book took the form of a step-by-step course, via a 'Personal Progress Chart', by which you could calibrate your success (or failure) in achieving the modules. The object was to captivate the man of your dreams. There was a lot to learn, for, quite aside from the obvious points – that every woman and girl, 'no matter how thin', should wear a girdle, and that all undesirable hair should be promptly removed – there were some more onerous recommendations. Keeping your earlobe at all times in line with your shoulder bone was one, and making circles with your feet whenever reasonably possible was another. King was impatient with the diversity of the human body. 'Normal legs, or ideal ones, are straight, and they touch at the ankles, calves, knees and thighs'; 'Whatever you do, don't go around looking flat-chested ... *Where God has forgotten, you can stuff with cotton!*' But happily, she believed firmly in cooperation, and her disciples formed cheerful alliances, such as the 'Better Bosom Boosters': 'With proper exercise, they often develop the CHEST two inches.'

To achieve such glorious results, the student had to work her way through the course handbook, first scrupulously weighing and measuring herself, and recording the dimensions of every part of the body, from ankle to bust, to be checked against King's chart. Suppose you were ten pounds over, or five inches bigger than the ideal, the prescription was thirty minutes' callisthenic exercise a day, and a thirty-minute walk: 'Walk fast. Wear low heels. Take long strides. Breathe deeply.' Lists of dietary directions followed, involving broiled lamb chops, clear soup and Ryvita. Effective, maybe – if a little joyless. But the successful dieters who wrote to Mrs King were jubilant – this testimonial is typical: 'Now that my lower extremities are under control, due to some wonderful exercises and diet, I can hardly believe the tape-measure when it reads 35½ inches around the hips.'

Ninety years on, such women sound like the echo of their grandmothers – 'Matilda',* for example, back in the 1860s – who commanded her maid to tighten her stays by an inch a day, till her waist became slender enough for her husband's requirements. Had women in the second half of the twentieth century really moved on? Or had they too, like their

---

* See Chapter 1, page 46.

predecessors, gone to extreme lengths to reshape the bodies they were born with, whether to gain other women's admiration, or to make men desire them?

Black Perfection

This avalanche of beauty and diet advice was almost completely directed at readers who were light-skinned. But this was the time of the civil rights movement. In *Beauty Shop Politics: African American Women's Activism in the Beauty Industry* (2010), the historian and academic Tiffany M. Gill argues that the beauty industry contributed to the creation of Black female identity, and that the apparently frivolous salon became a space for incubating political change. Beauty parlours run by and for Black women flourished in the first half of the twentieth century. Within their environment of intimacy and pampering, of the nurturing of self-esteem and prettiness, Black women gave and received shampoos and manicures while sharing their dreams – under the radar – for a more equal society. These were places where women organised voter registration drives and boycotts, all while having their nails done. And in 1957 Martin Luther King Jr addressed the National Beauty Culturists' League on 'The Role of Beauticians in the Contemporary Struggle for Freedom'.

In 1945 the magazine *Ebony* was founded. Initially modelled on *Life* magazine, its coverage of politics, arts, science, lifestyle and beauty earned it a wide readership among the Black community. However, its covers often told a different story. Gorgeous women with flashing smiles were seemingly selected for their relatively fair skin, sleek hair and beauty queen figures.

Ebony 'cover girls' from the 1940s and 50s: *left*, Billie Holiday, 1949; *right*, Dorothy Dandridge, 1951

A cover picture of blues legend Billie Holiday has lightened her Black skin, adjusted her features to an improbable degree and flattened her hair to her skull. Singer Eartha Kitt, of African American and Cherokee descent, was pictured a few years later similarly smoothed out and gold-tinted; while a 1951 cover gave the beautiful rising film star Dorothy Dandridge a selection of reductively racist props to play with: a string of beads, hoop earrings and a drum. Yet her appealing pose seems to come from the world of beatific American wives that we recognise from 1950s refrigerator adverts.

Dorothy was in fact of mixed Black, white, Native American, Hispanic and Jamaican heritage, and as far as American society in the 1940s and 50s was concerned, that made her a 'Negro'. The management of one Las Vegas hotel told Dorothy they would tolerate having her because she was famous, but requested her to stay away from their public areas; another ordered her not to use their swimming pool.

Meanwhile, a slightly less airbrushed Dorothy Dandridge was the first Black woman to feature on the cover of *Life* magazine. Dorothy had been chosen to star in the movie of *Carmen Jones* (1954), Oscar Hammerstein's musical adaptation of Bizet's opera *Carmen*, reimagined with an all-Black cast and directed by Otto Preminger. Dorothy's Carmen interpretation – of a feisty woman who refused to have her life determined by men – gained rave reviews, and secured her the first Best Actress Academy Award nomination ever given to a Black woman – though the award would go that year to the blonde, peach-skinned Grace Kelly for *The Country Girl*.

'What was I?' reflected Dorothy, in a memoir published after her death:

> That outdated 'tragic mulatto' of earlier fiction? Oddly enough, there remains some validity in this concept, in a society not yet integrated. I wasn't fully accepted in either world, black or white. I was too light to satisfy Negroes, not light enough to secure the screen work, the roles, the marriage status available to a white woman.

Dorothy Dandridge, her talent and her grace, fell into the chasm exposed by a racist interpretation of beauty. As an

Oscar nominee, she turned down a role playing a slave girl in *The King and I* (1956), on the grounds that it was a demeaningly racist part, as well as being too low-level for an actress of her stature. After this the movie industry closed ranks, and the offers stopped coming. 'If I were white,' she fantasised, 'I could capture the world.' *Carmen Jones* was to be the peak of a short, caged and crushed career; at the age of forty-two, Dorothy Dandridge was found dead in her apartment in Los Angeles, having probably overdosed on anti-depressants. But whether she had taken them deliberately or by accident was never determined.

———

Just as *Ebony*'s covers disseminated a certain image of African American women, so its advertisement space promoted products that its readers could aspire to. Noticeably, the adverts were heavy on cosmetics, particularly bleaching creams like Nadinola – 'Wonderful things happen when your complexion is clear, bright, Nadinola-light'. Wonderful things indeed. Nadinola was white-owned, and unfortunately the product, which had been insufficiently tested, started causing its users to go blind. Hair straightening products like Long-Aid ('helps short, thin, too-curly hair look longer in just 3 days!') were also heavily promoted.

'Give romance a chance! Don't let a dull, dark complexion deprive you of popularity.' Advertisement in *Ebony*, 1959

Though *Ebony* fostered racial pride, it also bought into the idea that a well-groomed Black woman should approximate as nearly as possible to the standards paraded on catwalks and red carpets by white icons. Almost as much as by their skin colour, Black women were judged by their hair, which was ironed, disciplined, straightened and squashed.* 'Straightened was respectable,' explained one woman. 'It was what we did ... decent people. We don't look unkempt.' Another added: 'You always knew that it was not a good thing to have nappy hair ...

---

* Straighteners, or relaxers, still generally contain a chemical called lye, also used in drain clearers and oven cleaners. Lye can cause scalp irritation, scarring, dermatitis and ulcers. The other method was a hot comb – a 'press' with a heated-up metal attachment that was used to flatten out curls and kinks.

One of the first things you learned about taking care of your own hair was how to straighten it.'

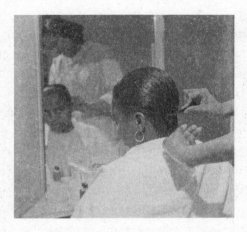

A scene familiar to Black women: the
beauty shop where hair is straightened

In its early years *Ebony*'s fashion editor was Elsie Archer. An African American who had worked with Black teenagers in Harlem and carved out a career for herself as a journalist, Archer joined the staff of *Ebony* in the 1950s. Smart and savvy, she could see that there was a gap in the market – and the time had come for someone to tell young Black women how they too could make the best of themselves. So in 1959 she wrote and published *Let's Face It: A Guide to Good Grooming for Negro Girls*.

Archer recognised that the world could sometimes feel hostile towards her readers: 'The color of your skin can cause a feeling of being unwanted or unloved ... [But] there is no medicine that will change it, so you just might as well be satisfied.' Her tone changes to that of an imperious aunt as she issues her teenage readers with beauty rules: learn to refuse second helpings; get rid of unwanted hair; clean away every particle of make-up before you go to bed. And stop wishing for a fairy godmother to come down and touch you with the magic wand that will give you a new head of hair. You can put your time to better use!

White women were under ever greater pressure to persevere and come closer to 'perfection'. But for Black women those pressures were magnified, as they strove to resemble the images that surrounded them on screens and in magazines. Elsie Archer's book emphasised the need for poise and femininity. Keep slim, look the part, don't wear slacks, get your teeth fixed, choose tasteful accessories:

> Remember the days of the gold hoop earrings? . . . Schoolteacher's blood boiled when girls paraded into classrooms looking like Zulu queens with gold loops larger than arm bracelets. This was one example of carrying a fashion fad a little bit too far.

———

In pre-civil rights America the photographer Eve Arnold set out to document Harlem's community fashion shows. These were private events, in which the mannequins themselves created the clothes and modelled them in front of a paying audience. Arnold caught backstage moments with intimacy and spontaneity, often photographing the star model Charlotte Stribling, aka Fabulous, whose hair was dyed a spectacular platinum blonde, and producing a series of studies of young Black women full of energy, insight and humour.

Eve Arnold's photo of Fabulous in an evening gown,
waiting to emerge onto the catwalk

Arnold hoped that *Harper's Bazaar* would feature her pictures, but the editors turned her down. Through the 1940s
and 50s Black women's style had been deferential to the ideals
of Eurocentric white beauty. But that orthodoxy would soon
change. In 1966, reacting to a growing awareness of this branch
of racial discrimination, *Ebony* ran an article entitled 'The
Natural Look':

Today . . . an increasing number of Negro women are turning their
backs on traditional concepts of style and beauty by wearing their
hair in its naturally kinky state.

And it quoted twenty-three-year-old Suzi Hill, a worker on Martin Luther King's civil rights campaign: 'We, as black women, must realise that there is beauty in what we are, without having to make ourselves into something we aren't.' From there, it was a short jump to regarding hot combs and hair relaxers as racist. The challenge to white beauty standards and rehabilitation of African-identified traits like tightly curled hair can be seen as counterparts to the burgeoning civil rights campaign.

A Stone in the Heart

Jean Lucey Pratt was looking for Mr Right. But for sure, Mr Right would recoil when he observed her waistline, her horrible nails and her flyaway hair.

We glimpsed the teenage Jean in the 1920s (Chapter 4), agonising in her diary about her physical shortcomings. But most of all, as the years went by, she agonised about being left on the shelf. Eventually, in June 1941, she recorded 'the death of an Old Maid', having lost her burdensome virginity at the age of thirty-one. But why, she kept asking herself, was she doomed to be single? Was there something wrong with her, that she had failed to attract a mate? She believed herself to be basically good-looking – so what was the problem?

Jean's thirties passed. It is revealing – and moving – to track her diaries as she tries and fails to reconcile herself to the inevitable waning of youth and bloom. In 1949 she turned forty: 'I am extremely tired and feel [I am] looking older day by day, and it terrifies me. A stone in the heart. I see a woman in the mirror with untidy greying hair that I don't recognise.' She fluctuates between the pleasure and pride conferred by good clothes, good grooming and good hair, and the fatalism of a middle-aged woman who recognises that lipstick and New Look dresses are decreasingly likely to tempt potential husbands. But a year or two later, though she could see that she should be cherishing herself, the effort and expense were starting to outweigh the rewards:

> God help me, grooming is a life's work, and quality is getting almost beyond my means nowadays. I get more sluttish at home, and when I go out seem to have no time to prepare myself. To get one's hair, hands, skin and clothes into decent condition after months of neglect needs at least a week's hard work on them beforehand.

At the same time, comfort was starting to win over glamour. In 1952 Jean's diary records that she bought a pair of flat fleece-lined bootees and Marks & Spencer's indestructible woolly underpants for winter ('hideous but warm and cheap').

The following year, she was beginning to find her 'silly amorous adventures' laughable; and yet – appearance-worry persisted. One day, Jean set off to London wearing a horrible hat. The hat didn't seem horrible when she put it on, but shortly into her journey the truth dawned: '[It] was hideous on me.' As a result, her outing was ruined by a type of heartache and humiliation that many women will recognise: the feeling that one small sartorial mis-step is an indicator of overall bad taste, failure and inadequacy. Jean endured a day of anguish. Then she went home, ripped the offending hat to pieces and set about remodelling it from scratch. And being in the habit of questioning her reactions in writing, Jean now asked herself: 'Does it matter what one looks like?' Why did she mind so much? Who was she trying to impress? This was no longer a sex/mating game. The marriage marketplace was behind her, and she was happy with her cats. But there remained, she concluded, the need to look 'easy on the eye', 'well groomed' and not over-conspicuous. There was a balance to be struck between neat and gaudy. 'One should try to be as pleasant as possible to look at.' Poised. Perfected. And so, the battle continued: 'I am determined to master the hair and hat problem.'

That determination propelled her back to the hairdresser, even against her better judgement. In 1950s England, hair salons were part of the boom economy, catering to women's need for gleaming curls and perfect perms. A new one had just opened in Slough, and Jean booked herself an appointment – 'It was quite terrifying.' The salon placed its clients in rows. They sat there, in serried ranks: the shampooed ladies, identically robed, waiting to have their hair wrapped up in curlers, placed along one wall, while those whose hair was already curled were facing them under rows of identical dryer hoods like machinery parts, obediently reading their magazines.

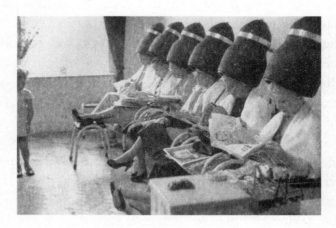

A 1950s hair salon

Something in Jean rebelled.

As I sat waiting, watching all the other women in stages of disarray, they seemed indistinguishable one from the other. We are being moulded to one pattern, made to look as the hairstylist and fashion designer dictates. We haven't a chance to be individual.

A moment of recognition. The quest for perfection demanded mindless compliance, passivity. It did not allow for improvisation or spontaneity. As Jean noted, fashion and beauty had become dictatorial. Married or single, young or old, women were enslaved not only by their horrible hats but also by the sinister metallic helmets that – once a week, or once a fortnight – were plugged in over their heads like the machines in *The Matrix*, harvesting human powers, and dehumanising their captives.

———

Like many other women, Jean Lucey Pratt dieted, though she was not fat. '[I am] living on a Hauser* diet. I can't speak highly enough of this system,' she noted in her diary in May 1955. By the 1950s slimming had become normalised. You could do it the hard way, with callisthenics and Ryvita. But a raft of technologies and gimmicks – lucrative to their inventors – was now available to women who wanted to 'reduce'. Writing in the *Tatler*, Jean Cleland described a visit to Helena Rubinstein's London salon, where she underwent 'galvanism' to re-shape her ankles: 'Pads soaked in saline are strapped round the ankles,

---

* Gayelord Hauser was the American author of *Eat and Grow Beautiful* (1936) and *Look Younger, Live Longer* (1950); his diet books became movie-star bibles and made him a fortune.

and this acts as an electrolyte, which drives the heat through the tissues.'

This was followed by 'faradism', and massage which distributed acid secretions and broke up fatty deposits. The following year, Rubinstein's salon introduced the 'traction rhythmic couch', designed to stretch muscles and redistribute flabby flesh. The client was harnessed to the couch and the motor switched on, to jiggle the muscles into motion. The same salon also innovated the Traxator: this supposedly diminished fat on specific areas, by applying vacuum cups which pumped waste products away from the body. Or you could try an in-demand method for shedding inches introduced by beautician Thelma Holland in 1958: the Slenderella Table, which toned your muscles and shrank your waistline. Yet again, the experts were keeping count: 'One client ... has lost 10½ inches in five weeks, and if that isn't exciting, I don't know what is,' commented Mrs Holland. Meanwhile, Frenchwomen retained their *gamine* figures by standing naked in a shower cubicle and being power-hosed with jets of liquid mud.

In August 1955 the *Tatler* ran a page which one can only read with a heavy heart, since its subject-matter has become a familiar annual frenzy: 'With holidays by the sea fast approaching, the day of reckoning is upon us.'

Beach panic was the name of the game. Look in the mirror, urged *Tatler*'s beauty correspondent, and tell yourself you don't need to lose some pounds ahead of your summer holiday on the Côte d'Azur. So, get down on the floor and start rolling. Then, sit-ups. Then get in a masseuse or, if you can't afford that, rub all your bulgy bits with a loofah, whack them with your fist and follow up with a painful regime of 'pull and pinch, pinch and pull' to break up the fatty tissues. Cut down your food intake. Say no to potatoes. Take wax baths and use electric blankets. Nothing could be simpler if you want to look slim when you swim. The message was still alive and well sixty years later, when the manufacturers of Protein World's Weight Loss Collection controversially advertised their food substitute across the London Underground with a slender bikini-clad model, under the slogan 'Are You Beach Body Ready?'*

The cascade of products and processes designed to remove excess inches bears witness to a kind of mania: a huge sector of women panic-stricken at the prospect of being betrayed by their fleshy thighs or bulgy tummies; women fearful at the inevitable revelation of their deficiencies in a teeny bikini. Never before had they been subjected to such exposure, or such pressure to look acceptable. These were women and young girls whose fat-awareness mindset was permanently switched to 'on' – and they were the targets of manufacturers who realised there was a willing and profitable market for anything that would turn them from fat to thin.

The Turkobath 'turns an ordinary home bathtub
into a steam cabinet – ideal for slimming'

---

* Protesters defaced the posters with graffiti, and fifty thousand people signed an online petition calling on Protein World to remove them, on the grounds that they promoted an unhealthy body image and were sexist and harmful. Transport for London removed the posters.

Take, for example, the Turkobath, a plastic cape, available for 15 shillings, that fastened around the neck and attached to the sides of the bathtub, keeping the steam in so that you sweated out the surplus fat. Or take the Rallie Home-Massage Belt, which had a moment in the late 1950s: its selling point was slimming without effort: 'Relax and ease away the inches.' Just five minutes a day, and you'll soon be taking in your waist-band. Or try the Slenda-Suit – a onesie made from vinyl, that also used the steam bath principle: you could 'just loll around' wearing it, and swelter away the excess pounds.

The Slenda-Suit, advertised in *Screenland*, 1953

Meanwhile, a new tummy-crunch goddess, Eileen Fowler, was becoming almost as well-known as Prunella Stack, as she was appointed the BBC Radio voice of the keep-fit movement. Fowler broadcast daily at 6:45 a.m. and her catchphrase 'Down with a bounce – with a bounce, come up!' became an inspiration to many early risers.

But stage and screen idols were even more influential. In March 1953 Oscar-nominated actress Jeanne Crain shared her slimming secrets with the readers of *Screenland*. She advocated push-ups, a lunch menu of raw vegetables and skimmed milk; and 'a colonic when first starting the four-day diet is very effective and helpful'. The following year, the Hollywood fanzine *Modern Screen* published a 'Beauty Fair Analysis Chart', which gave merciless details of the stars' figure measurements. Elizabeth Taylor, for example, was size 12 but unfortunately had a 'post-pregnancy weight problem'. 'You all know what happened. Liz gained thirty-five pounds during her pregnancy, twenty of which stayed on after the baby's birth.' She was cast in a film and given three weeks to lose twelve pounds: 'It was a painful experience consisting of appetite-curbing pills, steam baths and strenuous massage.'

At this time crispbread brands took off – like Ryvita, which was synonymous with shapeliness, Bisks – 'the natural safe way to lose those unwanted inches' and Energen – 'starch reduced ... they keep you slim and fit'. Alternatively, there were food supplements on the market – such as Larson's Swedish Milk Diet, which you could substitute for food every other day – that promised happiness and weight loss. Easy-to-take slimming tablets were regularly advertised. For only $2, candy-tasting VXM tablets 'will rid you of 10 pounds in 14 days!' Ayds would help you 'slim the way the stars slim', without dieting. StataVar tablets (just $1.95) would get rid of 'that ugly fat now!'

If you preferred not to self-medicate, support garments could be relied upon to flatten out the midriff. The American fashion designer Anne Fogarty attributed her eighteen-inch waist to the constant wearing of a restraining 'cinch', or wide, tight belt – 'The theory is very much akin to the old Japanese tradition of binding feet to keep them small,'* she wrote in *The Art of Being a Well Dressed Wife* (1959). The Shape-O-Lette corset made you 'bewitchingly beautiful – instantly!' Ambrose Wilson's 'famous rubber reducing corset ... cut in the fashionable manner' controlled the body with unyielding discipline. One woman remembered these garments with horrified amusement: 'I had one of the Playtex rubberised roll-ons – it had little perforated breathing holes all over, so that when you wrenched it off, the areas where the holes had been stood up on your skin like pimples.'

Slimming had become an international obsession. So it isn't surprising to see a parallel increase in reports of women damaging themselves, and sometimes dying, from dieting. In 1952 the *Daily Mirror* gave front page coverage to the terrible story of the ATTRACTIVE GIRL [WHO] SLIMMED HERSELF TO DEATH. Thirty-five-year-old Jessie Dennis from Birmingham had been 'a fine figure of a girl', auburn-haired and healthy, weighing about 9½ stone. Inexplicably, she started slimming; she lived off dry toast and cups of tea, and reduced her weight to five stone. Nobody could persuade her to eat; she would tell her family, 'I don't feel like it.' Jessie aged visibly, and became weak. Eventually she was taken to hospital, where she died. Jessie's brother told the *Mirror*'s reporter, 'We can only hope the tragedy of my sister's death may act as an object lesson and warn other women who develop this stupid craze to slim.' The following year saw the death of Katherine Reed from Burnley, whose diet caused her

---

*   Fogarty mistook her traditions. Small feet were regarded as beautiful by the Chinese, and this custom, whereby the feet of young girls were broken and tightly bound, causing terrible pain and resulting in disabilities, prevailed over nearly a thousand years. Initially the practice was confined to upper-class women, but by the nineteenth century it is estimated that 40 to 50 per cent of all Chinese women bound their feet. The practice was banned in 1912, but took until the 1950s to disappear entirely. Poor women in rural areas were the last to abandon foot-binding.

weight to plummet from 13 to just 4 stone. 'There was nothing
wrong with her mind,' Katherine's mother told the coroner.
Doctors agreed she was 'not insane in any way. It was just a
psychological illness.'

In 1957 twenty-two-year-old Joyce Ley from Romford in
Essex lost thirty-five pounds in four months. 'She got this stupid
craze from the other girls in her office,' her father told the *Daily
Mirror*. Depression and insomnia set in, and she died from an
overdose of sleeping pills. Elsie May Collins from Coventry
started to refuse food in her teens. She died, emaciated, in hospital, aged twenty-nine. Her mother blamed a 'slimming craze
which came over from America'.

Whether or not this was correct, it was the same story
on the other side of the Atlantic. Caren Crabbe, daughter
of a Hollywood actor famous for his role as Tarzan, died
in her sleep aged twenty – she weighed only sixty pounds (a
little over four stone). Caren was reported to have been 'on
a strict reducing diet'. And the screen goddesses themselves
crash-dieted and burned out. Barbara La Marr, one of the
best-known among the 1920s vamps, took dieting to an
extreme and died of TB and nephritis at the age of twenty-
nine, and it was rumoured that movie actress Renée Adorée
had met the same fate. The talented Maria Montez, aged
thirty-nine, who had been following a course of slimming
treatments that included taking very hot baths, died in her
tub, while the B-movie starlet Simone Silva – who made headlines when she removed her bikini top for a photocall at the
1954 Cannes film Festival – was found dead in her Mayfair
apartment in 1957; friends believed her crash-dieting habit
had contributed to her death.

The *Sunday Mirror* sounded the alarm. Women were buying
dodgy dieting pills which caused morbid conditions, it warned.
Emaciated and starving, their bodies became incapable of

accepting normal nourishing meals. 'Doctors everywhere are worried ... Adolescent girls are the main victims of the slimming craze. They are not wise enough to heed warnings and yet are most sensitive to the jeers of playmates or the nickname "Fatty".'

Concern was growing about cases of anorexia nervosa – which was increasingly being diagnosed in cases of self-starvation. But anorexia was still largely attributed to psychological imbalances; to paranoia, to sexual disturbance, or to a longing for death. Freud had associated food fixations with unconscious sexual urges, equating loss of appetite with loss of libido, resulting in 'melancholia'. In other words, eating disorders were seen as a side effect of another mental illness. There was no discussion, at this time, of women's body image,* or of the relationship between public icons and the pressures to conform to them. Few asked – why are women so dissatisfied with their appearance, and what is it that propels them to try to make themselves thinner? And nobody questioned whether it was right or wrong to bombard the public with a profusion of glorified, perfectly formed, beach-body-ready imagery, or for charlatans to get rich by selling them Shape-O-Lettes and Slenda-suits, based on the falsehood that they, too, could look like Brigitte Bardot.

_____

In the 1950s equality still seemed a very long way off, but at least it was visible on the horizon. The healthy economy of the

_____

*   See Meera Schanbhag, 'A Historical Perspective on the Cultural Connotations surrounding Eating Disorders' (2020). Schanbhag points out that 'disturbance of body image' was not formally categorised among the diagnostic criteria for anorexia nervosa until 1980. Bulimia was not linked diagnostically to body image until 1987.

mid-1950s seemed to hand out opportunity to all. And there was plenty of food for everybody. But here were women damaging their bodies and starving themselves to death. So what *was* going on?

A group of Italian psychiatrists and psychologists* have argued that, historically, in heavily patriarchal societies where women's roles have been limited to homemaking and motherhood, those women rarely suffered from self-starvation. Moreover, in developing countries, where food was insufficient, there were no case reports of anorexia nervosa. In contrast, more 'egalitarian' and affluent cultures 'witnessed spiralling cases of self-starvation'. The report's authors cited a leading Italian psychiatrist, Marina Palazzoli, who recalled working at the Institute of Clinical Medicine in Milan between 1938 and 1950:

> During the whole period of World War II in Italy ... there were dire food restrictions and no patients at all were hospitalised at the Clinic for anorexia. Hospitalizations for anorexia started in 1948, concurrent with the explosion of the Italian economic miracle and the advent of the affluent society.

Industrialised, developed countries were opening their doors to women, and welcoming, too, the fashions that liberated them: trousers, shorter skirts made from lighter, more revealing fabrics, simplified undergarments – and swimwear that no longer hid their bodies. And these countries celebrated this new manifestation of femininity with a blizzard of impossibly slender imagery; fat-free, shapely and size 10.

---

* Liliana Dell'Osso, Marianna Abelli, Barbara Carpita, Stefano Pini, Giovanni Castellini, Claudia Carmassi and Valdo Ricca, 'Historical Evolution of the Concept of Anorexia Nervosa and Relationships with Orthorexia Nervosa, Autism, and Obsessive-Compulsive Spectrum' (2016).

In a world of increasing women's rights, technological advance, societal wealth and an abundance of food, the essential message to women remained: be thin. But the imperatives of an earlier more patriarchal age still prevailed. The femininity fairy tale was as alive as ever: that comfort-story which reassured every girl, as she grew up, that grace, poise, perfection and Prince Charming could be hers, provided she conformed physically, and provided she was thin.

Society was finally starting to offer women empowerment and emancipation – or so it seemed. In reality the entire package amounted to a swindle. But it wasn't until 1978, when the psychotherapist Susie Orbach wrote her ground-breaking diet-buster *Fat is a Feminist Issue*, that the whole racket would be comprehensively uncovered. Building on second-wave feminism, and on the basis of John Berger's underlying insight, Orbach was able succinctly to explain how female dependency and thinness were interconnected. Marriage and motherhood, she explained, could only be attained through 'catching' a man. 'To get a man, a woman has to learn to regard herself as an item, a commodity, a sex object.' And this narcissism was fuelled by a glut of imagery on TV, on billboards and in magazines, which contributed to a woman's self-image as seen through men's eyes. The fashion and diet industries played an equal part. It was tacitly understood that self-presentation, and conformity to the ideal, were essential to catching a man. Orbach was specific: 'To do this she must look appealing, earthy, sexual, virginal, innocent, reliable, daring, mysterious, coquettish and thin.' Corseted and crinolined, Princess Alexandra had appealed to Prince Edward to love her and marry her for her beauty. But, more than a century later, had the fundamentals of women's relationship to men, and to their own appearance, really changed?

In the Mirror

Nella Last was by now in her sixties, and the marriage marketplace was a distant memory for her, and for the matrons of Barrow-in-Furness. Nevertheless, she took pride in her trim figure and spruce appearance. Why did she bother? Who cared about being thin, once you'd got your man? Why not – having achieved your objective – simply rejoice in the licence of old age, throw out all that tight underwear and give in to the temptation of all those chocolate biscuits, newly off the ration? Instinctively, we know the answer. As often as not, it's about looking good in other women's eyes. For just as we can't escape the public images of beautiful thin women all around us, so we are constantly shamed if we reflect back to them anything less than an 'adequate' appearance. In this context, it's revealing to examine, through Nella's critical eyes, the older woman's relationship to beauty in an era which prized perfection. Her diaries also offer a non-metropolitan perspective, while giving some penetrating glimpses into the priorities of ordinary, post-war British women.

One rainy April evening in 1950 Nella was roped in to help organise a dinner for members of the Women's Voluntary Service, which, during the war, had been a lifeline for her. Nella did the honours, greeting Mrs Diss, the local Barrow-in-Furness WVS head, who had invited her counterpart from Birkenhead to address the guests. Afterwards, these two women chatted to Nella, who was shocked to discover that, since they had last met, both of them had ballooned:

> She had so gone to seed, not only put on weight but badly needed a decent corset and hairdo ... She and Mrs Diss, who has put on at least three stones since wartime days, teased me with my

'girlish' figure, asking the secret. I said, 'Perhaps a nervy tummy that keeps me more or less on a diet – and I don't like chocolates', a little dig at Mrs Diss, who rarely has one out of her mouth.

Elsewhere, Nella is scornful of Mrs Diss for her neglect of the niceties, despite the fact that her husband was a wealthy jeweller and they lived in a lovely house: 'Her shoes always look run down and dirty, her permed hair always looks as if it needs a trip to the hairdresser's.' And she was scandalised by the WVS secretary, Mrs Newall: '[She] looks like a tinker's wife. She wears no corsets on her spreading figure.' Nella was equally unforgiving about another of her co-workers from the Service: 'Poor thing, she was a devastatingly plain-faced woman, with horrible jumbled teeth, unmarried and getting fat. She had not got much out of life.'

Meanwhile, Nella herself stayed respectable on a tight budget of £4 10s a week. That meant one perm a year, and a shampoo and set at the hairdresser's every three or four weeks. She was lucky with her 'girlish' figure, though she conscientiously wore her Spirella corsets – repaired and altered – through thick and thin. A highlight – which speaks eloquently of our mothers' and grandmothers' priorities – is Nella's description of a shopping trip to Blackpool, with £1 7s to spend, and her dream-come-true moment in the millinery department of Ledgerwood's:

> I saw A HAT . . . just the kind of coarsely woven straw, the exact shade of wine colour, the perfect *dream* of a hat – and only 16s 11d. I took it off the stand, tried it on and said 'I'll take it please.'

A few minutes later she was on her way, carrying the wine-coloured treasure in a green paper bag, suffused with the kind of contentment that comes only with the purchase of a covetable bargain.

Nella Last's diaries – like those of Jean Pratt, written when both were mature and no longer aspiring to find a mate – give a different slant on women's relationship with their looks. Good – and bad – hat days and regular visits to the hairdresser were common to both. And both of them were battling on, doing their best to look 'neat but not gaudy'. But Nella Last's diary reminds us that, at her stage of life, women's judgements often matter more than men's. Her own beady, sometimes merciless verdicts – from which she herself emerges superior – uncover a strand of competitive female fault-finding and evaluation that most women will recognise.

But usually, the fount of such fault-finding is self-doubt and uncertainty about one's own appearance. As Susie Orbach says, we are required to be our own judges, measuring ourselves against models of perfection: assessing our own fatness or slimness, our height and width, our preferences in underwear, our hairiness, our smelliness, and our taste in hats. We are urged to watch the inches, to climb on the scales and calculate the excess pounds and ounces. It's as habit-forming as any drug.

The mirrors surround us. The diktats of beauty don't disappear just because a woman finds a husband; patriarchal, commercial and media influences persist. A woman of sixty may 'let herself go' – or she may continue to do daily battle with those unforgiving imperatives. Either way, she is in their grip. Jean Pratt frets that she has neglected herself, and struggles to groom her skin and nails; Nella Last repairs her corset for the umpteenth time and alters her skirt 'to London length'. 'I feel quite up to date.'

It's not blameworthy to dress up, or to want to be gorgeous at any age. Clothes and grooming are genuine pleasures. It is probably more blameworthy to criticise other women for their beauty choices. But the commercial/media/patriarchal messages have grown in size and volume over the years, attempting to dazzle and deafen us. It seems the propaganda is all we hear.

Left: 1957 – a cover photo of 'blonde bombshell' Jayne Mansfield. The focus on Mansfield's large breasts verged on the freakish. She also typified the trend for sexy women to appear feather-brained. Right: 1899 – a woman in a whale-boned corset

In the 1950s representations of women were becoming preternatural, distorted and ever more unattainable. What average woman could ever approach the extremity of a body like Jayne Mansfield's: 40D–21–36? Her unreality was echoed in the distorted body proportions of the Barbie doll, introduced in 1959.

For most women attempting to increase their top halves and decrease their bottom halves, the numbers didn't add up. In one sense, women had reverted to the late nineteenth century, when an hourglass figure was a requisite for every well-attired lady. Back then, the woman with the eighteen-inch waist was both incapacitated for any kind of useful labour, while at the same time scoring points on the marriageability register.

The Victorian lady's S-bend anatomy could be remodelled from the outside in, and those dramatically unnatural mammary curves could be more or less achieved with the help of buckram, whalebone and laces. Ninety years later, clothing had simplified and minimised. The body itself was visible, and in a bikini or swimsuit, it stood to be judged on its intrinsic merits and metrics. If your boobs didn't measure up (or down) on the beach, there wasn't much you could do about it.

———

Or was there? In the 1950s, mammoplasty, hormonal treatment and implants were becoming available to those who sought a more perfect figure. Some women's bosoms were uncomfortably large. Huge, pendulous breasts equated with the primitive and the proletarian and, Jayne Mansfield notwithstanding, did not conform to modern versions of elegance, which privileged sportiness over motherhood and lactation. Surgeons like Dr Leslie Gardiner (author of *Faces, Figures and Feelings: A Cosmetic Surgeon Speaks* [1959]) were willing and able to restore them to 'normality'. Surgical reduction brought relief to numerous women who suffered from hypertrophic breasts. 'I am twenty-eight years old,' one of them wrote to him. 'I don't know what it is like to wear a swimsuit or a beautiful gown, to lead a normal, free existence, out of "harness".'

But more problematic was the plight of women who came to see doctors like Gardiner, complaining of the inadequacy of their breasts:

> I want to marry very soon. The prospect brings on inexplicable anxiety . . . I have indulged in exercises of every description. I have even consulted a psychiatrist and undergone hypnotic treatment. All to no avail. My bustline remains insignificant.

This woman had got herself a husband – but her body was selling him short. Gardiner had the greatest sympathy for these luckless individuals: 'The young girl whose breasts fail to grow normally during and after adolescence is denied part of that profound experience which she undergoes while she blossoms into womanhood.'

'Whatever you do, don't go around looking flat-chested.' How hard it could be. Joan, a twenty-year-old stenographer from North Carolina, was also in despair when she wrote to her local paper's advice columnist, Dr George Crane, in January 1955:

> Dr Crane, my life is simply miserable.
>
>   For my bust is so small. I try to conceal that fact with a special uplift type of bra but why can't I develop an attractive bust like other girls?

Dr Crane's no-nonsense response was probably not what she hoped for. The breasts, he explained, could only be enlarged by weight gain, exercise and pregnancy. Joan should stop stressing and start boosting the male ego instead:

> Millions of wives have flat busts, but their husbands proposed marriage to them because those girls were charming in their total personality.

So quit developing a complex over the size of your bust ...
Turn your attention off yourself by paying honest compliments
to your male companions. For if you make a boy feel happy and
proud of himself, he'll think you are wonderful, even if you have
no bust at all.

As usual, there were products that claimed to help – like
Charmode Flatterettes – breast-shaped foam inserts ('gives new
glamour to your figure', just 77 cents), or Chesties – down-filled
latex bust forms.

Gardiner experimented with hormonal therapies, but
they didn't work. He counselled against the introduction of
implants using sections of fat excised from the buttocks, as
after a short time the fat tended to be reabsorbed into the
body. Non-absorbable synthetic substances seemed a better
bet, and around 1958 doctors started experimenting with the
insertion of soft, resilient polyvinyl sponges. Unluckily, once in
position, they rapidly started to lose their spongy qualities, and
became rock-like, causing inflammations and infections. Scar
tissue formed around the implants, and the breasts shrank and
became strangely warped. 'Happiness can be bought at too high
a cost,' was Dr Gardiner's gloomy judgement on this useless
procedure.

These were the early days of silicone. A flexible, durable,
unreactive chemical substance, it had been produced industri-
ally for twenty years for use in insulating electrical components,
and as a sealant for caulking navy ships. It went unmentioned
by Dr Gardiner. But its properties were allegedly discovered in
the 1940s by Japanese sex workers, who injected it in gel form
into their breasts in order to improve their chances with the
GIs stationed in Japan. Word reached the American press, and
one magazine ran an article entitled 'Bosoms Can be Increased
2 Inches – Without Pain'. The piece was directed at 'women

only', since evidently such operations fell into the category
of sex, secrets and lies. Nobody was supposed to know that
the young, blonde lady from Boston described in the article
had paid just $35 for a fuller bosom that was actually a fake.
The article described the 'before' and 'after' effects of her ten-
minute appointment at a Japanese beauty parlour: 'Above the
waist she was almost flat-chested – shaped like a boy. Soon
she would have a more "normal" bosom.' Her turn came, and
she was given two simple hypodermic injections, each one
painlessly administering 70 cubic centimetres of liquid silicone
oil into her breasts: 'Within 10 minutes she lost her inferiority
complex and gained pride in her womanhood.' The procedure,
which had been performed in secret on thousands of English
and American women over four years, promised no negative
after-effects.

But the reality was extremely risky. Creepily, the injections
could cause a condition described as 'silicone rot' – in which
the flesh of the breasts began to decompose. The substance
could also cause longer-term complications, ranging from lung
embolism to gangrene, and from cancer to death.

———

As Elizabeth Haiken has pointed out,* cosmetic surgery is just
one of the components of the American Dream: a dream pursued by a society rapidly abandoning its rural roots: a society
increasingly obsessed by self-presentation, 'in which wrinkles
were no longer facts to be accepted, but "problems" to be
conquered'.

Cosmetic practitioners were discovering lucrative new strands
of work, devising facelifts and extreme exfoliation techniques for

---

*   In 'The Making of the Modern Face: Cosmetic Surgery' (2000). Haiken is
also the author of *Venus Envy: A History of Cosmetic Surgery* (1997).

eradicating loose skin, wrinkles, eye bags, freckles and blemishes. The *American Weekly* applauded the advances made in surgery that could 'change a patient's whole outlook on life'. Inferiority complexes, career lapses, self-consciousness and 'maybe a completely warped personality' could all be rectified by the skill of surgeons who performed miracles on the eyes, jawline, ears and nose. 'The operation may cost hundreds – or a few thousand ... Whatever the cost, it will be worth it.'

As Dr Peter Steincrohn told his *Evening Star* readers in Washington DC, 'Paying for a pretty new nose is one sure way of buying happiness.'

Meanwhile, those hundreds, or thousands, of dollars promised to make many doctors extremely happy too. And the prospect of this wealth meant there would be no let-up in research around cosmetic surgery. By 1962 tests were underway to place a silicone breast implant into the chest cavity of a dog named Esmeralda, and before long surgeons were starting to inject silicone into women's lips as fillers or plumpers. Around the same time work was starting to surgically remove the fatty portions of the thighs – this would evolve into the technique of liposuction. The prospect of a body extensively remodelled to conform to fashion was now within reach.

———

I began this book by remembering my own summers spent at Charleston in the late 1950s, and how I would pull out the dressing-up clothes from behind the curtain and transform myself into my fantasy princess. Even before I could read, fairy tales and Greek myths were my favourite stories. Rapunzel, Cinderella, Danaë, Persephone, the Little Mermaid were all firmly lodged in my imaginative world, and they were all 'as beautiful as the day'. Princesses, goddesses and goosegirls – whether manacled to rocks, locked in towers, transformed into laurel trees or sent to sleep for a hundred years – are always beautiful, always aspirational. In the stories, Beauty always triumphs, the curse is broken, the Beast or frog is transformed into a handsome prince, and the slipper fits.

There is another way that female appearance beguiles. Historically and in myth, ugliness and deformity have been the features of evil. Witches had snaggle teeth and hairy moles. Medusa, whose head was female, with writhing snakes for hair, could – terrifyingly – turn anyone to stone with a single look. In an irreligious age do we cultivate beauty as a way of imposing order and harmony on a malign and hostile world? Every day our hands and feet, our torsos and faces, grow a little older. Our hair goes a little greyer. Of all the human characteristics, beauty is the most transient. Up against the clock, we are impatient for answers, and the stupendous achievements of science seem to offer ways to postpone the inevitable passing of time – even mortality. We start a new diet, buy another pot of face cream, put on a new dress, get some highlights, book a Botox appointment, and hope for the best. We try to remedy the ills of our world by changing how we look. A new, wrinkle-free countenance seems to embody the prospect of achievable happiness.

But the mirror never lies:

> Looking-glass, Looking-glass, on the wall,
> Who in this land is the fairest of all?

If anyone in *Snow White* had a facelift, it would have been the Evil Queen Grimhilde in Disney's version of the German folk tale, with her lurid make-up and sculpted eyebrows – 'a beautiful woman, but proud and haughty, and she could not bear that anyone else should surpass her in beauty'. The story of Snow

White as told by the Brothers Grimm is grisly, but it also reads like a parody of the beauty myth.

Wanting to get rid of her beautiful young stepdaughter, the queen sends her into the forest, accompanied by the huntsman, who is ordered to kill the maiden and return bearing her lungs and liver. The huntsman takes pity on Snow White and instead kills a boar. He returns with its viscera, which the queen then eats. But now the truth-telling mirror reveals to the queen that Snow White is still alive. She visits the dwarves' house disguised as a peddler, and offers Snow White a pair of laced-up bodices. Tightening them round her waist, she tries – but fails – to asphyxiate the maiden. She next attempts to kill Snow White by tempting her with a beautiful poisoned hair comb – 'It pleased the girl so well that she let herself be beguiled.' The story tells us that a woman who is afraid of her ageing appearance may go to extreme lengths to ensure her beauty is unrivalled. Finally, the queen poisons Snow White with an apple, and this time the girl remains as if dead until a king's son liberates her from the spell.

Beautiful Snow White is carried off to the prince's castle, where they are married, while the evil queen, who is invited to the wedding, is forced to put on iron shoes heated red-hot in the fire, and dance until she drops down dead. All the animals of the forest rejoice.

These are the nursery fables so many of us have grown up with, and internalised: the fictitious fantasies that tell us again and again that a woman can stay forever young, that she has no agency, that her face is her fortune, that youth and beauty are rewarded, while the ageing woman is punished. In the fairy-tale cast of characters, witches, wicked stepmothers and older stepsisters all get their comeuppance, while the beauty of younger daughters is rewarded. Grimms' tales normally tell the story of a young, white, lovely heroine – as often as not 'so beautiful that her equal could not be found anywhere on earth'. They tell us that a boy must grow up to be a manly warrior, and that youth is better than age. And they tell us that things will work out, that all adventures end with a wedding, that death will be defeated, and that 'they all lived happily ever after'.

It's a fiction that we can never live up to.

We need to rewrite the story.

Afterword

> Every woman knows that, regardless of all her other achievements, she is a failure if she is not beautiful. She also knows that whatever beauty she has is leaving her, stealthily, day by day.

In 1999 Germaine Greer, author of *The Female Eunuch* (1970), was still angry: 'Thirty years on femininity is still compulsory for women.'

In the twenty-first century we are still, every day and unavoidably, bombarded with images of the women men seem to desire: perfect, thin, smooth women with unattainable bodies. But, every day and unavoidably, men see those images too. They are fantasy-fulfilment pictures: airbrushed and enhanced. We are in dreamworld. Women try to look as desirable as the unattainable women men fantasise about, while men continue to project their unattainable fantasies back onto the objects of their desire.

We need to undress one final icon: she is an imaginary modern woman. Picture her in all her slender, toned glory. Her garments are no longer the focus of admiration – they barely conceal her breasts and thighs, her belly and bottom. Instead, her beautiful, visible body is on trial. This beauty has been achieved by hours sweating in the gym. An army of paid professionals has supported her efforts: manicurists, beauticians, stylists and dentists. She has bought expensive products to improve the appearance of her eyelids, her ankles, her skin. She has deprived herself of nourishment and self-medicated in order to stay slender, and inflicted pain on her body with needles, lasers and scalpels. Measurements dominate her day. The aesthetic surgeon has played his part in enhancing, shaping and sculpting her face and body. She may be fifty, but she looks youthful. She has even had the unseen parts of her body reshaped by 'aesthetic gynaecologists'. She has the phoney, photoshopped, synthetic quality of a Barbie doll.

Yet still this woman feels that she has failed. Still, she feels judged. Like the Victorian woman in her corset and bustle, she is a captive. But when the Victorian woman got undressed, her body was still her own, unscathed.

This imaginary contemporary woman is a composite, but looking to the future, the evidence is unnerving. Instagram, TikTok and Love Island create the mirage on the road ahead: heroin chic, thigh gap, bikini bridge, skinny bitch, ribcage bragging, big booty – and where next? Body image is now on the list of diagnostic criteria linked to eating disorders. In 2023 the charity BEAT* estimated that 75 per cent of the 1.25 million people in the UK afflicted with eating disorders were female. A 2020 survey conducted by the Women and Equalities Committee showed that less than 20 per cent of women in the UK felt positive about their body image most of the time, while 9 per cent of adults had had suicidal thoughts related to their appearance. Diet culture, atypical representations of women and lack of imagery showing older women were at the root of this, above all via social media. And in 2022 an audit of

---

*   Formerly the Eating Disorders Association.

cosmetic surgery* revealed that the number of procedures – of which 28,883 (93 per cent) were undertaken by women – had increased overall by 102 per cent compared to the previous year. Breast augmentation was up by 66 per cent, and liposuction by 134 per cent.

Meanwhile, statistics tell us that bias hasn't gone away. A woman of colour is likely to do better in life if she straightens her hair, and if her skin is paler in colour; by 2027 the skin-lightening industry is projected to be worth over $24 billion. Thin women get promoted more than fat ones, and research published in the *European Eating Disorders Review* in 2022 showed that 21 per cent of the fashion models surveyed had BMIs below 17, which is viewed as severely underweight. We can spend time and money striving to look like a cosmetically enhanced film star or a plastic doll and be viewed as misguided narcissists – or we can suffer society's rebukes. We are damned if we do, and damned if we don't.

Meanwhile, for men too times are getting harder. Just as for years the media have objectified and dehumanised women, today they also objectify and dehumanise men. Social media is almost as permeated with imagery of muscle-packed hunks as it is of impossibly thin women. Some men 'bulk up' by taking anabolic steroids. Many now groom and use make-up products. There is a boom among men wanting aesthetic surgery and even excruciating leg-lengthening procedures which can increase height by as much as three inches. And yes, for around $15,000 a man can have a piece of silicone inserted into his penis to increase its length and girth. We hear of binge eating, and cases of anorexia increasing among males.

I would say, and I think many women might echo: 'Welcome to my world.'

---

* The BAAPS (British Association of Aesthetic Plastic Surgeons) National Audit.

And yet who knows? Maybe, we will see change – because at last there are some men whose eyes have finally been opened to the female condition.

––––––––––

One of the aims of this book has been to demonstrate how, as the progress towards equality and liberation has gathered momentum, the demands and pressures made on the female body have escalated in parallel. All along, corporate greed, the diffusion of visual media and men's fear of losing their power base have rendered women ever more exposed and vulnerable. The final chapter culminated in 1960, with the undressed woman standing trembling on the shore. There is nowhere left for her to hide, as her bikini has denuded her of all but the bare minimum.

But the forward march of feminism did not grind to a halt in 1960; on the contrary, it got into a new gear. Since then, legislation and changes in attitude have given women unprecedented freedom. Male power over Western women has largely contracted, and in many respects we have a more unimpeded, tolerant society. In my generation's lifetime there have been several successful new waves of feminism that have broken down many of the fences standing in the way of women's progress. In 1965 the magazine *Nova* started featuring Black models. 1968 saw women's liberation groups protesting outside the Miss America contest in Atlantic City. Early in 1970 a movement was born when the first National Women's Liberation Conference was held in Oxford. That same year the Equal Pay Act was passed, and 1975 saw the Sex Discrimination Act signed into law, making direct and indirect discrimination on the basis of sex illegal.

In 1978 Susie Orbach changed the vocabulary of slimming with *Fat is a Feminist Issue*. Then, in 1991, Naomi Wolf's uncovering of the beauty industry and its associated advertising was published as *The Beauty Myth*. And more recently, new, game-changing feminist voices began to be heard – like those of Caroline Criado-Perez, Laura Bates, Alexandra Ocasio-Cortez, Malala Yousafzai, Heather Widdows, Caitlin Moran and Jia Tolentino.

Over the same period awareness has grown that dieting is exploitative and can do more harm than good. In 1969 the American author and academic Bill Fabrey founded the National Association to Advance Fat Acceptance. In 2004 there was a conspicuous anti-Barbie backlash when the Dove brand launched its 'Real Beauty' campaign. Billboards displayed photographs of women who weren't models, in their underwear; they were thin, fat, in-between, and of different ethnicities. In the wake of the campaign Dove's sales doubled, to $4 billion.

Meanwhile, with the help of social media, body positivity started to gain ground. And, seeing that Dove was increasing its market share, other brands jumped on the bandwagon. In 2013 model and 'body positivity activist' Tess Holliday created the hashtag #effyourbeautystandards and quickly gained hundreds of thousands of Instagram followers. Two years later Holliday – US size 22, 300 pounds, five feet five inches and heavily tattooed – signed with a top British modelling agency, and in 2018 she adorned the cover of Cosmopolitan. Since then she has spoken out about her struggles with her weight, and revealed that she is in recovery from the eating disorder atypical anorexia.

We live in a time of transition. And there are moments when the likeness in the mirror reflects back images of pride, joy, freedom and equality. We can now rejoice in fashion models with a variety of skin colours. Beauty may be fat, in a wheelchair, or use a hearing aid. They may be an amputee, or have various skin conditions. Tattoos and freckles, once unacceptable, are fashionable. In 2017, Rihanna launched her beauty brand Fenty to include all women. The oppressive social codes once transmitted by clothing have become blurred, and although public toilets are a site of controversy – with too many of them still identified by a stick symbol wearing a skirt – most of the women using them are likely to be wearing trousers; we are now so acclimatised to this extraordinary fact that it no longer seems like the genuine triumph that it is.

———

Sometimes – and maybe it has always been the case – just 'getting ready' can bring an intense hit of pleasure.

From the 'real ladies' of the 1860s in their superlative riding habits to Lucile's *fin-de-siècle* goddesses in their romantic tea gowns; from Mary Church Terrell in her radiant pink get-up to Roberta Cowell in eyeliner and ballgown, this book has told the story of a galaxy of women who loved to look luscious. And I do believe that self-enhancement and decoration can be more than indulgence; it can be an art. But now that my survey of past generations reaches its end, it feels right to look closer to home, and take a straw poll from some of the women I love.

My younger daughter comments, 'I think dressing up and putting on make-up are the fun, creative side of being a woman!' Just as I did at her age, she buys clothes from vintage shops, saving money and resources, while declaring herself as the inventive, colourful woman that she is. She rejects any suggestion that she is seeking male admiration: 'I dress mainly for myself. But I'm also very aware of what the women I work with wear. Often I meet a woman I look up to and they're the ones who I want clothing approval from the most.'

My daughter-in-law works in a high-pressure corporate setting, where suits and ties are the norm. East Asian, petite, with a cascade of lustrous black hair, she has evolved a strikingly individual style:

> I gravitate towards wearing bold colours, pattern and print; leaning in to stereotypically 'feminine' modes of dress: high waists, exaggerated sleeves, swishy skirts. Don't get me wrong, I love a great pantsuit, but I do like to challenge the almost subliminal conception that to do a job well or be taken seriously you need to dress like a man.
>
> A great outfit can be like a suit of armour; it can put me in the right frame of mind and give me an extra confidence boost when imposter syndrome kicks in.

Among women of my own generation, I admire and envy those who have the confidence to ignore trends. My sister is one. In her sense of style she is larger than life, while her artistry with a sewing machine complements her expertise in colour and design. She's a connoisseur of sparkly earrings; a lover of scarlet and black stripes, sapphire fingernails and red suede shoes. Another woman I have known all my life, who has always been a paradigm of originality and elegance, has for the last fifteen years been paralysed from the neck down and so uses a wheelchair. This means that her clothes are viewed from the front only, and she is always seen in a sitting position. Accordingly, she has adapted to circumstances. She wears softly woven tunics of muted cream and sand colours with extravagantly ruffled fronts, poetic jewellery that she designs made from seed pearls and buried metal artefacts, and velvet Moroccan slippers.

I also have an old friend, now well into her seventies, who stripes the fringe at the front of her thick, short grey hairstyle with a vibrant slick of magenta dye: a trademark message of vigour, energy and youthful frivolity. It's easy to think of more public women who adopt a signature, like the quirky, relatable children's author Jacqueline Wilson, who delights in an abundance of silver rings on her fingers, or Theresa May with her cheeky animal print kitten heels, treating the front bench like the front row. Wilson is seventy-eight, May is sixty-seven.

They're not alone. The @advancedstyle blog has over four hundred thousand Instagram followers, who love its street-style images of proudly wrinkled senior fashionistas in their unapologetic millinery and sunglasses, and outfits from the dressing-up drawer.

And confident, courageous women wear what *they* want: like the former editor of *Vogue* Alexandra Shulman, who refused to be shamed by the furore which erupted when she posted a photograph on Instagram of her curving fifty-nine-year-old self in a bikini. 'When it comes to that glorious sensation of the sun warming my stomach, I don't care that a one-piece might be more flattering,' she retorted in the *Daily Mail*. 'Flattering says who? My wearing a bikini is all about me. It's not about how other people think I look.'

And who can forget the sight of Lioness Chloe Kelly tearing off her top, whirling it above her head, and hurtling joyfully across the pitch at Wembley in her functional white sports bra after scoring for victory in front of 87,000 jubilant fans (not to mention another 17 million watching on TV)?*

As one of them commented, 'Chloe Kelly celebrating her goal in a sports bra is the feminist image of the decade.'

---

* Kelly's joyous gesture apparently brought a smile to the face of American footballer Brandi Chastain who also ripped off her top when she scored a conclusive penalty for the US against China in the 1999 Women's World Cup Final.

Chloe Kelly after the Lionesses' win at Wembley, 31 July 2022

———

Perhaps the goalposts are shifting.

In 2018 the young American actress Lili Reinhart stood on the platform at *Glamour*'s Women of the Year summit and spoke about women's relationship with their bodies:

There is no easy fix to the ideas of women that have existed for hundreds of years, so that leaves us with one option: changing ourselves. Showing what's real, with no filter, and certainly with no shame ...

You can be naturally beautiful with acne, or scars, cellulite or curves. So let's celebrate each other and ourselves as we are, as we will be, and as we were meant to be, unique, imperfect, beautiful – and so incredibly powerful.

Words like this have laid the ground for a new attitude to appearance. Two years later the British-Asian actor and TV presenter Jameela Jamil spoke to the ET Style YouTube channel, and explained how, after years of anorexia, body dysmorphia and self-hatred, she had called an end to hostilities with her body:

The first time I recognised beauty ... was probably watching a Disney princess and thinking that beauty was long blonde hair and white skin and a waist that was *that* big [holding her fingers about two inches apart], and I think that probably haunted me up until, well, now!

And she described how she had made peace with her own body image:

It's a lot of pressure to have to love something that you hate ... I prefer neutrality ... I can't love my body, but I can accept my body, and just get on with it and not think about it and not worry about it as much.

I think that the only problem I have with this kind of 'love your body' movement is that it's still forcing us to stay trapped in the obsession of our bodies ... I think women would have a lot to gain from thinking less about our bodies and more about our bank accounts and our social lives and our love lives and our families and our educations.

I think that's where our priority should lie if we're going to catch up with men.

Historically, many men have been in a position where they are able to feel indifference towards their bodies. For women, it's never been so easy.

It seems as if, whatever their gender, Gen Z are mostly pro-inclusivity, anti-diet and sceptical about manipulative brand campaigns. Body neutrality has been described as an active rebellion, in which we are released from the constant, chaotic scrutiny of appearance. We cease to love our body, or to hate it. We reject labels that cynically use bodies to sell products. We stop wearing uncomfortable clothes. Instead we change our perceptions of our self-worth by simply accepting and respecting our bodies as practical and functional entities: they breathe, they digest food, they feel heat, cold, pain and pleasure. And they can think, comprehend and imagine.

Will we ever declare a truce on the beauty frontline, that danger zone which for so long has kept women from parity and peace of mind?

If we are ever going to find that equilibrium, we need to understand the past, and reimagine the future.

Appendix

In order to get some idea of what people lived on in the period discussed in this book, the following figures, which give approximate equivalents (rounded up or down to the nearest £) of one old penny and one pound to today's money (2023 figures) will be useful.

Until decimalisation was introduced in 1971, there were 12 pennies to a shilling, 20 shillings to a pound, and 240 pennies to a pound.

	£0 0s 1d	£1
1860	0.40p	£155
1870	0.41p	£152
1880	0.42p	£154
1890	0.47p	£164
1900	0.64p	£157
1910	0.59p	£151
1920	0.26p	£57
1930	0.31p	£84
1940	0.32p	£72
1950	0.18p	£44
1960	0.12p	£29

Sources CPI inflation calculator and MeasuringWorth.com

Notes on Sources

Prologue

6 'I am not my hair ...': *Glamour*, 6 April 2021

1: Victoriana

13 'an acknowledged Queen ...': *Leicester Journal*, 13 March 1863
14 'fine full eyes': *Leicester Journal*, 13 March 1863
14 'fine full forehead': *Leicester Journal*, 13 March 1863
14 'the most charming of brides': *Leicester Journal*, 13 March 1863
14 'She glittered like the morning star ...': *Chelmsford Chronicle*, 31 March 1863
19 'Ladies ... real ladies ...': Sala, *Twice Round the Clock*
20 'Your lady's maid ...': cited in Randall, *The Model Wife*
20 'Oh, [they were] delightful ...': Raverat, *Period Piece*
22 'long hours of work ...': *Daily Telegraph*, 22 June 1863
22 'The Danaës!': Sala, *Twice Round the Clock*
24 'If young ladies from the country ...': *The Times*, 9 January 1862
24 'No good-looking girl ...': *The Times*, 17 January 1862
24 'It never occurs ...': *The Times*, 21 January 1862
26 'Confined ... in cages ...': Wollstonecraft, *A Vindication of the Rights of Woman*
27 'I can see no business ...': cited in Riegel, 'Women's Clothes and Women's Rights'
29 'Narrow indeed is the path ...': Warren, *How I Managed my Children from Infancy to Marriage*
29 '... a little French ...': Nevill, *Under Five Reigns*
33 'A country girl, she was ...': Hudson, *Munby – Man of Two Worlds*
34 'I wound my way through the crowd ...': Stanley, ed., *The Diaries of Hannah Cullwick*
34 'I say, Massa ...': Hudson, *Munby – Man of Two Worlds*

35 'Eh, I wouldna be a lady ...': Stanley, ed., *The Diaries of Hannah Cullwick*
37 'a monstrous disfigurement ...': Hale, *A Slender Reputation*
37 'He alleged various reasons ...': cited in James, ed., *The Order of Release*
41 'They generally wear ...': *Daily News*, 1 May 1868
41 'unmentionable nether garments': *Liverpool Weekly Courier*, 12 October 1872
43 'No discussion of the feminine body ...': Brownmiller, *Femininity*
45 'No young lady could go ...': *Englishwoman's Domestic Magazine*, March 1867
45 'As a gentleman I admire ...': cited in Roberts, 'The Exquisite Slave'
46 'dundrearies', 'Brobdingnagian moustaches ...': Sala, *Twice Round the Clock*
47 'a source of extreme annoyance ...': Humphry, *How to be Pretty though Plain*
47 'singeing with glowing nut-shells': Saalfeld, *Lectures on Cosmetic Treatment*
48 'Consumption is ... a flattering malady': cited in Day, *Consumptive Chic*
48 'no better exercise ...': Pullan, *Maternal Counsels to a Daughter*
49 'Ladies do not work ...': Cobbe, *Life of Frances Power Cobbe, by Herself*
50 'Englishwomen are famed ...': Professional Beauty, *Beauty and How to Keep It*
52 'Freckles are the enemy ...': ibid.
52 'perfectly harmless': *The Queen*, 25 December 1897
52 'You can't blame men ...': Sears, Roebuck Catalog, cited in Brumberg, *The Body Project*
53 'on taking them off ...': Professional Beauty, *Beauty and How to Keep It*
53 'It is impossible ...': ibid.
55 'We are trapped like birds in a cage': cited in Bannerji, 'Textile Prison'
56 'this attire [was] ...': ibid.
58 'On coming to England ...': Das, *A Bengali Lady in England*
60 'The ordinary Englishwoman ...': ibid.
61 'Do not begin to paint ...': Professional Beauty, *Beauty and How to Keep It*
61 'A violently rouged woman ...': ibid.
61 'If Satan has ever ...': Montez, *The Arts of Beauty*
62 'laughing was strictly forbidden ...': Saalfeld, *Lectures on Cosmetic Treatment*
63 'foul and filthy doings': cited in Rappaport, *Beautiful for Ever*

2: Belle Epoque

67 'Those were the days ...': Asquith, *Autobiography*
67 'No party was complete ...': Marlborough, *Laughter from a Cloud*
68 'There's a lovely lady ...': reproduced on the Langtry fan website lilliel-angtry.com
72 'A virtuous woman ...': Staffe, *The Lady's Dressing Room*, cited in Pike, *Human Documents of the Age of the Forsytes*
72 'A young lady ...': cited in Pearsall, *The Worm in the Bud*

73 'highly recommended ...': cited in Hawthorne, 'From Rags to Riches'
75 'delicately shaded, at the summit ...': d'Orchamps, *Tous les Secrets de la Femme*, cited in Steele, *Fashion and Eroticism*
75 'A ripple of excitement ...': Zola, *Nana*, translated by Virginia Nicholson
76 'Pictures of Lily': lyrics by Pete Townshend. Copyright © T.R.O. Inc.
78 'conspicuous consumption': Veblen, *The Theory of the Leisure Class*
79 'I wish you could see ...': Lieber, *The Stranger in America*
79 'On those occasions ...': cited in Pike, *Human Documents of the Age of the Forsytes*
80 'The poor were people ...': Hardy, *As It Was*
80 'but her face ...': Maud Pember Reeves, cited in Horowitz, *Strong-Minded Women*
80 'I had nothing ...': Mayhew, *London Labour and the London Poor*, cited in ibid.
81 'The fondness for dress ...': cited in Pike, *Human Documents of the Victorian Golden Age*
82 'To dye gloves ...': *Girls' Own Paper*, 9 September 1893
82 'You will hardly find ...': *Girls' Own Paper*, 15 July 1893
82 'It is evident ...': *Girls' Own Paper*, 29 July 1893
86 'She would beg them ...': Thornycroft, *Time Which Spaces Us Apart*
87 'She had great beauty ...': Cooper, *The Rainbow Comes and Goes*
88 'A lady in full dress ...': Oliphant, *Dress*
89 'Whenever you can, count': cited in *New Yorker* 24 January 2005
89 'I use a needle ...': Galton, *Memories of My Life*
90 'Their plenty involves ...': *Aberdeen Evening Express*, 23 April 1889
90 'best stock': Galton, *Memories of My Life*
92 'Throughout many periods ...': Dame Mary Beard, *Radio Times*, cited in *Guardian*, 9 February 2021
93 'Nowadays mothers ...': St Helier, *Memories of Fifty Years*
95 'their breasts enlarge ...': cited in Berney, 'Streamlining Breasts'
95 'Many women go childless ...': ibid.
95 'If nature has not ...': ibid.
96 'We liked our women ...': Brown, *Brownstone Fronts and Saratoga Trunks*
96 'that burning clime ...': cited in Jia Tolentino, 'The Ozempic Era', *New Yorker*, 27 March 2023
99 'I am confident ...', *et seq*: cited in the *Staunton Vindicator*, 15 April 1881
104 'a girl so alluring ...': Downey, *Portrait of an Era as Drawn by C. D. Gibson*
104 'Fifth Avenue': Joseph Pennell, cited in Sullivan, *Our Times 1900–1925*
107 'Many well-meaning people ...': Aida Overton Walker, 'Colored Men and Women on the Stage', *Colored American Magazine*, October 1905
108 'The fact of the matter ...': Overton Walker, 'Colored Men and Women on the Stage'
108 'a dusky, vivacious young person ...': *Truth*, 21 May 1903
110 'In this age ...': Overton Walker, 'Colored Men and Women on the Stage'
111 'In obedience ...': *Colorado Statesman*, 24 October 1914
112 'Of course Elsie and I ...': Duff Gordon, *Discretions and Indiscretions*
112 'gone away to London ...': ibid.

113 'We were both very curious ...': ibid.
116 'sinuous, dreamy [and] velvet-eyed': cited in Evans, *The Mechanical Smile*
116 'I soon learned ...': ibid.
116 'wonderful swaying step': ibid.
116 'Orders flowed in ...': Duff Gordon, *Discretions and Indiscretions*
116 'They were invited ...': cited in Evans, *The Mechanical Smile*
117 'Romance came very often ...': cited in ibid.
117 'The slimming craze ...': Duff Gordon, *Discretions and Indiscretions*
118 'We have no successor ...': ibid.
119 'How on earth ...': Stringer, *Golfing Reminiscences*
120 'I thought I was never ...': Hardy, *As It Was*
120 'An extreme slit ...': *South Bend News-Times*, 12 September 1913
123 'She is upon us ...': Harper, *Revolted Women*
123 '[She] has sacrificed ...': cited in Fletcher, *Women First*
124 'The saddle is ...': *New York Journal*, 19 July 1896
125 'Several boys ...': Peel, *Life's Enchanted Cup*
125 'My sister and I ...': Londonderry, *Retrospect*
126 'The woman bicyclist ...': *Wichita Daily Eagle*, 12 June 1895
126 'The advent of the bicycle ...': Anson, *Victorian Days*
126 'Let me tell you ...': cited in Maria Popova, 'Wheels of Change: How the Bicycle Empowered Women', The Marginalian, 23 March 2011
127 'Don't be a fright ...': ibid.

3: New Century

129 'Greek – everything must be Greek ...': Cooper, *The Rainbow Comes and Goes*
129 'Christ, I am so fat!': cited in Ziegler, *Diana Cooper*
133 'I don't suppose ...': cited in ibid.
133 'dewdrops': Cooper, *The Rainbow Comes and Goes*
134 'Diana's clothes fell ...': cited in Ziegler, *Diana Cooper*
136 'Marriage must inevitably remain ...': Greville, *The Gentlewoman in Society*
140 '... the many women broken ...': Roberts, *The Classic Slum*
140 'It feels sad ...': Brittain, *Testament of Youth*
141 'I was suffocating ...': cited in Riddell, *Death in Ten Minutes*
142 'How *can* you send your daughter ...': Brittain, *Testament of Youth*
142 '[They are] for the most part ...': *Illustrated London News*, 27 August 1910
142 'A womanly woman ...': *Nuneaton Observer*, 13 November 1908
142 'The appearance ...': *Northwich Guardian*, 16 April 1912
143 'The greatest charm ...': Walker, *The Pretty Girl Papers*
144 'She saw herself ...': Starkie, *A Lady's Child*
148 'I have *cut my hair off*!': cited in Moore, *E. Nesbit*
149 'A flapper': *The Times*, 20 February 1908
150 'a glimpse of stocking': *Aberdeen Evening Express*, 3 February 1914
150 'When their hair is put up ...': *Yorkshire Evening Post*, 15 July 1913

150 'The newest girl ...': *Birmingham Daily Gazette*, 25 April 1914

152 'conspicuous outrage': Q. Bell, *On Human Finery*

153 'clean, sober ...': Bundles, *Self Made*

154 'to contribute to the economic ...': cited in Walker, *Style and Status*

154 'He answered my prayer': Bundles, *Self Made*

155 'I had to make ...': Whitfield, *A Friend to all Mankind*

156 'It was easy ...': Garvin Fields, *Lemon Swamp and Other Places*

163 'A bell rang ...': Cierplikowski, *Autobiographical Reminiscences*

164 'the first of the moderns': Duff Gordon, *Discretions and Indiscretions*

164 'The primary effect ...': Beaton, *The Glass of Fashion*

166 'I have tried to destroy ...': cited in Scott, '"Their Campaign of Wanton Attacks"'

166 'I didn't like the way ...': ibid.

168 'The suffragette of today ...': *Votes for Women*, 30 July 1908

168 'Be guided by ...': cited in Atkinson, *The Suffragettes in Pictures*

170 'Opposite the windows ...': Rhondda, *This Was My World*

170 'Fashionable young women ...': see Cally Blackman, 'How the Suffragettes used Fashion to Further Their Cause', Stylist.co.uk

171 'He said to me ...': Londonderry, *Retrospect*

172 'The woman shall not wear ...': Deuteronomy 22:5, Bible: King James Version

172 'the first man ...': *Penrith Observer*, 7 December 1915

172 'the fellers would laugh': Peel, *Life's Enchanted Cup*

173 'In case it should be thought ...': Londonderry, *Retrospect*

174 'Most of us ...': *Vogue,* April 1917

174 'that female costume ...': de Frece, *Recollections of Vesta Tilley*

175 'a delicate piece ...': de Frece, *Recollections of Vesta Tilley*

176 'varying from an impassioned declaration ...': de Frece, *Recollections of Vesta Tilley*

177 'You are the creature ...': cited in ibid.

177 'It was not a time ...': Hale, *A Slender Reputation*

181 'The touch of your hand ...': cited in Roper, 'Nostalgia as an Emotional Experience in the Great War'

181 'Some of the tissue paper ...': ibid.

182 'I have come to tell you ...': Essex, *Woman in a Man's World*

185 'Try out the several different shades ...': *Chicago Tribune*, 25 February 1928

188 'feminine persuasion': cited in 'Happy 100th Birthday to the Facelift', *Tatler*, 22 February 2016

189 'If soldiers whose faces ...': Thorek, *A Surgeon's World*

191 'Medical skill ...': *Daily Mirror*, 23 November 1906

192 'content to lie ...': cited in Vickers, *The Sphinx*

193 'Isn't it awful?': ibid.

194 'Oh ... is that a cinema?': ibid.

194 '[A] girl came in one day ...': Walker, *The Pretty Girl Papers*

195 'Facial wrinkles eradicated ...': *Tatler*, 7 January 1931

196 'Women may spend thousands ...': Miller, *Cosmetic Surgery*

197 'A huge plethora ...': Peters and Fornasier, 'Complications from Injectable Materials used for Breast Augmentation'

198 *LADIES!!: Daily Mirror*, 8 October 1914
199 'that curious pneumatic look ...': Asquith, *Diaries*
200 'To think that ...': Noël, *La Chirurgie Esthetique*, translated by Virginia Nicholson

4: Jazz Age

208 'Mrs Dudley Ward was wearing ...': *Daily Mirror*, 28 January 1926
208 'This Spring will see ...': *Daily Mirror*, 19 February 1936
208 'Mrs Dudley Ward, looking lovely ...': *Tatler*, 28 June 1922
208 'Mrs Dudley Ward, about ...': *Tatler*, 31 March 1920
208 'whining, dull ...': diary entry for 23 June 1924 in Heffer, ed., *Henry 'Chips' Channon, The Diaries*
208 'exaggerated feminine allure ...': Beaton, *The Glass of Fashion*
210 'She has that air ...': Cartland, *We Danced All Night*
213 '"Don't bind your breasts ..."': Brownmiller, *Femininity*
214 'naughty': cited in Trethewey, *Before Wallis*
214 'from the crest ...': ibid.
215 'It was like seeing': ibid.
218 'One might as well ...': cited in John, *Turning the Tide*
218 'Oh, how I hated ...': Rhondda, *This Was my World*
219 'right hand *man*': ibid.
230 'People weren't figure-conscious ...': Powell, *Below Stairs*
231 'In less than a week ...': *Leeds Mercury*, 20 April 1926
231 'I am twenty-six ...': *Leeds Mercury*, 15 June 1926
231 'From what you tell me ...': *Lucky Charm*, 1930
232 'I was bulging with puppy fat': Devas, *Two Flamboyant Fathers*
233 'I wish I wasn't ...': Garfield, ed., *A Notable Woman*
233 'You have interesting lines ...': Devas, *Two Flamboyant Fathers*
235 'restaurants have become ...': *Daily Mirror*, 16 July 1927
236 'The new fashions ...': Cramp, *Fooling the Fat*
237 'Why should anyone ...': cited in 'The Slimming Tips of the Silent Screen Stars', Glamourdaze.com, 23 November 2018
237 'I do know ...': *Girls' Cinema*, 17 November 1923
237 'Every day bananas ...': Cartland, *We Danced All Night*
239 'Josephine Baker, our lives ...': Wood, *The Josephine Baker Story*, cited in Sowinska, 'Dialectics of the Banana Skirt'
240 'Paris is the dance ...': cited in Wood, *The Josephine Baker Story*
241 'What's the name ...': ibid.
242 'broker in beauty ...': cited in Evans, *The Mechanical Smile*
242 'A top model ...': Clayton, *The World of Modelling*
242 'I know that when you go ...': cited in Quick, *Catwalking*
243 'At the films': Powell, *Below Stairs*
245 'To be an actor ...': 'Hooray for Hollywood', lyrics by Jonny Mercer. Copyright © Peermusic Publishing
246 'The little shop-girl ...': Aretz, *The Elegant Woman*
246 'But then, when you catch sight ...': Mitford, *Hons and Rebels*
248 'She had almost given up ...': ibid.

248 'She was the first …': Cartland, *We Danced all Night*
248 'to appearing perpetually …': *New York Times*, 28 January 1952
249 'She made a fetish …': Atherton *Adventures of a Novelist*
250 'My brain seemed …': cited in Wortis Leider, *California's Daughter*
251 'I have seen myself …': *New York Times*, 4 December 1935
251 'Miss Atherton appeared …': ibid.
252 'a watery, washed up …': Newhall, ed., *The Daybook of Edward Weston*
252 'I take your hormones regularly …': ibid.
253 'The young woman of to-day …': *Westminster Gazette*, 19 March 1924
253 'The truly natural woman …': Greville, *Vignettes of Memory*
254 'a famous beauty …': *Sunday Post*, 7 August 1927
254 'Plenty of fresh air …': *Berwickshire News and General Advertiser*, 5 October 1926
254 '[She] proceeded immediately …': Bettman, 'Plastic and Cosmetic Surgery of the Face'
254 'No wrinkles mar …': *New York Times*, 4 August 1920
255 'Foreigners react …': Passot, *Sculpteur de Visages*, cited in Martin, *Suzanne Noël*
255 'I will kill myself …': Le Henaff, 'Cosmetic Surgery on Trial'
257 'The following day …': Passot, *Sculpteurs de Visages*
257 'I agreed to undertake …': ibid.
260 'the most perfectly developed …': *Leeds Mercury*, 5 October 1903
260 'the ladies were …': ibid.
260 'Height, 5ft 4¼ …': *Dundee Evening Post*, 25 November 1903
262 'Generally, men lined …': Roberts, *The Classic Slum*
263 'disinterested judges': in Paul Popenhoe, *Applied Eugenics* (1918)
263 'Examine these women …': Wiggam, *The Fruit of the Family Tree*
264 'This improvement of life …': ibid.

5: Modern Girls

269 'Twenty years old …': *Daily Herald*, 13 June 1935
269 'My dream is a world …': Stack, *Building the Body Beautiful*
270 'Prunella is …': *How I Train My Daughter*, Mollie Stack, *Daily Express*, 15 November to 4 December 1928
270 'I suffered the usual …': Stack, *Movement is Life*
270 'The arena … was filled …': *Sunday Times*, 26 April 1931
271 'The lights shine out …': 'Health and Beauty Display at Wembley', British Pathé, 1939
273 'Through an ethic …': Matthews, 'They Had Such a Lot of Fun'
273 'The modern girl …': Stack, *Building the Body Beautiful*
273 'I have drunk …': Stack, *Movement is Life*
274 'It's a marriage …': 'Glasgow Cathedral', British Pathé, 29 September 1938
274 'Nothing more exquisite …': cited in Matthews, 'They Had Such a Lot of Fun'
275 'I'm glad you don't …': Stack, *Movement is Life*

275 'Her lovely complexion ...': *Portsmouth Evening News*, 24 November 1927
276 'Youth is glorious ...': Stack, *Building the Body Beautiful*
277 'I am an old-fashioned feminist ...': *Time and Tide*, 31 October 1924
278 'I cannot see now ...': Ellis, *My Life*
278 'Don't go out ...': cited in Bill, 'Attitudes Towards Women's Trousers'
278 'Can a woman ...': *Eastbourne Gazette*, 23 August 1933
278 'Yes – but you'd better ...': cited in Bill, 'Attitudes Towards Women's Trousers'
279 'strange creatures ...': *Liverpool Echo*, 17 August 1933
280 'congenital invert': Havelock Ellis, referenced in Cline, *Radclyffe Hall*
281 'acts of the most horrible ...': cited in ibid.
283 'One morning ...': Jivaka/Dillon, *Out of the Ordinary*
284 'Is that a man ...': ibid.
286 'I consider that ...': *Western Mail*, 10 May 1935
287 'I ask, is it advisable ...': *Hartlepool Northern Daily Mail*, 18 March 1937
287 'Her back was bare ...': *Eastbourne Gazette*, 16 August 1933
288 'The Englishwoman ...': *Liverpool Echo*, 17 August 1933
288 'In the summer of 1932 ...': Fielding, *Mercury Presides*
290 'she wore sunburn ...': Beaton, *The Glass of Fashion*
290 I think she invented ...': cited in Stewart, *Painted Faces*
291 'I passed a local ...': Mass Observation Day Surveys, Respondent 080, Grace Hickling, March 1937
291 'I devote no expense ...': Mass Observation Directive, Respondent 1405, Hope Sykes, April 1939
292 'The chief reason ...': Mass Observation Directive, Respondent 1336, Sylvia Terry-Smith, February 1939
292 'I'm content ...': Mass Observation Directive, Respondent 1544, Nora Corfe, January 1939
293 'Should I be ...': Mass Observation Directive, Respondent 1068, Dorothy Brant, February 1939
293 'I devote 75% ...': Mass Observation Directive, Respondent 1002, Margaret Hedges, March 1939
294 'I vowed I would die ...': Garfield, ed., *A Notable Woman*
296 'neglect and malnutrition': Forrester, *Twopence to Cross the Mersey*
297 'Coming towards me ...': Bhatia, *Passage Across the Mersey*
297 'horrible with varicose veins': Forrester, *By the Waters of Liverpool*
297 'Girls did not look ...': ibid.
298 '[they] were my single ...': ibid.
298 'You'll have to stop ...': ibid.
299 'There was no one ...': ibid.
300 'Every little speck ...': Keenan, *Women We Wanted to Look Like*
300 'I've got to hide ...': ibid.
303 'The implicit assumption ...': Pilgrim, 'The Mammy Caricature'
304 'Keep young and beautiful ...': lyrics by Al Dubin, music by Harry Warren
306 'It is, though most people ...': Cierplikowski, *Autobiographical Reminiscences*
307 'We ... first assembled ...': Lees-Milne, *Another Self*
307 'I went to London ...': Cierplikowski, *Autobiographical Reminiscences*

308 'Your finger tips . . .': *Londonderry Sentinel*, 17 August 1937
309 'The whole operation . . .': *Leicester Evening Mail*, 5 May 1932
310 'evils of the no-corset fad': *Corsets and Lingerie*, November 1921
312 'It was almost a madness . . .': Cartland, *The Isthmus Years*
312 'Women who deliberately . . .': *Daily Mirror*, 9 July 1936
312 'She brought on . . .': *Daily Mirror*, 3 September 1935
313 'How proud she was . . .': Letitia Simpson, 'My Day Before Yesterday', Burnett Collection of Working-Class Autobiographies, Brunel University
314 'There was nothing . . .': cited in Herzig, *Plucked*
314 'First of all . . .': cited in Cox, *Good Hair Days*
315 'She was in acute distress . . .': *Daily Gazette for Middlesborough*, 12 May 1939
315 'I look at least . . .': *Leicester Daily Mercury*, 28 November 1934
316 'To appear young . . .': Harpole, *Leaves from a Surgeon's Case-Book*
318 'Until I met Mr Willi . . .': *Tatler*, 26 February 1930
322 'The plastic surgeon . . .': cited in Ludovici, *Cosmetic Scalpel*

6: Beauty is a Duty

325 'Here the legs . . .': *Life*, 7 June 1943
326 'Girls, it seems . . .': 'Battle of the Bulges', British Pathé, 1941
327 'Legs are running riot . . .': *Evening Star* (Washington DC), 17 January 1943
327 'Betty Grable's legs . . .': *Life*, 7 June 1943
327 'Even her extensively . . .': *Time*, 23 August 1948
327 'I can act a little . . .': *Evening Star* (Washington DC), 26 September 1943
327 'Her talents are unremarkable . . .': *Time*, 23 August 1948
328 'There we were . . .': Westbrook, '"I Want a Girl, Just like the Girl that Married Harry James"'
328 'hideously painted lips': J. P. Mayer, *British Cinemas and their Audiences*, cited in Williams, *Betty Grable*
328 '[She's] cheerful and vulgar . . .': Picture Ballot Aug–Sept 1944: Soldiers and Pin-ups, Mass Observation Archive
329 'How could a young girl . . .': cited in Williams, *Betty Grable*
329 'Life is very drab . . .': David Lean, 'Brief Encounter', *The Penguin Film Review* London, Penguin, 1947
330 'nervous as a cat . . .': *Evening Star* (Washington DC), 26 September 1943
330 'She had so much pain . . .': Warren, *Betty Grable*
330 'and that was that': ibid.
331 'I love lipsticks': cited on the Vintage Venus: Beauty in Classic Hollywood blog
332 'She sure doesn't . . .': Warren, *Betty Grable*
332 'Unlike the Nazi frau . . .': *Britannia and Eve*, 1 April 1941
333 'Bare legs are not respectable . . .': Forrester, *Lime Street at Two*
333 'all the women met their Führer . . .': Junge, *Until the Final Hour*
334 'girls he could dominate . . .': Kershaw, *Hitler*
335 '[They] hailed Herr Hitler . . .': *Time*, 23 September 1935

336 'The League performed ...': Stack, *Movement is Life*

337 'The full horror ...': Stack, *Movement is Life.*

337 'which hid her swastika badge': *Daily Mirror*, 8 March 1939

337 'Her face is freckled ...': *Evening Standard*, 7 March 1939

337 'She prefers a shiny ...': *Nottingham Journal*, 14 March 1939

340 'We're just off motoring ...': *The Letters of Virginia Woolf*, Virginia Woolf to Violet Dickinson, 18 April 1935

340 'Nerves rather frayed ...': *The Diary of Virginia Woolf*, 9 May 1935

345 'I am resigned ...': ibid., 23 June 1919

345 'To be fitted ...': Woolf, *Moments of Being*

345 'quite atrociously': letter to Harold Nicolson, 19 December 1922, in Nicolson, ed., *Vita and Harold*

346 'the everchanging and turning world ...': Woolf, *A Room of One's Own*

347 'I was ... no more fitted ...': Baldwin, *I Leap Over the Wall*

350 'It would be [a] calamity ...': cited in Summers, *Fashion on the Ration*

350 'a thing of beauty ...': *Daily Mirror*, 23 September 1940

351 'Women's and maids' dresses ...': cited in Peter McNeil, 'Put Your Best Face Forward'

352 'Come to us ...': White, *D for Doris, V for Victory*

355 'Here's your brassière ...': Kerr, *The Girls Behind the Guns*

355 'Gone are the boyish ...': cited in Summers, *Fashion on the Ration*

356 'If Mr Hitler's coming ...': cited in ibid.

356 'His corset would ...': *Daily Express*, 225 July 1944

357 'The uniform is ...': *Bradford Observer*, 6 December 1941

357 'Joining the WRENs ...': Lamb, *I Only Joined for the Hat*

358 'I learnt that ...': interview with Pat Bawland, in Nicholson, *Millions Like Us*

358 'They arrive unsuitably shod ...': cited in Tyrer, *They Fought in the Fields*

359 'Town girls ...': cited in ibid.

359 'Somehow khaki breeches ...': Joseph, *If Their Mothers Only Knew*

359 'like Humpty Dumpty ...': Hardie, ed., *Digging for Memories*

360 'Felling trees ...': 'Jolly Good Fellers', British Pathé, 1942

361 'You are *not* going to church ...': cited in de la Haye, *Land Girls*

363 'There's no need ...': *Reveille*, 5 January 1942

363 'rather blonder than Nature ...': *Britannia and Eve*, 1 October 1942

364 'Cosmetics are ...': ibid.

365 'I had two years ...': interview with John W. Mills, *Sculptor to the Nation*, for North Hertfordshire District Council, March 2019

366 'The jumble sale tat ...': cited in Gibson and Mollan, eds, *Representations of Peace and Conflict*

366 'Don't depict women ...': ibid.

367 'I can't get why ...': BBC News Magazine, 6 August 2008

367 'touching and beautifully sculpted ...': comment posted Jackie R, Tripadvisor, May 2016

367 'This monument is ...': comment posted by BonnieNimmo, Tripadvisor, July 2016

367 'dumbfounded': comment posted by Jill O, Tripadvisor, July 2018
367 'The monument to the women ...': Carolyn Dougherty, 'Women's Erasure from War Memorials', The F Word, June 2011

7: New Look

372 'Ah, Cannes!': Bardot, *Initiales B.B.*
373 'I shall fight ...': *Daily Mirror*, 21 October 1950
373 'Photographs of women ...': *Birmingham Daily Gazette*, 4 November 1953
373 'You go on the beach ...': *Shields Daily News*, 9 October 1950
373 'Young girls ...': cited in Bensimon, *The Bikini Book*
379 'alimoniously rich': cited in Smith, *Reflected Glory*
379 'terribly sexy ...': *Sunday Times*, 8 May 1994
381 'She had very nice ...': cited in Smith, *Reflected Glory*
381 'I like a woman ...': ibid.
385 'a very English post-war look ...': Princess Katya Galitzine, cited in 'Meet Jean Dawnay, Dior's English rose', www.vam.ac.uk
386 'Now it hardly ever ...': Dawnay, *Model Girl*
387 'steaks and salads': Dawnay, *How I Became a Fashion Model*
388 'We couldn't have looked sexy ...': Jennifer Hocking, cited in Clayton, *The World of Modelling*
389 'She never reads ...': Malcolmson, eds, *Nella Last in the 1950s*, 19 February 1951
389 'She even buys ...': ibid., 7 June 1952
389 'I saw rows ...': ibid., 14 June 1952
393 'There's a reason ...': *O, The Oprah Magazine*, October 2005
394 'I was born ...': cited in Brittain, *Lady into Woman*
395 'dressing up like film stars': cited in Nicholson, *Perfect Wives in Ideal Homes*
395 'yet new clothes ...': see Russell, *The Tamarisk Tree* and *We Called on Europe*
397 'HOW THE MANAKADS ...': *Birmingham Daily Gazette*, 20 June 1952
398 '[We] spent our lunch hour ...': Evans, *A Good School*
399 'Superficially, my life ...': Cowell, *Roberta Cowell's Story*
402 'I earnestly believe ...': Cowell, *Roberta Cowell's Story*
403 'You are a woman ...': Atwood, *The Robber Bride*
405 'radiant with success ...': cited in King, *Glorify Yourself*
405 'Remember, love at first sight ...': Alton, *Painting with Light*
406 'I just can't believe ...': *Yorkshire Evening Post*, 22 August 1946
407 'Her legs had to be ...': Morley, *The 'Miss World' Story*
408 'The decision to abandon ...': *Civil & Military Gazette* (Lahore), 13 June 1956
408 'Religious leaders ...': *Birmingham Daily Post*, 13 June 1956
409 'I purloined a razor ...': Brownmiller, *Femininity*
411 'Now that my lower extremities ...': cited in King, *Glorify Yourself*
414 'What was I?': cited in River, *Dorothy Dandridge*

416 'Straightened was respectable': Craig, 'The Decline and Fall of the Conk'
416 'You always knew ...': ibid.
419 'Today ... an increasing number ...': *Ebony*, June 1966
420 'the death of an Old Maid': Garfield, ed., *A Notable Woman*, 8 June 1941
420 'I am extremely tired ...': ibid., 6 December 1949
421 'God help me ...': ibid., 5 January 1952
421 'hideous but warm and cheap': ibid., 22 November 1952
421 'silly amorous adventures': ibid., 15 February 1953
421 'It was hideous ...': ibid., 22 June 1954
422 'It was quite terrifying': ibid., 5 April 1959
423 '[I am] living on ...': ibid., 3 May 1955
423 'Pads soaked ...': *Tatler*, 4 April 1956
424 'One client ...': *Tatler*, 28 May 1958
424 'With holidays ...': *Tatler*, 10 August 1955
427 'post-pregnancy weight problem': *Modern Screen,* November 1954
428 'I had one ...': author interview with Flora Calder, cited in Nicholson, *Perfect Wives in Ideal Homes*
428 'ATTRACTIVE GIRL ...': *Daily Mirror*, 23 January 1952
429 'There was nothing wrong ...': *Burnley Express*, 5 August 1953
429 'She got this ...': *Daily Mirror*, 3 September 1957
429 'on a strict ...': *Evening Star* (Washington DC), 12 April 1957
430 'Doctors everywhere ...': *Sunday Mirror*, 11 March 1951
431 'witnessed spiralling cases ...': Dell'Osso et al., 'Historical Evolution of the Concept of Anorexia Nervosa'
433 'She had so gone to seed ...': Malcolmson, eds, *Nella Last in the 1950s*, 22 April 1950
434 'Her shoes always look ...': ibid., 27 October 1951
434 '[She] looks like ...': ibid.
434 'Poor thing ...': Malcolmson, eds, *Nella Last's Peace*, 6 November 1946
434 'I saw A HAT ...': Broad and Fleming, eds, *Nella Last's War*, 27 April 1942
435 'to London length': Malcolmson, eds, *Nella Last's Peace*, 2 January 1948
438 'I am twenty-eight ...': Gardiner, *Faces, Figures and Feelings*
438 'I want to marry ...': ibid.
438 'Dr Crane ...': *The Daily Record* (Dunn, NC), 25 January 1955
439 'Happiness can be bought ...': Gardiner, *Faces, Figures and Feelings*
441 'change a patient's ...': *American Weekly*, 13 May 1945
441 'Paying for a pretty new nose ...': *Evening Star*, 12 June 1958
442 'Looking-glass, Looking-glass ...': Grimm Brothers, 'Little Snow-White'

Afterword

445 'Every woman knows ...': Greer, *The Whole Woman*
450 'I think dressing up ...': in conversation with the author
451 'I gravitate towards ...': in conversation with the author

452 'When it comes ...': *Daily Mail*, 19 June 2022

453 'Chloe Kelly ...': Twitter post, cited by Lucy Ward in 'Pure joy and a sports bra: the phot that encapsulates England Women's Euros win', *Guardian*, 1 August 2022

454 'There is no easy fix ...': speech at the *Glamour* 2018 Women of the Year Summit, available at Glamour.com, 11 November 2018, and on YouTube

454 'The first time ...': Jameela Jamil, ET Style via YouTube, 28 January 2020

Bibliography

Much of the research for this book was undertaken during the Covid-19 pandemic 2020–21, thus it relied heavily on digitised source material, as well as the London Library's impressive postal service. There is a vast abundance of material about the history of fashion and beauty, in print and online. The following lists are not exhaustive.

Biography, Memoirs, Diaries, Autobiography, Oral Histories

Andrée, Rosemary, pseud., *My Life Story*, London, 1951

Anson, Lady Clodagh, *Victorian Days*, London, Richards Press, 1957

Anstee, Margaret Joan, *Never Learn to Type: A Woman at the United Nations*, Chichester, John Wiley, 2003

Argyll, Margaret Campbell, Duchess of, *Forget Not: The Autobiography of Margaret, Duchess of Argyll*, London, W. H. Allen, 1975

Asquith, Cynthia, *Remember and be Glad*, London, J. Barrie, 1952

Asquith, Lady Cynthia, *Diaries 1915–18*, London, Hutchinson, 1968

Asquith, Margot, *The Autobiography of Margot Asquith 1864–1945*, London, Eyre & Spottiswoode, 1962

Atherton, Gertrude, *Adventures of a Novelist*, London, Jonathan Cape, 1932

Atkinson, Diane, *Love and Dirt: The Marriage of Arthur Munby and Hannah Cullwick*, London, Macmillan, 2003

Baker, Jean-Claude and Chris Chase, *Josephine: The Hungry Heart*, New York, Cooper Square Press, 1993

Bakewell, Joan, *The Centre of the Bed*, London, Sceptre, 2003

Baldwin, Monica, *I Leap Over the Wall: A Return to the World after Twenty-Eight Years in a Convent*, London, Hamish Hamilton, 1950

Bardot, Brigitte, *Initiales B.B., Mémoires*, Paris, Grasset, 1996

Battiscombe, Georgina, *Queen Alexandra*, London, Sphere, 1972

Beaton, Cecil, *The Wandering Years: Diaries 1922–1939*, London, Weidenfeld & Nicolson, 1961

Beatty, Laura, *Lillie Langtry: Manners, Masks and Morals*, London, Vintage, 2000

Beckwith, Muriel Beatrice, Lady, *When I Remember*, London, I. Nicholson & Watson, 1936

Bhatia, Robert, *Passage Across the Mersey*, London, Harper, 2017

Bloom, Ursula, *Trilogy*, London, Hutchinson, 1954

Bloomer, Dexter C., *Life and Writings of Amelia Bloomer*, Boston, Arena Publishing Co., 1895

Brewer Kerr, Dorothy, *The Girls Behind the Guns*, London, Hale, 1990

Bricktop with James Haskins, *Bricktop*, New York, Athenaeum, 1983

Briggs, Julia, *A Woman of Passion: The Life of E. Nesbit*, Harmondsworth, Penguin, 1987

Brittain, Vera, *Testament of Youth: An Autobiographical Study of the Years 1900–1925*, Victor Gollancz, 1933

Broad, Richard and Suzie Fleming, eds, *Nella Last's War: The Second World War Diaries of Housewife, 49*, London, Profile, 2006

Brooks, Gwendolyn, *Maud Martha*, London, Faber & Faber, 2022

Bundles, A'Lelia, *Self Made: The Life and Times of Madam C. J. Walker*, London, John Murray, 2020

Burnett, John, *Useful Toil: Autobiographies of Working People from the 1820s to the 1920s*, Allen Lane, 1974

Burnett, John, *Destiny Obscure: Autobiographies of Childhood, Education and Family from the 1820s to the 1920s*, London, Allen Lane, 1982

Cartland, Barbara, *The Isthmus Years, Autobiographical Reminiscences of the Years 1918–1939*, London, Hutchinson & Co., 1943

Cartland, Barbara, *The Years of Opportunity, 1939–1945*, London, Hutchinson & Co., 1948

Cartland, Barbara, *We Danced all Night*, London, Hutchinson, 1970

Chanda, Monica, ed. Malavika Karlekar, *Of Colonial Bungalows and Piano Lessons: Memoirs of a young Indian Woman*, London, Routledge, 2019

Chitty, Susan, *The Diary of a Fashion Model*, London, Methuen & Co., 1958

Cierplikowski, Antoine, *Autobiographical Reminiscences*, London, W. H. Allen & Co, 1946

Cline, Sally, *Radclyffe Hall: A Woman Called John*, London, John Murray, 1997

Cobbe, Frances Power, *Life of Frances Power Cobbe, by Herself*, London, R. Bentley & Son, 1894

Cooper, Diana, *The Rainbow Comes and Goes*, Harmondsworth, Penguin, 1961

Cooper, Diana, *Trumpets from the Steep*, Harmondsworth, Penguin, 1964

Cooper, Duff, *Old Men Forget*, London, Rupert Hart-Davis, 1954

Cousins, Sheila, (pseud. Ronald de Couves Matthews), *To Beg I am Ashamed*, London, Richards Press, 1953

Cowell, Roberta, *Roberta Cowell's Story*, London, Heinemann, 1954

Das, Kamala, *My Story*, New Delhi, Sterling, 1988

Das, Krishnabhabini, trans., ed. and introduced Somdatta Mandal, *A Bengali Lady in* England (1885), Newcastle, Cambridge Scholars Publishing, 2015

Dawnay, Jean, *Model Girl*, London, Weidenfeld & Nicolson, 1956

Dawnay, Jean, *How I Became a Fashion Model*, London, Thomas Nelson & Sons, 1958

Dawnay, Jean, *Working for Christian Dior*, London, Zuleika, 2019

Deb, Chitra, trans. Smita Chowdry and Sona Roy, *Women of the Tagore Household*, Haryana, Penguin, 2010

De Frece, Lady (Matilda Alice Powles), *Recollections of Vesta Tilley*, London, Hutchinson & Co., 1934

Devas, Nicolette, *Two Flamboyant Fathers*, London, Collins, 1966

Diliberto, Gioia, *Debutante: The Story of Brenda Frazier*, New York, Knopf, 1987

Dolson, Hildegarde, *We Shook the Family Tree: Reminiscences*, London, Hammond, Hammond & Co., 1952

Downey, Fairfax, *Portrait of an Era as Drawn by C. D. Gibson: A Biography*, New York, C. Scribner's Sons, 1936

Duncan, Isadora, *My Life*, New York, Boni and Liveright, 1927

Duff Gordon, Lucy, Lady, *Discretions and Indiscretions*, London, Jarrolds, 1932

Ephron, Nora, 'A Few Words About Breasts', *Esquire*, 1 October 1973

Essex, Rosamund, *Woman in a Man's World*, London, Sheldon Press, 1977

Evans, Mary, *A Good School: Life at a Girls' Grammar School in the 1950s*, London, Women's Press, 1991

Fielding, Daphne, *Mercury Presides*, London, Eyre & Spottiswoode, 1954

Fields, Mamie Garvin with Karen Fields, *Lemon Swamp and Other Places: A Carolina Memoir*, New York, Free Press, 1983

Forrester, Helen, *Lime Street at Two*, London, Bodley Head, 1985

Forrester, Helen, *By the Waters of Liverpool*, London, HarperCollins, 1993

Galton, Francis, *Memories of My Life*, London, Methuen & Co., 1908

Gänzl, Kurt, *Lydia Thompson, Queen of Burlesque*, New York and London, Routledge, 2002

Garfield, Simon, ed., *Our Hidden Lives: The Remarkable Diaries of a Forgotten Britain, 1945–1948*, London, Ebury, 2004

Garfield, Simon, ed., *A Notable Woman: The Romantic Journals of Jean Lucey Pratt*, London, Canongate, 2016

Godfrey, Rupert, ed., *Letters from a Prince: Edward, Prince of Wales, to Mrs Freda Dudley Ward, March 1918–January 1921*, London, Little, Brown & Co., 1988

Greville, Lady Violet, *Vignettes of Memory*, London, Hutchinson, 1927

Hale, Kathleen, *A Slender Reputation: An Autobiography*, London, Frederick Warne, 1994

Hall, Ruth, *Marie Stopes: A Biography*, London, Deutsch, 1977

Hardy, Lady Violet, *As it Was*, London, C. Johnson, 1958

Harpole, James, *Leaves from a Surgeon's Case-Book*, London, Cassell & Co., 1939

Harrison, Rosina, *My Life in Service*, London, Cassell, 1975

Heffer, Simon, ed., *Henry 'Chips' Channon, The Diaries 1918–38*, London, Hutchinson, 2021

Henrey, Mrs Robert, *The Little Madeleine: The Autobiography of a Young French Girl*, London, Dent, 1951

Henrey, Mrs Robert, *London Under Fire, 1940–45*, London, Dent, 1969

Hodgkinson, Liz, *From a Girl to a Man: How Laura Became Michael: The Story of the World's First Female-to-Male Transsexual*, London, Quartet, 2015

Holman-Hunt, Diana, *My Grandmothers and I*, London, Hamish Hamilton, 1960

Holmes, Beatrice Gordon, *In Love with Life: A Pioneer Career Woman's Story*, London, Hollis & Carter, 1944

Hooper, Barbara, *Mary Stocks, 1891–1975: An Uncommonplace Life*, London, Athlone, 1996

Horowitz Murray, Janet, *Strong-Minded Women: And Other Lost Voices from Nineteenth-Century England*, Harmondsworth, Penguin, 1984

Hudson, Derek, *Munby, Man of Two Worlds: The Life and Diaries of Arthur J. Munby 1828–1910*, London, John Murray, 1972

Hulanicki, Barbara, *From A to Biba*, London, Hutchinson & Co., 1983

Hurst, Margery, *No Glass Slipper*, London, Arlington, 1967

Jebb, Miles, ed., *The Diaries of Cynthia Gladwyn*, London, Constable, 1995

Jivaka, Lobzang/Dillon, Michael, *Out of the Ordinary: A Life of Gender and Spiritual Transitions*, New York, Fordham University Press, 2016

John, Angela V., *Evelyn Sharp: Rebel Woman 1869–1955*, Manchester, Manchester University Press, 2009

John, Angela V., *Turning the Tide: The Life of Lady Rhondda*, Cardigan, Parthian, 2013

Jopling, Louise, *Twenty Years of my Life 1867–1887*, London and New York, John Lane, 1925

Joyce, Peggy Hopkins, *Men, Marriage and Me*, London, Geoffrey Bles, 1930

Kenward, Betty, *Jennifer's Memoirs: Eighty-five Years of Fun and Functions*, London, HarperCollins, 1992

Keppel, Sonia, *Edwardian Daughter: Reminiscences*, London, Hamish Hamilton, 1958

Kurth, Peter, *Isadora: A Sensational Life*, London, Abacus, 2003

Lamb, Christian, *I Only Joined for the Hat: Redoubtable Wrens at War: Their Trials, Tribulations and Triumphs*, London, Bene Factum, 2007

Lambert-Huxley, Siobhan and Sunil Sharma, eds, *Atiya's Journeys: A Muslim Woman from Colonial Bombay to Edwardian Britain*, New Delhi, Oxford University Press, 2010

Langtry, Lillie, *The Days I Knew*, London, Hutchinson & Co., 1925

Lawrence, Gertrude, *A Star Danced*, London, W. H. Allen, 1945

Lees-Milne, James, *Another Self*, London, Hamish Hamilton, 1970

Lees-Milne, James, *A Mingled Measure: Diaries, 1953–1972*, London, John Murray, 1994

Lees-Milne, James, *Caves of Ice: Diaries, 1946–47*, London, John Murray, 1996

Lees-Milne, James, *Midway on the Waves: Diaries, 1948–49*, London, John Murray, 1996

Leider, Emily Wortis, *California's Daughter: Gertrude Atherton and her Times*, Stanford, Stanford University Press, 1991

Lewis, Alfred Allan and Constance Woodworth, *Miss Elizabeth Arden*, London, W. H. Allen, 1973

Llewelyn Davies, Margaret, *Life as We Have Known It: By Co-Operative Working Women*, London, Hogarth Press, 1931

Londonderry, Marchioness of (Edith Helen Vane Tempest Stewart), *Retrospect: Reminiscences*, London, F. Muller, 1938

Long, Helen, *Change into Uniform: An Autobiography 1939–1946*, Lavenham, T. Dalton, 1978

Ludovici, L. J., *Cosmetic Scalpel: The Life of Charles Willi, Beauty-Surgeon*, Bradford-on-Avon, Moonraker, 1981

MacCarthy, Fiona, *Last Curtsey: The End of the Debutantes*, London, Faber & Faber, 2006

MacCarthy, Mary, *A Nineteenth-Century Childhood*, London, Constable, 1985

Macdonald, Eleanor, *An Autobiography of a Pioneer Business Woman: Nothing by Chance*, Alton, Nimrod, 1987

Mackworth, Margaret Haig Thomas, Viscountess Rhondda, *This Was my World*, London, Macmillan & Co., 1933

Malcolmson, Patricia and Robert, eds, *Nella Last's Peace*, London, Profile, 2008

Malcolmson, Patricia and Robert, eds, *Nella Last in the 1950s: Further Diaries of Housewife, 49*, London, Profile, 2010

Mannin, Ethel, *Rolling in the Dew*, London, Jarrolds, 1940

Mannin, Ethel, *Young in the Twenties: A Chapter of Autobiography*, London, Hutchinson, 1971

Marlborough, Laura Spencer-Churchill, Duchess of, *Laughter from a Cloud*, London, Weidenfeld & Nicolson, 1980

Marshall, Cherry, *The Cat-Walk*, London, Hutchinson, 1978

Martin, Paula J., *Suzanne Noël: Cosmetic Surgery, Feminism and Beauty in Early Twentieth-Century France*, London, Routledge, 2016

Masters, Brian, *Great Hostesses*, London, Constable, 1982

Mazumdar, Shudha, *A Pattern of Life: Memoirs of an Indian Woman*, New Delhi, Manohar, 1977

Michelmore, Cliff and Jean Metcalfe, *Two-Way Story: An Autobiography*, London, Hamilton, 1986

Milburn, Clara, ed. Peter Donnelly, *Mrs Milburn's Diaries: An Englishwoman's Day-to-Day Reflections, 1939–1945*, London, Abacus, 1979

Mirza, Begum Khurshid, ed. Lubna Kazim, *A Woman of Substance: The Memoirs of Begum Khurshid Mirza 1918–1989*, New Delhi, Zubaan, 2005

Mistinguett, trans. Lucienne Hill, *Mistinguett, Queen of the Paris Night*, London, Elek, 1954

Mitchison, Naomi, *All Change Here: Girlhood and Marriage*, London, Bodley Head, 1975

Mitford, Jessica, *Hons and Rebels: An Autobiography*, London, Victor Gollancz, 1960

Moore, Doris Langley, *E. Nesbit: A Biography*, London, Ernest Benn, 1967

Morton, James, *Lola Montez: Her Life and Conquests*, London, Portrait, 2007

Mosley, Charlotte, ed., *Love from Nancy: The Letters of Nancy Mitford*, London, Sceptre, 1994

Nevill, Lady Dorothy, ed. Ralph Nevill, *Under Five Reigns*, London, Methuen, 1910

Nevill, Lady Dorothy, ed. Ralph Nevill, *My Own Times*, London, Methuen, 1912

Nevill, Ralph, *The Life & Letters of Lady Dorothy Nevill*, London, Methuen & Co., 1919

Newhall, Nancy, ed., *The Daybook of Edward Weston*, New York, Horizon Press, 1961

Nicolson, Nigel, ed., *Vita and Harold: The Letters of Vita Sackville-West and Harold Nicolson 1910–1962*, London, Weidenfeld & Nicolson, 1992

Ogden, Christopher, *Life of the Party: The Biography of Pamela Digby Churchill*, London, Little, Brown, 1994

Partridge, Frances, *Memories*, London, Phoenix, 1996

Paul, Brenda Dean, *My First Life: A Biography*, London, John Long, 1935

Pawar, Urmila, trans. Maya Pandit, *The Weave of my Life: A Dalit Woman's Memoirs*, Kolkata, Stree, 2008

Pearl, Cora, ed. William Blatchford, *The Memoirs of Cora Pearl*, London, Panther, 1984

Pearson, John, *The Private Lives of Winston Churchill*, London, Bloomsbury, 2011

Peel, Mrs C. S., *Life's Enchanted Cup: An Autobiography (1872–1933)*, London, John Lane, 1933

Picardie, Justine, *Coco Chanel: The Legend and the Life*, London, HarperCollins, 2010

Pike, E. Royston, *Human Documents of the Age of the Forsytes*, London, Allen & Unwin, 1969

Pike, E. Royston, *Human Documents of the Lloyd George Era*, London, Allen & Unwin, 1972

Pike, E. Royston, *Human Documents of the Victorian Golden Age*, London, Allen & Unwin, 1972

Powell, Margaret, *Below Stairs*, London, Peter Davies, 1968

Powell, Margaret, *Climbing the Stairs*, London, Peter Davies, 1969

Powell, Margaret, *Servants' Hall*, Bath, Firecrest, 1980

Rappaport, Helen, *Beautiful for Ever: Madame Rachel of Bond Street: Cosmetician, Con-Artist and Blackmailer*, London, Vintage, 2012

Raverat, Gwen, *Period Piece*, London, Faber & Faber, 1952

Raynes, Rozelle, *Maid Matelot*, Southampton, Nautical Publishing Co., 1971

Richardson, Joanna, *Enid Starkie*, London, John Murray, 1973

Riddell, Fern, *Death in Ten Minutes: The Forgotten Life of Radical Suffragette Kitty Marion*, London, Hodder & Stoughton, 2019

Riddell, Fern, *Death in Ten Minutes: Kitty Marion: Activist, Arsonist, Suffragette*, London, Hodder & Stoughton, 2018

River, Charles, *Dorothy Dandridge: The Life and Legacy of One of Hollywood's First Successful Black Actresses*, n.p., Charles River Editors, 2020

Rosenblum, Constance, *Gold Digger: The Outrageous Life and Times of Peggy Hopkins Joyce*, New York, Henry Holt, 2000

Russell, Dora, *The Tamarisk Tree, Vol. 3 Challenge to the Cold War*, London, Virago, 1985

Sharp, Evelyn, *Unfinished Adventure: Selected Reminiscences from an Englishwoman's Life*, London, John Lane, 1933

Shrimpton, Jean, *Jean Shrimpton: An Autobiography*, London, Ebury, 1990

Smith, Sally Bedell, *Reflected Glory: The Life of Pamela Churchill Harriman*, New York, Simon & Schuster, 1996

Sorabji, Cornelia, *India Calling: The Memories of Cornelia*, New Delhi and Oxford, Oxford University Press, 2001

Spanier, Jenny Yvonne, *It Isn't All Mink*, Bath, Cedric Chivers, 1971

St Helier, Lady, Mary Jeune, *Memories of Fifty Years*, London, E. Arnold, 1909

Stack, Prunella, *Movement is Life: The Autobiography of Prunella Stack*, London, Collins, 1973

Stanford, Peter, *Bronwen Astor: Her Life and Times*, HarperCollins, 2000

Stanley, The Hon Eleanor, *Twenty Years at Court: From the Correspondence of the Hon Eleanor Stanley, Maid of Honour to Her Late Majesty Queen Victoria, 1842–1862*, London, Nisbet & Co., 1916

Stanley, Liz, ed., *The Diaries of Hannah Cullwick: Victorian Maidservant*, London, Virago, 1984

Starkie, Enid, *A Lady's Child: An Autobiography*, London, Faber & Faber, 1941

Stenn, David, *Clara Bow: Runnin' Wild*, London, Ebury, 1989

Stringer, Mabel E., *Golfing Reminiscences*, London, Mills & Boon, 1924

Swanson, Gloria, *Swanson on Swanson*, Feltham, Hamlyn, 1981

Tedder, Valerie, *Post-War Blues*, Leicester, Leicester City Council, Living History, 1999

Terrell, Mary Church, *A Colored Woman in a White World*, Lanham, Rowman & Littlefield, 2020

Terry, Dame Ellen, *The Story of my Life*, London, Hutchinson & Co., 1922

Thorek, Max, *A Surgeon's World: An Autobiography*, Philadelphia, J. B. Lippincott, 1943

Thornycroft, Rosalind and Chloe Baynes, *Time Which Spaces Us Apart*, Batcombe, n.p., 1991

Trethewey, Rachel, *Before Wallis: Edward VIII's Other Women*, Stroud, History Press, 2018

Vickers, Hugo, *The Sphinx: The Life of Gladys Deacon*, London, Hodder & Stoughton, 2020

Waller, Angela, *Before there were Trolley Dollies*, Long Preston, Dales, 2011

Warren, Doug, *Betty Grable: The Reluctant Movie Queen*, Robson Books, 1982/2016

Warwick, Frances, Countess of Warwick, *Life's Ebb and Flow*, London, Hutchinson, 1929

Wells, Maureen, *Entertaining Eric: A Wartime Love Story*, Long Preston, Magna, 2008

White, Doris, *D for Doris, V for Victory*, Oakleaf Books in association with People's Press, Milton Keynes, 1981

Whitehorn, Katharine, *Selective Memory*, London, Virago, 2007

Whitfield, John H., *A Friend to all Mankind: Mrs Annie Turnbo Malone and Poro College*, n.p., CreateSpace, 2015

Willmott, Phyllis, *A Green Girl*, London, Peter Owen, 1983

Willmott, Phyllis, *Coming of Age in Wartime*, London, Peter Owen, 1988

Willmott, Phyllis, *Joys and Sorrows: Fragments from the Post-war Years*, London, Peter Owen, 1995

Wood, Ean, *The Josephine Baker Story*, London, Sanctuary, 2000

Woolf, Virginia, ed. Jeanne Schulkind, *Moments of Being: Autobiographical Writings*, London, Chatto & Windus for Sussex University Press, 1976

Woolf, Virginia, ed. Anne Olivier Bell, *The Diary of Virginia Woolf*, London, Hogarth Press, 1980

Woolf, Virginia, ed. Nigel Nicolson, *The Letters of Virginia Woolf*, London, Chatto & Windus, 1980

Wordsworth, Dame Elizabeth, *Glimpses of the Past*, London and Oxford, A. R. Mowbray & Co., 1912

Wyndham, Joan, *Love is Blue*, London, Flamingo, 1987

Wyndham, Joan, *Love Lessons: A Wartime Diary*, London, Virago, 2001

Ziegler, Philip, *Diana Cooper*, London, Hamish Hamilton, 1981

History, Sociology, Psychology, Advice

Adburgham, Alison, *Shops and Shopping: Where, and in what Manner the Well-dressed Englishwoman bought her Clothes*, London, George Allen & Unwin, 1964

Agnew, Eadaoin, *Imperial Women Writers in Victorian India*, Cham, Palgrave Macmillan, 2017

Alton, John, *Painting with Light*, New York, Macmillan, 1949

Angell, Shirley, *Pinnacle Club: A History of Women Climbing*, Glasgow, Pinnacle Club, 1988

Archer-Straw, Petrine, *Negrophilia: Avant-Garde Paris and Black Culture in the 1920s*, London, Thames & Hudson, 2000

Archer, Elsie, *Let's Face It: A Guide to Good Grooming for Negro Girls*, Philadelphia and New York, J. B. Lippincott Co., 1959

Aretz, Gertrude Kuntze-Dolton, trans. James Laver, *The Elegant Woman, from the Rococo Period to Modern Times*, London, G. G. Harrap & Co., 1932

Aronson, Theo, *The King in Love: Edward VII's Mistresses*, London, Corgi, 1988

Atkinson, Diane, *The Suffragettes in Pictures*, Stroud, Sutton, 1996

Balfour, Patrick, 3rd Baron Kinross, *Society Racket: A Critical Survey of Modern Social Life*, London, John Long, 1933

Ballin, Ada S., *The Science of Dress: In Theory and Practice*, London, Sampson Low, Marston, Searle & Rivington, 1885

Banner, Lois W., *American Beauty*, New York, Knopf, 1983

Bates, Laura, *Everyday Sexism*, London, Simon & Schuster, 2014

Bax, Clifford, *The Beauty of Women*, London, F. Muller, 1946

Bayard, Marie, *Toilet Hints: Or, How to Preserve Beauty and How to Acquire it*, London: Weldon & Co., 1883

Beaton, Cecil, *The Glass of Fashion*, London, Weidenfeld & Nicolson, 1954

Beauty, Its Attainment and Preservation, New York, Butterick, 1892

Beerbohm, Sir Max, *The Pervasion of Rouge: A Defence of Cosmetics*, New York, Dodd, Mead & Co., 1922

Beeton, Isabella Mary, *Book of Household Management*, London, Ward Lock & Co., 1936

Bell, John C., *Natural Beauty*, London, 1927

Bell, Quentin, *On Human Finery*, London, Hogarth Press, 1947

Bensimon, Kelly Killoren, *The Bikini Book*, London, Thames & Hudson, 2006

Berger, John, *Ways of Seeing*, Harmondsworth, Penguin, 1972

Bird, Walter, *Andrée, Britain's Venus*, Elstree, Camera Studies Club, 1943

Black, Elsa, *Beauty for Every Woman*, London, The Star, [1935]

Booth, Charles, ed., *Life and Labour of the People in London*, London, Williams & Northgate 1889–91

Bordo, Susan, *Unbearable Weight: Feminism, Western Culture, and the Body*, Berkeley, University of California Press, 2004

Bowley, Arthur L., *Wages in the United Kingdom in the Nineteenth Century*, Cambridge, Cambridge University Press, 1900

Branca, Patricia, *Silent Sisterhood: Middle Class Women in the Victorian Home*, London, Croom Helm, c. 1975

Brittain, Vera, *Lady into Woman: A History of Women from Victoria to Elizabeth II*, London, A. Dakers, 1953

Brown, Judith, *Glamour in Six Dimensions: Modernism and the Radiance of Form*, Ithaca, Cornell University Press, 2009

Browning, H. Ellen, *Beauty Culture*, London, Hutchinson & Co., 1898

Brownmiller, Susan, *Femininity*, New York, Open Road, 1984

Brumberg, Joan Jacobs, *The Body Project: An Intimate History of American Girls*, New York, Random House, 1997

Campbell, Gertrude Elizabeth Blood (Lady Colin Campbell), *Etiquette of Good Society*, London, Cassell & Co., 1911

Caplin, Madame Roxey A., *Health and Beauty: Or, Woman and Her Clothing*, London, Kent & Co., 1864

Carey, Tanith, *Never Kiss a Man in a Canoe: Words of Wisdom from the Golden Age of Agony Aunts*, London, Box Tree, 2009

Cartland, Barbara, *Marriage for Moderns*, Jenkins, 1955

Cartland, Barbara, *Barbara Cartland's Etiquette Handbook: A Guide to Good Behaviour from the Boudoir to the Boardroom*, London, Random House, 1962

Chamberlain, Mary, *Fenwomen: A Portrait of Women in an English Village*, London, Virago, 1977

Chernin, Kim, *The Obsession: Reflections on the Tyranny of Slenderness*, New York, Harper Perennial, 1994

Clark, Kenneth, *Feminine Beauty*, London, Weidenfeld & Nicolson, 1980

Clayton, Lucie, *The World of Modelling*, London, Tandem, 1969

Clephane, Irene, *Ourselves: 1900–1930*, London, John Lane, 1933

Collins Brown, Henry, *Brownstone Fronts and Saratoga Trunks*, New York, E. P. Dutton, 1935

Comettant, Oscar, *Trois ans aux États-Unis: Etude de moeurs et coutumes américaines*, Paris, Pagnerre, 1857

Conn, Mrs Josef, *Let there be Light, Mothers!*, Kensington, Farmer & Sons, 1907

Cooke, Dorothy M., *Keep Fit Work for Women*, London, Sir Isaac Pitman & Sons, 1937

Cooley, Arnold James, *The Toilet and Cosmetic Arts in Ancient and Modern Times*, London, Robert Hardwicke, 1866

Costelloe, Rachel, *Our Freedom and its Results*, London, Leonard & Virginia Woolf, 1936

Cox, Caroline, *Good Hair Days: A History of British Hairstyling*, London, Quartet, 1999

Craig, Maxine Leeds, *Ain't I a Beauty Queen? Black Women, Beauty, and the Politics of Race*, Oxford, Oxford University Press, 2002

Crow, Duncan, *The Edwardian Woman*, London, Allen & Unwin, 1978

d'Orchamps, Baronne, *Tous les Secrets de la Femme*, Paris, Albin Michel, c. 1925

Dabiri, Emma, *Don't Touch my Hair*, London, Penguin, 2019

Dahl, Arlene, *Always Ask a Man: Arlene Dahl's Key to Femininity*, London, Frederick Muller, 1965

David, Alison Matthews, *Fashion Victims: The Dangers of Dress Past and Present*, London, Bloomsbury, 2015

Davidoff, Leonore, *The Best Circles: Society, Etiquette and the Season*, London, Croom Helm, 1974

Dawes, Frank, *Not in Front of the Servants*, London, Wayland, 1973

Day, Carolyn A., *Consumptive Chic: A History of Beauty, Fashion and Disease*, London, Bloomsbury, 2017

de Beauvoir, Simone, trans. Constance Borde and Sheila Malovany-Chevalier, *The Second Sex*, London, Vintage, 2009

de Courcy, Anne, *Debs at War 1939–1945: How Wartime Changed their Lives*, London, Weidenfeld & Nicolson, 2005

de Courcy, Anne, *Chanel's Riviera: Life, Love and the Struggle for Survival on the Côte d'Azur, 1930–1944*, London, Weidenfeld & Nicolson, 2019 de la Haye, Amy, *Land Girls: Cinderellas of the Soil*, Brighton, Royal Pavilion and Museums, 2009

Dean, Teresa H., *How to Be Beautiful – Nature Unmasked: A Book for Every Woman*, London, Trübner & Co., 1890

Dengel, Veronica, *Personality Unlimited: The Beauty Blue Book*, London, Faber & Faber, 1949

Dengel, Veronica, *All About You*, London, Faber & Faber, 1954

Donnelly, Antoinette, *How to Reduce: New Waistlines for Old*, New York and London, D. Appleton & Co., 1921

Douglas, Fanny, *The Gentlewoman's Book of Dress*, London, Henry & Co., 1895

Ellis, Havelock, *My Life*, London, Houghton Mifflin 1939

Entwistle, Joanne and Elizabeth Wissinger, eds, *Fashioning Models: Image, Text, and Industry*, London and New York, Berg, 2012

Erskine, F. J., *Lady Cycling*, London, Walter Scott, 1897

Evans, Caroline and Minna Thornton, *Women and Fashion: A New Look*, London, Quartet, 1989

Evans, Caroline, *The Mechanical Smile: Modernism and the First Fashion Shows in France and America 1900–1929*, New Haven, Yale University Press, 2013

Evans, Hilary, with the Mary Evans Picture Library, *The Oldest Profession: An Illustrated History of Prostitution*, Newton Abbot, David & Charles, 1979

Every Woman's Book of Health and Beauty, London, Amalgamated Press, 1935

Ferguson, Marjorie, *Forever Feminine: Women's Magazines and the Cult of Femininity*, London, Heinemann, 1983

Fletcher, Sheila, *Women First: The Female Tradition in English Physical Education, 1880–1980*, London, Athlone, 1984

Fogarty, Anne, *The Art of Being a Well-Dressed Wife*, London, V&A, 2011

Forth, Christopher E. and Ivan Crozier, eds, *Body Parts: Critical Explorations in Corporeality*, Lanham and Oxford, Lexington, 2005

Fox, Dr George Henry, *The Use of Electricity in the Removal of Superfluous Hair: And the Treatment of Various Facial Blemishes*, Detroit, George S. Davis, 1886

Foxcroft, Louise, *Calories & Corsets: A History of Dieting over 2000 Years*, London, Profile, 2011

Freedman, Rita, *Beauty Bound*, London, Columbus, 1988

Friedan, Betty, *The Feminine Mystique*, New York, W. W. Norton, 1963

Fryer, Peter, *Mrs Grundy: Studies in English Prudery*, London, Dobson, 1963

Gabor, Mark, *Pin-Up: A Modest History*, London, Pan, 1973

Gallagher, Catherine and Thomas Laqueur, eds, *The Making of the Modern Body, Sexuality and Society in the Nineteenth Century*, Berkeley and London, University of California Press, 1987

Gallichan, Walter Matthew, *Modern Woman and How to Manage Her*, London, T. Werner Laurie, 1913

Gardiner, Leslie Elgar, *Faces, Figures and Feelings: A Cosmetic Surgeon Speaks*, London, Robert Hale, 1959

Gattey, Charles Neilson, *The Bloomer Girls*, London, Femina, 1967

Gent, Helena, *Health and Beauty, with a Series of Simple Home Exercises*, London, Health & Strength, 1909

Gernsheim, Alison, *Victorian and Edwardian Fashion: A Photographic Survey*, London, Faber & Faber, 1963

Gibson, Stephen and Simon Mollan, eds, *Representations of Peace and Conflict*, London, Palgrave Macmillan, 2012

Gill, Eric, *Clothes: An Essay upon the Nature and Significance of the Natural and Artificial Integuments worn by Men and Women*, London, Jonathan Cape, 1931

Gill, Tiffany M., *Beauty Shop Politics: African American Women's Activism in the Beauty Industry*, Champaign, University of Illinois Press, 2010

Gilman, Sander L., *Making the Body Beautiful: a Cultural History of Aesthetic Surgery*, Princeton, Princeton University Press, 1999

Gordon, Jane [pseud. Peggy Graves], *Technique for Beauty*, London, Faber & Faber, 1940

Gordon, Jane, *Slimming*, London, Gordon Graves, 1951

Gordon, Jane, *Jane Gordon's Beauty Book*, London, André Deutsch, 1953

Graves, Robert and Alan Hodge, *The Long Weekend: A Social History of Great Britain 1918–1939*, London, Penguin, 1971

Green, Jonathon, *It: Sex Since the Sixties*, London, Secker & Warburg, 1993

Greer, Germaine, *The Whole Woman*, London, Doubleday, 1999

Greville, Violet, Lady, ed. W. H. Davenport Adams, *The Gentlewoman in Society*, London, Henry & Co., 1891

Greville, Lady Violet, *The Gentlewoman's Book of Sports*, London, Pushkin Press and the London Library, 2016

Guenther, Irene, *Nazi Chic? Fashioning Women in the Third Reich*, Oxford, Berg, 2004

Gundle, Stephen, *Glamour: A History*, Oxford, Oxford University Press, 2009

Haiken, Elizabeth, *Venus Envy: A History of Cosmetic Surgery*, Baltimore and London, Johns Hopkins University Press, 1997

Hands, Joseph, *Beauty and the Laws Governing its Development*, London, E. W. Allen, 1882

Hardie, Melissa, ed., *Digging for Memories: The Women's Land Army in Cornwall*, Penzance, Hypatia Trust, 2006

Harland, Marion, *Eve's Daughters, or Common Sense for Maid, Wife and Mother*, New York, John R. Anderson & Henry S. Allen, 1882

Harper, Charles G., *Revolted Women, Past, Present and to Come*, London, Elkin Mathews, 1894

Hartley, C. Gascquoine, *The Truth About Women*, London, Eveleigh Nash, 1913

Hauser, Gayelord, *Eat and Grow Beautiful*, London, Faber & Faber, 1939

Haweis, Mary Eliza Joy, *The Art of Beauty*, London, Chatto & Windus, 1878

Hawthorn, Jane, *How to Look Your Best: Woman and her Powder Puff*, London, Fountain Press, 1926

Hawthorne, Rosemary, *Bras: A Private View*, London, Souvenir Press, 1992

Hawthorne, Rosemary, *Knickers: An Intimate Appraisal*, London, Souvenir Press, 1999

Herzig, Rebecca M., *Plucked: A History of Hair Removal*, New York, NYU Press, 2015

Holden, Ivie Priestnall, *Every Woman's Guide to Beauty: Comprehensive Advice for the Attainment of Perfect Beauty of the Face and Figure*, London, Link House, 1935

Hornibrook, Arthur F., *The Culture of the Abdomen: The Cure of Obesity and Constipation*, London, William Heinemann, 1924

Hornibrook, Ettie A., *Stand Up and Slim Down: Being Restoration Exercises for Women*, Garden City, Doubleday, Doran & Co., 1934

Hughes, M. V., *A London Home in the Nineties*, London, Oxford University Press, 1937

Hughes, M. V., *A London Family Between the Wars*, London, Oxford University Press, 1940

Humphry, Mrs C. E., *How to be Pretty though Plain*, London, J. Bowden, 1899

Inch, Thomas, *Inch on Fitness*, London, George Newnes, 1923

'Isobel', ed., *The Art of Beauty: A Book for Women and Girls*, London, C. A. Pearson, 1899

James, William, ed., *The Order of Release: The Story of John Ruskin, Effie Gray and John Everett Millais told for the First Time in their Unpublished Letters*, London, John Murray, 1948

John, Angela V., *By the Sweat of their Brow: Women Workers at Victorian Coal Mines*, London, Croom Helm, 1980

Johnson, Cecil Webb, *Why Be Fat?*, London, Mills & Boon, 1923

Johnson, Kim K. P. and Sharron J. Lennon, eds, *Appearance and Power*, Oxford, Berg, 1999

Jones, Geoffrey, *Beauty Imagined: A History of the Global Beauty Industry*, Oxford, Oxford University Press, 2010

Joseph, Shirley, *If Their Mothers Only Knew: An Unofficial Account of Life in the Women's Land Army*, London, Faber & Faber, 1946

Junge, Traudl, trans. Anthea Bell, *Until the Final Hour: Hitler's Last Secretary*, London, Orion, 2004

Keenan, Brigid, *Women We Wanted to Look Like*, London, Macmillan, 1977

Kellerman, Annette, *Physical Beauty: How to Keep It*, London, William Heinemann, 1919

Kershaw, Ian, *Hitler*, London, Allen Lane, 1998

King, Eleanore, *Glorify Yourself: A Complete and Up-to-date Course on Beauty and Charm*, Marple, Academy of Charm & Beauty, 1953

Koonz, Claudia, *Mothers in the Fatherland: Women, the Family and Nazi Politics*, London, Routledge, 2013

The Lady's Maid: Her Duties, and How to Perform Them, London, Houlston and Sons 1877

Lambert, Miles, *Fashion in Photographs 1860–1880*, London, Batsford, 1991

Laver, James, *Taste and Fashion from the French Revolution until To-day*, London, George G. Harrap & Co., 1937

Laynard, Boyd, *Secrets of Beauty, Health, and Long Life*, London, Hammond, Hammond & Co., 1900

Lesnik-Oberstein, Karin, ed., *The Last Taboo: Women and Body Hair*, Manchester, Manchester University Press, 2006

Lethbridge, Lucy, *Servants: A Downstairs View of Twentieth-Century Britain*, London, Bloomsbury, 2013

Lewis, Reina, *Gendering Orientalism: Race, Femininity and Representation*, London, Routledge, 1996

Lewis, Roy and Angus Maude, *The English Middle Classes*, Harmondsworth, Penguin, 1953

Lieber, Francis, *The Stranger in America, Comprising Sketches of the Manners, Society, and National Peculiarities of the United States, in a Series of Letters to a Friend in Europe*, London, R. Bentley, 1835

Linton, E. Lynn, *The Girl of the Period and Other Social Essays*, London, R. Bentley, 1883

Löbel, Sali, *Glamour and How to Achieve it*, London, Hutchinson & Co., 1938

Macdonald, Charlotte, *Strong, Beautiful and Modern: National Fitness in Britain, New Zealand, Australia and Canada 1935–1960*, Wellington, Bridget Williams, 2011

Macdonald, Eleanor, *Live by Beauty*, London, Secker & Warburg, 1960

Mackern, Mrs Louie and M. Boys, eds, *Our Lady of the Green: A Book of Ladies' Golf*, London, Lawrence & Bullen, 1899

Mackworth, Margaret Haig Thomas, Viscountess Rhondda, *Leisured Women*, London, Hogarth Press, 1928

Malcolmson, Patricia, *Me and My Hair: A Social History*, Gosport, Chaplin, 2012

Margetson, Elisabeth Bertram, *Living Canvas: A Romance of Aesthetic Surgery*, London, Methuen & Co., 1936

Margetson, Stella, *The Long Party: High Society in the Twenties and Thirties*, Farnborough, Saxon House, 1974

Margueritte, Victor, trans. Brian Stableford, *The Bacheloress*, Tarzana, Black Coat Press, 2015

Marwick, Arthur, *Beauty in History: Society, Politics and Personal Appearance c. 1500 to the Present*, London, Thames & Hudson, 1988

Mayhew, Henry, *London Labour and the London Poor*, London, Griffin, Bohn and Co., 1861–62

McClingtock, Anne, *Imperial Leather: Race, Gender and Sexuality in the Colonial Contest*, New York, Routledge, 1994

McCrone, Kathleen E., *Sport and the Physical Emancipation of English Women, 1870–1914*, London, Routledge, 2014

McIntosh, Peter C., *Physical Education in England since 1800*, London, Bell & Hyman, 1968

Milcoy, Katharine, *When the Girls Come Out to Play: Teenage Working-class Girls' Leisure Between the Wars*, London and New York, Bloomsbury, 2017

Mill, John Stuart, *The Subjection of Women*, London, Longmans, Green, Reader, and Dyer, 1869

Miller, Charles Conrad, *Cosmetic Surgery: The Correction of Featural Imperfections*, Philadelphia, F. A. Davis Co., 1924

Montez, Lola, Countess of Landsfeld, *The Arts of Beauty*, London, James Blackwood, 1858

Moore, Constance, *The Way to Beauty*, London, Ward Lock & Co., 1955

Morley, Eric, *The 'Miss World' Story*, Maidstone, Angley, 1967

Müller, Jørgen Peter, *My System for Ladies*, London, Ewart, Seymour & Co., 1914

'Myrene', *The Lady Beauty-Book*, London, *The Lady* Offices, 1900

Nath, Ipshita, *Memsahibs: British Women in Colonial India*, London, C. Hurst & Co., 2022

Nevill, Ralph, *Mayfair and Montmartre*, London, Methuen & Co., 1921

Newton, Stella Mary, *Health, Art and Reason: Dress Reformers of the 19th Century*, London, John Murray, 1974

Nicholson, Virginia, *Singled Out: How Two Million Women Survived Without Men after the First World War*, London, Viking, 2007

Nicholson, Virginia, *Millions Like Us: Women's Lives in War and Peace, 1939–1949*, London, Viking, 2011

Nicholson, Virginia, *Perfect Wives in Ideal Homes: The Story of Women in the 1950s*, London, Viking, 2015

Noakes, Lucy and Juliette Pattinson, eds, *British Cultural Memory and the Second World War*, London, Bloomsbury, 2013

Noël, Suzanne, *La Chirurgie Esthetique: Son Rôle Social*, Paris, Masson et Cie., 1926

Noble, Peter, and Yvonne Saxon, eds, *Glamour: Film, Fashion and Beauty*, London, Burke, 1953

Oliphant, Mrs Margaret, *Dress*, London, Macmillan and Co., 1878

Orbach, Susie, *Fat is a Feminist Issue: How to Lose Weight Permanently without Dieting*, London, Paddington Press, 1978

Parmelee, Maurice, *Nudism in Modern Life: The New Gymnosophy*, Garden City, Garden City Publishing Co., 1931

Passot, Raymond, *Sculpteur de Visages: Les Secrets de la Chirurgie Esthétique*, Paris, Denoël et Steele, 1933

Pearsall, Ronald, *The Worm in the Bud: The World of Victorian Sexuality*, Harmondsworth, Penguin, 1971

Peters, Dr Lulu Hunt, *Diet and Health: With Key to the Calories*, Baltimore, Riley and Lee, 1918

Phelps, Elizabeth Stuart, *What to Wear?*, London, James R. Osgood and Co., 1874

Pitman, Joanna, *On Blondes*, New York, Bloomsbury, 2008

Pomeroy, Florence, Viscountess Harberton, *Reasons for Reform in Dress*, London, Hutchings & Crowsley, 1884

Pool, Daniel, *What Jane Austen Ate and Charles Dickens Knew: Fascinating Facts of Daily Life in the Nineteenth Century*, London, Robinson, 1998

Poucher, W. A., *Eve's Beauty Secrets*, London, Chapman & Hall, 1926

Pringle, Margaret, *Dance Little Ladies: The Days of the Debutante*, London, Orbis, 1977

Professional Beauty, A, *Beauty and How to Keep it*, London, Brentano's, 1889

Pugh, Martin, *Women and the Women's Movement in Britain, 1914–1959*, London, Macmillan, 1992

Pullan, Matilda, *Maternal Counsels to a Daughter*, London, Darton and Co., 1855

Quick, Harriet, *Catwalking: A History of the Fashion Model*, London, Hamlyn, 1997

Randall, Rona, *The Model Wife, Nineteenth-Century Style*, London, Herbert, 1989

Riordan, Teresa, *A History of the Innovations That Have Made Us Beautiful*, New York, Broadway Books, 2004

Roberts, Robert, *The Classic Slum: Salford Life in the First Quarter of the Century*, Harmondsworth, Penguin, 1973

Robinson, Jane, *Bluestockings: The Remarkable Story of the First Women to Fight for an Education*, London, Viking, 2009

Rolt-Wheeler, Ethel, *Famous Blue Stockings*, London, Methuen, 1910

Romm, Sharon, *The Changing Face of Beauty*, London, Mosby, 1992

Ross, Alexander, *Superfluous Hairs, and Their Means of Removal*, London, A. Ross, 1880

Russell, Jane, *Success and Happiness through Charm*, London, Odhams Press, 1939

S— G—, *The Art of Being Beautiful: A Series of Interviews with a Society Beauty*, London, Henry J. Drane, 1902

Saalfeld, Dr Edmund, trans. J. F. Halls Dally, *Lectures on Cosmetic Treatment: A Manual for Practitioners*, London, Rebman, 1910

Sackville-West, Vita, *The Women's Land Army*, London, Michael Joseph, 1944

Sala, George Augustus, *Twice Round the Clock: or, Hours of the Day and Night in London*, London, J. & R. Maxwell, 1859

Santos, Lucy Jane, *Half Lives: The Unlikely History of Radium*, London, Icon, 2020

Schireson, Henry Junius, *As Others See You: The Story of Plastic Surgery*, New York, Macaulay Co., 1938

Scott, Linda M., *Fresh Lipstick: Redressing Fashion and Feminism*, New York and Basingstoke, Palgrave Macmillan, 2005

Sen, Indrani, *Woman and Empire: Representations in the Writings of British India, 1858–1900*, Hyderabad, Orient Longman, 2002

Sheba, etc., *Women Who Fascinate and Why*, London, Vail & Co., 1924

Shewell-Cooper, Wilfred, *Land Girl: A Manual for Volunteers in the Women's Land Army 1941*, Stroud, Amberley, 2011

Short, Don, *Miss World: The Naked Truth*, London, Everest, 1976

Shorter, Edward, *A History of Women's Bodies*, London, Allen Lane, 1983

Shulman, Alexandra, *Clothes … and Other Things that Matter*, London, Cassell, 2020

Simon, Linda, *Lost Girls: The Invention of the Flapper*, London, Reaktion, 2017

Smith, Alison, ed., *Exposed: The Victorian Nude*, London, Tate, 2001

Squire, Alexander Balmanno, *Superfluous Hair and the Means of Removing it*, London, J. & A. Churchill, 1893

Stack, Mary Bagot, *Building the Body Beautiful*, London, Chapman & Hall, 1931

Staffe, Baronne, trans. Lady Colin Campbell, *The Lady's Dressing Room*, London, Cassell, 1892

Steele, Valerie, Fashion and Eroticism: Ideals of Feminine Beauty from the Victorian Era to the Jazz Age, New York and Oxford, Oxford University Press, 1985

Steele, Valerie, *The Corset: A Cultural History*, New Haven, Yale University Press, 2001

Stein, Elissa, *Here She Comes … Beauty Queen*, San Francisco, Chronicle, 2006

Stewart, Susan, *Painted Faces: A Colourful History of Cosmetics*, Stroud, Amberley, 2017

Strauss, Rita, *The Beauty Book*, London, Cassell & Co., 1924

Streatfeild, Noel, ed., *The Years of Grace: A Book for Girls*, London, Evans Brothers, 1950

Strings, Sabrina, *Fearing the Black Body: The Racial Origins of Fat Phobia*, New York, NYU Press, 2019

Suleiman, Susan Rubin, ed., *The Female Body in Western Culture: Contemporary Perspectives*, Cambridge, MA and London, Harvard University Press, 1986

Sullivan, Mark *Our Times 1900–1925: I – The Turn of the Century*, New York, Charles Scribner's Sons, 1926

Summers, Julie, *Fashion on the Ration*, London, Profile, 2015

Summers, Leigh, *Bound to Please: A History of the Victorian Corset*, Oxford, Berg, 2001

Sutherland, Millicent, Duchess of, *That Fool of a Woman, and Four Other Sombre Tales*, London and New York, G. P. Putnam's Sons, 1925

Sylvia's Book of the Toilet: A Ladies' Guide to Dress and Beauty, London, Ward, Lock & Co., 1881

Syme, Alison, *A Touch of Blossom: John Singer Sargent and the Queer Flora of Fin-de-Siècle Art*, University Park, Pennsylvania State University Press, 2010

Tapert, Annette and Diana Edkins, *The Power of Style*, New York, Crown, 1994

Tarlo, Emma, *Clothing Matters: Dress and Identity in India*, London, Hurst and Company, 1996

Thomas, E. Wynne, *The House of Yardley, 1770–1953*, London, Sylvan Press, 1953

The Toilet, London, Ward Lock & Co., 1897

Tolentino, Jia, *Trick Mirror*, London, Fourth Estate, 2019

Trasko, Mary, *Daring Do's: A History of Extraordinary Hair*, Paris, Flammarion, 1994

Trivedi, Lisa, *Clothing Gandhi's Nation: Homespun and Modern India*, Bloomington, Indiana University Press, 2007

Troubridge, Lady Laura, *The Book of Etiquette*, London, Associated Bookbuyers' Co., 1931

Tweedsmuir, Susan, *The Edwardian Lady*, London, Duckworth, 1966

Tyrer, Nicola, *They Fought in the Fields: The Women's Land Army: The Story of a Forgotten Victory*, London, Sinclair-Stevenson, 1996

Veblen, Thorstein, *The Theory of the Leisure Class*, London, George Allen & Unwin, 1924

Vicinus, Martha, ed., *Suffer and Be Still: Women in the Victorian Age*, Bloomington and London, Indiana University Press, 1972

Walker, Emma E., *The Pretty Girl Papers*, Boston, Little, Brown, 1910

Ward, E. & Co., *The Dress Reform Problem: A Chapter for Women*, London, Hamilton, Adams & Co., 1886

Warner, Marina, *Monuments and Maidens: The Allegory of the Female Form*, London, Weidenfeld & Nicolson, 1985

Warren, Eliza, *How I Managed my Children from Infancy to Marriage*, London, Houlston and Wright, 1865

Watling, Sarah, *Noble Savages: The Olivier Sisters*, London, Vintage, 2019

Watson, J. Forbes, *The Textile Manufactures and the Costumes of the People of India*, London, Wm. H. Allen, 1867

Waugh, Norah, *Corsets and Crinolines*, London, Batsford, 1954

West, Rebecca, *1900*, London, Weidenfeld & Nicolson, 1982

Wiggam, Albert Edward, *The Fruit of the Family Tree*, Garden City, Garden City Publishing Co., 1925

Williams, Florence, *Breasts: A Natural and Unnatural History*, New York, W.W. Norton, 2012

Williams, Neville, *Powder and Paint: A History of the Englishwoman's Toilet, Elizabeth I–Elizabeth II*, London, Longmans, Green & Co., 1957

Willis, Deborah, *Posing Beauty: African American Images from the 1890s to the Present*, W.W. Norton, 2009

Wilson, Elizabeth, *Adorned in Dreams: Fashion and Modernity*, London, I.B. Tauris, 2003

Wojtczak, Helena, *Women of Victorian Sussex: Their Status, Occupations and Dealings with the Law, 1830–1870*, St Leonards, Hastings Press, 2003

Wolf, Naomi, *The Beauty Myth: How Images of Beauty are used Against Women*, London, Chatto & Windus, 1990

Wollstonecraft, Mary, *A Vindication of the Rights of Woman*, first published 1792

Wood, Maggie, *"We Wore What We'd Got": Women's Clothes in World War II*, Exeter, Warwickshire Books, 1989

Woodforde, John, *The Strange Story of False Hair*, London, Routledge & Kegan Paul, 1971

Woolf, Virginia, *A Room of One's Own*, London, Hogarth Press 1929

Woolf, Virginia, *Three Guineas*, London, Hogarth Press, 1938

Wyatt, Roy, *Sussex Maidens*, London, The Naturist, 1953

Zweiniger-Bargielowska, Ina, ed., *Women in Twentieth-century Britain*, Harlow, Longman, 2001

Fiction, Drama, Poetry

Atherton, Gertrude, *Black Oxen*, London, John Murray, 1923

Atwood, Margaret, *The Robber Bride*, Toronto, McLelland and Stewart, 1993

Austen, Jane, *Mansfield Park*, London, Thomas Egerton, 1814

Beerbohm, Max, *Zuleika Dobson*, London, William Heinemann, 1911

Brontë, Charlotte, *Jane Eyre*, London, Smith, Elder & Co., 1847

Carroll, Lewis, *Through the Looking-Glass, and What Alice Found There*, London, Macmillan, 1871

Dickens, Charles, *David Copperfield*, London, Bradbury & Evans, 1850

Dickens, Charles, *Little Dorrit*, London, Bradbury & Evans, 1857

Fitzgerald, F. Scott, *Tender is the Night*, New York, Charles Scribner's Sons, 1934

Gissing, George, *The Odd Women*, London, Lawrence & Bullen, 1893

Grimm Brothers, trans. and ed. Margaret Hunt, *Grimm's Fairy Tales*, London, Routledge & Kegan Paul, 1948

Hall, Radclyffe, *The Well of Loneliness*, Paris, Pegasus Press, 1928

Loos, Anita, *Gentlemen Prefer Blondes: The Illuminating Diary of a Professional Lady*, New York, Boni and Liveright, 1925

Mitchell, Margaret, *Gone with the Wind*, New York, Macmillan, 1936

Patmore, Coventry, *The Angel in the House*, London, Macmillan, 1863

Shakespeare, William, *The Tempest*, 1611

Stowe, Harriet Beecher, *Uncle Tom's Cabin*, Boston, John P. Jewett and Co., 1852

Swift, Jonathan, *Gulliver's Travels*, London, Benjamin Motte, 1726

Woolf, Virginia, *Orlando*, London, Hogarth Press, 1928

Woolf, Virginia, *The Waves*, London, Hogarth Press, 1931

Yeats, W. B., 'A Woman Young and Old', first published 1929

Zola, Émile, *Nana*, Paris, Charpentier, 1880

Newspapers, Magazines

BRITISH

Aberdeen Evening Express

Belfast Telegraph

Berwickshire News and General Advertiser

Birmingham Daily Gazette

Blackpool Gazette and Herald

Bradford Observer

Britannia and Eve

Burnley Express

County Down Spectator and Ulster Standard

Daily Express

Daily Gazette for Middlesborough

Daily Herald

Daily Mirror

Daily News

The Daily Telegraph

Dundee Evening Post

Dundee Evening Telegraph

East Kent Gazette

Eastbourne Gazette

The Englishwoman's Domestic Magazine

Evening Standard

Evening Star

Falkirk Herald

The Girl's Own Annual

The Girl's Realm Annual

Girls Own Paper

The Guardian

Hartlepool Northern Daily Mail

Health and Efficiency

The Illustrated London News

The Illustrated Sporting and Dramatic News

Leeds Mercury

The Leisure Hour Magazine

Liverpool Echo

Londonderry Sentinel

The Manchester Guardian

Mother and Daughter

Music Hall and Theatre Review

New Ross Standard

News Chronicle

Northwich Guardian

Nottingham Journal

Nuneaton Observer
The Observer
The Penrith Observer
The People
Portsmouth Evening News
Psychology Today
Reveille
Shields Daily News
The Stage
The Sunday Times
The Tatler
Taunton Courier and Western
    Advertiser

Time and Tide
The Times
Truth
Vogue
Votes for Women
Washington Evening Star
Western Mail
Westminster Gazette
Woman and Beauty
Yorkshire Evening Post
Yorkshire Post and Leeds
    Intelligencer
The Young Ladies Journal

AMERICAN

American Weekly
Brooklyn Daily Eagle
The Colorado Statesman
Colored American Magazine
The Daily Gazette,
    Wilmington, DE
The Daily Record, Dunn, NC
Ebony
Esquire
Girls' Cinema
Indianapolis Times
Kinematograph Weekly
The Lancaster Daily Intelligencer

Lucky Charm
Modern Screen
New York Journal
The New York Journal
The New Yorker
O, The Oprah Magazine
Screenland
The Staunton Vindicator
Time
The Wichita Daily Eagle
Yank
The Yorkville Enquirer
The Youth's Companion

Journals, Scholarly Articles, Theses

Aston, Elaine, 'Male Impersonation in the Music Hall: The Case of
    Vesta Tilley', New Theatre Quarterly, 4:15, 1988
Baker-Sperry, Lori and Liz Grauerholz, 'The Pervasiveness and
    Persistence of the Feminine Beauty Ideal in Children's Fairy Tales',
    Gender and Society, 17:5, October 2003
Bannerji, Himani, 'Textile Prison: The Discourse on Shame (Lajja) in the
    Attire of the Gentlewoman (Bhadramahila) in Colonial Bengal',
    Canadian Journal of Sociology, 19:2, spring 1994
Basow, Susan, 'The Hairless Ideal: Women and their Body Hair',
    Psychology of Women Quarterly, 15:1, March 1991

Bennette, Rebecca, 'The Meaning of Dress: Nationalism, Feminism, and Fashion in Early Twentieth-Century Ireland', *Proceedings of the Harvard Celtic Colloquium*, 18/19, 1998/1999

Berney, Adrienne, 'Streamlining Breasts: The Exaltation of Form and Disguise of Function in 1930s Ideals', *Journal of Design History*, 14:4, 2001

Bettman, Adalbert G., 'Plastic and Cosmetic Surgery of the Face', *Northwest Journal of Medical Sciences*, 19:205, 1920

Bill, Katina, 'Attitudes Towards Women's Trousers: Britain in the 1930s', *Journal of Design History*, 6:1, 1993

Brownell, Michaela, 'Fashioning a Feminist Utopia: The Significance of Dress in Charlotte Perkins Gilman's *Herland*', masters thesis, University of St Thomas, 2020

Craig, Maxine, 'The Decline and Fall of the Conk; or, How to Read a Process', *Fashion Theory*, 1:4, December 1997

Cramp, Dr Arthur, 'Fooling the Fat: How "Slendaform" Reduces the Pocketbook', *Hygeia*, December 1923

Davidoff, Leonore, 'Mastered for Life: Servant and Wife in Victorian and Edwardian England', *Journal of Social History*, 7:4, summer 1974

Dell'Osso, Liliana, Mariana Abelli, Barbara Carpita, Stefano Pini, Giovanni Castellini, Claudia Carmassi and Valdo Ricca, 'Historical Evolution of the Concept of Anorexia Nervosa and Relationships with Orthorexia Nervosa, Autism, and Obsessive-Convulsive Spectrum', in *Journal of Neuropsychiatric Disease and Treatment*, 12, July 2016

Evans, Caroline, 'The Ontology of the Fashion Model', *AA Files*, 63, 2011

Fields, Jill, '"Fighting the Corsetless Evil": Shaping Corsets and Culture, 1900–1930', *Journal of Social History*, 33:2, 1999

Gardner, Kirsten E., 'Hiding the Scars: A History of Post-Mastectomy Breast Prostheses, 1945–2000', *Enterprise and Society*, 1:3, September 2000

Gottlieb, Julie V. and Matthew Stibbe, 'Peace at Any Price: The Visit of Nazi Women's Leader Gertrud Scholtz-Klink to London in March 1939 and the Response of British Women Activists', *Women's History Review*, 26:2, September 2016

Haiken, Beth, 'Plastic Surgery and American Beauty at 1921', *Bulletin of the History of Medicine*, 68:3, fall 1994

Haiken, Elizabeth, 'The Making of the Modern Face: Cosmetic Surgery', *Social Resarch*, 67:1, spring 2000

Harnett, Kerry A., 'Appearing Modern: Women's Bodies, Beauty, and Power in 1920s America', BA thesis, Boston College, 2009

Hawthorne, R., 'From Rags to Riches', *Journal of the Association of Chartered Physiotherapists in Women's Health*, 104, spring 2009

Heller, Michael, 'London Clerical Workers 1880–1914: The Search for Stability', PhD thesis, University College London, 2003

Jackson, Veronica, 'Restructuring Respectability, Gender, and Power: Aida Overton Walker Performs a Black Feminist Resistance', *Journal of Transnational American Studies*, 10:1, 2019

Johnson, Kim, Sharron J. Lennon and Nancy Rudd, 'Dress, Body and Self: Research in the Social Psychology of Dress', *Fashion and Textiles*, 1, 2014

Keller, Susan L., 'The Riviera's Golden Boy: Fitzgerald, Cosmopolitan Tanning, and Racial Commodities in "Tender is the Night"', *F. Scott Fitzgerald Review*, 8, 2010

Le Hénaff, Yannick, 'Cosmetic Surgery on Trial: How the Dujarier Case Impacted its Practice and Structure in France during the Interwar Period', *Social History of Medicine*, 32:1, February 2019

Mason, Meghann, 'The Impact of World War II on Women's Fashion in the United States and Britain', masters thesis, University of Nevada Las Vegas, 2011

Matthews, Jill Julius, 'They Had Such a Lot of Fun: The Women's League of Health and Beauty Between the Wars', *History Workshop Journal*, 30:1, autumn 1990

McNeil, Peter, '"Put Your Best Face Forward": The Impact of the Second World War on British Dress', *Journal of Design History*, 6:4, 1993

Newman, Richard, '"The Brightest Star": Aida Overton Walker in the Age of Ragtime and Cakewalk', *Prospects: An Annual of American Cultural Studies*, 18, October 1993

Nicholson, Claire Violet, 'In Woolf's Clothing: An Exploration of Clothes and Fashion in Virginia Woolf's Fiction', PhD thesis, Anglia Ruskin University, 2013

Park, Lora E., Ariana F. Young and Paul W. Eastwick, '(Psychological) Distance Makes the Heart Grow Fonder: effects of Psychological Distance and Relative Intelligence on Men's Attraction to Women', *Personality and Social Psychology Bulletin*, 2015

Parker, Michelle I., 'The Truth is in the Lye: Soap, Beauty, and Ethnicity in British Soap Advertisements', undergraduate thesis, University of Washington Tacoma, 2014

Pennell, E. R., 'Around London by Bicycle', *Harper's Monthly Magazine*, 95, June 1897

Peters, Walter and Victor Fornasier, 'Complications from Injectable Materials used for Breast Augmentation', *Canadian Journal of Plastic Surgery*, 17:3, autumn 2009

Petty, Margaret Maile, 'Threats and Promises: The Marketing and Promotion of Electric Lighting to Women in the United States, 1880s–1960s', *West 86th: A Journal of Decorative Arts, Design History, and Material Culture*, 21:1, 2014

Pilgrim, David, 'The Mammy Caricature: Anti-Black Imagery', Jim Crow Museum, Ferris State University, October 2000

Quittkat, Hannah L., Andrea S. Hartmann, Rainer Düsing, Ulricke Buhlmann and Silja Vocks, 'Body Dissatisfaction, Importance of Appearance, and Body Appreciation in Men and Women Over the Lifespan', *Frontiers in Psychiatry*, 10:864, 2019

Rhode, Deborah L., 'Appearance as a Feminist Issue', *SMU Law Review*, 69:4, January 2016

Riegel, Robert E., 'Women's Clothes and Women's Rights', *American Quarterly*, 15:3, autumn 1963

Roberts, Helene E., 'The Exquisite Slave: The Role of Clothes in the Making of the Victorian Woman', *Signs*, 2:3, spring 1977

Rolley, Katrina, 'Cutting a Dash: The Dress of Radclyffe Hall and Una Troubridge', *Feminist Review*, 35, summer 1990

Roper, Michael, 'Nostalgia as an Emotional Experience in the Great War', *Historical Journal*, 54:2, June 2011

Schanbhag, Meera, 'A Historical Perspective on the Cultural Connotations Surrounding Eating Disorders', *Inquiries Journal*, 12:9, 2020

Scott, Helen E., '"Their Campaign of Wanton Attacks": Suffragette Iconoclasm in British Museums and Galleries during 1914', *Museum Review*, 1:1, 2016

Serafine, Amelia Earhart, '"Let's Get Together and Chew the Fat": Women, Size and Community in Modern America', PhD dissertation, Loyola University Chicago, 2017

Showalter, Elaine and English Showalter, 'Victorian Women and Menstruation', *Victorian Studies*, 14:1, September 1970

Sowinska, Alicja, 'Dialectics of the Banana Skirt: The Ambiguities of Josephine Baker's Self-Representation', *Michigan Feminist Studies*, 19, fall 2005–spring 2006

Threlfall-Sykes, Judy, 'A History of Women's Cricket, 1880–1939', PhD thesis, De Montfort University, 2015

Westbrook, Robert B., '"I Want a Girl, Just Like the Girl that Married Harry James": American Women and the Problem of Political Obligation in World War II', *American Quarterly*, 42:4, December 1990

Willett, Julie, 'Susannah Walker. *Style and Status: Selling Beauty to African American Women, 1920-1975*', *American Historical*

Review, 113:1, February 2008

Williams, Melanie and Ellen Wright, *Betty Grable: An American Icon in Wartime Britain, Historical Journal of Film, Radio and Television*, 31:4, 2011

Zweiniger-Bargielowska, Ina, '*The Culture of the Abdomen*: Obesity and Reducing in Britain, circa 1900–1939', *Journal of British Studies*, 44:2, April 2005

Zweiniger-Bargielowska, Ina, 'The Making of a Modern Female Body: Beauty, Health and Fitness in Interwar Britain', *Women's History Review*, 20:2, 2011

Archives, Websites

The Bank of England Inflation Calculator is helpful for reckoning the purchasing power of money in the past: https://www.bank-ofengland.co.uk/monetary-policy/inflation/inflation-calculator

The British Newspaper Archive gives access by subscription to millions of pages of local and national British newspapers: www.britishnewspaperarchive.co.uk

The Burnett Collection of Working-Class Autobiographies at Brunel University is an impressive collection of first-hand unpublished material 1791–1945: https://www.brunel.ac.uk/life/library/ArchivesAndSpecialCollections/Burnett-Archive-of-Working-Class-Autobiographies

Cosmetics and Skin, includes timelines and product details from depilatories to lipsticks: http://www.cosmeticsandskin.com/index.php

Cycling History includes the history of women and bicycles: https://cyclehistory.wordpress.com/

Feminism in India, a platform for Indian women: https://feminisminindia.com/

Fashion-Era gives details of the history of fashion, from sleeves to mourning dress: www.fashion-era.com

The Internet Archive is a non-profit library of millions of free digitised books and other material: https://archive.org/

JSTOR is a library of primary research, journals and books, accessed via subscription: https://www.jstor.org/

The Library of Congress allows free search of its collection of digitised American newspapers: https://chroniclingamerica.loc.gov/newspapers/

Mass Observation specialises in material about everyday life in Britain, from 1937 to the 1950s: http://www.massobs.org.uk/mass-observation-1937-1950s

Media History Digital Library – the history of film, broadcasting and recorded sound: https://mediahistoryproject.org/

Millennium Memory Bank Oral History Collection held at the British Library: https://www.bl.uk/collection-guides/major-national-oral-history-projects-and-surveys

The *Oxford Dictionary of National Biography*, accessed through subscribing institutions, has a searchable database of more than sixty thousand biographies of individuals who shaped British history: www.oxforddnb.com

Pathé News is a searchable archive of thousands of newsreel archives, 1896–1984: https://www.britishpathe.com/

Project Gutenberg is a library of more than seventy thousand free ebooks, mostly out of copyright: https://www.gutenberg.org/

Russell, Dora, *We Called on Europe – The Story of the Women's Caravan of Peace, 1958*, unpublished, held in the Feminist Archive, University of Bristol

The Wellcome Library catalogues works on health, science and art; many items in its collection have been digitised: https://wellcome-collection.org/collections

Acknowledgements

Many people have supported me in the research and writing of *All the Rage*, and this is an opportunity to show my appreciation in print. So – thank you very much: to my very well-dressed Virago editors: both the wonderful Rose Tomaszewska who began the process, and the equally wonderful Lennie Goodings who picked up where Rose left off and has demonstrated the most hands-on commitment any author could ask for. Rose and Lennie showed robust belief in this book throughout. Thank you too to Lennie's wise and watchful colleague Zoe Gullen, and to their associates at Virago: Linda Silverman, Niamh Anderson, Katy Brigden and Louise Harvey. I have been equally lucky to be supported by my lovely agents, Caroline Dawnay and her encouraging colleague Kat Aitken. And this is also the right place to salute the memory of my dear friend the late, great Dame Carmen Callil who applauded my debut with the illustrious publishing imprint she founded, who always believed in my books, but who sadly has not lived to see this one launched.

My family has been indispensable throughout. I can never be grateful enough to Bill for his patience and wisdom; loving thanks too to my daughters Maria and Julia Nicholson, who are both, in my eyes, models of female beauty and feminist principles. All three cheered me on, read the book in draft, and made clever suggestions and criticisms. Special thanks to my brother Julian Bell, to my stylish sister Cressida Bell, and to her colleagues Jaap Van Der Schaaf and Alex Fenner who made thoughtful and informed contributions. Luca Nania and my son Teddy Nicholson played important parts too, with their vital knowledge of computer software. And particular thanks to my gorgeous daughter-in-law Rachel Chang for sharing her unfailing enthusiasm for fashion.

My gratitude also goes to my friend, the beautiful and elegant Romilly Saumarez Smith, for her help and her patience, and to the dazzling Alison MacLeod for her clever suggestions. I also had morale-boosting encouragement and practical assistance from many other friends and acquaintances. Thank you to Annabel Abbs, Drusilla Beyfus, Rupert Christiansen, Richard Cohen, Clare Fanthorpe, Regina Marler, Anne Morrison, Juliet Nicolson, Charlie Porter, Charles Saumarez Smith, Jenny Shelley, Nicola Shulman, Joelle Stockley, Aron White, Charlotte Wickenden and Tom Wills. Other people who helped me navigate the research labyrinth are Sandy Nairne, Katie Flanagan from Brunel University, Katie Fallon from the Adam Matthew Group who support the Mass Observation project, and Peter Jones from King's College, Cambridge. My friend Carol Sanford directed me to her contacts in Charleston, South Carolina – Pastor Kylon Middleton and Dr James Ward – to help me with queries about their home city. And special thanks too to Amanda Foreman and Justine Picardie.

The staff of the London Library deserve a special mention for making it possible to continue researching at the height of the Covid-19 lockdown of 2020.

In addition, the author gratefully acknowledges the kind permission of copyright holders to quote from a number of authors and sources, as follows:

The extracts on pages 58–60 have been sourced from Krishnabhabini Das's original Bengali travelogue *Englande Bangamahila* (1885) translated into English by Somdatta Mandal as *A Bengali Lady in England* (Cambridge Scholars, 2015). Acknowledgements to Nella Last (author) and Patricia and Robert Malcolmson (editors) for excerpts from *Nella Last in the 1950s: Further Diaries of Housewife, 49*, published by Profile Books Ltd, 2010. Excerpts from *A Notable Woman: The Romantic Journals of Jean Lucey Pratt*, edited by Simon Garfield, Canongate, London (2015) reproduced with permission of the Licensor through PLSclear; excerpts from *A Slender Reputation: An Autobiography* by Kathleen Hale (Frederick Warne, 1994), reproduced by kind permission of David Higham Associates.

Image Credits

Index